Love, Death, Fame

Poetry and Lore from the Emirati Oral Tradition

Letter from the General Editor

The Library of Arabic Literature makes available Arabic editions and English translations of significant works of Arabic literature, with an emphasis on the seventh to nineteenth centuries. The Library of Arabic Literature thus includes texts from the pre-Islamic era to the cusp of the modern period, and encompasses a wide range of genres, including poetry, poetics, fiction, religion, philosophy, law, science, travel writing, history, and historiography.

Books in the series are edited and translated by internationally recognized scholars. They are published in parallel-text and English-only editions in both print and electronic formats. PDFs of Arabic editions are available for free download. The Library of Arabic Literature also publishes distinct scholarly editions with critical apparatus.

The Library encourages scholars to produce authoritative Arabic editions, accompanied by modern, lucid English translations, with the ultimate goal of introducing Arabic's rich literary heritage to a general audience of readers as well as to scholars and students.

The publications of the Library of Arabic Literature are generously supported by Tamkeen under the NYU Abu Dhabi Research Institute Award G1003 and are published by NYU Press.

Philip F. Kennedy
General Editor, Library of Arabic Literature

About this Paperback

This paperback edition differs in a few respects from its dual-language hardcover predecessor. Because of the compact trim size the pagination has changed. Material that referred to the Arabic edition has been updated to reflect the English-only format, and other material has been corrected and updated where appropriate. For information about the Arabic edition on which this English translation is based and about how the LAL Arabic text was established, readers are referred to the hardcover.

Love, Death, Fame

Poetry and Lore from the Emirati Oral Tradition

BY

Al-Māyidī ibn Ẓāhir

TRANSLATED BY
Marcel Kurpershoek

FOREWORD BY
David F. Elmer

REVIEWED BY
Sultan Alameemi

VOLUME EDITOR
Philip F. Kennedy

NEW YORK UNIVERSITY PRESS
New York

NEW YORK UNIVERSITY PRESS
New York

Library of Congress Cataloging-in-Publication Data

Names: Ibn Ẓāhir, al-Mājidī, author. | Kurpershoek, P. M., translator. | Elmer, David F., writer of introduction. | ʿUmaymī, Sulṭān ʿAlī ibn Bakhīt, 1974– editor.
Title: Love, death, fame : poetry and lore from the Emirati oral tradition / Al-Māyidī ibn Ẓāhir ; translated by Marcel Kurpershoek ; foreword by David F. Elmer ; reviewed by Sultan Alameemi.
Other titles: Dīwān. English
Description: New York : New York University Press, [2023] | Includes bibliographical references and index. | Summary: "Poems and tales of a literary forefather of the United Arab Emirates"— Provided by publisher.
Identifiers: LCCN 2023000781 | ISBN 9781479825806 (paperback) | ISBN 9781479825813 (ebook) | ISBN 9781479825837 (ebook)
Subjects: LCGFT: Poetry.
Classification: LCC PJ7765.I35 D5913 2023 | DDC 892.7/14—dc23/eng/20230309
LC record available at https://lccn.loc.gov/2023000781

Series design and composition by Nicole Hayward
Typeset in Adobe Text

Manufactured in the United States of America

10 9 8 7 6 5 4 3 2 1

For Tonny Scherft, my mother,
and Betsy Udink, my wife,
who steadied me on this road.

Contents

Letter from the General Editor / iii
Abbreviations / xi
Foreword / xiii
Introduction / xix
Map: Names of Places in the Poetry of Ibn Ẓāhir and the Narratives / liv
Map: The Gulf Region and Oman in Ibn Ẓāhir's Day / lv
Note on the Text / lvi
Notes to the Introduction / lxvii

Poems / 1
1: Graybeard's Song / 3
2: Lightning's Laughter / 8
3: Agony of Love / 11
4: Death and Revival / 15
5: Wisdom Poem / 21
6: Dance of the Zephyr / 27
7: Don't Be Hard on Friends / 30
8: Rain Poem / 33
9: Tears at the Court of Love / 39
10: Torn to Shreds by Passion's Agony / 43
11: Glittering Mirage Led You Astray / 49
12: Fatal Attraction / 53
13: I Dared the Devil to Ride His Horse / 57
14: She Left Me Baffled / 60

15: Muzzleloader's Ramrod / 65
16: Intelligent Speech and Borders of the Land / 69
17: Daughter's Elegy / 75

Narratives / 79
18: Gift of Poetry / 81
19: Ibn Ẓāhir's Camel / 85
20: Fishing and Pearl Diving / 89
21: Guests and Riddles / 96
22: Daughters of Ibn Ẓāhir / 110
23: Search for a Grave / 115

Notes / 119
Bibliography / 215
Further Reading / 223
Index / 225
About the NYU Abu Dhabi Institute / 245
About the Abu Dhabi Poetry Academy / 246
About the Translator / 247
The Library of Arabic Literature / 248

Abbreviations

n.	noun
sg.	singular
pl.	plural
lit.	literally
cf.	compare
CA	Classical Arabic or Modern Standard Arabic
ref.	refer to
MS	manuscript
MSS	manuscripts

Foreword

DAVID F. ELMER

To enter the world of al-Māyidī ibn Ẓāhir is to enter a world that seems impossibly distant from the glittering modern metropoles of Abu Dhabi and Dubai, even as it retains a timeless presence in the collective Emirati self-consciousness. With a distinctive blend of lyrical longing and didacticism, Ibn Ẓāhir's *qāṣidah*-style poems offer evocative glimpses of vast desert expanses, delicate oases, and Bedouin caravans. Rooted in the seventeenth century and transmitted across generations by oral tradition, the poems depict an idealized way of life that remains an essential touchstone even in modern Emirati society.

Since the 1930s, the study of oral poetry has been conducted largely in the shadow of Milman Parry, who transformed our understanding of Homer and Homeric poetry by conducting methodical fieldwork on an analogous oral epic tradition in what was then Yugoslavia. Marcel Kurpershoek brings to his edition and masterful translation of these poems expertise laboriously acquired in the course of his own extensive fieldwork in the Arabian Peninsula. But the tradition represented by the poems in this volume is fundamentally different in certain important respects from the one observed by Parry in the Balkans. Parry, whose comparative project was further elaborated by Albert Lord, described a practice of "composition in performance": his Bosnian, Croatian, and Serbian singers composed their songs anew each time they performed them, relying on a specialized language of formulaic expressions that enabled the singers to sing their tales in metrical verse without committing a specific sequence of verses to memory. The formulaic character of Homeric epic reflects a similar technique. The *qāṣidah* tradition, however, is distinguished by a marked separation between the acts of composition and performance. Texts composed with care by poets are entrusted to others—"reciters" or "messengers"—for performance and transmission. A complex system of rhymes ensures that texts remain notably stable from performance to performance, especially by comparison with the relatively more fluid texts of the epics collected by Parry and Lord.

The separation between composition and performance—so different from Parry's model of Homeric composition or from the South Slavic epics he collected—means that the poems of Ibn Ẓāhir always stage a certain distance, a gap between the voice of the performer and the voice of Ibn Ẓāhir himself. The "signature verses" with which the poems begin insist that we hear the words of the poet. Poem 7, "Don't Be Hard on Friends," offers a typical example: "These are the words of al-Māyidī, a discerning poet / whose well-knit verses find favor with reciters." But the signature speaks of Ibn Ẓāhir in the third person, emphasizing that the performer of the verses, one of the "reciters," is *not* the great poet, and that Ibn Ẓāhir himself remains absent from the scene of performance. The sense of absence, programmed, so to speak, by the gap between composition and performance, animates also many of Ibn Ẓāhir's most powerful recurrent themes, such as the longing for an absent lover or nostalgia for lost days of youth.

There is, however, one striking image that brings flashes of urgent immediacy to Ibn Ẓāhir's landscape of longing and absence. The poems are punctuated by desert rainstorms whose waters bring forth dense beds of flowers from otherwise barren sands. These rainstorms, described in vivid detail, invite multiple interpretations. They figure the insistent presence of erotic desire: the poet prays for storms to "drench" the land of his beloved, imagining the clouds as they "roll by and roar like studs in rutting season"

("Graybeard's Song," lines 55–57). At the same time, the rains—or, more precisely, the desert flowers they engender—figure the satisfaction of desire. Ibn Ẓāhir concludes his longest description of desert rains by declaring that the storms have occasioned reunion with his beloved ("Intelligent Speech and the Borders of the Land," lines 72–73):

From afar, the tribe of my beloved drew near
  to raise its lofty tents on carpets of herbage.
Worries dispelled, I enjoyed the soundest sleep:
  from afar they brought my sweetheart, straight to me!

But there is still more to this image, for the waters that flow in the desert represent also the invigorating force of poetic inspiration as it is channeled through the words of Ibn Ẓāhir. So, in "Lightning's Laughter," as a "deafening drum of drops hammer[s] the earth" the poet prays, "Let the rains wash our dusty minds . . . as a torrent restores life to a desiccated wadi" (lines 12–13).

Bearing in mind this association between life-giving rain and the inspired poetry that Ibn Ẓāhir pours out for his "thirsty" followers ("Lightning's Laughter," line 3), we can discern in the lengthy rain section of "Intelligent Speech and the Borders of the Land" (again, the longest such section in the corpus) more than just an expression of desire and its fulfillment. As Kurpershoek notes in his introduction to the poem, the description of rains that "drenched lands from east to west / in an embrace of all terrain that borders Oman" (line 58) offers, in the form of a catalogue of wadis, oases, and towns, a virtual map of the territory of today's United Arab Emirates. To envision this territory as universally inundated by rain is also to assert the all-encompassing aspirations of the poetry of Ibn Ẓāhir, whose invigorating "waters" likewise flow throughout Emirati lands. In the universal scope of these ambitions we can detect the truly Homeric dimensions of the figure of Ibn Ẓāhir: just as the Homeric tradition aspired to speak to and for all ancient Hellenes, so too does the poetic voice of Ibn Ẓāhir position itself as speaking to and for all Emiratis. Indeed, a comparison of ancient biographical accounts of Homer with the fascinating tales about Ibn Ẓāhir collected in this volume would reveal a number of interesting similarities between the two figures, all speaking to their common stature as embodiments of traditions that aim for universal appeal.

As a representative of traditional Emirati society, Ibn Ẓāhir speaks, necessarily, with a conservative voice. The conservatism of his persona is perhaps most vividly crystalized in his traditional antagonism toward his poetically gifted daughter, who is named Salmā in some accounts but who most often remains anonymous. As Kurpershoek notes, Ibn Ẓāhir is said to have felt threatened by Salmā's poetic talents, and to have forbidden her from composing poems (or to have physically silenced her: "Introduction," pp. xlvi). This forceful assertion of patriarchal authority, though contextualizable within the traditional culture of decades past, is out of step with the modern Emirates, where striking progress has been made with regard to women's rights; since 2006, for instance, the United Arab Emirates have ranked ahead of all other Arab states on the United Nations' Gender Inequality Index. It is striking, however, that the tradition nevertheless endows Salmā with a powerful, poetically confident voice, expressed in verses woven "from exquisite twigs in the palm's core" ("Daughter's Elegy," line 2). The tradition allows Salmā to speak back to her father, and in this sense transcends the conservatism in which it is rooted.

A further dimension to the figure of Ibn Ẓāhir's daughter is suggested by the tale that describes his doubts regarding the paternity of one of his three daughters ("Daughters of Ibn Ẓāhir," §§22.3–7). Two of the girls compose verses, in which Ibn Ẓāhir "recognized enough of himself . . . to know for sure that they were his offspring." But the third, youngest daughter shows no inclination for poetry and thus arouses her father's suspicion. Only in the mortal agony of the test to which her father himself subjects her does she versify—thus putting Ibn Ẓāhir's doubts to rest. Setting aside the cruelty of the test, this story can be interpreted in terms of the dynamics of oral tradition, with the father's suspicion reflecting the challenge of determining the "authenticity" of an orally circulating poem. In the absence of an established canon of written texts, even an aficionado of Ibn Ẓāhir's poetry might occasionally hear a recitation of an unfamiliar poem attributed to the master: how might one judge whether such a poem is genuinely the "offspring" of Ibn Ẓāhir, or instead a supposititious child making its way in the world under false pretenses? The tale suggests that the quality of the verses themselves will reveal the father's identity.

We return, however, to the daughter whose own distinctive poetic voice is preserved in "Daughter's Elegy" (whether she is the same as the one who was doubted is unclear). This daughter, it is suggested, may even have surpassed her father's talent ("Daughters of Ibn Ẓāhir," §22.10). Her defiant insistence that her father does not "have a monopoly on poetry" (§22.11) is an assertion not only that an authentic poetic voice will always be recognizable on its own terms, but also, more remarkably, that not even the authoritative voice of the very father of the tradition can escape scrutiny and criticism. Salmā, the rebellious daughter, is an indication that the tradition of Ibn Ẓāhir, as it evolves in tandem with Emirati society, is a tradition under negotiation.

David F. Elmer
Harvard University

Introduction

Al-Māyidī ibn Ẓāhir[1]

Al-Māyidī ibn Ẓāhir and his poetry are inextricably intertwined with the United Arab Emirates.[2] Through his *qaṣīdah*-style poems and the anecdotal stories that feature him as a feisty sage, the poet was embraced as a proto-Emirati in the young country's search for its cultural foundations. The first *dīwāns*, his collected work, were published under the auspices of the ruler of Dubai, Shaykh Rāshid ibn Saʿīd Āl Maktūm (1963), and the ruler of Abu Dhabi, Shaykh Zāyid ibn Sulṭān Āl Nahāyān (1967).[3] The poetry's descriptions of rain (*maṭariyyāt*) are cited as evidence that the borders of the country that came into being in 1971 were traced so as to include the places Ibn Ẓāhir singled out in his prayers for these heavenly blessings on his homeland's arid grounds (Poem 16).

Shaykh Zāyid is known as the Father of the Nation; Ibn Ẓāhir is considered the poet who epitomizes an oral culture that antedates the state by almost three centuries.[4] In this view, his work and legend demonstrate that the Emirates, far from being a fortuitous creation, are largely congruous with preexisting characteristics. The attention lavished on Ibn Ẓāhir has imbued generations of Emirati citizens with his poetry's wise and mildly skeptical spirit. In marked contrast, the narrative lore presents the poet as a resourceful, quick-witted, sly, defiant, and outrageously generous underdog, a financially struggling, sometimes ruthless family man who overcomes the odds and his poetic rivals through mastery of his art and sheer pluckiness.

Historical Background

While the Emirates celebrates Ibn Ẓāhir as a national poet, little is known for certain about his person and tribal affiliation.[5] The picaresque stories about his life clearly reflect the concerns of a society that looks back on an imagined past, much as the people of ancient Greece looked back to the Trojan War "as an important symbolic event, perhaps for the very foundation of their own communities."[6] In his poetry, there is a remarkable paucity of names and events that are recorded in chronicled history. Based on a few verses in one poem (§§13.27–33), Emirati literary historians have concluded that he lived to witness the reign of Sayf ibn Sulṭān al-Yaʿrubī, a powerful ruler of the Omani dynasty of al-Yaʿāribah (r. 1692–1711).[7]

In another verse, the poet evokes nostalgic memories of "intrepid stalwarts, gallant men of Banū Hilāl" (§1.63). Understandably, many have interpreted this as a reference to the migrations of Banū Hilāl from the Arabian Peninsula to North Africa and its legend as perpetuated in the cycle of epic storytelling and verse (*Sīrat Banī Hilāl*) in Arabia, Egypt, and other countries. However, the eleventh-century migration of Banū Hilāl headed to the west, as expressed in the term *taghrībah*, "westward journey." There are no known movements of Banū Hilāl toward the east.

There is a more compelling argument. The historical and literary sources leave no doubt that the Banū Hilāl mentioned by Ibn Ẓāhir are the descendants of Hilāl, a brother of the most prominent Jabrid ruler, Ajwad ibn Zāmil, who died in 1507.[8] Hilāl's grandson Qaṭan ibn ʿAlī, and later Qaṭan ibn Qaṭan, and Qaṭan ibn Qaṭan ibn Qaṭan, inherited the Jabrid dominions in Oman, and played a prominent part in the struggles against the principal founder of the Yaʿāribah rule, Nāṣir ibn Murshid ibn Sulṭān al-Yaʿrubī, the first imam of the dynasty (r. 1624–49).

In the Omani chronicles, the name of Qaṭan ibn Qaṭan al-Hilālī is frequently mentioned. Dislodged from a number of fortresses by the imam's generals, he continued raiding the former Jabrid territories in Oman from his base in al-Aḥsāʾ, the lineage's original seat of power in eastern Arabia. With the armies of the Yaʿrubī imam in hot pursuit, he would shelter in the desert redoubt of Līwā, the home province of today's rulers of Abu Dhabi and the Emirates. The Omani chronicles mention that on one occasion the governor of al-Buraymī, the province most exposed to the Hilālī depredations, launched an expedition to capture the camel herds of Qaṭan ibn Qaṭan with the aim of crippling his mobility, a clear indication of the Jabrid Banū Hilāl's Bedouin roots.[9] After a final act in the back and forth of his yearly raids into Oman, Qaṭan ibn Qaṭan withdrew to al-Aḥsāʾ, and after 1645 there is no further mention of his name in the Omani works of history.

For centuries, the history of the Emirates has been an inseparable part of the history of Oman.[10] Culturally, however, the area of present-day United Arab Emirates has probably been closer to eastern Arabia, and through it to central Arabian Najd. The poetry of Ibn Ẓāhir provides early and eloquent testimony to this connection. This influence continues to be felt: Nabaṭī poetry has not developed in Oman and seems to stop at the Emirati–Omani border. By far the largest contingent of non-Emirati participants in the *Million's Poet* competition in Abu Dhabi hails from Saudi Arabia. Omani participants have had to learn its style. Therefore, one might argue that the current border between the Emirates and Oman coincides with an older border of cultural and religious identity. The Emirates' Jabrid past may offer a historical explanation.

The Jabrids

Half Bedouin, the Jabrid rulers seem to have been fond of poetry. From this period stem the first monuments of Nabaṭī poetry, closely related to early classical desert poetry, with which it shares large amounts of vocabulary, imagery, and prosody. Qaṭan ibn Qaṭan plays a prominent role in these poetical exchanges and has remained a legendary figure in Arabian folklore until today.[11]

The tradition of Jabrid eastern Arabian court poetry was continued in al-Aḥsāʾ with the rise of the successor regime of Āl Ḥumayd, popularly known as Ibn ʿurayʿir, in the second half of the seventeenth century until its destruction by the House of Saud in 1793. If indeed Ibn Ẓāhir flourished toward the end of the seventeenth century, it is inconceivable that he should not have been aware of Jabrid poetry and the role of the Jabrid Banū Hilāl. Ḍank, the only place in his rain poems outside the borders of today's United Arab Emirates, where according to oral tradition Ibn Ẓāhir worked in palm cultivation, was one of the last fortresses of the Jabrid Banū Hilāl to be subjected by the powerful Omani imams of the al-Yaʿāribah dynasty. The Omani chronicles provide ample evidence of the long struggle between al-Yaʿāribah and Banū Hilāl.[12]

Jabrī is the tribal kinship designation used by members of al-Jubūr, a branch of the Banū ʿĀmir in Najd who established their authority in the eastern Arabian oases of al-Aḥsāʾ and al-Qaṭīf around the middle of the fifteenth century on territory occupied in earlier centuries by the states of al-Qarāmiṭah (the Qarmatians) and al-ʿUyūniyyūn. The founder, Zāmil al-Jabrī, was succeeded by his sons Sayf and Ajwad. In 1471, Ajwad expanded the frontiers to include Bahrain, Oman, and large swaths of Najd to become the strongest ruler in the Arabian Peninsula at the time.[13] Ajwad prided himself on the patronym of "Ibn Jabr" and he enjoined his sons to keep it.

Ajwad died in 1505/1506, not long before a Portuguese fleet commanded by Alfonso de Albuquerque entered the Gulf in late summer of 1507. Ajwad divided his realm among three sons: Sayf, Muḥammad, and ʿAlī.[14] Sayf had subjected large parts of Oman to his father's rule starting in 1487. In 1511, the king of Hormuz captured Bahrain and al-Qaṭīf. Ten years later, the Jabrid ruler Muqrin ibn Zāmil was killed in fighting against the king and the Portuguese.[15]

Ḥusayn ibn Sayf ibn Ajwad turned the tables on the king of Hormuz by expelling him from the Omani port of Sohar. Jabrid rule in Oman was continued by the descendants of Ajwad's brother, Hilāl ibn Zāmil: in 1524, Hilāl's branch took the reins of power in the person of Qaṭan ibn 'Alī ibn Hilāl ibn Zāmil. In 1525, Jabrid rule of its center, al-Aḥsā', was overthrown by a force from Basra. Henceforward, "their only power and influence was concentrated in Oman under the leadership of the branch called Banū Hilāl."[16] A century later, the Banū Hilāl were still politically active in Oman. The history of *Tuḥfat al-a'yān fī sīrat ahl 'Umān* by al-Sālimī mentions Āl Qaṭan ibn Qaṭan in the chronicled events of 1615. According to this work, Nāṣir ibn Nāṣir ibn Qaṭan's forces were domiciled in the "northern Bedouin region" (*bādiyat al-shamāl*) and took part in ever-shifting political alliances. The chronicle of *Kashf al-ghammah* adds that Nāṣir ibn Nāṣir ibn Nāṣir ibn Qaṭan was accompanied by 'Alī ibn Qaṭan ibn Qaṭan ibn Qaṭan ibn 'Alī ibn Hilāl.[17] When Nāṣir ibn Murshid ibn Sulṭān ibn Mālik ibn Abī l-'Arab al-Ya'rubī was installed as the new imam of Oman, he took the town of Samad al-Shān from 'Alī ibn Qaṭan al-Hilālī. Another town, al-Ghabbi, was in the hands of groups of "Bedouin and sedentary Āl Hilāl." Yanqal belonged to Nāṣir ibn Qaṭan al-Hilālī, and so did Tawām (the common name for al-Buraymī and al-'Ayn). The Banū Hilāl, put on the defensive by the imam, withdrew to Ḍank, the oasis near al-Buraymī and al-'Ayn where Ibn Ẓāhir is said to have started his working life.[18]

The camel herds of Qaṭan ibn Qaṭan fell into the hands of the new ruler and were returned to Banū Hilāl in exchange for their fortress in Ḍank, an example of the differing priorities in Bedouin and sedentary culture that marked the struggle. The imam put himself at the head of an army that laid siege to Yanqal. In consequence, Nāsir ibn Qaṭan ibn Jabr fled to al-Jaww, an area near al-'Ayn and al-Buraymī, and from there to Līwā, a string of small oases at the edge of the Empty Quarter. According to the chronicles, Līwā was then in the possession of al-Jubūr. Internal strife caused one faction of the tribe to flee to "the Christians" (the Portuguese) in Sohar.

Next, the imam added Līwā to his dominions thanks to the assistance given to him by the Hilālī faction of Nāṣir ibn Qaṭan ibn Qaṭan.

After the loss of Yanqal, Nāṣir ibn Qaṭan had withdrawn to al-Aḥsā', from where he launched yearly raids on Oman. One year, when intercepted by the troops of the imam, he sought refuge in Līwā with the locally preeminent Banū Yās, the tribal confederation to which the present ruling house in Abu Dhabi belongs, and negotiated a truce. Reinforced with the Banū Yās Bedouin of the al-Ẓafrah region (now the western desert region of the Emirates bordering Saudi Arabia), he launched an attack on the fortress of al-Jaww, with considerable support from al-Jaww's inhabitants. In retaliation, one of the generals of the imam marched from Nizwā and destroyed all the fortresses of al-Jaww. Again, his Hilālī opponents fled to the "Christians" in Sohar and Julfār (present-day Rās al-Khaymah). His camels were confiscated by the imam's forces. In his turn, Nāṣir ibn Qaṭan raided the camels of Bedouin tribes along the Omani coast.

The impression given by the chronicles is that the governors of the imam kept rounding up the camels of Banū Hilāl, who kept plundering other camels in Oman with raids from their strongholds at the Banū Yās settlements in al-Ẓafrah and Līwā. Like the Wahhābī chroniclers in Saudi Arabia, the Omani dynastic historians naturally show a strong bias toward the imam's religious authority. The rightful possessions of "the believers" (*al-ʿibbād*) are contrasted with wanton violence and thievery on the part of the Bedouin "lawless oppressors and perfidious tyrants" (*al-bughāt al-ṭughāt al-nākithīn*).[19] Hence the imam's orders to his commanders "to march to the north and confiscate the camels of Nāṣir ibn Qaṭan, because he draws on these resources to commit his outrages. The commander marched at the head of his troops and clashed with Banū Yās who stood in defense of the camels near a place called al-Shuʿaybah, near al-Ẓafrah." This pattern of desultory warfare repeated itself for a number of years: the Bedouin launched raids, plundered parts of Oman, and made their escape toward the safety of "the endless wastes" (*al-fayāfī*) on their hardy camels. In the end, the imam made an all-out effort to put an end to these Bedouin depredations. He put himself at the head of a large army and commanded the tribal chiefs. Nāṣir ibn Qaṭan withdrew toward al-Aḥsāʾ. The last mention of Ibn Qaṭan and Banū Hilāl in chronicled history is not long before the death of the Yaʿrubī imam Nāṣir ibn Murshid in 1649.[20]

Conceivably, Ibn Ẓāhir drew on living memory to set the departure scene of his Bedouin beloved in the context of the gallant exploits of these scions of the Omani Banū Hilāl.[21] If he did so, it does not necessarily contradict his fulsome praise for Sayf ibn Sulṭān al-Yaʿrubī, who pacified Oman during the poet's lifetime.[22] By then, memory of the marauding incursions by the last of the Jabrids may have provided a suitably nostalgic backdrop for the lovers' heartbreak at her tribe's departure.

Jabrid and Other Poetry of Ibn Ẓāhir's Era

Such a tentative chronology for Ibn Ẓāhir's floruit, based on efforts to match fleeting references in verse to chronicles, cannot go beyond the realm of plausible conjecture. However, the argument gains strength if literary influences from the central Arabian province of Najd are taken into account. In the absence of any information on Ibn Ẓāhir's life and times, the only way to gain a measure of understanding of his poetry's character, its approximate position in the early centuries of Arabian Nabaṭī poetry (ca. 1300–1800), and its originality in relation to this corpus is by comparison with what is known, sometimes with somewhat greater historical certainty. Najdī and other Arabian poetry, especially *qaṣīdah*-style works of poets in the Jabrid cultural sphere, probably comes closest to a literary context for Ibn Ẓāhir's work.[23] This brings to light a significant number of interlocking legends connected with these poets, close parallels in style and wording, and even a Jabrid poet's verses migrating into the *dīwān* of Ibn Ẓāhir. Thus, features of the otherwise blank face of Ibn Ẓāhir emerge from a fragmented composite of similarities and differences. Beyond this, his persona, as distinct from his oral legend, remains shrouded in mystery.

Jabrid poetry and lore show striking examples of how legend became part of poetry and in turn gave birth to new verse. On account of certain parallels, explicit or hinted at in the oeuvre of Ibn Ẓāhir, the following may offer a loose framework for further interpretation.

The Jabrid prince Qaṭan ibn Qaṭan al-Hilālī, alluded to by Ibn Ẓāhir in his verse, was in poetic correspondence with the Najdī poet al-ʿUlaymī from Wādī Ḥanīfah in the al-ʿĀriḍ region of present-day Riyadh.[24] Al-ʿUlaymī's poem is purportedly sent from Oman to his hometown:

> O visitor to Oman, you've come before dark raises
> its wings, while people are sunk in sleep;
> Worn out, you traveled from Najd to Malaḥ,
> across endless wastes and bleak deserts;
> I am far from you in the Wādi of Oman,
> and you in Wādi Ḥanīfah, let it be blessed by rain.[25]

From there, the verses move through the usual themes in the *qaṣīdah* style of his period up to the poem's "message," his eulogies of Prince Qaṭan. Then it abruptly ends with a vague complaint: according to the poet, the nature of his laments should be obvious and can easily be surmised from the poet's pitiable mental and physical condition. Therefore, the assumption of commentators has been that the poet seeks advice on how to cure his lovesickness.

The legend tells that the ruler of al-ʿUlaymī's town connived with his mother-in-law to seize his beautiful wife in exchange for a princely sum. The poet traveled to Oman and appeared at Qaṭan's court to make his complaint and appeal for help. Miraculously, the sultan decided to accompany the poet on the long journey back to Najd and artfully succeeded in delivering a happy end by summarily dispatching the usurper on the night of his wedding with the poet's wife.[26]

As in the case of Ibn Ẓāhir's poems and the legend purportedly explaining certain verses, the text of the poem itself shows no trace of such a tale: the legend was woven by narrators whose flights of fancy took the mysterious last verses as their point of departure and by analogy with other legends of the kind. Such an oral cultural interpretation of the poem fits existing patterns at the time. For instance, later transmission confused elements from al-ʿUlaymī's Qaṭan ibn Qaṭan poem-cum-legend with a similar exchange between the Jabrid poet al-Shuʿaybī and Barakāt al-Sharīf, a prince of the al-Mushaʿshaʿ dynasty, who in turn was mistakenly identified with one of the sharifs of Mecca.[27] Here the dramatic events were set in motion by the false aspersions cast on Barakāt by his stepmother when he spurned her erotic advances, another motif with a long pedigree.[28]

In similar fashion, Qaṭan ibn Qaṭan saves the marriage of Abū Ḥamzah al-ʿĀmirī, the earliest known Nabaṭī poet, from the murderous intrigues of his mother, who acts in cahoots with his fellow tribesmen. By amazing coincidence, and anachronistically, Qaṭan's raiding trajectory led him to the place where Abū Ḥamzah's beloved wife, Umaymah, had been abandoned in the desert by her misled husband.[29]

The story of the wronged and humiliated hero's revenge and the restitution of his nuptial rights plays out in similar fashion in the legends surrounding the poetry of Abū Zayd al-Hilālī and the Hilālī-like saga of Shāyiʿ al-Amsaḥ, an ancestor of the Shammar tribe in northern Arabia.[30]

In a long poem that is considered one of the finest in the Nabaṭī tradition, Barakāt al-Sharīf in his turn cites an even earlier poem said to have been composed by a religious functionary, ʿAbd al-Raḥīm al-Tamīmī, one of the "martyrs of love," nicknamed Muṭawwaʿ Ushayqir.[31] The pious poet is said to have composed his verses in his dying moments when his kinfolk forced him to divorce a woman he had secretly married for love. Barakāt recalled him fondly:

I was stirred by old verses I heard recited
to emulate al-Tamīmī's message of love.[32]

In a further twist of Jabrid legend entangling poetry and vice versa, al-Shuʿaybī (a poet who corresponded with Barakāt al-Sharīf from his hometown of al-ʿUnayzah in al-Qaṣīm) included two verses from Abū Ḥamzah al-ʿĀmirī, the pre-Jabrid poet whose marriage was said to have been saved by the Jabrid prince Qaṭan ibn Qaṭan. These verses are preceded by two other verses of al-Shuʿaybī that are repeated almost verbatim by Ibn Ẓāhir (§10.46, §10.49). In the essentially oral culture of Nabaṭī poetry, motifs and verses traveled freely over great distances of space and time in a continuous process of cross-fertilization.

The demise of the homegrown tribal state may have imbued the later poems of the Jabrid bard ʿĀmir al-Samīn with a tone of regret that was not mitigated by the role the Omani branch continued to play.[33] But Jabrid poetry lived on long after the dynasty's political power had passed into oblivion. Al-Samīn was cited in a poem by ʿAbd Allāh al-Sayyid, a poet as much attached to the al-Ghurayr princes of Āl Ḥumayd as al-Samīn was to the Jabrids, at a comparable tragic moment: their rule of more than a century in al-Aḥsāʾ was being upended in 1793 by Saʿūd ibn ʿAbd al-ʿAzīz. Fittingly, when al-Sayyid addressed the new Saudi ruler, he cited Barakāt al-Sharīf.[34]

In light of these cultural precedents in eastern Arabia, the interaction with Najd, Arabia's poetic powerhouse, and the common literary heritage of early Nabaṭī poetry (fifteenth–eighteenth centuries), Ibn Ẓāhir may have had in mind Qaṭan ibn Qaṭan's succor to love-stricken poets when he lamented the departure of Banū Hilāl, a tradition of chivalrous romance appropriate to his elegiac verses at the deserted campsite. There is no hint that he bemoaned the waning of the lineage's political power.

The argument in favor of a literary interpretation is reinforced by the mention of cheetahs in Ibn Ẓāhir's verse that precedes his passionate invocation of Banū Hilāl. In Nabaṭī poetry, the use of cheetahs for hunting gazelle occurs in odes to the Jabrid princes, who used to spend winters in the desert and summers in the palm oases of al-Aḥsāʾ, and in the orally transmitted poetry of the Banū Hilāl saga.[35] On the other hand, the first sign in Nabaṭī poetry of a new hunting technique introduced by the Portuguese, a brief mention of firearms, occurs in al-Shuʿaybī's ode to Barakāt al-Sharīf. In Ibn Ẓāhir's work, a man's character is compared to the mechanism of a flintlock. In sum, his verses on Banū Hilāl (the Omani branch of the Jabrids) are to all appearances a nostalgic literary throwback to an era of Bedouin dominion. And since the subject is the departure of the beloved, seated in her swaying camel-borne litter, it is a fair assumption that all similar scenes in Ibn Ẓāhir's *dīwān* are colored by memories of a bygone age.

In another turn of the wheel of history, the earliest manuscripts with Ibn Ẓāhir's *qaṣīdah*s were compiled and scripted by literate men from al-Aḥsāʾ, teachers and religious scholars who in the early twentieth century came to the Emirates at the invitation of wealthy pearl merchants.[36] This explains why their manuscripts are in large part devoted to poetry from other parts of Arabia, with a special emphasis on the eastern province.[37]

The Signature Verse

Ibn Zayd, one of the Jabrid poets who described a royal hunt with cheetahs, begins his odes with a signature verse, a characteristic of the poetry attributed to Banū Hilāl bards whose peregrinations took them to the Maghreb coasts of North Africa. This practice is followed by Ibn Ẓāhir in all of his poems.[38]

One of Ibn Zayd's poems opens:

> These lines of wisdom were composed by the poet Ibn Zayd:
> challenging verses for the benefit of reciters.[39]

It shows an uncanny resemblance to the first verse of the second of Ibn Ẓāhir's poems presented here:

The discerning poet al-Māyidī builds his verses,
wise sayings repeated by poets and reciters.[40]

Not only the wording chimes: the poems have the same rhyme (*-ād*) and meter, known as *hilālī*, a variation of the classical *ṭawīl* ("long"). More than half of Ibn Zayd's poems open on the steady note of this *hilālī* signature verse, in which Ibn Ẓāhir likewise proclaims his name and credentials as a poet. Ibn Zayd and Ibn Ẓāhir also share much of the opening verse's vocabulary and phrasing: the verb "to build" (*bnā*, CA *banā*) for their construction of verse;[41] "new, original verse" (*jdād al-gīl*); "popular with raconteurs" (*bēn ar-rwāt tgāl*); "uplifting verses of wisdom" (*amthāl, mithāyil*); "amazing, extraordinary (verses)" (*ʿajīb, gharīb*); "intelligent" (*fihīm, fāhimīn*); and, of course, "to speak" (*gāl*, CA *qāl*) and "speech," (*gōl, gīl*, CA *qawl*)—that is, "to compose and recite verses of poetry."[42]

Ibn Zayd's next verse continues with a close parallel to a Hilālī poem:

Recite my verse, my messengers who set out
on lean camels that cover great distances in one day.[43]

Ibn Ẓāhir's verse §9.38 is a literal borrowing from that same Hilālī poem's last verse.

The verses of Ibn Zayd, the poet of Ajwad ibn Zāmil (r. 1471–1506), reflect the rulers' Bedouin character. In Jabrid poetry, religion hardly played a role. Hunting with cheetahs and falcons was their pastime. And in his poems, Ibn Zayd vaunts their seasonal migrations:

They own rich estates near Ḥizwā, a shelter
from midsummer heat in the cool shade of lush palm gardens
[. . .]
They camp in al-Dahnā's sands after copious rains,
and in al-Aḥsāʾ when the clusters of dates have ripened.[44]

Like the Bedouin of Ibn Ẓāhir and of his daughter's poem, the ruling house of Banū Jabr took part in the seasonal summer trek to the palm oases.[45]

Apart from Ibn Zayd, the only other Jabrid poet conspicuous for his use of the *hilālī* signature verse is Fayṣal al-Jumaylī, who is cited in a verse by the then ruler of Rawḍat Sudayr, Rumayzān ibn Ghashshām (d. 1669):

> In these verses I emulate Fayṣal al-Jumaylī:
> wisdom's poetry is passed on among the intelligent.[46]

And the wording of Rumayzān's verse parallels Ibn Ẓāhir's opening of §5.1:

> Al-Māyidī ibn Ẓāhir polishes his verses with finesse—
> elegant masterpieces, spread from mouth to mouth.

However, by Rumayzān's time poetry had acquired a taste for rhetorical flourishes that stands in marked contrast to the rough-hewn *hilālī* style.[47]

Rumayzān kept up an active poetic correspondence with Jabr ibn Sayyār, a close kinsman and artistic predecessor of the eighteenth-century innovator Ḥmēdān al-Shwēʿir, who opens two of his poems with a signature verse. In later eighteenth-century poetry there are no further examples of this *hilālī* feature. The Najdī chronicles mention Rumayzān's role in his town's power struggles of 1642.[48] This date coincides with the last mention of the Jabrids—that is, Qaṭan ibn Qaṭan al-Hilālī—in the Omani chronicles. One may conclude, therefore, that by then the *hilālī* style in poetry had by and large run its course in Najd.

The life and times of al-Khalāwī, the Najdī poet to whom Ibn Ẓāhir, in the opinion of Emirati critics, bears the greatest resemblance, can only be speculated about. Like Ibn Ẓāhir and al-Jumaylī, he signs off on his verses with a double name, one of them an adjective denoting descent (*nisbah*): Rāshid al-Khalāwī, or literally as he puts it in his lines, "These are the verses of al-Khalāwī and al-Khalāwī Rāshid."[49] Estimates of his floruit vary from the fifteenth to the late eighteenth century.[50] This does not fit entirely with the commonly held view among experts that he is one of the first poets to emerge after the poet heroes of Banū Hilāl and that he followed their style while making a significant contribution of his own. As in the case of Ibn Ẓāhir, many myths have sprung up about his origins and name: a *khalāwī*, "a lone man, an outcast in the wilderness," and *rāshid*, "a man who knows his way and survives thanks to his unfailing intelligence and wisdom."[51]

Without exception, these stories are based on oral tradition and may have their origin in fanciful interpretations of intriguing verses, such as the legend of Qaṭan ibn Qaṭan that sprouted from the final verses of al-ʿUlaymī, and the legend of Sharīf Barakāt, who as a poet embroidered on the even older legend of the religious Muṭawwaʿ Ushayqir and his accession to the ranks of martyrs of love. However, al-Khalāwī's poetry has not only been preserved in oral tradition but also in manuscripts.[52] His work must have been in high demand, probably as much for practical as for aesthetic reasons. Somewhat in the style of medieval books of hours, al-Khalāwī details the seasons, the weather, and the winds according to the astronomical calendar for purposes that vary from agriculture to seafaring. In addition, he presents a comprehensive catalogue of the gnomic wisdom current at the time. In the centuries that followed, much of it was repeated and recast by Arabian poets until it was compiled in the great Najdī dictionaries of proverbs and sayings.[53]

For all of these reasons, Emirati students of poetry consider al-Khalāwī the principal precursor of Ibn Ẓāhir. Like verses of al-Shuʿaybī's ode to Barakāt al-Sharīf and lines taken from the Banū Hilāl saga, versions of al-Khalāwī's wisdom verses have been incorporated into Ibn Ẓāhir's work.[54] Clearly, these *dīwān*s were in demand as secular manuals for survival, practical guides in a society that depended on oral culture for information in people's day-to-day affairs.[55]

The majority of pre-eighteenth-century Nabaṭī poets known from manuscripts did not open their *qaṣīdah*-style poems with a signature verse. Many of that era's Najdī poems had political significance: poets engaged in poetic correspondence, and often spoke in praise or defense of rulers and with a view to social and political interests. In consequence, it is possible to put an approximate date on many of these poems by reference to chronicles of the period. Presumably, the Banū Hilāl cycle and its associated poetry continued to circulate in oral culture. In addition, its influence occasionally shows in the more sophisticated poetry of the Jabrid period, as in the work of the two Jabrid poets who employed the signature verse.[56]

Notably, there is no trace of it in the work of Abū Ḥamzah al-ʿĀmirī, a Nabaṭī poet who has been dated to the early fourteenth century and therefore should be closest in time to the historical Banū Hilāl.[57] In his *al-Muqaddimah* (*Prolegomena*), the historian Ibn Khaldūn (732–808/1332–1406) gives examples of *hilālī*-style "Bedouin" poetry with opening verses similar to the ones employed by Ibn Ẓāhir.[58] Most likely, Ibn Khaldūn culled the verses from oral tradition or written versions of it. Therefore, these two types of Nabaṭī poetry, the sophisticated tradition of al-ʿĀmirī and the Hilālī, may have coexisted as early as the fourteenth century. At that time, Nabaṭī poetry may have been current in the elite's cultural communication in parallel with popular legend perpetuated for entertainment and instruction. The *hilālī*-style opening verses of two Jabrid poets may suggest that both currents existed side by side and mingled.

A further remarkable feature of Ibn Ẓāhir's work and other early Nabaṭī poetry is the recurrence of vocabulary, imagery, motifs and themes, sayings and proverbs, and prosodic characteristics. Therefore, literary analysis may serve as an auxiliary tool in rough dating to supplement the scarce information from historical sources.

Rhyme, in particular, evolved in recognizable patterns.[59] A quantitative comparison of the rhymes used by Ibn Ẓāhir and other early Nabaṭī poetry from the fifteenth to the late eighteenth centuries indicates that these rhymes are synchronous with the occurrence of the signature verse. A quick scan leads to the conclusion that Ibn Ẓāhir's rhymes are mostly aligned with the poetry of Banū Hilāl, followed closely by semilegendary Najdī poets who adopted the *hilālī* style: Shāyiʿ al-Amsaḥ, Rāshid al-Khalāwī, and the Jabrid poets, in that order. The degree of congruity with Ibn Ẓāhir's verse falls off steeply with pre-nineteenth-century poetry dated to the rule of the Āl Ḥumayd dynasty established in al-Aḥsāʾ province by Barrāk ibn Ghurayr in 1669 and which lasted until 1793.

These considerations result in slightly contradictory data when used to suggest approximate dates for Ibn Ẓāhir's period. If Ibn Ẓāhir lived to witness the rule of Sayf ibn Sulṭān al-Yaʿrubī, he flourished more than 150 years after Ibn Zayd, the poet of Ajwad al-Jabrī, and several decades separate him from the last appearance of the Jabrid Omani branch in Omani chronicles. Prima facie evidence suggests that *hilālī* stylistic elements in his poetry are difficult to reconcile with the era of Sayf ibn Sulṭān's rule. Such a conclusion would be premature, however, in the absence of more information about the state of Nabaṭī poetry in the area that constituted today's Emirates at that time. Conceivably, Ibn Ẓāhir represents a local tradition that continued elements of the Jabrid Hilālī tradition for longer than is otherwise known. Or Ibn Ẓāhir, for reasons of taste and literary effect, may have availed himself of the oral cycle of the Banū Hilāl saga, including its poetry, that continued to flourish in Arabia until recent times. After all, examples of such a predilection were in evidence until the end of the twentieth century.[60]

In oral tradition, such nuances have been lost in the mists of time. Twentieth-century storytellers in the Emirates make no distinction between the Banū Hilāl who trekked to North Africa and the Banū Hilāl of the Jabrid branch who were tribal overlords in parts of Oman from the fifteenth century to almost the middle of the seventeenth century. They have lost the ability to distinguish between Abū Zayd al-Hilālī of the saga of *taghrībat Banī Hilāl*, and Qaṭan ibn Qaṭan al-Hilālī, the equally legendary poet prince and lovers' pillar of strength. For them, they have become one Banū Hilāl, the epitome of tribal romance.[61] Likewise, Ibn Ẓāhir's more philosophically inclined poetry possibly alludes to both traditions.

Ibn Ẓāhir's Poetry

Ibn Ẓāhir's poetry shows the influence of Jabrid, Hilālī, and other early Arabian Nabaṭī traditions of poetry, and the early classical poetry of the Arabian desert. However, his work remains fundamentally different, if not at first glance.

His oeuvre of sixteen poems (or seventeen, if one includes the poem attributed to his daughter) is striking for its unity of tone, motifs, imagery, and thought. Taken as a metatext, it seems to reflect on itself. Compared to other Nabaṭī poetry of the age, it is peerless and leaves one wondering about the poet's larger purpose: it can hardly be meant as poetry for poetry's sake. Serious intent pervades his philosophical lyricism and makes for a sharp contrast with the playfulness and tongue-in-cheek sauciness of the poet's narrative lore.

His themes are familiar from earlier Jabrid bards, and Najdī poetry in general, but are adapted to an inner world of reflection. Early Najdī poetry ranges from the voice of a boisterous, tribal collective (Banū Hilāl, al-Ḍayāghim); to verses in amatory ghazal style as a prelude to encomia, often dressed up as advice or complaints that are sent to rulers, patrons, and important friends; to collections of gnomic wisdom and descriptions of seasonal phenomena. Except for tribal voices, these are compositions by individuals seeking to distinguish themselves vis-à-vis fellow poets, and indeed Ibn Ẓāhir is not shy about proclaiming his preeminence in this arena. Yet in his work there is no mention of a *mamdūḥ*, the prestigious personality to whom the Nabaṭī *qaṣīdah*s of his predecessors are addressed, often accompanied by vivid descriptions of hardships on the way, designed to elicit the patron's sympathy.

In Ibn Ẓāhir's work, customary tribal and personal boasting are not in evidence, apart from poetic prowess and critical acclaim vaunted in the introductory verses; nor are the Najdī bards' virile calls for (bloody) deeds to match challenges hurled in words. The Najdī poet's hard-nosed, often jocular, occasionally rambunctious verses; his taste for rhetorical flourishes and mostly down-to-earth concerns such as sending messages of condolence and prayers for a plague on the house of a friend's enemies—such humdrum concerns have bowed out and Ibn Ẓāhir has rearranged the stage props to accommodate a dreamlike and pensive setting for the theater of his mind.

His spectacular rain sections (*maṭariyyāt*) are not a gambit for a patron's reward, but prayers for blessings on the whereabouts of a beloved and her memory. Socially, he is at a far remove from the Jabrid poet's penchant for grumbling about his treatment at the hands of his own group: Ibn Ẓāhir's tribal affiliation is unclear.

In affairs of the heart, Ibn Ẓāhir is tender and spiritual, though without a tendency toward platonic love, whereas the Najdī poets are often unabashedly physical and delight in details of the female body.[62] It is questionable whether the beloved for whom he pines is a refined and beautiful woman or the embodiment of an amorous ideal. While Ibn Ẓāhir's poetry must be understood in the context of classical and early Nabaṭī traditions, another key to understanding it is provided by the *dīwān* itself, for if read as one text, parts may explain the whole and vice versa.

For instance, the first poem offers a key to the high-pitched emotions of his ghazal sections. It opens on the elegiac note of the classical *qaṣīdah*: a bleak desert scene filled with nostalgia for the beloved who has departed with her tribe. A dove's obsessive litany of cooing awakens memories of his affair's ups and downs.[63] So far there is nothing unusual about the thematic progress. That is, until the lady's camel-borne litter fades away in the distance and the poet himself becomes the object of pursuit: his black raven (that is, his youthful head of hair) is chased away and its perch seized by the white-spotted owl (the first appearance of gray hairs).

In twenty-five verses, the poet spells out the essence of life's drama as he sees it: the brimming cornucopia of youth is passed around in a joyous carousel. Glorious youth seems to last forever. The shock comes when reality shows its grim face unannounced. The poet's heart freezes in horror at the first appearance of white in the black hairs of his head: the white-spotted owl. Then he pulls himself together and musters all his courage to gird for battle in defense against the onslaught of old age.

In the three-way fracas that follows, the poet seeks to enlist youth as an ally against the gray monster. The attempt fails when his young friend absconds: as the poet lunges for him, he seems to have dissolved into thin air. The graybeard watches the scene with sarcastic bemusement. Gradually it dawns on the poet that resistance is futile and that he will not escape humanity's common fate. He imagines the ravages of senility that lie in wait for him. He screams with terror on finding all ways out of his nightmares barred. Finally, his feverish mood abates. Calmed by his acceptance of reality, he finds himself on firmer ground as his mind opens to the eternal truths of the scriptures and the dicta of wisdom.

In another twist, the poet's grave musings are interrupted by a frivolous burst of impious thought: "God be with you, days of youthful frolics!" The palanquin of his wasp-waisted darling is readied and the colorful scene of the caravan's departure is enacted once more. His only sorrow is that he must wait another year before seeing her return. All he can do is pray for rain on her lands, clouds that "roll by and roar like studs in rutting season" (§1.57). His imaginary thunderstorm delights the Bedouin of Banū Hilāl, with their "tents made of red leather, cheetahs for the hunt" (§1.61). It proves no more than a dream (§§1.65–66):

. . . ruins, barren scenes of old.
The traces of former splendor, vanished,
lost forever, like a misty bank of fog.

There is no trace of romance in the plaint that ends a similar scene of knife-wielding close combat with youth and old age (§8.71):

While we play and bustle about, life passes like a dream:
in the final act a treacherous stab, the curtain falls.

In yet another poem, imagery of seafaring is harnessed to the same purpose (§13.14, §13.17):

Dizzy and nauseated, my sick seamen swooned [. . .]
My vessel was sprayed by a wave of hoariness:
I bailed and bailed, fearful of drowning in the deep.

In the poem of Ibn Ẓāhir's daughter (Poem 17), the ship of youth flounders in the middle of the sea.

In the end, the violent knee-jerk response to youth's farewell, fought in an abstract battle of the mind, stands out as the poem's most poignant and true-to-life section. It is the poem's moving idea and, one could argue, the thread that runs through the entire oeuvre, here presented in a straightforward manner and embedded within life's wider canvas as a subject for reflection. With the poet's intentions unveiled, one is emboldened to search for more hidden meaning under the cover of this deft use of convention.

A keyword such as "old age" (*shayb*, *mishīb*) has a relatively high incidence in Poems 1 and 8, and in Poem 1 this is also the case with "amorous love" (*tiṣābī*, *ṣibā*) and "youth" (*shibāb*).[64] Other poems are also notable for trigger words such as "camel-borne litters" (*ẓaʿan*, i.e., the departure or return of the beloved), "separation" (*fargā*, *frāg*),[65] "blind fate" (*dahar*), and "the world" (*dunyā*, as an active agent in human affairs).[66]

Keywords in certain classes are interchangeable. In Poem 4, the lovelorn poet feels that "now one thirsty for my soul watches me," that is, the angel of death. The "world" wages incessant war on him, similar to the surprise attack carried out by old age (§4.29):

> You're assaulted without warning
> or reconnaissance by camel-mounted spies.

In Poem 5, the infidelity of Amor (*ṣibā*) pushes the poet over the brink (§§5.58–59):

> When my hair became flecked with gray—
> the color of haggard wolves with spotted fur—
> I felt certain that gray was extinction's harbinger:
> youth's halcyon days were not here to stay.

And again the "dreaded guest arrived, at a breathless gallop," to hit him "in the eyes, teeth, everywhere" (§5.65, §5.67). This poem shows a balance across the gamut of keywords, but it is especially rich in wise sayings.

From this repetition in different guises emerges the thrust of Ibn Ẓāhir's thought. Beauty of natural life, art, and poetry; spellbinding spectacles of rainstorms; the Bedouin's colorful transport of a mass of animals and people; the game of love and its electrifying sign language—these delights are there to be enjoyed to the full. The poet is no hermit who shrinks in disgust from sampling such pleasures, living in abstinence to preserve the purity of his soul. Even more alien to Ibn Ẓāhir's mind are attempts to wipe the world clean—a tabula rasa as a highway to the hereafter, as in the Wahhābī doctrine that a century later manifested itself on his Gulf shores. A Sufi's spiritual path to individual salvation is perhaps the closest to his outlook.[67]

In his verses, religious commandments play a modest role, mainly as an adjunct to gnomic wisdom and metaphysical endorsement of its generally overlapping obligations. The poet is surprisingly modern in his eclectic use of heritage when he gives advice on navigating life's pitfalls. For Ibn Ẓāhir, the touchstone is how one deals with the element of time that ineluctably forces the truth to emerge from the world's jamboree of false appearances.

Like Tolstoy in *The Death of Ivan Ilyich*, Ibn Ẓāhir considers that a bad life is always an obstacle to dying well.[68] If the world befuddles people and tricks them into throwing themselves into futile enterprises, the poet's wisdom verses serve as waymarks to keep to the golden mean and take a large enough view of life to act sensibly. In the signature verses of the prelude, he designates himself as a "discerning poet" (*fihīm*), as do other poets of his era.[69] Even if there is an element of conventional hyperbole, it is likely that poets such as Rāshid al-Khalāwī and Ibn Ẓāhir, who specialized in folksy wisdom, truly regarded themselves as counselors and advisors for those who depended on oral information and advice. This would explain Ibn Ẓāhir's claim that his orally composed verses should be accorded equal status with scripted (religious) learning (§§15.36–37):

> My compositions for you are being told and retold,
> heritage in scripted lines, irrefutable compositions.
> Sheets lined with writing: books read by eyes;
> my speech wells up straight from the heart.[70]

Ibn Ẓāhir's long *qaṣīdah*s are constructed from sections that are often seamlessly welded together by barely perceptible transitions: the classical amatory prologue, the *nasīb*, has been replaced by a signature verse, and by verses in which the poet vaunts the excellence of his compositions and prides himself on his devoted audience. The sections that follow feature fleeting moments of felicity enjoyed in the company of his sweetheart; their tormented relationship; imaginary dialogues on the rights and wrongs of the lovers' pleas; and her departure when the Bedouin set out on their yearly migration. Passion's storm calms when it is channeled into the timeless perspective of popular wisdom and, to a lesser degree, the eternal truths of the scriptures.

His mental balance regained, the poet's heart is quickened by the arrival of pitch-black clouds, heavy with rain and flashes of lightning.[71] As the poet fancies the exhilaration of his beloved's tribe at the lush meadows that burst from rain-drenched desert soil, he is transported to his days of exuberance and merrymaking. From there, another bout of lover's blues calls for a dose of soothing wisdom. This is the general pattern, but the order and emphasis vary. For instance, the prologue may immediately usher in a section of gnomic wisdom, followed by the spectacle of thunderstorms, love and its agonies, and so on.

This explains why an uninterrupted reading of the poems creates a mesmerizing kaleidoscope effect: the compelling bass beat of great themes rivets the attention on a slow, trancelike dance of modulated motifs. Like Sufi chants, the sonorous repetition and variation might raise spirits to the state of bliss that Ibn Ẓāhir inspires in his audience, as he claims in his signature prologues.[72] In a more granular look at the corpus, the major poems revolve around three main themes: love, conflated with nostalgic memory and a sense of loss as a result of the workings of Time and the World (*al-dunyā*); wisdom presented in sound-bites of binary opposition as a medium to regain equanimity and composure;[73] and rain poems as metaphor for healing forces that revive nature and human spirits.[74] The workings of memory encompass them all.

For his original use of time-honored motifs, Ibn Ẓāhir draws on a broad register of tradition. His signature verse and its poetic self-praise are a further development of *hilālī* opening verses as attested by Ibn Khaldūn's samples, Jabrid poetry, verses of Shāyiʿ al-Amsaḥ, and especially Rāshid al-Khalāwī. While other opening lines vaunt the composer's traditional virtues of generosity and bravery, al-Khalāwī and Ibn Ẓāhir revel in the popular appeal of their verses.

The wording and phrasing of his verses on the departure of his Bedouin love are redolent of the eighth-century poet Dhū l-Rummah (d. 117/735–36), and also of Ibn Sbayyil, the nineteenth-century village poet in thrall to Bedouin beauties, who in his turn is indebted to a tradition established by the seventh-century ghazal poet ʿUmar ibn Abī Rabīʿah (23–93 or 103/644–712 or 721). The sources for

Ibn Ẓāhir's rain sections run the gamut from pre-Islamic poetry to other early Nabaṭī poetry. One can point to such pedigrees for all his themes, motifs, and tropes.

In Ibn Ẓāhir's work, this profusion of inherited riches has been bent to his poetic purpose. Many of his compositions are underpinned by wise sayings and proverbial expressions.[75] As with other Nabaṭī poems salvaged from oral tradition, the value attributed to these signposts of wisdom within the poetry's broader frame must have been a compelling reason for their preservation. Though a conventional motif, the poet has indeed been vindicated in his bold claim (§§4.5–6):

> Sonorous verses spread and read by the crowds:
> till the Day of Resurrection its lines are recited.
> Perhaps, once we're gone, we will not be forgotten
> like discarded utensils scattered in desert wastes.[76]

The Legendary Ibn Ẓāhir

Folktales that were spun into Ibn Ẓāhir's enduring legend have sustained interest in his poetry. In the Emirates, the stories of his saga—or, as one narrator put it, "his comings and goings" (*sīrātah w-yayyātah*)[77]—enjoy great popular appeal, judging by the many versions that have been recorded from narrators with various tribal backgrounds and from different parts of the Emirates. There is a wide gulf between the gravitas of the poems and the humorously mischievous sage who cleaves with fierce single-mindedness to an independence that is under constant threat from his own outrageous generosity.[78] Arguably, the Emirati image of Ibn Ẓāhir as the nation's cultural fountainhead is more reflected by the colorful legend than by the poetry, though the latter must be closer to the poet's original persona.

Interaction between society and legend has its parallel in a putative relation between individual verses and the anecdotal stories. The poet's advertisement of his verses as immunization against the ills of life may have given birth to the story of Ibn Ẓāhir's higher calling. Initially, there had been no sign of a heavenly gift. He must have been in his forties when he carried a load of dates from his palm garden in Ḍank, just across today's border in Oman, toward his tribespeople. As he crossed a rough patch of stony desert and led his camel by the reins at night, he halted at the sound of human-like shrieks: they belonged to a female desert spirit, a jinni with her infant daughter.[79] From her gestures, he understood that she was in desperate need of water. He poured her a generous quantity from his skin and cut a lump of dates from the bunches on his camel. This loosened her tongue and she explained that she had always been a mute (*balmā*) but had been healed by his kindness. In gratitude, she prayed for him to become a learned and wise man (*fāhim wa-ʿālim*): a poet.[80] The inhospitable stretch of desert where the incident took place has been named Hōr al-Balmā ("desert flats of the female mute"). On his return, and to the bewilderment of his kin, he began to recite poetry that had been revealed to him.

The enthralling story of a dreamlike encounter with mysterious forces in the desert has cemented Ibn Ẓāhir's reputation as a poet of a special caliber. As with prophets, the poet is caught unawares when he receives the call to his new vocation from supernatural forces. The story helps explain why his poems were composed at a ripe age: as a young man, he had neither the interest or the talent.[81] Instead, he wasted his time in frivolous pursuits (§§13.21–22):

A reckless teen, I dared the Devil to ride his horse;
  I jumped into the saddle, held the reins with firm grasp,
Went on a rampage, and committed sin after sin:
  I hid what I did, but God knows only too well.[82]

Folk culture demands meanings that are personalized and have the touch and smell of real life, not abstractions of literary convention. In circles of Emirati oral culture, it is taken as a fact that Ibn Ẓāhir's divine gift means that he only speaks the truth and nothing but the truth, and that these truths are handed down faithfully from one generation to the next through oral transmission.[83] His gnomic folk wisdom is taken as a natural appendix of his having been chosen for a higher mission.[84] For others, it is a reason to reject the Hōr al-Balmā story as an ignorant fantasy.[85]

The story of Ibn Ẓāhir's beginnings as a poet on a divine mission revolves around his personal development. So does the story about the end of his life, which he spent traveling to different locations of the Emirates in search of a suitable grave.[86] In the narratives, the story is related to the verse (§13.33):

> From desert plains to coast, and waterholes in between,
> this is the place where the eye sleeps in peace.[87]

He did so by burying different objects (a spool of wool, camel hair, and a skin with clarified butter are mentioned) in the ground and checking on their condition one year later. The only place where the object showed no trace of decay, a location near Rās al-Khaymah, was chosen and made ready. In the narrative, the grave, situated at the edge of the sands, became a meeting place for Bedouin on their way to the market. There they vied in displays of hospitality and exchanges of poetry—a scene reminiscent of festive congregations at the tombs of saints. Again, some narrators object, saying that, according to the faith, bodies of the dead are destined to be consumed by worms.

In between these episodes, Ibn Ẓāhir's story tells how he made a precarious living in various trades, struggled to provide for his dependents as a dedicated family man, and especially how he became an unlikely celebrity who emerged victorious whenever visitors challenged him to live up to his reputation.

The most intriguing and unusual series of narrative episodes concerns the poet's relationship with his daughter. It must have originated in the *qaṣīdah* (Poem 17) that in the manuscripts is attributed to "the daughter of Ibn Ẓāhir" (*bint Ibn Ẓāhir*). In some of the oral traditions, her name is given as Salmā. As always, details vary, but the common thread through the stories is that Ibn Ẓāhir has three or four daughters, and no son. His wife is not named: she and her husband call each other *yā fulān*, "So-and-So." Her role is to be in the background, quietly putting up with her husband's eccentricities. Yet her auxiliary role is important. She understands her husband, sometimes better than he himself, and, as was the wont of Bedouin women, received unannounced guests in his absence.

One of the daughters did the same but with too much exuberance: she rushed to meet and welcome visitors. Therefore, she was called "the hostess" (*marḥabaniyyah*, literally "girl always ready to welcome visitors"). People talked behind her back, and for that reason she was the only daughter to become a spinster. It is not made entirely clear, but she might have been the daughter who was left behind in Oman (that is, the area of al-Buraymī just across the border) as an infant and who rejoined the family later. At some point, Ibn Ẓāhir started to doubt his parenthood of her: if she spoke, it was in monosyllables and then only when asked a direct question. Unlike her sisters, she did not sing or recite poetry when they teamed up to do their chores. After consulting his wife ("Do as you see fit!"), he devised a cruel test: he had her plant a tall bundle of firewood in the backyard, lashed her to the improvised pole, and waited huddled over a fire while she was exposed all night to an ice-cold winter gale without protective clothing. When she almost froze to death, and thought that her motionless father had dozed off over the embers, she spoke a sentence or two resembling verse as a final sigh of despair. He asked her to repeat it, and when she did, he freed her and carried her in his arms to the fire and the supper that had been kept for her.

The reconciliation did not last long. Warned early on by displays of her strong-minded independence (in analogy with her shrewd trick that made unwilling camels cross a creek that was an arm of the sea), he became uncomfortable with her growing success as a poet. When he feared being surpassed by his daughter, and angered by her boast in the first line of her poem in this collection, he again put her to a test with difficult conditions.[88] She nevertheless overcame the hurdles. For lack of an alternative, he resorted to the only means left to him: he asserted his patriarchal authority. He congratulated her and in the same breath enjoined her to henceforward abstain from composing poetry. In versions now deemed more acceptable, she did as she was told.[89] According to harsher readings, he cut her tongue, either entirely or by slashing it through the middle, or simply killed her.[90]

In another series of episodes (the one that features him as a celebrity poet and which for that reason is considered the most relevant episode), a daughter reappears who has been married to a well-to-do but frugal trader. Ibn Ẓāhir's son-in-law (*nisībih*) and his wife own herds of camels, sheep, and goats that are kept around their house, which is situated on a sand hill.[91] His father-in-law is lodged on top of the facing dune, dressed in tattered workman's clothes. Because he shares with visitors whatever food comes his way, his food stores are always running low or depleted. When a group of visitors arrives, the son-in-law makes a bet with his wife that her father will not find the wherewithal to feed them. She remains steadfast in her faith in her father and God's succor of him. Unsurprisingly, she wins, and she collects the camels he promised (on penalty of divorcing her if he did not keep his promise) and drives them to her father.

Apart from showing that a father takes precedence over the husband in Bedouin society, the story uses the flat character of the son-in-law as a foil, throwing the protagonist into relief as a champion of generosity, the supreme virtue. As in the case of other martyr-heroes of hospitality, such as Ḥātim al-Ṭāʾī and his Nabaṭī equivalent, Shāyiʿ al-Amsaḥ, Ibn Ẓāhir of the saga is expected to be generous to a fault.[92] His family has no choice but to wholeheartedly support him in his material self-destruction and take part in the sacrifice. In this, he is like a saint: "One of God's favorites because he shares whatever he has" (*kirīm ḥabīb allāh*).[93]

As a rule, the poet's visitors are driven by purpose.[94] They come to test his reputation for savviness, reckless generosity, unfailing wit, and powers of improvisation. Only by seeing and hearing for themselves can they attain peace of mind: either by demolishing the mystique that attracted them or by satisfying themselves that he is deserving of his reputation so as to put an end to their wrangles on the issue. They take along one of their strongest poets with the aim of sending him into the arena as Ibn Ẓāhir's challenger. The visitors' local poetic tough flexes his muscles for what he thinks will be a walkover: his aim is to render Ibn Ẓāhir perplexed and speechless (*taʿjīzih*).[95]

Amid the twists and turns of the versions, two stand out. In one, the hard-up poet surreptitiously seizes the pack camel of a friend on his way to stock up for his family at a coastal market, slaughters it, and regales his guests with the roast. Subsequently, he confounds them by solving their riddle with one of his own devising and with another sly language-based puzzle. Their poet proves unable to make sense of it.[96] Next morning, on departure, they leave a number of camels in token of their appreciation. His unfortunate friend is more than compensated for his patience by being allotted two of them.

In the second version, Ibn Ẓāhir is intercepted as he makes his way through the desert on foot, while his children are carried on his only camel. The visitors install themselves near his halting place and wait for him to invite them over. On the pretext of fetching water from a well, he rides away, returns with bags full, and at a short distance from the camp slaughters the beast. The guests come running to stop him but it is too late.[97] Again the same scenario unfolds: he baffles them with his impromptu virtuoso performance and the next morning is richly rewarded for his trouble.

Unlike Najdī poetry of the era, Ibn Ẓāhir's verses are not especially remarkable for their pugnacious character. One must assume, therefore, that the gentle dueling in the tales bears some relation to the conventional gauntlet the poet threw down in his preludes. In the final analysis, it is not so much the celebration of poetic stardom as the triumph of humility that draws attention. Unlike the classical tribal "outlaw poets" (*ṣaʿālīk*), Ibn Ẓāhir is intensely social. Like Shāyiʿ al-Amsaḥ before him, and Ḥmēdān al-Shwēʿir after him, his underdog position is a conceit that lends him an ideal vantage point from which to take aim and puncture vanity and false pretentions. In all versions, visitors who have come riding from afar to meet the storied hero-poet ask for directions from an old man dressed in rags and carrying a bundle of firewood—without realizing that this is their man.[98] The graybeard points to a *ghāf* tree on the dune and then extends them an invitation himself, an offer they unceremoniously reject. This is only the first of the lessons they are going to be taught. One imagines the old man's sly smirk and chuckle to himself as he sizes up the self-assured travelers. His habitual dissemblance (*tanakkur*) is a thread that runs through all tales. The message is that one should not go by appearances if one wishes to avoid fatal mistakes of judgment.

A master of dissemblance, Ibn Ẓāhir knows how to hide his identity while roaming his lands like a king on an incognito inspection tour. When the local emir's tax collectors demand their tithe for the fish he has just sold, he refuses with the argument that he is not a well-to-do owner of majestic palms or a seagoing ship (*būm*). He only has what he has procured with his own labor and the bare minimum for the upkeep of his family. Instead, he tells them to bring their masters the verses he improvises for the occasion. Predictably, the emirs recognize the composer. They hasten to have him called to their assembly room and shower him with praise and gifts. Nevertheless, he departs and makes for Jumayra beach near Dubai to join the local self-employed pearl divers in the coastal waters (*qaḥḥah*). Angry at the trifling sum the harvest of his weeks of toil fetches in the market, he tosses the money into the sea, to the dismay of the other divers.

Finally, he is enlisted by the captain of a large pearling ship as one of the crew members whose task it is to haul up the divers from the bottom of the sea. When he is brought to the ship owner's daughter for inspection, she does not even deign to cover her face at seeing him and protests that such a decrepit old man will serve no useful purpose. But the captain says that he could find no one else to complement his crew. At sea, it turns out that the old man has unsuspected reserves of strength and hauls as strongly as a powerful winch while singing his own seaman's verses. The captain discovers his identity and spares him from further hard work. Sent to shore in a lighter vessel (*tishshālah*),[99] he is received with full honors by the owner's daughter, who this time makes sure to wear a veil as a sign of her respect.

By now, Ibn Ẓāhir has had his fill of life at sea and the commercial exploitation of labor that comes with it.[100] He retrieves the camel that was left to pasture inland and makes for his family. There he discovers that his neighbor has been doing just as well or better without entering the coastal labor market, leading him to declare (§20.14):

> My dears, best to live off the desert:
> I have no business toiling at sea.

He then takes his family north, and on the crest of sand near Rās al-Khaymah where he decides to settle, he joyfully proclaims: "From the dune, I saw my desert abode: the new as of old" (§20.12).

The Poet and the Tales

As a cultural monument, Ibn Ẓāhir is identical with the poems found in manuscripts, themselves of uncertain origin, and the narrative saga as told, retold, and remolded in oral transmission.[101] Beyond the name given to the poet, we have no reliable historical information about when, where, for what audience, and how the *qaṣīdah*s were composed. Therefore, one must make do with "these amusing compilations of folktale and legend."[102]

In the Emirates, it is taken as axiomatic that Ibn Ẓāhir is a proto-Emirati of Bedouin stock.[103] Narrative details such as his scorn for life at sea and his exulting at his retreat into the desert are thought to underscore the correctness of this assumption. This cannot be taken at face value. With the transformation of the Arab Gulf economies from traditional occupations, such as pearling, to oil-based welfare states, people's self-definition as "Bedouin" is often used as a shorthand reference to local tribal roots. The designation evokes the hallowed glow of an inherited authentic regional past of desert purity and chivalry, which is celebrated in such pastimes as camel racing and falconry. This has more to do with the use of heritage as a signifier in quasi-aristocratic and social stratification through pageants and games than with the economic and social realities that underlie original meanings.

Even in the narrative lore of the poet's legend, the term "Bedouin" carries a meaning that is far removed from the culture of "pure" camel nomads such as the Rwala Bedouin whose manners and customs were studied by Alois Musil.[104] The word for his dwelling (*bēt*, CA *bayt*) might refer to a Bedouin's "house made of goat hair," a Bedouin tent, in northern Arabia. But Ibn Ẓāhir's dwelling, as described by the storytellers, is a cabin made of palm fronds and branches, dry brushwood, palm leaf matting, and woven material, with a small enclosure in front of the single door for the cooking fire and to keep goats out.[105]

His "Bedouin" life may have shared some characteristics with that of the fifteenth- and sixteenth-century Jabrid rulers in eastern Arabia who influenced the culture along the northern Omani coast of today's Emirates: they spent winters in the sands of al-Dahnāʾ desert and summers at the palm oases of al-Aḥsāʾ. Similarly, as stated in the dramatic last verses of this collection of poems, at the end of the hot season the Bedouin left the coastal oases and moved south, inland toward al-ʿAyn and al-Buraymī.[106] The storytellers point out that Ibn Ẓāhir spent winters in Umm al-Khayūs (a location in Rās al-Khaymah) and summer in al-Hīlī (a location near al-Buraymī).[107] In addition, even at that time few of the areas covered by today's states of the Emirates and Oman were not intimately connected with the sea and its economy of travel, trade, fishing, and pearling.[108] For instance, the last of the Jabrid Banū Hilāl (who, according to the old Omani chronicles, were often in league with Banū Yās, the tribal confederation of the present rulers of the country) took refuge in the "Christian" (that is, Portuguese) fortress of Sohar on the Omani coast when they were hard-pressed by the new Omani Yaʿrubī imam at their stronghold in Līwā, a location at the edge of the Empty Quarter and as far inland as it is possible to reach in the Emirates (see p. xiv).

The narrative saga of the poet as a jack-of-all-trades presents an entertaining overview of lifestyles and occupations in pre-oil society, reflecting certain traits of character dear to an audience that values Ibn Ẓāhir as a cultural precursor. Anachronisms that abound in this presumably centuries-old lore (such as the designation of a group of visitors on camelback as "Saudis" or the money the poet receives for his pearls as Indian coinage (paisas and rupees)) and other features might point to late nineteenth- or early twentieth-century origins for many of the details. This does not preclude Ibn Ẓāhir's saga from having been in gestation for a much longer period of time.

The legend's enduring appeal, and the fact that it was recorded and expertly noted for the first time in the late 1990s and early 2000s, gained from the contrast between the poet's utterly simple yet fulfilling life and the rapid transformations wrought by oil wealth and the influx of foreign labor and lifestyles. Like the old Phrygian peasants Philemon and Baucis of the Greek saga, who lived contentedly in a hut roofed with reeds and thatch, and who survived a flood thanks to their warm hospitality offered to incognito visiting gods, Ibn Ẓāhir may have come to stand for a lost paradise of honest and unpretentious simplicity.[109] In the eyes of some, his legacy kept alive a nostalgic dream of finding clues for this idealized past's recovery in one form or another—like the longing glances Ibn Ẓāhir cast at the tail end of the Hilālī caravan as it faded into shimmering hot air and carried off his beloved and his own youth. And even Ibn Ẓāhir could not escape becoming a member of Abū Zayd al-Hilālī's team.[110]

Ultimately, the question leads back to the poetry. If one adopts a comprehensive view of the verses, against the background of the other poetry of the era taken in a broad sense, it is hard to escape the impression that the poet looks at his world from a sedentary point of view. This would not preclude vast experience with life in the desert, if only for the purpose of travel. Like Ibn Sbayyil, the nineteenth-century central Arabian oasis poet who fell in love with the Bedouin, Ibn Ẓāhir looks at the Bedouin with admiration and sympathy.[111] Again like Ibn Sbayyil, he sees them depart and arrive, but there is no hint that he ever joined them on their migrations. This in itself is not conclusive: artistic motifs and themes that stretch back for over a thousand years do not necessarily provide clues about their users' backgrounds. Likewise inconclusive are similes borrowed from the oases and their systems of irrigation, pearling, and foreign merchandise sold at coastal markets. Yet, on basis of the poetry, the only perhaps partly reliable information about Ibn Ẓāhir as a person, it would feel counterintuitive to designate him as Bedouin. The prominence of maxims and gnomic wisdom; the unrelenting focus on Time, Fate, the World, and human destiny; the overarching transcendental thrust of his verses; his vocabulary and phrasing—such specifics point to roots in the world of sedentary civilization.

Ibn Ẓāhir and the United Arab Emirates

One of the earliest modern researchers on the poet and his work wrote that the first editions of Ibn Ẓāhir's poetry were in tune "with popular sentiment in the region starting in the 1960s when people were looking for cultural symbols to unite them under the new umbrella of the Union, symbols that would give expression to their characteristics and identity as a people. Ibn Ẓāhir fitted that bill to perfection: he provided the right symbol on account of his unique work and his legend that had been preserved as part of popular oral heritage."[112] In addition, his rain sections (in particular in Poem 16) seemed to delineate almost exactly the current borders of the newly founded state (see the map on p. xxxix).[113] The place names scattered in his verses and in the stories about his ceaseless traveling in search of a livelihood or a burial site, or to rejoin his family, contributed to a sentiment that he truly belonged to all of the Emirates. As expressed by the narrators: "There is nowhere he did not visit. He lived in every place."[114]

Generally considered the true originator of Nabaṭī poetry in the Emirates, Ibn Ẓāhir and his published *dīwān* provided the impetus for a subsequent wave of editions of other works in Nabaṭī style.[115] As the embodiment of things truly Emirati, he is credited with inventions of great simplicity: he is said to have been the first to introduce the little boat made of palm fronds and their thick bases, a *shāshah*, that he used for fishing in the coastal waters, from the Omani coast farther south.[116] And among storytellers, the name Rās al-Khaymah, literally "the top of the tent (or cabin)" is attributed to him: he had fitted a lamp on top of his shack, itself on top of a sand dune near the sea, which served as a beacon for sailors in the dark of night on their way to the shore.[117] Already for the people who preceded the current generations, the combative, kindhearted, witty, resourceful, hard-bitten, scruffy poet of the folktales had become a towering figure admired for his art and uplifting strength of character. As put by another poetical icon considered typical for the style and humor of the Emirates, Ibn ʿAtīj al-Hāmilī (1855–1909):

> The times of Ibn Ẓāhir, an age bygone,
>   were ashamed of reciting a wretched line;
> Our poems are the offspring of their lucid verse,
>   a murmur of little rills after thundering torrents.[118]

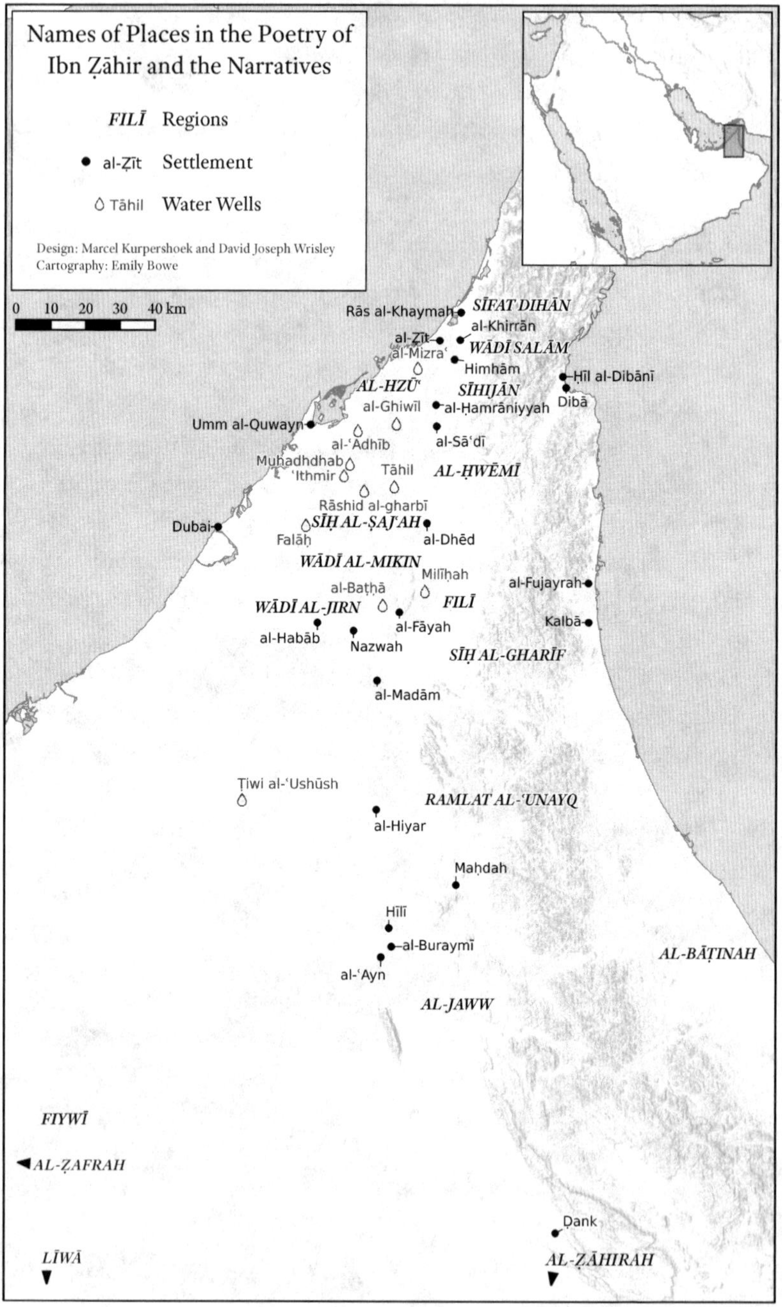

Names of Places in the Poetry of Ibn Ẓāhir and the Narratives
FILĪ Regions
al-Ẓīt Settlement
Ṭāhil Water Wells
Design: Marcel Kurpershoek and David Joseph Wrisley
Cartography: Emily Bowe
0 10 20 30 40 km
Rās al-Khaymah
SĪFAT DIHĀN
al-Khirrān
al-Ẓīt
al-Mizraʿ
WĀDĪ SALĀM
Himhām
Ḥīl al-Dibānī
Dibā
AL-HZŪʿ
SĪHIJĀN
al-Ghiwīl
al-Ḥamrāniyyah
Umm al-Quwayn
al-ʿAdhīb
al-Sāʿdī
Muhadhdhab
ʿIthmir
Ṭāhil
AL-ḤWĒMĪ
Rāshid al-gharbī
Dubai
SĪḤ AL-ṢAJʿAH
al-Dhēd
Falāḥ
WĀDĪ AL-MIKIN
Milīḥah
al-Fujayrah
al-Baṭḥā
WĀDĪ AL-JIRN
FILĪ
Kalbā
al-Habāb
al-Fāyah
Nazwah
SĪḤ AL-GHARĪF
al-Madām
Ṭiwi al-ʿUshūsh
RAMLAT AL-ʿUNAYQ
al-Hiyar
Maḥdah
Hīlī
al-Buraymī
al-ʿAyn
AL-BĀṬINAH
AL-JAWW
FIYWĪ
AL-ẒAFRAH
Ḍank
LĪWĀ
AL-ẒĀHIRAH

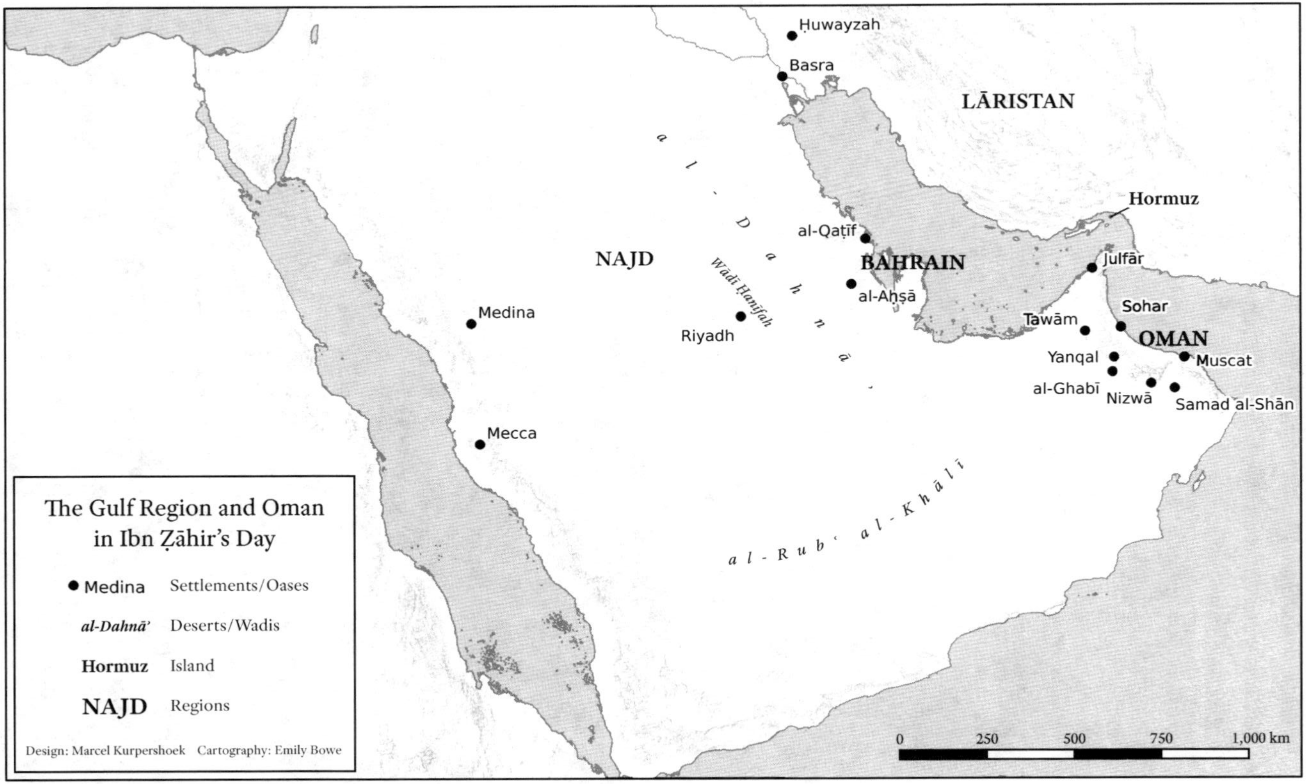
The Gulf Region and Oman in Ibn Ẓāhir's Day
Medina Settlements/Oases
al-Dahnā' Deserts/Wadis
Hormuz Island
NAJD Regions
Design: Marcel Kurpershoek Cartography: Emily Bowe
Ḥuwayzah
Basra
LĀRISTAN
Hormuz
al-Qaṭīf
BAHRAIN
al-Aḥsā
Julfār
Sohar
OMAN
Tawām
Yanqal
al-Ghabī
Nizwā
Muscat
Samad al-Shān
NAJD
Medina
Mecca
Riyadh
Wādī Ḥanīfah
al-Dahnā'
al-Rub' al-Khālī
0 250 500 750 1,000 km

Note on the Text

Language, Meter, and Rhyme

The idiom of the poems is fundamentally different from the language of the narratives. Obviously, the language of poetry is never merely a version of common daily usage, literary and other prose, and recorded narrative speech. In this collection, the contrast is particularly stark because the poetry is centuries older (though its language must have undergone changes in the course of transmission) and is part of the highly stylized, often mannerist conventions of that era. At the time of composition, the culture of this type of Nabaṭī poetry was shared by the elite in the oases of al-Yamāmah in central Najd and the eastern Arabian oasis of al-Aḥsā', from where it reached the coasts and hinterland of the areas that were then vaguely defined as northern Oman. The earliest manuscripts date from the 1920s and, while the notation varies, many features of the notation reflect aspects of Emirati usage in the modern age. Whether they also reflect features of the spoken language in Ibn Ẓāhir's age, we cannot know for certain.

The stories, on the other hand, are told in the language of today's usage, or, more precisely, in that of Emiratis whose age ranged from sixty to ninety years at the time of recording in the late 1990s and early 2000s. All of them were known storytellers and much of their vocabulary stems from the pre-oil traditional economy of the Arabian Gulf littoral and inland areas. Recorded and noted to reflect the speech of the narrators, it is artful speech: storytelling by persons steeped in the area's narrative lore, composed of elements inherited and constantly remolded through oral transmission. In its recorded state, it may well reflect these stories' stage of development in the second half of the nineteenth century or in the early twentieth century.

That is not to say that the language of the poetry is entirely different from that of the tales. The poetry partakes of the artistic idiom of the sixteenth- to eighteenth-century Nabaṭī tradition of the wider eastern and central Arabian area. In many respects, it is an Emirati subspecies, one closer to aspects of the eastern Arabian than the central Arabian tradition, as might be expected in light of long-standing political and cultural ties. But even here, Ibn Ẓāhir's corpus differs more from eastern Arabian poetry than the latter does from the central Arabian Nabaṭī "norm."

The Emirati dialect is part of the Arabic spoken along the Arabian side of the Gulf. For a comprehensive description and analysis of the linguistic aspects, see the studies of Clive Holes, in particular the volumes of his series *Dialect, Culture, and Society in Eastern Arabia*. For the Nabaṭī poetry of Central Arabia and its historical aspects, refer to the works of Saad Sowayan and other works listed in the bibliography.

Most poems are in a meter that corresponds to the classical *ṭawīl* ("long"), in Nabaṭī poetry called *masḥūb* ("drawn out"), and which is considered one of the Hilālī meters. Three poems (1, 14, and 16) are in a meter that corresponds to the classical *hazaj* ("trilling"). Poem 8 is in a shorter meter that corresponds to the classical *mutaqārib* ("with short steps").[119] Three other poems (5, 11, and 13) are in a meter that resembles the classical *rajaz* ("trembling"). As in classical Arabic poetry, the meters are quantitative and of a fixed length that in principle is the same in each hemistich.[120] And as in the poetry of Ḥmēdān al-Shwēʿir, there are patterned variations, mostly at the end of the line. In Nabaṭī poetry, it is not possible to have a succession of two short syllables.[121] The technique of scansion in Nabaṭī poetry is explained in detail in a number of studies in English and Arabic.[122]

Rhyme, as discussed above, shows remarkable correspondences with other *hilālī*-style verses of the early centuries of Nabaṭī poetry. The poems are, without exception, composed with a single rhyme at the end of each verse. Since the nineteenth century, it has become customary for Nabaṭī poets to end each column of hemistiches with a separate rhyme.[123]

Text of the Poems and Narratives

The text of the poems is based on nine manuscripts. A compact disc with copies of these manuscripts was given to me by the director of the Abu Dhabi Academy of Poetry, Sultan Alameemi. Some of these had been preserved in the National Library of Abu Dhabi. Perhaps due to reorganizations and the move to temporary offices of the library's parent organization pending the availability of new offices, these could not be traced by the staff. Therefore, I was not able to see the originals. Fortunately, the copies were in a good state and probably no less readable than the originals. Later, I obtained other copies from Fālīh Ḥanẓal, the author of several works on Emirati traditional culture and history, among them a dictionary of Emirati expressions that has been referenced in notes to this volume's text. Ḥanẓal's copies did not contain texts not already found on Alameemi's compact disc.

Nabaṭī poetry boasts a history of some seven centuries (the earliest known poem has been dated to the early fourteenth century), but the earliest known manuscripts were acquired in Arabia and brought to Europe by the French scholar Charles Huber during his travels in 1878 and 1883–84.[124] The manuscripts cannot have been older than a few decades at that time. In the Emirates, the first manuscript dates from 1926. Collecting poetry and writing it by hand in manuscripts continued until the 1970s, at which time it was supplanted by printed editions.

Many manuscripts with Nabaṭī poetry may have been lost as a result of the resurgence of radical Wahhabism after the resumption of Saudi rule in Riyadh in 1902 and the campaign of conquest waged by the Saudi *Ikhwān* troops. One of the first scholars along the Omani coast to record poetry in MSS was the poet Aḥmad ibn ʿAbd al-Raḥmān Bū Sanīdah, a clerk for Shaykh Sālim ibn Sulṭān al-Qāsimī, the ruler of Sharjah until 1883, and after that for Shaykh Ṣaqr ibn Khālid al-Qāsimī. He was renowned for his beautiful handwriting and for his activities as a prolific producer of MSS, which later he came to see as a sinful activity. He burnt all MSS in his possession before his death in 1913. The work of the poet Sālim ibn ʿAlī al-ʿUways fared no better: the collected poetry of his friend Shaykh Sulṭān ibn Sālim al-Qāsimī, the ruler of Rās al-Khaymah, was lost at sea on the way to India where it was to have been printed.

More successful preservation work began as part of a cultural and scholarly effort in Abu Dhabi, Dubai, and Sharjah. Aḥmad ibn Khalaf al-ʿUtaybah, a wealthy pearl merchant with a solid business reputation throughout the Gulf, and a poet himself, decided to bring teachers for the school his father had started in the 1920s before government schools had opened.[125] He came to an agreement with teachers from al-Aḥsāʾ. Culturally linked to the northern coast of Oman since the days of the Jabrid rule in the fifteenth and sixteenth centuries, al-Aḥsāʾ was a natural port of call for this cultural and educational enterprise. The teachers played an important role in the production of manuscripts with poetry. They took an active part in the literary and cultural sessions in the Abu Dhabi majlis of Khalaf al-ʿUtaybah, the Arabian equivalent of a literary salon where poetry was recited and discussed, exactly as depicted by Ibn Ẓāhir in some of his preludes. Friends who came to visit Khalaf brought manuscripts as a gesture of friendship.

Some of the earliest manuscripts bear the names of the teachers and men of letters from al-Aḥsāʾ: al-Sayyid ʿAbd Allāh al-Hāshimī, a teacher in the school of Khalaf's father; ʿAbd Allāh ibn ʿAbd al-Qādir, a poet and a cultured man, *adīb*, from al-Aḥsāʾ (1873–1926); and

Aḥmad ibn ʿUthmān al-Khaṭīb, also from al-Aḥsāʾ, whose manuscript (1926) is the first dated collection of Emirati poetry, followed a year later by that of al-Hāshimī. They were a tight-knit community, as one can tell from the fact that al-Khaṭīb's and ʿAbd al-Qādir's manuscripts included poems by al-Hāshimī.

Their MSS run to hundreds of pages, but the share of poets from the Omani coast is modest. Prominent among them are Ibn Ẓāhir, Ibn Muḥīn, and Khalaf al-ʿUtaybah. The majority of names stem from the scribes' homeland in eastern Arabia and the ubiquitous great names from Najd, such as Barakāt al-Sharīf, Ibn Liʿbūn, Muḥsin al-Hazzānī, ʿUbayd ibn Rashīd, and Muḥammad ibn ʿAbd Allāh al-Qāḍī.

In Dubai, the most active part was played by Shaykh ʿUbayd ibn Jumʿah Āl Maktūm, a lover of poetry. At his request, Muḥammad ibn Ḥāfiẓ produced a number of anthologies in manuscript, four of which survived. The first (1939) is devoted to the poet Mubārak al-ʿUqaylī (1939). A second MS (1940) covers more or less the same ground as the Abu Dhabi MSS: besides the great Arabian names, they include Ibn Ẓāhir and Ibn Muḥīn, and poets from Dubai. A third MS presents the poems of Shaykh Sulṭān ibn Ṣaqr al-Qāsimī of Sharjah. Other manuscripts were produced in Sharjah and ʿAjmān. Ḥamad Khalīfah Bū Shihāb, who co-authored an early edition of Ibn Ẓāhir's work, one of the three used for this edition, was a pivotal figure in the cultural life of ʿAjmān and a close friend of many poets whose work he collected. But again, most of what he collected was lost.[126]

Currently, twelve MSS with poetry of Ibn Ẓāhir are known to exist.[127] For the edition on which this translation was based, nine of these were used. The MSS show the usual variations in wording, number, and order of verses; parts of poems are found in more than one place in the same MS; and some MSS give only part of a poem.[128] Nevertheless, some full versions of poems occur and the existing MSS have provided sufficient basis for the Emirati editions: each line is traceable to MSS (with only one known MS for Poems

6 and 13). Variations in wording are relatively minor. A comparison of the MSS pages devoted to Ibn Ẓāhir and oral versions shows that the existing texts must have their source in more than one earlier manuscript, of which no trace has been found.[129] At the time of recording in the late 1990s and early 2000s, the oral versions were far more fragmentary than the written texts. Analysis has shown that a number of poems attributed to Ibn Ẓāhir in five of these MSS are unlikely to be part of his work.[130]

Al-Māyidī ibn Ẓāhir has always been seen as the Emirati poet par excellence. His first printed *dīwān* was published in 1963 at the expense of the ruler, Shaykh Ḥamdān ibn Rāshid Āl Maktūm, at the Omani Presses (*al-Maṭābiʿ al-ʿUmāniyyah*, founded by a scion of a family of teachers from al-Aḥsāʾ, al-Sayyid Hāshim ibn al-Sayyid Riḍā l-Hāshimī).[131] The next edition, *Jewels from the Poetry of Ibn Ẓāhir* (*Dīwān al-jawāhir fī shiʿr Ibn Ẓāhir*), appeared in Abu Dhabi in 1967 at the orders of the first head of state, Shaykh Zāyid ibn Sulṭān Āl Nahayān, and was prepared by Muḥammad Sharīf al-Shībānī, the poet of the court in Abu Dhabi, originally from Bahrain.[132]

For the Arabic text used as the basis for this translation, this volume has relied on three scholarly editions based on manuscripts. The first and least scholarly of these was published in 1989 by Abū Shihāb and Abū Malḥah in 1989 in Dubai. The earliest of the principal works is a massive volume published in 1999 by Aḥmad Rāshid Thānī (1962–2012), which aimed at the documentation of all that was known about Ibn Ẓāhir and his work at that time. An important inclusion is the annotated and well-documented recordings of the narrative saga of the poet.

Thānī's work was continued by Sultan Alameemi, whose edition includes an even more thorough review of sources with the added benefit of fresh analysis of the materials. In particular, Alameemi's edition includes two new poems of Ibn Ẓāhir that came to light in hitherto unknown manuscripts (Poems 6 and 13). As it turned out, the latter poem offered confirmation of the only mention that can be related to chronicled fact: the rule of the Yaʿrubī imam Sayf ibn

Sulṭān. The verses with the imam's name had been in oral circulation, but thanks to the discovery they found their place in a full poem. This work also followed in Thānī's footsteps with the addition of an edition of recordings of the narrative materials, enriched with a linguistically precise rendering of the dialectal texts and explanatory notes.[133]

The edition of Alameemi, who was this volume's reviewer, has been taken as the point of departure for the Arabic text of the *qaṣīdah*s. A relatively modest number of changes reflect preferred readings of MSS, whether in agreement with the two other editions or not. Depending on their importance, these changes were discussed with Alameemi in the course of his review.[134] As even these changes were generally of minor importance for the overall thrust of verses and poems, they have not been detailed in the notes.[135] Also, several sessions were devoted to points that had remained somewhat obscure. On some vexed issues, Alameemi would call on other experts in oral culture for their opinion.[136]

In his edition, Thānī has divided the recordings of the transmitters into sections and distributed these over thematically arranged episodes.[137] These recordings were made in 1996–97 during sessions in the Rās al-Khaymah area.[138] His order of thematic progression has an internal logic that has been followed in this edition. In Alameemi's edition, each narrator has been given a separate chapter, which is subdivided into thematic headings that are more or less common to all chapters.[139] This edition's narrative section follows a thematic arrangement and a selection of text borrowed principally from Alameemi and supplemented with passages from Thānī's work.[140] While the edition aims at consistency, this has not always been possible and is perhaps not even desirable for such material. The result has been reviewed and explained with the assistance of Alameemi.

As noted by Emirati researchers, authors, and participants in poetry sessions (see n. 136), much of Ibn Ẓāhir's work remains somewhat recondite because of the linguistic evolution of the poetry over the centuries and an absence of comparative material. For this volume, solutions have been found by expanding the context. Other clues can be found in Najdī, Emirati, and Omani dictionaries of proverbs and sayings.[141] Even though there are no known poets in the area of today's Emirates contemporary with Ibn Ẓāhir, he hardly composed a line that does not have an equivalent in the fifteenth- to eighteenth-century poetry of eastern Arabia and Najd, especially the poetry that appeared with the encouragement of the Jabrid dynasty, which had its center in the oasis of al-Aḥsāʾ. In addition, Ibn Ẓāhir's poetry shows Hilālī influence in prosody, vocabulary, and images, particularly in the manner of later Hilālī-style poets such as Shāyiʿ al-Amsaḥ and Rāshid al-Khalāwī, who became legends in their own right. In many respects, his work also shows kinship with Najdī poets from the second half of the seventeenth century and whom we know from chronicles, such as Rumayzān ibn Ghashshām and Jabr ibn Sayyār, the immediate predecessor of Ḥmēdān al-Shwēʿir. The poetry from these centuries offers numerous keys to further understanding Ibn Ẓāhir.

Similarly, Arabian poetry of the classical era offers an indispensable treasure trove of kindred material (vocabulary, figures of speech, themes and motifs, images, composition, and thought) that has been soaked up by the work of Ibn Ẓāhir and permeates its every capillary. One example of telling detail is an element in the description of the powerful male camel that carries the palanquin of the beloved. The beast is praised for being "civet-scented behind the ears" (§14.14, "behind the ears," *dhifārīh*, is more precisely "the bone behind the ear," here in dual). The same wording, meaning, and intent are found in verses by the late-eighth-century poet Dhū l-Rummah:

> Like pepper rolled into grains by the secretion
> of sweat streaming from the cavities behind their ears.

And like Ibn Ẓāhir's sweetheart, Dhū l-Rummah's beloved is whisked off while seated on carpets of the same make as Ibn Ẓāhir's:

Their backs adorned with colorful Syrian coverings
hung over the curved litter poles of the doe-eyed beauty.[142]

While the comparative material is vast, the most intensive use has been made of *al-Mufaḍḍaliyyāt*, especially its Arabic scholion, and the *dīwān* of Dhū l-Rummah. Their geography and the context of Arabian desert culture make the area's early Nabaṭī poetry a natural outgrowth of these works. Dhū l-Rummah was buried in the sands of al-Dahnā', where the Jabrid princes began hunting with cheetahs some five centuries later—the same princes whose Hilāl branch brought this culture of poetry to the northern shores of Oman where Ibn Ẓāhir flourished another two or three centuries later. If little light is shed on these literary developments by the chroniclers, the nature of classical Arabian desert poetry and its Nabaṭī offspring leaves no doubt about the intimate connection of these two.

Translation

This is the first translation of Ibn Ẓāhir's work and the narrative saga recorded from oral transmitters. In the United Arab Emirates, the poet is venerated as a national icon, but outside his native area he remains virtually unknown in the Arab world, and to a large extent even in neighboring Gulf states.

In transliteration from classical Arabic, the poet's name is written as al-Mājidī ibn Ẓāhir, but here as al-Māyidī ibn Ẓāhir. Because his work is in the idiom of Emirati vernacular poetry, called Nabaṭī poetry, names are transliterated in a way that more closely reflects the pronunciation of this predominantly oral poetry (recited on social occasions), and that is accepted among specialists. In this Introduction, names of towns and other geographical features mentioned in the poetry, and the names of early Nabaṭī poets and other names of persons, are transliterated according to their standard classical Arabic spelling to facilitate identification. Occasionally, as appropriate, names and words that occur in the vernacular text may be given in the Introduction and the endnotes (for example, if they occur in book titles or as official family names) according to the classical Arabic transliteration, such as the tribe al-Nuʿaym, and not an-Nʿēm. Also, classical transliteration is preferred where the vernacular might lead to misunderstanding. For instance, the Arabic word for the star Canopus, *suhayl*, is *shēl* in the vernacular, pronounced *(i)s-hēl*; a village near Rās al-Khaymah, Dihān, is pronounced Dhān (iD-hān). The transliteration in these parts of the volume will also hew closer to the classical Arabic practice in other respects and details. Even though in the vernacular all final vowels are long by definition, for this volume the choice has been made to place a macron over all long vowels, again to facilitate identification for those with a background in classical Arabic.

The English translation closely follows the Arabic original, but it is far from a literal translation. For those interested in more background on the Arabic original, a limited glossary of some of the poetry's vocabulary will appear as part of the web-based materials for this edition on the Library of Arabic Literature's website at www.libraryofarabicliterature.org. The endnotes of this edition provide explanations of various aspects of the verses and the narrative text. In particular, they have been amplified with equivalents from classical and modern standard Arabic, lines by predominantly early classical Arabic poets and Nabaṭī poets of Ibn Ẓāhir's era in a wider sense, and other information conducive to a more detailed understanding of the verse and its literary and cultural context. The text, both poetry and narratives, has been extensively cross-referenced, not only with other parts of the text, but to an even greater extent with early Nabaṭī poetry from the period 1300–1800, with some instances of nineteenth- and twentieth-century poetry, and the early classical period from about 500–800, mainly Saad Sowayan's works on Nabaṭī poetry, C.J. Lyall's edition and translation of *al-Mufaḍḍaliyyāt*, and the *dīwān* of Dhū l-Rummah and other poets from the Arabian desert areas. More detailed descriptions of some subjects of special interest for interpretation, such as the practice of opening poems with a "signature verse," can be found at p. xxix.

In the harsh environment of central Arabia and the Arabian Gulf littoral, geography and natural conditions saw little change during the fifteen hundred years or so of its poetry until the advent of modernity (for lack of a better word) and the radical transformations brought about by the oil economy. During these centuries of rare continuity, this environment remained woven into the texture of cultural expression, part of the artists' daily life, though elsewhere in the Arab world its elements turned into metaphor or came to be seen as tedious harking back to archaic cliché. In truth, the ancient genres and themes showed remarkable development, and time-honored motifs acquired new metaphorical meanings and were put to work in remodeled *qaṣīdah* structures. Ibn Ẓāhir's work, for instance, is an example of semantic and stylistic integration of elements borrowed from a conventional heritage for a purpose that makes of it an original artistic creation. His achievement can only be truly appreciated if his work is put in the context of the broader traditions of Arabian poetry—in fact, by treating the entire Arabian (as distinct from "Arabic"—that is, referring to the Arabian Peninsula and adjoining related tribal areas) tradition in poetry as one huge metatext to be cross-referenced and thereby understood in all its aspects. This explains the need for a relatively voluminous apparatus of notes, especially for an oeuvre about whose creator and immediate historical context so little is known. In such a case, the only available tool for interpretation is the work itself and all the materials that may have been part of the creator's mental makeup.

Notes to the Introduction

1 In the published editions, including the study and edition (2004) of this volume's reviewer, Sultan Alameemi (Sulṭān al-ʿAmīmī in Library of Arabic Literature transliteration style), the first part of the poet's name is spelled al-Mājidī. This represents an effort to bridge the linguistic difference with modern standard Arabic. For this edition, the reviewer has expressed a preference for writing the name's *jīm* as *yāʾ*, al-Māyidī, in accordance with Emirati pronunciation and the spelling of names in earlier editions of Nabaṭī poetry in the Library of Arabic Literature.

2 Among the many poets in the manuscript of al-Khaṭīb (1926), Ibn Ẓāhir's section is introduced with the words: "These are the verses of Ibn Ẓāhir from Oman" (*mimmā qāl Ibn Ẓāhir rāʿī ʿUmān*). The first printed collection was published by "Oman Press" (*al-Maṭbaʿah al-ʿUmāniyyah*) in Dubai (1963). In the area of today's Emirates, Oman was a common geographical designation used to refer to the area of al-ʿAyn and al-Buraymī that straddles the inland border between the modern states of the Emirates and Oman. Narrative lore locates Ibn Ẓāhir's early days partly among the palm gardens in Ḍank, just across the border from al-ʿAyn in Oman.

3 Ibn Ẓāhir, *Dīwān al-shāʿir al-shaʿbī Ibn Ẓāhir*; Muḥammad Sharīf al-Shaybānī, *Dīwān al-jawāhir fī shiʿr Ibn Ẓāhir, Shāʿir al-Khalīj*.

4 Abū Shihāb and Abū Malḥah, *al-Mājidī ibn Ẓāhir: Ḥayātuh wa-shiʿruh*, 13.

5 Ibn Ẓāhir has been claimed by many tribes in the Emirates. Alameemi speculates that his name is a poetic moniker: in his view, al-Māyidī/

al-Mājidī is derived from *majd*, "glory," and Ẓāhir means "prominent, highly visible," two qualities that are accompanied by the epithet *fihīm*, "intelligent, discerning," in the opening verse of twelve of the sixteen poems (*Bint ibn Ẓāhir*, 104). Candidates among the tribes that are mentioned include al-Miṭārīsh of al-Misāfrah (sg. Maṭrūshī) and the Bedouin of Banū Kāsib (al-Mikāsib of al-Misāfrah), some of whom live in Ḍank, both of al-Nuʿaym; al-Misāfrah, who belong to al-Khawāṭir in Rās al-Khaymah (Thānī, *Ibn Ẓāhir: Baḥth tawthīqī fī shiʿrih wa-sīratih al-shakhṣiyyah*, 410); and numerous others. Al-Mawājid and al-Ẓawāhir are also mentioned, on account of the poet's name. In a lucid overview of all that has been said and written about his name, tribe, and place of birth, Alameemi concludes that these claims stem from oral tradition, and are mutually contradictory and mere speculation. It is unlikely that more credible information will surface. Alameemi, *al-Mājidī ibn Ẓāhir: Sīratuh wa-ashʿāruh wa-qaṣāʾid tunshar li-awwal marrah*, 141–46.

6 Richard P. Martin's introduction to Richmond Lattimore's *The Iliad of Homer*, 3.

7 Nicknamed Qayd al-Arḍ ("Land Registrar") because he ushered in a policy of land and property registration, he was praised for his conquests, agriculture, the security he brought to his lands, and the construction of a system of irrigation channels (*al-falaj*) to transport water from sources in the mountains to palm gardens. His tomb in al-Rustāq was destroyed by Saudi Wahhābī forces. Ḥamīd ibn Muḥammad ibn Razīq, *al-Fatḥ al-mubīn fī sīrat al-sādah Āl Bū Saʿīdiyyīn*, 295–300.

8 The Egyptian historian Ibn Iyās (852–930/1448–1524) described Muqrin, a successor of Ajwad, as "the absolute lord of the Arab nomads of the East" (al-Juhany, *Najd before the Salafi Movement: Social, Political and Religious Conditions during the Three Centuries preceding the Rise of the Saudi State*, 52).

9 Aḥmad ʿUbaydalī, *Kashf al-ghammah al-jāmiʿ li-akhbār alummah li-muṣannif majhūl*, 362.

10 Fāliḥ Ḥanẓal, *al-Mufaṣṣal fī ta'rīkh al-Imārāt al-ʿArabiyyah al-Muttaḥidah*, 3, 7.

11 E.g., the story "The Son of al-ʿUlaymī and Prince Qaṭan ibn Qaṭan" (ʿAbd al-Karīm al-Juhaymān, *al-Asāṭīr al-shaʿbiyyah min qalb jazīrat al-ʿarabiyyah*, 3:195–214). Also see n. 24 below on the Jabrid poet al-ʿUlaymī.

12 For information on the historical background to Ibn Ẓāhir's work, one may refer to events chronicled in early Omani history works listed in the bibliography. See ʿUbaydalī, *Kashf al-ghammah*; Nūr al-Dīn ʿAbd Allāh ibn Ḥamīd al-Sālimī, *Tuḥfat al-aʿyān*; Ḥamīd ibn Muḥammad ibn Razīq, *al-Fatḥ al-mubīn*; and ʿAbd al-Laṭīf ibn Nāṣir al-Ḥumaydān, "al-Ṣirāʿ ʿalā as-sulṭah fī dawlat al-Jubūr: Bayn mafāhīm al-qibaliyyah wa-l-mulk."

13 In al-Samhūdī's history, he is described as "the chief of the people of Najd and the sultan of Bahrain and al-Qaṭīf" (ʿAlī ibn ʿAbdallāh Samhūdī, *Wafā' al-wafā' bi-akhbār dār al-muṣṭafā*).

14 The chronicles mention Muḥammad's arrival in Mecca in 1515 at the head of an impressive pilgrimage caravan.

15 Muqrin ibn Ajwad was killed in 1521 by the Portuguese invaders who captured Bahrain and the Omani coast. The inland territories of al-Aḥsā' were overrun by a tribal leader of al-Muntafiq and later were ruled by an Ottoman governor (Al-Juhany, *Najd*, 53).

16 Al-Ḥumaydān, "al-Ṣirāʿ," 84; the foregoing is based on his article.

17 In other cases, it is often difficult to ascertain who of the many bearers of this and other names used by these princelings is meant.

18 George Percy Badger, *The Imāms and Seyyids of ʿOmān by Salīl ibn Razīq from A.D. 661–1856*, 73.

19 Ḥamīd ibn Muḥammad ibn Razīq, *al-Fatḥ al-mubīn*, 269.

20 ʿUbaydalī, *Kashf al-ghammah*, 363.

21 Fāliḥ Ḥanẓal (*Amīr al-shiʿr al-nabaṭī al-Mājidī ibn Ẓāhir*, 29–30) and Sultan Alameemi (*Ibn Ẓāhir*, 156–57) pose the question and do not exclude the possibility.

22 "The Yaʿrubi era was, for the most part, one of internal peace and prosperity, during which wealth increased and learning flourished;

it was remarkable for a sudden and extraordinary development of naval power." See "Rule of the Yaʿaribah 1625–1744" in John Gordon Lorimer, *Gazetteer of the Persian Gulf, ʿOman, and Central Arabia.*

23 See the subsection "Ibn Ẓāhir and Jabrid Poets" in the "Glossary on Style, Themes, and Motifs" in the "Book Supplements" section of the website for the Library of Arabic Literature, at http://www.libraryofarabicliterature.org/extra-2/.

24 In his analysis of versions of the poems in different editions and manuscripts, Sowayan comes to the conclusion that al-ʿUlaymī's ode must have been addressed to Qaṭan ibn Qaṭan ibn Qaṭan ibn ʿAlī ibn Hilāl ibn Zāmil al-Jabrī (Saad Sowayan, *al-Shiʿr al-nabaṭī: Dhāʾiqat al-shaʿb wa-sulṭat al-naṣṣ*, 346). A historical as well as a legendary personality, he is commonly referred to as Qaṭan ibn Qaṭan. The names of Qaṭan and Nāṣir are common in later generations of the Jabrid Banū Hilāl and their bearers are often indistinguishable from one another.

25 *yā-zāyirin fī ʿMānin gabl yinjālī, jinḥ ad-dijā wa-l-malā bi-n-nōm dhhālī / yā-ṭūl khaṭwatk min Najdin ilā Malaḥin, w-min dūnik al-bīd gafrin ṣaḥṣaḥin khālī / anā bi-wādī ʿMānin ʿanki mintizḥin, w-anti b-wādī Ḥanīfah ʿālā l-awshālī* (Sowayan, *al-Shiʿr al-nabaṭī*, 353).

26 Sowayan, *al-Shiʿr al-nabaṭī*, 346–52.

27 Sowayan, *al-Shiʿr al-nabaṭī*, 351. Barakāt al-Sharīf, a son of Sayyid Mubārak ibn Muṭṭalib ibn Badrān al-Mushaʿshaʿī, the governor of Shah ʿAbbās I in ʿArabistān and Ḥuwayzah, died in 1615 or 1610 (Sowayan, *al-Shiʿr al-nabaṭī*, 362).

28 Sowayan, *al-Shiʿr al-nabaṭī*, 363.

29 Sowayan, *al-Shiʿr al-nabaṭī*, 255–59.

30 In oral tradition, verses with similar rhyme from Shāyiʿ's legend became entangled with verses of Ibn Ẓāhir. See n. 344 to §14.28, and also n. 92 below.

31 So called after his town, Ushayqir in the al-Yamāmah province of Najd, and for being a *muṭawwaʿ*, a man who devotes his life to religion and may volunteer to perform certain religious functions, such as leading prayers.

32 *giltih ʿalā bētin gidīmin simiʿtih, ʿalā mithl mā gāl at-Timīmī li-ṣāḥibih* (Sowayan, *al-Shiʿr al-nabaṭī*, 368–69).

33 Sowayan, *al-Shiʿr al-nabaṭī*, 336.

34 Sowayan, *al-Shiʿr al-nabaṭī*, 521–27; H. St. J. B. Philby, *Saʿudi Arabia*, 82–83.

35 See n. 33 to §1.61 and "Banū Hilāl and Hunting with Cheetahs" in the online "Glossary of Style, Themes, and Motifs."

36 See n. 125 below.

37 See the "Signature Verses" section in the online "Glossary of Style, Themes, and Motifs."

38 See the "Signature Verses" section in the online "Glossary of Style, Themes, and Motifs." For Ibn Zayd, see Sowayan, *al-Shiʿr al-nabaṭī*, 299–314.

39 *yigūl Ibn Zaydin gōl rāʿī mithāyil, migālin ʿalā kill ar-rwāt mikād* (Sowayan, *al-Shiʿr al-nabaṭī*, 300).

40 §2.1: *yigūl al-fihīm al-Māyidī illī binā, wa-l-amthāl mā bēn ar-rwāt tʿād.*

41 See "Building Poetry" in the online "Glossary of Style, Themes, and Motifs."

42 The lines of Ibn Zayd: *yigūl Ibn Zaydin gīl bānī mithāyil, jdādin guwāfīhā gharībin ʿgūdhā* and *yigūl Ibn Zaydin gil bānī mithāyil, jdād al-bnā li-l-fāhimīn tishūg* (Sowayan, *al-Shiʿr al-nabaṭī*, 304, 312). For similar expressions in Ibn Ẓāhir's work, see §7.1, §8.1, §11.1, and §16.1.

43 The Hilālī original reads: "My messengers from ʿUqayl who set out / on lean camels curved like bows." The Hilālī word for "to set out" (*tigallalaw* "to pack up and carry loads," CA *istaqalla* "to lift; transport") occurs with the same meaning in Dhū l-Rummah's verse: "They packed up and departed for good, / cutting off our neighborly relations though they meant no harm" (*thumma staqallū fa-batta l-baynu wa-jtabadhat, ḥabla l-jiwāri nawan ʿawjāʾu fa-nbatarā*) (Dhū l-Rummah, *Dīwān Dhī l-Rummah*, 1153). In other poems of Ibn Zayd, the word is found in the same position and context: *fa-gul ayyuhā r-rakb allidhī qad tiqallalaw* (Sowayan, *al-Shiʿr al-nabaṭī*, 300, 304; the hemistich is identical in both poems). It usually occurs at the end

of the first hemistich: its syllable structure v – v – fits the metrical requirements of the meter in that position. For the Hilālī verse, see n. 222 to §9.38. It can hardly be incidental that Ibn Zayd mentions Ḥizwā (Ḥuzwā), Dhū l-Rummah's favorite sand hill, where he was buried at his explicit instructions. See n. 458 to §23.2.

44 Sowayan, *al-Shiʿr al-nabaṭī*, 306. See for Ḥizwā (CA Ḥuzwā) the previous note and Kurpershoek, *Arabian Satire*, 93, 156.

45 The trek is called *al-miḥḍār*, from the same root as *ḥaḍar*, "villagers, settled people," and CA *ḥaḍārah* "civilization." See §17.30 and n. 408 on "summering." Their original homeland was located in the general area of al-Dahnāʾ sands, the tribal haunts of the classical Bedouin poet Dhū l-Rummah, whose beloved Mayy follows a similar movement with the seasons: "My greetings to both abodes of Mayy [i.e., her summering in a palm oasis and cool season in the desert] / will the days of yore ever return? [. . .] Their camel-borne litters stop in the desert and at other times / at the sweet waters of an oasis, untainted by frogs" (*a-manzilatay Mayyī salāmun ʿalaykumā, hali l-azmunū llātī maḍayna rawājiʿū* / [. . .] / *ẓaʿāʾinu yaḥlulna l-falātawa-tāratan, maḥāḍira ʿadhbin lam takhuḍhu l-ḍafādiʿū*) (*Dīwān*, 1273, 1282).

46 There is no information on al-Jumaylī besides his poetry. Because he is cited by Rumayzān, Sowayan categorizes him with the Jabrid poets (Rumayzān's verse: *giltih ʿalā bēt al-Jmēlī Fayṣal, wa-l-amthāl yarthāhā min an-nās fāhimih*, Sowayan, *al-Shiʿr al-nabaṭī*, 392; Ibn Ẓāhir's verse §5.1: *yigūl al-fihīm al-Māyidī illī binā, bidʿin tarāthāh r-rwāt w-shāʿ*). The verses of Rumayzān and Ibn Ẓāhir share these terms: the poet's name, the transmission of poetry (lit. "to inherit," *tarāthā, yarthāhā* (CA *waritha*)), and the intelligence of the poet and his audience (*fāhim, fihīm*).

47 In one poem, Rumayzān's brother, Rushaydān, employs the signature verse: "Rushaydān al-Tamīmī recites his wisdom verses: / an unfailing beacon for the elite" (*yigūl Rshēdān at-Timīmi mithāyil, tarāhinn l-akhyār ar-rjāl thbāt*) (Sowayan, *al-Shiʿr al-nabaṭī*, 430).

48 Sowayan, *al-Shiʿr al-nabaṭī*, 404.

49 Ibn Khamīs, *Rāshid al-Khalāwī: Ḥayātuh, shiʿruh, ḥikamuh, falsafatuh, nawādiruh, ḥisābuh al-falakī*, 51.

50 In his poetry, al-Khalāwī addresses laudatory verses to a chief named Manīʿ ibn Sālim, without further clarification of his identity. According to one view, Mānīʿ was a Jabrid chief at the time of the Portuguese conquests (Sowayan, *al-Shiʿr al-nabaṭī*, 293). Others believe that al-Khalāwī flourished as late as the rule of Āl Ḥumayd, popularly known as Ibn ʿUrayʿir, established in 1669 by Barrāk ibn Ghurayr in al-Aḥsāʾ after his expulsion of the Ottoman overlords (Ibn Khamīs, *al-Khalāwī*, 20–21; Philby, *Saʿudi Arabia*, 27, 83).

51 Al-Saʿīd, *al-Mawsūʿah al-nabaṭiyyah al-kāmilah*, 163–66.

52 Like the poetry of Barakāt al-Sharīf, al-Khalāwī's work has been included in Emirati manuscripts together with that of Ibn Ẓāhir and many other Arabian poets; see Note on the Text, p. lx.

53 ʿAbd al-Karīm al-Juhaymān, *al-Amthāl al-shaʿbiyyah fī qalb al-jazīrah al-ʿarabiyyah* and Muḥammad ibn Nāṣir al-ʿUbūdī, *al-Amthāl al-ʿāmmiyyah fī Najd*.

54 See the "Ibn Ẓāhir and Jabrid Poets" and "Ibn Ẓāhir and the Najdī Ethos" in the online "Glossary of Style, Themes, and Motifs."

55 Kurpershoek, *Arabian Satire*, xxii.

56 As Sowayan observes, unlike early Nabaṭī poetry and its recognizable historical framework, orally transmitted poetry of Banū Hilāl and Āl Ḍaygham (al-Ḍayāghim) clearly shows traces of more recent vernacular usage (*al-Shiʿr al-nabaṭī*, 253).

57 In his verse, al-ʿĀmirī praised the sharif of Mecca, Kubaysh ibn Manṣūr ibn Jammāz al-Sharīf al-Ḥusaynī, who ruled in Medina from 1325 to 1327/28 (Sowayan, *al-Shiʿr al-nabaṭī*, 255–56).

58 Examples are: *qāla l-Sharīf ibn Hāshim ʿAlī*; *taqūl fatātu l-ḥayyi Saʿdā wa-hāḍahā*; *yaqūl bi-lā jahlin fatā l-jūdi Khālid*; *taqūl fatāt al-ḥayyi Ummu Salāmah* (Ibn Khaldūn, *Muqaddimat Ibn Khaldūn*, 587–93).

59 See "Ibn Ẓāhir, Jabrid, and Other Early Nabaṭī Poetry: Frequency of Rhymes" in the online "Glossary of Style, Themes, and Motifs."

60 The poet al-Dindān (d. 2004), for instance, was familiar with Hilālī poetry, and opened five of his poems with a Hilālī-style signature

verse. Kurpershoek, *The Poetry of ad-Dindān: A Bedouin Bard in Southern Najd.*

61 E.g., an Emirati narrator in a comment on §17.26, §17.28: "The people who took those beauties as booty, as mentioned in this poem, who were they? She talks about the Banū Hilāl. They are the ones about whom she said, 'They took from me what suited them, leaving little; done with me, the rascals made themselves scarce'" (Alameemi, *Ibn Ẓāhir*, 274). There may be a kernel of truth, though, since in the Omani chronicles, the Banū Hilāl (of the Jabrids) are decried as inveterate robbers, see p. xxiv.

62 See "Ibn Ẓāhir and the Najdī Ethos" in the online "Glossary of Style, Themes, and Motifs." This also applies to one of Ibn Ẓāhir's main themes: old age and youthful dalliance (*al-shayb wa-l-taṣābī*). Short descriptions of physical decay are in the nature of vignettes and do not exhibit the graphic detail of classical and Nabaṭī poetry from Najd, e.g., ʿAbīd ibn al-Abraṣ and, especially, Ḥmēdān al-Shwēʿir, who makes no bones about the sexual details of the classical motif, "where spouses mocked their aged partners and their inability to satisfy them" (Arazi, "al-Shayb wa 'l-shabāb" in *EI2*; Kurpershoek, *Arabian Satire*, 3, 15). Neither does Ibn Ẓāhir follow the playful example of classical poets in their literary games (*ikhwāniyyāt*, also noted in Ḥanẓal, *Amīr al-shiʿr al-nabaṭī al-Mājidī ibn Ẓāhir*, 19 and Thānī, *Ibn Ẓāhir*, 40) and the seventeenth-century Nabaṭī exchanges in the same mannerist style between Jabr ibn Sayyār, Ḥmēdān's immediate predecessor, and Rumayzān and others. For instance, the poet Ibn Dawwās (an otherwise unknown contemporary of Jabr ibn Sayyār, d. 1708, see *Arabian Satire*, xiv) employs the conceit of consoling Jabr on his diminished sexual prowess by pointing to advantages of his age, such as his wealth of experience and venerable reputation: "He complains about old age, but gray hairs are a source of pride: / venerable, he is mentioned with approval by men of religion" (*yashkī l-shayb wa-l-shayb fīh iftikhār, maʿa waqārin hal ad-dīn yanbūnih*) (Arazi, "al-Shayb wa 'l-shabāb"; Sowayan, *al-Shiʿr al-nabaṭī*, 482). In §1.24, the poet's rage against gray hair abates and he declares

himself resigned to God's decree, but then sounds doubtful when he expresses the hope that he may find some benefit in old age. For Ibn Ẓāhir, the subject remains deadly serious.

63 See "Doves" in the online "Glossary of Style, Themes, and Motifs."

64 See "Love, Youth, and Old Age" in the online "Glossary of Style, Themes, and Motifs."

65 See "Departure, Separation, and Loss" in the online "Glossary of Style, Themes, and Motifs."

66 See "The World, Fate, and Time: Appearances and Truth" in the online "Glossary of Style, Themes, and Motifs."

67 In §5.54, Ibn Ẓāhir compares dancing girls with the motions of worshippers of the al-Rifāʿī and al-Badriyyah Sufi orders during their chants. Sufi influences were known to have existed in the eastern parts of the Arabian Peninsula, such as al-Aḥsāʾ, Bahrain, and al-Qaṭīf, during the Jabrid reign. For instance, in the sixteenth century the order of al-Kawwāziyyah, named after Muḥammad Amīn al-Kawwāz, came to Basra from al-Aḥsāʾ by way of Shaykh Aḥmad ibn Mūsā al-Minbāwī, a prominent member of al-Shādhiliyyah order. Similarly, the order of Ibrāhīm al-Rudaynī, a Sufi shaykh originally from Yemen, came to Basra from al-Aḥsāʾ (al-Ḥumaydān, "al-Ṣirāʿ," 76–77).

68 As Ivan Ilyich discovers just in time: "This is wrong. Everything you have lived by, and still do, is a lie, a deception that hides life and death away from you." Tolstoy, *The Death of Ivan Ilyich and Other Stories*, 215. As in Ibn Ẓāhir's work, the point is that Ivan Ilyich had done nothing particularly bad, but wasted his time on the common vanities and petty ambitions of his privileged class of magistrates and government officials.

69 Ḥmēdān al-Shwēʿir: "This eloquent graybeard, a sage (*fāhimin*) steeped in savoir faire"; "These are the words of a learned and discerning (*fihīm*) poet"; "Listen (*iftihim*) to my verses of wise counsel, in such high demand"; "Listen carefully (*iftihim*), my boy, to this wise old man (*fihīm*)"; "Listen carefully (*ifham*) to these polished verses" (Kurpershoek, *Arabian Satire*, 7, 41, 35, 105, 119). Rāshid al-Khalāwī:

"Listen carefully to this learned man with a lifetime of experience" (*ṣikh w-istimiʿ min ʿālimin māras al-warā*) (Ibn Khamīs, *al-Khalāwī*, 142). ʿĀmir al-Samīn calls himself "perspicacious" (*biṣīr*) in the verse after his signature verse (Sowayan, *al-Shiʿr al-nabaṭī*, 344). The characterization has been perpetuated in oral tradition recorded in modern times: "Ibn Ẓāhir has a deep insight into the affairs of the world (*mitbaṣṣir bi-d-dunyā*); no one is more discerning than he" (Thāni, *Ibn Ẓāhir*, 525); and in less highbrow fashion: "The guy is not dumb" (*w-rayyāl hab hayyin*) (Thāni, *Ibn Ẓāhir*, 531).

70 See n. 379 to §15.37.

71 See "Clouds, Rain, and Winds" in the online "Glossary of Style, Themes, and Motifs."

72 The narrators of the poet's folktales made the same observation, e.g., Ḥamad ibn Khamīs al-ʿAlīlī: "When a poem of Ibn Ẓāhir is recited, you know at once, without being told, that it is his composition—without anyone telling you. You know that he is the poet: all his poems resemble one another" (*intah yōm bi-yʿad ʿālēk giṣīd bin Ẓāhir, tifhamah inhā giṣīdtah lī gālhā min awwalhā lēn ākhirhā, rūḥik tifhamhā, tʿarifhā nhā muwallifah, giṣīdah yitshābah*); and Muḥammad ibn Khalfān ibn Ḥzēm al-Flāsī: "The poems of Ibn Ẓāhir are all very similar to one another" (*hādhā giṣīd bin Ẓāhir giṣīdah ṭāl ʿumrik killah yitshābah*) (Alameemi, *Ibn Ẓāhir*, 172, 247).

73 See "Wisdom and Maxims" in the online "Glossary of Style, Themes, and Motifs."

74 Poems with a substantial presence of each of these three themes are Poems 1, 8, 10, 14, and 16. Poems 1, 10, and 14 open on the theme of love, and 8 and 16 with verses of wisdom. These might be considered quintessential Ibn Ẓāhir poems. See "Main Themes in Ibn Ẓāhir's Poetry" in the online "Glossary of Style, Themes, and Motifs."

75 The total number of wisdom verses is around two hundred, roughly one-fourth of the total number of 823, depending on how they are counted. Some of them might be regarded as purely religious advice, for instance, and others as mere inveighing against the treachery of the world for causing the lover's heartbreak.

76 In a chest-beating passage of sixty-one verses about his poetic prowess, Rāshid al-Khalāwī was even more daring in his boast: "If it weren't poetry, you'd say, this is revealed by the angel Gabriel." See n. 379 to §15.37. And more modestly in the second half of the nineteenth century, ʿAdwān al-Hirbīd: "Carry these verses on light-footed camels: / you're my messenger to generations to come" (*min shālhin yingal ʿalā l-fiṭṭar al-fīḥ, maʿ wāḥdin yatnā migābīl al-ajyāl*) (Saad Sowayan, *Ayyām al-ʿArab al-awākhir: asāṭīr wa-marwiyyāt shafahiyyah fī l-taʾrīkh wa-l-adab min shamāl al-jazīrah al-ʿarabiyyah maʿa shadharāt mukhtārah min qabīlat Āl Murrah wa-Subayʿ*, 214).

77 Alameemi, *Ibn Ẓāhir*, 184.

78 Thānī observes that the popular "biography (*al-sīrah al-shaʿbiyyah*) that is still being told in different parts of the Emirates" demonstrates how deeply the poet has become ingrained in the collective consciousness; even books and studies about the poet have not escaped the tendency to make no distinction between "Ibn Ẓāhir as a historical poet and as a legendary hero in folktales" (Thāni, *Ibn Ẓāhir*, 63). This duality has been a given since the earliest days of Arabian poetry. For instance, al-Ḥuṭayʾah in his guise as an often outrageous caricature in the *Book of Songs* (*Kitāb al-Aghānī*), admixed with some of his verse, is not readily identifiable with the serious poet and his deep knowledge of desert life found in his collected poetry. The examples are legion: they are part and parcel of an Arabian oral culture with fifteen hundred years of continuity.

79 See "Jinn" in the online "Glossary of Style, Themes, and Motifs."

80 In another version: "Do you want to become a learned man or a tyrant?" (*tibā ʿālim willa ẓālim*) (Alameemi, *Ibn Ẓāhir*, 192, 232).

81 "As a young man he did not compose poetry. It is said that he did not become a poet until he had reached the age of forty or above" (*hū mā giṣad awwal shibābah, ygūlūn, giṣad illā min baʿad wiṣal al-arbaʿīn w-fōg*) (Alameemi, *Ibn Ẓāhir*, 235).

82 "Riding the Devil's horse" is a conventional trope in poetry on the theme of the graybeard and amorous youth. The forty years the poet says he was consumed by passion is seen as evidence for the same, §§12.8–9 (Thānī, *Ibn Ẓāhir*, 406).

83 "After he turned forty, he received inspiration, through a jinni's intervention. He was not an ordinary poet. [. . .] There is no forgery in Ibn Ẓāhir's poetry. His every word is nothing but the truth; whatever he says is honestly as it is. [. . .] Even in his love poetry he gives the unadorned truth. Normally, poets draw an exaggerated picture or leave out what doesn't suit them, but he doesn't lay it on thick. [. . . .] All his ghazals give a fair account." (*w-min baʿad al-arbaʿīn sinat ʿimrah kān, bas istilhām sha l-būghah yatah, w-illā mā kān shāʿir bas* [. . .] *giṣīd bin Ẓāhir mā fīh tazyīf, kil kilmah ygūlhā hī al-ḥagg, ṣidg, kil kalāmah ṣidg* [. . .] *ḥattā fī l-ghazal ḥaggah. al-ghazal, kil an-nās ash-shaʿarā yzaydūn w-ynagṣūn fīh, hū mā yzayyid fī l-ghazal* [. . .] *kil al-ghazal ḥaggah ykūn mitsāwī* (Alameemi, *Ibn Ẓāhir*, 235). And concerning transmission: "He cut her tongue, the graybeards of old were absolutely sure about it. Our grandfathers and fathers said that he cut her tongue because of her verse [i.e., her signature verse, §17.1]. She meant, my verses are better than yours, that's why. A true report. The old men of those days did not lie. They say that he cut her tongue because of this issue" (Thānī, *Ibn Ẓāhir*, 515); "There is his grave, take my word. Where they built a wall next to it. The graybeards of the old days know it, without fail" (*w-hādhāk gabrah tismaʿ wēn binī ʿalēh ydār, hādhāk yʿarfūnah sh-shiwwāb al-gabliyyīn, ydallūnah*) (Alameemi, *Ibn Ẓāhir*, 206).

84 "He read the Qur'an and other works. He knows the Qur'an since his knowledge of it shows in his poetry and genius: he always brings Qur'anic wisdom into his verses and sayings of the Prophet. [. . . .] The poets who came before him did not work it into their poetry to the extent he did." (*girā al-Gūrān, w-girā ḥājāt, lannah hū ʿalā maʿriftah bi-sh-shiʿr w-nibāghtah fī sh-shiʿr dāyim iyyīb ʿannah w-ʿan ar-rasūl* [. . .] *kill ash-shaiʿarā illī gālū min gabl hādhā sh-shāyy, mā iyyībūn bi-ṭ-ṭarījah hādhī*) (Alameemi, *Ibn Ẓāhir*, 236–37). Some narrators maintain that Ibn Ẓāhir built a mosque, and that he was deeply religious (*hū insān dayyin*) (Alameemi, *Ibn Ẓāhir*, 223).

85 To make such a distinction offers additional evidence for the prevailing tendency to regard the "biography" (*sīrah*) as factual, though opinions may vary on details.

86 See "Graves" in the online "Glossary of Style, Themes, and Motifs."

87 The verse and a few other lines were only known from oral transmission until the entire poem was rediscovered in a hitherto unknown manuscript. It is regarded as an apt description of the Emirates' coastal areas and an encomium to the excellent quality of the land at Rās al-Khaymah, the location of the poet's grave.

88 As one narrator pithily put it: "He devised an impossible task for her in order to make her give up poetry" (*ṭalab ʿalēhā miʿjizah* (CA *muʿjizah* "miracle") *sawwā lhā yōm baghā ywaggif ʿalēhā l-giṣīd*) (Thānī, *Ibn Ẓāhir*, 511).

89 To a remarkable degree, Salmā's story parallels and overlaps elements of her father's saga, depending on the version of the narrative. For instance, like the female jinni who endowed her father with his talent for poetry, she is initially taciturn or even, like the jinni (or in other versions, her father), a mute (*balmā*, according to Alameemi, *Ibn Ẓāhir*, 241) before she becomes a poet. Like Ibn Ẓāhir, she is reckoned to have been about forty years old, and unmarried, when she composed the despairing verses included in this collection. These verses show an uncanny resemblance to individual verses in her father's oeuvre. In sum, she looks like the female repressed alter ego of the famous poet—the poet she could have been and one to outshine him, according to the Emirati storytellers.

90 Curiously, these narrators still maintained that the murdered girl was buried side by side with her father and the rest of the family. This chapter of the tales shows the protagonist as a man devoted to sustaining his family and at the same time a ruthless patriarch who expects the womenfolk of his household to toe the line laid down by him (and by social tradition of his time).

91 Even the son-in-law is associated with poetry by the storytellers. In a minority version, his daughter helped her husband to compose verses that enabled him to defeat his father-in-law in a contest in which two lines of dancers, *razfāt*, fire volleys of improvised verse at each other, and Ibn Ẓāhir threatened to cut her tongue for that reason (Thāni, *Ibn Ẓāhir*, 508–9).

92 Similarly, Shāyiʿ was visited by a group of fellow tribesmen who showed up at night, claiming that they had been despoiled of their riding camels by robbers, knowing that he was hard up, in order to put him to the test in extreme conditions (*jimāʿatih yastamḥinūnih*) (Sowayan, *Ayyām al-ʿarab*, 267).

93 Thāni, *Ibn Ẓāhir*, 467.

94 The word used by a narrator, *gaṣṣādah,* is related to the original meaning of the classical word for *qaṣīdah*, a long poem, derived from the verb *qaṣada*, "to aim for, endeavor to reach an end," i.e., the person or persons a poet wishes to address. In this case, it refers to travelers who endeavor to reach the poet: "They rode and rode until they saw this graybeard herding a few sheep and goats, an old man [. . . .] They greeted him and he returned their greetings, and said, 'Welcome, welcome, my guests!' 'No,' they said, 'we are heading for him (*niḥin gaṣṣādah*).' 'Where do you want to go?' he said. They said, 'We are heading for Ibn Ẓāhir's group.'" And in almost the same words, another narrator: "They said, 'Where is Ibn Ẓāhir?' 'Nearby,' he said. 'You're my guests tonight!' 'No,' they said, 'We are on our way to meet someone.' 'Good,' he said. 'Come this way, there ahead of you'" (*gālū: wēn bin Ẓāhir? gāl: jirīb, yā ḥayykum ṣōbnā l-lēlah. galū: lā niḥin gāṣdīn. gāl: ʿiyal minnā taʿālū, hniyyah jiddāmkum*) (Alameemi, *Ibn Ẓāhir*, 193–94).

95 At this point, narrators add the accepted wisdom: "As you know, a poet loathes another poet, as a shaykh loathes another shaykh and as a *muṭawwaʿ* can't stand another man of religion" (*ʿād tʿarf ash-shāʿir mā ydānī sh-shāʿir, wa-sh-shēkh mā ydānī sh-shēkh, wal-mṭawwaʿ mā ydānī l-mṭawwaʿ*) (Alameemi, *Ibn Ẓāhir*, 173).

96 "He was visited by tribal men (*ʿarab*), may God guide you, who were looking for him. With them was a Wahībī or a member of the al-Durūʿ tribe who said, 'I am going to challenge Ibn Ẓāhir.' They were going to engage in a contest of exchanging riddles." (*yūh ʿarab, allāh yihdīk, yinshidūn ʿanah, w-wāḥid Wihībī aw Dirʿī, gālhum, b-asīr atḥaddā bin Ẓāhir. taghāṭaw, hum taghāṭaw*) (Alameemi, *Ibn Ẓāhir*, 202–3).

97 In a variation on this theme, a group of men comes riding from afar with the aim of purchasing his fabled she-camel, but instead are feasted on the slaughtered animal (Thānī, *Ibn Ẓāhir*, 454–57).

98 As expressed in §5.26: "A noble character stands tall even if dressed in rags; appearances deceive: a man is more than his trade"; and see n. 136 to §5.27. In these tales, Ibn Ẓāhir appears as sorely lacking in means, though confident that somehow with God's help he will pull through, thanks to his devotion to the principles of hospitality. The little boat he has built from palm fronds and branches (*shāshah*) "in truth is the boat made by the poor to catch fish; and he also went raiding, collected and sold firewood, and worked as a herder and a diver" (Thānī, *Ibn Ẓāhir*, 504). For a Bedouin, there was no stigma attached to robbing another tribe's camels. In Arabian society, only the poorest would make a living from cutting fire bush (*Arabian Satire*, 149n128).

99 Holes, *Dialect*, 3:424.

100 The hardship involved in pearling (the months at sea during the hot season, long days of heavy toil, separation from one's family) are the subject of many Emirati poems and stories. See Ghassān Aḥmad al-Ḥasan, *Tajalliyyāt al-ghawṣ fī al-shiʿr al-nabaṭī fī dawlat al-Imārāt al-ʿArabiyyah al-Muttaḥidah*.

101 Thānī observed that orally transmitted poetry of Ibn Ẓāhir at the time of his recording was often based on published versions (*Ibn Ẓāhir*, 50).

102 As said about Homer by Richard P. Martin in his introduction to Richmond Lattimore's translation of *The Iliad*, 36.

103 "He settled here in Rās al-Khaymah: he liked the place, the people, the Bedouin. He was a Bedouin person" (Thānī, *Ibn Ẓāhir*, 423); "his character is that of a Bedouin" (Alameemi, *Ibn Ẓāhir*, 184). "He did not move from Rās al-Khaymah until he died. His grave is there. He'd go to al-ʿAyn for the summer months. [. . . .] He'd say, 'This is my homeland. Its folks do not migrate to another land. It is a green oasis and its inhabitants do not go on migrations.'" (*mā intigal min Rās al-Khaymah līn māt, gabrah mawjūd, ysīr ḥiḍḍār līn al-ʿAyn.* [. . .] *ygūl,*

ad-dār dār, w-ahalhā mā yinyiʿūn l-dār [. . .] *khaḍrā w-ahalhā mā yinyiʿūn l-dār*) (Alameemi, *Ibn Ẓāhir*, 186).

104 According to one of the narrators, "he went to live in Rās al-Khaymah: the man was also a man of the sea—a Bedouin and a seaman" (Alameemi, *Ibn Ẓāhir*, 176–77). Another narrator avers: "At first he toiled to make a living in Oman and transported dates" (*imbūnah ykidd ʿMān, iyyīb tamr*) (Alameemi, *Ibn Ẓāhir*, 192).

105 Such a structure would also be called *khēmah* (CA *khaymah* "tent"). See Roger Webster, "Notes on the Dialect and Way of Life of the Āl Wahība Bedouin of Oman," for excellent detailed descriptions of the life and dwellings that were still being used at the time of the oil economy in comparable cultural conditions to the ones described by the transmitters of Ibn Ẓāhir's oral saga.

106 See "Departure and the Seasons" in the online "Glossary of Style, Themes, and Motifs."

107 Thānī, *Ibn Ẓāhir*, 450–51. "Emirati people at that time used to spend the summer in the oases, a custom called *al-khiṭārah* (i.e., to bring a visit outside one's place of residence)" (Thānī, *Ibn Ẓāhir*, 464, 484–86); it is more generally known as *al-miḥḍār* (see Muḥammad ibn Aḥmad ibn al-Shaykh Ḥasan, *al-ʿĀdāt wa-l-taqālīd fī dawlat al-Imārāt*, 48–49, and n. 408 to §17.30).

108 Perhaps to make him look more "Bedouin," the narrators maintain that he was forced to build his little boat of reed and palm branches (*shāshah*) and go fishing after the death of his fabled she-camel that he had earned with two years working as a herdsman (Thānī, *Ibn Ẓāhir*, 431).

109 Jennifer R. March, *Cassell Dictionary of Classical Mythology*, 623–24. Ibn Ẓāhir of the saga shares the Arcadian taste of the philologist al-Aṣmaʿī (d. 213/828), who in spite of his affluence "persisted in living as a poor man," which he regarded as "the pure Arab way of living," in tune with "the sincere piety of plain-living people." And to some extent, Ibn Zāhir's poetry reflects the stories of al-Aṣmaʿī's "meetings with poor bedouins and young girls who revealed to him

an unexpected and extraordinary insight into the mysteries of the divine love" ("al-Aṣmaʿī," *EI2*).

110 It was perhaps inevitable that Emirati oral culture should enlist Ibn Ẓāhir in the ranks of the elder, more famous Banū Hilāl from whom he inherited his signature verse, and not for what it probably was: a nostalgic throwback at the (Jabrid) Banū Hilāl. In the words of a then (2004) sixty-five-year-old in Sharjah: "He is said to have been one of the Banū Hilāl, as he has said in one of his poems, 'Tents made of red leather, cheetahs for the hunt [. . .] Intrepid stalwarts, gallant men of Banū Hilāl' (§1.61, §1.63) [. . .] This name, al-Māyidī, it is not a tribe: it is his moniker. Now this tribe is nowhere, it has disappeared from the Emirates. They migrated from this land. Banū Hilāl reached Tunis and North Africa and have settled there." (*hū ygūlūn min Binī Hlāl, innah ygūl hu hnāk fī giṣīdtah hāyyīk, yōm ygūl: binīna b-ḥimr w-ṣēd nimr / shaghārīf Binī Hlāl. bas al-Māyidī, hādhā al-Māyidī hub gibīlah, al-Māyiḍī lagab ḥaggah. bas hāy gibīlat Binī Hlāl hāy mā shay, al-ḥīn fī al-Imarāt mā shay minhā, hāy rāḥaw min ad-dār hādhī, Binī Hlāl wiṣlaw al-ḥīn ṣōb Tūnis w-shimāl Ifrīyā skinaw*) (Alameemi, *Ibn Ẓāhir*, 234–25). In another example, verses attributed to Abū Zayd al-Hilālī, in which he agonizes over having too little to spend on his guests, are in turn attributed to Ibn Ẓāhir (Thānī, *Ibn Ẓāhir*, 569).

111 Ibn Sbayyil's nineteenth-century affirmation of his inferiority to the Bedouin, as part of his subservience to his Bedouin beloved ("I am just a villager, they're redoubtable Bedouin"), itself sounds like a borrowing from protestations of not being on a par with the beloved's social rank in the verses of the legendary Hilālī-style poet dubbed al-Tamīmī who lived centuries before Ibn Ẓāhir: "She is a Bedouin and I am a sedentary man living in a village / chasing Bedouin girls is cruel torment for an oasis-dweller" (*wu-hū bādiyin w-anā maʿ al-ḥaḍar gāʿid, w-ṭard al-buwādī li-l-ḥaḍar ʿdhāb*) (Kurpershoek, *Arabian Romantic*, 117; Sowayan, *al-Shiʿr al-nabaṭī*, 390).

112 Thānī, *Ibn Ẓāhir*, 63.

113 In particular and most famously §16.59: “From the empty deserts in the south to the north, from al-Ẓafrah to the Gulf’s littoral at Dihān”; see Map 1, p. liv.

114 *Mā khallā big‘ah, sikan fī kil big‘ah* (Alameemi, *Ibn Ẓāhir*, 202). The same expression is used by other narrators, e.g.: “There isn’t a place he did not visit (*hū mā khallā big‘ah*)”; and another narrator: “He lived in the desert. [. . .] He went everywhere on his she-camel. You’d say he had been strapped to its back and spent all his days on it” (*ygūl lak mgazzar ḥayātah hū killahhā ‘alā nāgat hādhī*, a standard expression, as in the verse of the desert knight Shlēwīḥ al-‘Aṭāwī, “as though it (my heart) was bound by cinches to the saddle” (Kurpershoek, *Oral Poetry and Narratives from Central Arabia* , 2:165)). “He made the Mecca pilgrimage on it; he visited all places on this she-camel” (Thānī, *Ibn Ẓāhir*, 448–49).

115 Thānī, *Ibn Ẓāhir*, 63–64. Alameemi writes: “Ibn Ẓāhir’s poems hold a special position in Emirati popular culture. One part has been recorded in writing and preserved, and much of what has been written down in this way keeps circulating orally among the transmitters of poetry; and another part was not written down and was solely transmitted orally. In addition, many verses from other poems have been wrongly attributed to him” (Alameemi, *Ibn Ẓāhir*, 288). Also, “Ibn Ẓāhir is unique in that he is the only poet on the Omani coast” whose work has been preserved in manuscripts and in oral tradition in various readings (Alameemi, *Ibn Ẓāhir*, 287).

116 Thānī, *Ibn Ẓāhir*, 430.

117 Thānī, *Ibn Ẓāhir*, 425–26.

118 *Dīwān Ibn ‘Atīj*, 30 (*tīfān bin Ẓāhir w-‘aṣrin māḍī, ‘ēbin ‘alā bētin ygāl hizīl / w-ḥinnā amthālnā l-amthālhum, w-misāyilin titba‘ maghānī sīl*); Thānī, *Ibn Ẓāhir*, 51.

119 In the poetry of Ḥmēdān al-Shwē‘ir, this meter is reserved for poems with an emphasis on gnomic wisdom, but that is not the case here.

120 A good, but not staggering, number of verses show metrical flaws, a sure indication that changes have occurred in the course of transmission. On the whole, it seems no reason to doubt the overall integrity of the corpus.

121 See the heading "Language, Meter, and Rhyme" in the Introduction to Kurpershoek, *Arabian Satire*, xxxiii–xxxiv.

122 See the chapter "Prosody and Language: A Synchronic and Diachronic Overview" in Sowayan, *Nabaṭī Poetry*, 147–67; the chapter "al-ʿArūḍ" in Sowayan, *al-Shiʿr al-nabaṭī*, 145–86; and the sections on language and prosody in Kurpershoek, *Oral Poetry*.

123 Kurpershoek, *Arabian Satire*, xxxiii.

124 Kurpershoek, *Arabian Satire*, xxxvii, and Kurpershoek and Lorentz, "Charles Huber, voyageur en Arabie."

125 Pearl merchant: *ṭawwāsh*, pl. *ṭuwāwīsh*; the trade in pearls is called *aṭ-ṭwāshah* (al-Ṭābūr, *Rijāl fī ta'rīkh al-Imārāt al-ʿArabiyyah al-Muttaḥidah*, 65–67; Fāliḥ Ḥanẓal, *Muʿjam al-alfāẓ al-ʿāmmiyyah fī dawlat al-Imārāt al-ʿArabiyyah al-Muttaḥidah*, 428).

126 Alameemi, *Ibn Ẓāhir*, 26.

127 Alameemi, *Ibn Ẓāhir*, 33–34.

128 For instance, the al-Khaṭīb MS only reproduces the most popular proverbs and sayings from Poem 5.

129 Alameemi, *Ibn Ẓāhir*, 36.

130 Alameemi, *Ibn Ẓāhir*, 73–98. Accordingly, these have not been included in this edition.

131 Thānī, *Ibn Ẓāhir*, 17.

132 He is said to have received his information for the *dīwān* from Shaykha Salāmah, the mother of Shaykh Zāyid (Thānī, *Ibn Ẓāhir*, 17).

133 While Thānī limited himself to the area of Rās al-Khaymah, the presumed location where the poet lived for a longer period until his death, Alameemi sought out narrators who lived along the axes of the caravan routes and locations mentioned in the stories, from al-ʿAyn to Dubai. The eleven transmitters whose stories he recorded resulted in thirteen narratives, because he returned to two of them at a later date to make another recording of the same material and study it for discrepancies (Alameemi, *Ibn Ẓāhir*, 134–35). One of the transmitters, Khalīfah ibn ʿAlī l-Kitbī, was recorded by both Thānī and Alameemi. Because of the quality of his storytelling (detailed memory, consistency, clear narrative thread, colorful and apposite

language), he has also been chosen as a principal source for this edition.

134 In the notes to the translation, Alameemi's answers to my questions are referred to with the words "It was explained that." Unless otherwise stated, the assumption should be that this source is meant.

135 For instance, in §1.2 the printed editions read *darb* ("way, path") for *dhirb* ("mountainous outcropping"), but all MSS give the latter, which accordingly has been chosen for this edition.

136 "Some of the expressions remain obscure, not the thought behind it. The meaning of some verses has not been clarified so far, and for that reason transmitters and writers have expressed them in different ways" (Thānī, *Ibn Ẓāhir*, 39–40).

137 Thānī, *Ibn Ẓāhir*, 389–552.

138 Thānī recorded narratives from fifteen transmitters, listed in his *Ibn Ẓāhir*, 397–402. His section with stories opens with Khalīfah ibn ʿAlī al-Kitbī.

139 Alameemi, *Ibn Ẓāhir*, 166–288.

140 Where repetition occurs in some passages, as in §23.6, this is because it was deemed preferable to render more than one version, each of which found favor with narrators and presents distinctive interest. Redundancies are characteristic of storytelling, but most of these have been left out.

141 The Najdī works of al-Juhaymān and al-ʿUbūdī, Ḥanẓal's dictionary of Emirati proverbs and other Emirati collections, and the Omani dictionary of al-Rawāḥī.

142 *Ka-annahū fulfulun jaʿdun yudaḥrijuhū, naḍḥu l-dhafārā idhā jawlānuhū nḥadarā / shāfū ʿalayhinna anmāṭan shāmiyatan, ʿalā qanā alja'at aẓlāluhu l-baqarā* (*Dīwān*, 1150–51, 1295–96). Lane explains it as "the place that sweats in the back of a camel's neck behind the ear; two protuberances on the right and left of the small hollow in the middle of the back of the neck, derived from *dhafaru al-ʿaraqi*, 'the pungency of the odor of sweat,' because it is the first part that sweats in a camel" (*An Arabic-English Lexicon*, 967). Ibn Ẓāhir's imagery and wording resemble Dhū l-Rummah's verses, though from a different

perspective: Dhū l-Rummah describes the departure of the Bedouin from the desert toward their summer station at a palm oasis, whereas Ibn Ẓāhir does so from the perspective of an oasis dweller who watches in dismay as his Bedouin sweetheart departs from the oasis with a fresh supply of dates toward the desert.

Poems

Graybeard's Song

This key poem associates separation from the beloved with the passage of Time, the exposure of youthful illusions, and confrontation with life's realities. The ideas unfold against the backdrop of a nostalgic evocation of the Bedouin culture of the Jabrids and their Omani branch of Banū Hilāl. 1.0

In the solitude of a steep outcrop, buffeted by the winds, the poet takes in the scenery and pours out the emotions of his grief-stricken heart. A dove's cooing reminds him of a beloved who abandoned him, a love identified with farewell to youth and horror at the approach of old age. A furious dialogue with youth and Time's inveterate indifference ensues, only to give way to resignation, fortified by gnomic wisdom. Memories of a Bedouin beauty in her camel-borne palanquin leave the poet thirsting for more. His prayers for rain to fall on the tribe's desert pastures are the transition to the most famous verses. The Bedouin nobility of Banū Hilāl, gone before the poet's time, is marked by their hunting with cheetahs and tents made of red leather, a vignette characteristic of the beginnings of Nabaṭī poetry during Jabrid rule in eastern Arabia until about 1520. Similarly, only early Nabaṭī poetry features "Moses's appointment": a Qur'anic reference, understood as the forty days between rainfall and the growth of herbage alluded to in this poem.

1.1 These are the verses of al-Māyidī,
crafted to the tune of an inner urge;[1]
Whispers caught, after a steep ascent,
on the pinnacle of prominent elevations,
Buffeted by winds blowing from all sides:[2]
sand-raising breezes from east and west
Stir memories of a passionate love,
torments whipped up by a cooing dove[3]
1.5 Singing its heart out on a high perch,
from grief-stricken lament to quiet elegy.
I do not know what woe has befallen it,
nor was it told about my tribulations,
Fate's crushing blows in times long gone—
God's blessings on halcyon days of dalliance![4]
We dwelled in enchanted gardens of delight,
amid lush pastures, our camels full of milk.
I am careful not to offend my darling;
haughty, she spurns me as if we've never met.
1.10 Sweet love turned into distant memory:
a game of blame, not in our heart of hearts.
Destiny's bitter thrusts struck me down,
erased intimacy and imposed separation.
Like many dear ones, she rode away forever,
lost in an unknown place, beyond my reach.
In a relentless chase, I was hunted down:
black raven driven out, white-spotted owl[5]
Covered my head in horrid plumage:
hoariness from eyebrow to parting.[6]
1.15 Weighed down with impossible tasks,
by the withdrawal of joyous youth,
I cried in despair, "Don't leave! I need you!
It can't be! Forsaking your closest friend!
Abandoning me to that loathsome thing?[7]
Leave a fugitive in the lurch—how dare you!"

Furious, I lunged at him. "Fine," he said,
ready for the fight, then pulled back.[8]
"Graybeard," I said, "what to do with you?"
He said, "Have patience and fear not.
Do you think old age will pass you by?
How many have gone down that road? Join them!"
You wouldn't hesitate to redeem yourself,[9]
striking with swords and thrusting with lances.
I said, "Alas, a truce with you cannot last;
I play fair while you play fast and loose.[10]
A tender heart, with heedless innocence,
commits folly by baring its mind to you.[11]
To inveigh against God's Decree is of no avail—
maybe turning gray will bring some benefit.[12]
Farewell, companion in days of merriment,
though you do not suffer me at your side."[13]
Time's cudgels may hit a young person,
strike him down in the flower of youth;
So too, the old may be reprieved,
to be left alone until they reach senility:[14]
Eyesight fails, and instead of getting up,
he supports himself on all fours to move.
He does not see a hand waving before his eyes;
and he stays quiet even if called loudly.[15]
To him, little ones and grown-ups look alike:
a blur in a decrepit graybeard's vacant stare.
Nights are pregnant with dark forebodings,
steeped in poison secreted by venomous ants.[16]
A raging fire has set my heart ablaze,
red hot, like a boiling kettle's iron legs.
Anxiety and worries repel sweet slumber;
my eyes track the stars until they're gone.
This transient world lacks permanence;
our spirit is doomed to vanish, I believe;[17]

Inexorably, life is a prelude to death;
death is followed by Judgment Day:
There is no escape from these three—
Holy Scripture lays down their rule.[18]
An old board may fit perfectly on its own:
to make it fit another board will not do.[19]
My thoughts strayed back to the days of yore.
God be with you, days of youthful frolics![20]
Days of amorous pursuit and love's seduction,
when doves were caught in my hunter's net;
When a lover pines for beauty's lithe curves:
his darling gazelle, albeit one dressed in clothes;[21]
Wasp-waisted, she strides to her palanquin,
eyes lined with kohl, lovers' bane and blight.
They break camp, their minds set on travel:
they pull down the partitions of her tent,[22]
Bring her camel's chair and accoutrements;
lead up a dark-necked stud, eight years old,
Barrel-chested and calm: It won't be rushed,
until, fully decked out and caparisoned,
It runs, trappings aflutter like locusts' wings—
young ones: some airborne, others crawling still.
Colorful trimmings and rugs flap and wave;
ribbons dance to the camel's angry grunts:
The maiden's own embroidered handiwork—[23]
a lady who rebuffs my ardent courting.
A slip of the veil may reveal her tattoos,
glitter of teeth and sweetness of lips.
I remain circumspect, on my guard
lest malicious gossips pounce and gloat.[24]
My love with pearl-white teeth is whisked away
as we crane our necks to catch a glance,
Carried off, escorted by groaning camel mothers,
smooth, muscular necks held in gracious curves.[25]

She turned her back and left me empty-handed:[26]
fear of calumniators keeps her mute and impervious.
She bites her tongue and hides her feelings,
harboring no baleful intent toward me.
I shiver at the thought of waiting a year for her,[27]
like a man dying of thirst, desperate for a well.
Let the night clouds drench her land,[28] 1.55
year after year, wherever she sojourns!
While people sleep, the clouds hurry along,
release life-bringing rains from an overcast sky;
They roll by and roar like studs in rutting season;
torrents race down the wadis, fed from gullies.[29]
For a month, pastures' pools ripple with water
drawn by winds from clouds' entrails.[30]
Two weeks after the rains came pouring down,[31]
dense herbage mantles the earth;
Camel trains unload and lofty tents are pitched: 1.60
Bedouin who roam enemy lands without concern;[32]
Tents made of red leather, cheetahs for the hunt;[33]
black woolen tents, prominent, not hidden away.[34]
They take no ruler's orders, ride on sinewy mounts:
well-trained, obedient horses of pure Arabian stock.[35]
Intrepid stalwarts, gallant men of Banū Hilāl,[36]
unflinching when war's fire is set ablaze.
They dampen the flames fanned by their enemies:
the roar abates, red-hot embers crumble to ashes.[37]
I turn my gaze to their deserted quarters— 1.65
bleak desolation, ruins, barren scenes of old.
The traces of former splendor, vanished,
lost forever, like a misty bank of fog.
Say prayers for the Lord of Quraysh,[38]
as many as drops of rain from the clouds.

Lightning's Laughter

2.0 *In its lyrical simplicity, this poem displays the construction of an emotional arc: it runs the gamut from joyful pride to despair and back to rekindled passion—similar to the style of Ibn Sbayyil, a much later ghazal poet, who had never heard of Ibn Ẓāhir. In Arabia, wells that sustain desert life offer a natural metaphor for the burst of inspiration that wells up in a poet. The gushing water translates into rhyme, rhythm, sounds, and images. The poet's tongue serves as a bucket for hauling up the precious cargo. Abandoned by his youth, he concludes this upbeat prelude on a gloomy note: let others take their turn and hoist the heavy buckets. Relief comes in an absorbing spectacle of cloudbursts and life-bringing rain. Flowering meadows attract swarms of Bedouin and the poet's ultimate consolation: a ravishing damsel, a gazelle of the sort that hunts and haunts the hunter. As Ibn Ẓāhir puts it in verse thirteen of this ode to joy, rain's ultimate blessing is to wash people's "dusty minds."*

The discerning poet al-Māyidī builds his verses, 2.1
wise sayings repeated by poets and reciters.[39]
Inside me flows a stream of great renown:
my tongue is the bucket, hauled up by poetry.[40]
The sweet drink is quaffed by the thirsty throng:
devotees of verse, only dimwits doze off;[41]
He's awake when the empty-headed sleep;
his stubborn eyes fight to chase off slumber.
Dew sprinkles the earth, night is dead quiet, 2.5
around me people are immersed in dreams;
All night, wrecked by ghostly forebodings,
I ponder my life's doom-laden course.[42]
Recalling my halcyon days, I cry hot tears:
unattainable memories, etched on distant crests.[43]
Seduction's game brings no profit, that I knew;
the valley of foolish impudence is not my abode.
I'm done; the bucket is slung over my shoulder:
let others draw with new buckets if they like![44]
West on the horizon rose mighty thunderclouds; 2.10
rumbling, they cast a black pall over the lands.
Thunderclaps let lightning burst into laughter,[45]
heavy rains rattled and clattered on the ground:
A deafening drum of drops hammered the earth,
illuminated by blinding flashes from the sky.
Let the rains wash our dusty minds, I pray,
as a torrent restores life to a desiccated wadi.
Listen to the roar of water splashing on the soil:
floods carve out a course around hard obstacles.[46]
Night clouds filled Ḥawāmī's wells:[47] 2.15
soaked with water, the thirsty earth came to life.
Desert meadows burst into orgies of succulent green,
vying like neighbors in giving delicious presents.
Bedouin rushed in from distant lands,[48]
guided by wayfarers' gestures and descriptions.[49]

Clustered around Wādī l-Ghadīr, they marveled[50]
at dark eyes, rimmed with black streaks of kohl.
It happened among the well's frenzied crowds:[51]
a gazelle hunted me—has the game turned around?
2.20 I had no doubts, but why does she reveal tattoos,
no trace of horns, and docility unlike a gazelle?[52]
Her arms are plumper, her waist more waspish;
she's smart and refrains from bounding off.
Her smile shows what no gazelle ever had:
white rows of teeth evenly aligned, no gaps.

Agony of Love

Ostensibly, the poet makes a desperate plea to his beloved to stop snubbing him and show a little kindness. The connoisseurs of his poetry, which "flows like ink from his tongue," are moved by the suffering of this "martyr of love": the stepping-stone for a transition to the theme of love's agonies. Toward the end of his litany, it appears that the complaint is less about female charms than the fading away of the poet's youth, as in the first poem, and the onset of a riper age. A substantial section of gnomic wisdom about the unpredictability of fate (the first of several to come in other poems) ushers in the traditional scene of the beloved's departure with her Bedouin tribe. The poet's sorrows at this loss contrast painfully with the sweet delights of the date harvest, itself a symbol for the delicious joys of youth. As elsewhere, the scene is pictured from the poet's perspective as a settled oasis dweller fascinated by the Bedouin. The poem's first half is notable for its musical quality: assonance, alliteration, parallelism, and stylistic repetition are employed to great effect. 3.0

3.1 The discerning al-Māyidī ibn Ẓāhir speaks
in verses that flow from his tongue like ink;
The rhymes assault my poor, squirming heart
as locusts swarm from Tihāmah mountain.[53]
My own lines, not another poet's verse:
stray camels don't mix with homegrown stock.[54]
Connoisseurs of art and lore are dazzled,
arbiters of taste who flock to my entertainment:
3.5 If my poetry's devotees go into ecstasies,
they travel far: to memorize and profit.[55]
They speculate: "His amorous heart is in thrall
to art, his chants composed on windy peaks;[56]
A martyr of love, his disease is incurable,
in spite of doctors' frantic efforts to cure."
I tell them, "Sweet sleep has eluded me
in the two years of this ailment's torment."
Tears well up, run in streams from my eyes:
my cheeks are dripping wet from crying.
3.10 With my hand I wipe and wipe my face,
in vain: the more I wipe, the more I weep.[57]
Like *ghaḍā* wood under a boiling kettle,
my heart is set ablaze by a relentless fire.
Cool earth and mud, poured from shovels,
bring no relief to my agony and pangs:[58]
My ailment takes no comfort from wet soil
and cold water makes it no easier to bear.
None of the medical arts brought benefit:
they were blocked because of a mystery.[59]
3.15 Why greet her caprice with a gracious smile,
if bandages only make the bleeding worse?[60]
My love, I think you are fighting shy of me:
you've fallen in with enemies and enviers.
If I twist the ropes of hope and pay fealty,[61]
she is rude to me and loosens the knots.

With satisfaction unattainable, what guile
will gain my right from refusal and tyranny?
If hardship itself tired of your empty promises,
how about creditors whose debts remain unpaid?[62]
Such antics will not win you trusted friends:
professions of devotion are derided as pretense.
No matter how grievously I'm being wronged,
I seek to please her and keep her spite at bay:
I have been languishing for three long years
to appease her, though she ignores my claims,
Waiting for a rendezvous with youth, bygone,[63]
like my black hair, now streaked with gray.
If I miss our tryst today—it's too late:
Tomorrow the grim reaper will lie in wait.[64]
May God ward off evil on its approach,
protect the commonweal from woe.
A fire loses the scalding heat of its flames
as it dies down and its ashes are blown away.
A camel with two riders may outpace a fleet horse,
then droops, too knackered for a saddle.[65]
Fate won't spare you from biting the dust:
tribe after tribe was laid low by its scourge.[66]
Arid land shouldn't despair of rainy revival:
desolate wadis find relief in torrential floods.[67]
The sick should not despair of recovery;
the healthy cannot escape their doom.
The poverty-stricken may yet strike it rich,
or be granted the Lord's mercy, if God decrees.
The sore-eyed are not forever bereft of sleep:
their eyes will taste sweet slumber and leisure.
Let a hunter persevere if his quarry darts away:
when it returns at ease, he may bag it unawares.
Don't be lulled into complacency if a wolf is gone:
when your battle with sleep is lost, he'll appear.

3.35 A watchdog dozes off at night; a wolf steals up
on its sheep, hides, makes a choice, and pounces.
Poor heart racked with pain God willed for it:
on litters being led to desert meadows,
Stunning beauties are carried away by the studs;
all that's left: dark spots under the cooking pots.[68]
They whisked her away, not caring for me a whit,
though my tears ran freely, in streams and drops:
Like leaky water bags bouncing on a camel's back,
in such copious flows, my eyes spout their tears.[69]
3.40 A cultivator of palm trees pinning high hopes
on sweet dates only to see the Bedouin abscond: that's me.[70]
Alas, but for God's favor nothing succeeds;
nothing lessens if God wants it to increase.
If one endeavors to live one's life as He wills,
count on God not to contravene His promise.[71]
If dealt with churlishly by the world, a generous soul
may count on receiving from God a double reward.[72]
Pray for the most perfect of all creatures, Muḥammad,
as often as Qur'an reciters complete their readings.

Death and Revival

The poem revolves around the essentials of life and the human condition, the world and its end. It includes the holy scriptures and a local version of Noah's Flood to reinforce its point. The psychological and natural cycles of ambition and gusto; setbacks and loss; revival of flagging spirits and wilting herbage; defeat on the heels of joyful climax; and the all-important home stretch to the grave and the end of the world, "precariously balanced on the bull's horns," are repeated in the dense final verses on the flood's aftermath. The poet sees no permanence, except for his poetry. In his view, these verses are new creations on foundations lost in the depths of time, as the world itself is in perpetual flux while its vital questions remain the same. Those who cannot recognize that truth are lost. 4.0

Ibn Ẓāhir's claim to eternal fame, bolstered by his verses built like impregnable citadels, introduces a scene of fearsome desolation, presided over by the tawny owl whose eerie screeches send a chill up his spine. With passionate fervor, he describes the intimacy that prevailed between him and his sweetheart, a true soulmate. The perfidy and wiles of the World put an end to that, and the poet entrusts himself to the Lord who scripted "our faith, its Torahs and Psalms." His desiccated heart undergoes a revival with the advent of life-bringing rains. Thunder and lightning, "like a wedding party," bring the famous floods of al-Muʿayrīḍ and their creative destruction

(§§4.51–55), a subject that has received much scrutiny from commentators. On completion of the date season, the joyful ninety days, the poem ends on a gloomy note: the earth's bleak landscape in the wake of Apocalypse.

Discerning al-Māyidī ibn Ẓāhir molds and speaks: 4.1
verses of wisdom soaring high like lofty castles;[73]
Buildings raised with art, not mud and stone:
impregnable walls that can't be scaled.
If siege is laid by grimly determined enemies,
we beat them back with prayers for God's succor.
My canny audience rejoices in its novelty,
unaware that its beginnings are centuries old.[74]
Sonorous verses spread and read by the crowds:[75] 4.5
till the Day of Resurrection its lines are recited.[76]
Perhaps, once we're gone, we will not be forgotten[77]
like discarded utensils scattered in desert wastes.
I climbed soaring peaks to vent my spleen
in verses that heave in my raging breast,[78]
My gaze fixed on an abode abandoned by my love,
laid waste by the wheels of time and distance.[79]
Let melancholy winds tug at the empty haunt,[80]
bury the camp's remains under layers of dust:
Barren desolation without a trace of human life,[81] 4.10
the haunt of wild animals sniffing in the wind,[82]
The ghastly screeches of the tawny desert owl,[83]
like the harrowing shrieks of one lost and alone;[84]
An owl's repeated and plaintive hoots, forlorn[85]
as a drover's calls to stragglers far behind the herd.[86]
There a mourning dove coos: whisperings
of women terrified by alarming news,[87]
A lament of soft moans from its perch on hills
amid the murmur of chirping birds and pigeons.[88]
Until separation ends, I must suffer pain: 4.15
hellish torments in the quiet of night;[89]
Lashed by the spiked whip of my hankering
after a beloved, longing's unbearable burden.
In separation, her presence's heavenly bliss
turns into sorrow, an incurable affliction.

Whether near or far, she does me no wrong,
heedless of packs of lies whispered in her ear.
All my life, I've never uttered indiscretions,
until grief itself lodged its grievance against me.[90]
God forbid, I have shown her no discourtesy;
if only I had blinded my eyes with drops
Before feasting them on her youthful succulence;[91]
white teeth like a smile fresh from soft soil,
Chamomile petals glistening with a touch of dew,
a glimpse of her haunches' tantalizing curves![92]
Her gorgeous looks waft with a lovely scent:
fragrant perfume sprinkled on her locks.[93]
May God grant me forgiveness! She's as I say:
rays of light at dawn, chasing off the dark.
Her face, resplendent with ravishing smile,[94]
outshines the mundane beauties of other belles.
My love, you are both my ailment
and my medicine, you know it all![95]
You have strung me along for ages:
someone waiting to snatch my soul inches ever closer.[96]
May God requite a world at war without truce
or respite from disasters and twists of fate.
You're assaulted without warning
or reconnaissance by camel-mounted spies.[97]
She can't be bought off and acts at random:
no amount of tithe will give her satisfaction.
Don't trust the world and her conceited henchmen:[98]
you don't hurt a fly, yet she scares you to death.
On parting, a thought nestled inside me:[99]
it is hard to turn the quern of separation.[100]
We aim to manipulate the world's grindstone,
yet attempts at guiding her must come to naught.
She primps herself to strut like a pretty girl;[101]
she's fooled people by dolling up for ages.[102]

She dazzles us dimwits and takes us unawares,
hurls us from her back headlong into the grave.
Our praise is for Him who bestowed His favors,
Who scripted our faith, its Torahs and Psalms.[103]
My insides boil like water in a copper pot,
while the lid dances over cooked meat;[104]
Kindled with a flaming rag, a fire was set ablaze.
Steam that escapes from the lid's valve[105]
Brings relief, until my boiling insides erupt anew;[106]
when my nostrils are caressed by morning breezes,
Wafts of memories and passionate love cast aside
by Fate, ensconced high on its saddle.
So close she was, so far away they've taken her:
her loss crushed the splints of my broken legs.
Seized by despair, I surrendered to my sorrows,
though otherwise, caught amid such wreckage,
I remain tight-lipped, my mouth tied with thongs:[107]
you are the one to loose these fetters!
It takes a miserable friend to let down a friend:
absconding by stealth, not leaving a trace![108]
My travails stem from humiliation, felt deeply[109]
when I see that scorched earth can be revived:
Toward dusk, a heavy deck of clouds drifted in
to release its torrential load on parched valleys;
Rain to resuscitate the green from dead earth
with such abundance that sheep stay where they are.[110]
Shaking off dust, earth dressed in delightful robes;
sprinkled with dew, it spread a saffron scent.
Torrent beds thundered with swirling water
sent gushing over desiccated lands.
A wedding party: flying batons and lighted torches,
as lightning set eastern mountains aglow.[111]
In al-Muʿayrīḍ's flood, ninety thousand perished:
drowning Muslims and unbelievers alike.[112]

Al-Ḥīl's palm gardens were inundated;[113]
stems of the tallest trees stood in water;
Young, small palms lost bunches of dates:
Crashing waves left debris in the crowns.[114]
A sweet smell of palm blossom and pollen
recalls fragrance of perfumed, exquisite brides.[115]
4.55 Stewed for ninety days in midsummer's heat,
dates have ripened, palm fronds shed their fruits.[116]
Before us, multitudes have gone on their last journey,[117]
assigned to oblivion in unmarked burial sites.
We live as they lived; likewise we pass away:
life in repose is illusion, as God has decreed.
A cotton sheet wrapped around the body:
last washing and into the grave, that's all.
The world ends after mankind's departure,[118]
a harvest of seeds' last residue, I think.
4.60 Nothing remains but lifeless sandy plains,
littered with smooth stones, bed of empty seas.[119]
The angel blows the trumpet more than once:
on horns of a cosmic bull, earth is cleft asunder.[120]
Say prayers for the best of men, Muḥammad,
as many as pilgrims who hasten to Mecca.

Wisdom Poem

A quintessential Ibn Ẓāhir poem, this is especially famous in the United Arab Emirates on account of more than forty lines of verse devoted to popular wisdom. The insertion of this section is a good example of another of the poet's skills: the fluency of his transitions from one theme to the other, so seamless that in casual reading the transitions are hardly perceptible. This is the only poem with a relatively difficult rhyme based on the consonant ʿayn. In the prelude, poems are compared to a sack stuffed with sweet dates, and in the next verse to a fat sheep, not the lean type shunned by wolves: a train of association typical in Ibn Ẓāhir's wisdom poetry. Similarly, the end of the section (the conviction that hardship will be followed by relief, as verdure will follow drought) transitions into gripping scenes of rain. A remarkable touch is the comparison of palm trees tilting in the wind to the swaying of dancing Sufi devotees. The curves of the poem's emotional arc are no less daring: this upbeat section ends in utter defeat when the poet succumbs to the ravages of old age. 5.0

5.1 Al-Māyidī ibn Ẓāhir polishes his verses with finesse—
elegant masterpieces, spread from mouth to mouth:[121]
Poetry lovers came in throngs, flocked around me,
gesticulating like market buyers and sellers.[122]
When all and sundry display dubious wares,
not a single one of my fruits shows a rotten spot;
Sacks full of poems, succulent and tasty:
Fresh dates, picked with finicky care;[123]
5.5 Or like sheep grown fat on lush grazing—
not the scrawny sort, shunned by wolves.
If you are looking for friends as company,[124]
discriminate: choose a trustworthy gentleman!
Not one to leave you in the lurch, he saves you
with stout defense, clever tricks, helpers;
In a dinghy, pitching and rolling in roaring waves,
on high seas, sails reefed and jib hoisted.
Evil ventures will not earn you praise:
noble poise on arduous climbs brings acclaim.
5.10 If you've been of no use while alive,
your account at death is a resounding zero.
You can't escape from death's tribulations:
pleading for you on Judgment Day—that counts.
You, servile flunky sucking up to Mammon,[125]
be not beguiled! You're being led up the garden path!
Though you're coddled, drinking from her teats,[126]
soon you'll be weaned, bereft of contentment.
You depart from this world with a scrap,
like a date sack emptied by pincers.[127]
5.15 Does it make you happy to stride into your mansion?
Remember, your true abode measures an arm's length.[128]
It is natural to rejoice on returning to one's home;[129]
to be lowered into the ground—frightening!
A prisoner tied down forever in a dusty grave,
waiting to be released by a terrifying shout.[130]

Be wise, use your lifetime to do some good
while you can, and ward off punishment.[131]
Even birds, on the wing all day long,
must alight to spend the night.[132]
Don't you see how a bird needs feathers to fly,
how it remains earthbound if its wing is cut?[133]
You may call for succor: God is alive and present!
If you go stealing, don't think He doesn't notice.
He is all-knowing: things either plain to see or hidden,[134]
the invisible world, folded inside future's chest.
If God has made you well-to-do and prosperous,
shame on you for being a scrounging miser!
Provide for those worthy of support: widows, orphans,
hard-up travelers who ply the roads—they're your gain![135]
It doesn't hurt even though divine decree is immutable:
as bandages help to soften pain caused by wounds.
A noble character stands tall even if dressed in rags;
appearances deceive: a man is more than his trade!
Don't be fooled by a peregrine's dust-colored feathers:
if you look for glossy black, a starling will do.[136]
Some people are best avoided; don't get close:
you risk your fingers by brushing against them:
Make sure to count the bones one by one,
lest some of your wristbones are missing.
Beware of a spiteful churl's company:
illicit progeny of vicious scandalmongers;
An ingrate who disowns his benefactors:
his sense of good old virtue extirpated;[137]
A wretch who'd sell his grandmother for a pittance,
to buy execrable rubbish wherever it's for sale.
Given a chance, he hunts with the wolves;
smelling a rat, he hurries to warn the shepherd.[138]
To a guest he serves a supper of leftovers;
he leaps with joy at an invitation to a meal;[139]

If you attend a banquet, he is yellow with envy,
while uninvited he calls on you at dinnertime.[140]
If subsistence comes by force, not by God's will,
why do lions go hungry while dogs eat their fill?[141]
Some folks will woo you with honeyed words:
shifty bastards, dodgy like crafty foxes;
A fat mongrel barks at you from his kennel,
while lions keep to their den, proud and aloof;
His solemn pledges are the assurances of women,
singing girls who make you any promise,[142]
The way a boiling pot bubbles and spills over,
while the ladling cook is not paying attention;
Or as a wayward horse in need of a tight rein
throws off a rider who forgets to keep his grip.
Beware of stroking a viper's soft, smooth skin:
sit motionless and keep a sharp eye on it![143]
Don't be deceived by its body's silky touch:
venom flows like spittle round its incisors.
Human beings come in various kinds:
misers, noble spendthrifts, cowards, and stalwarts.
Bravery is of two sorts: before or against the wind;
some ships sail a steady course, others lie still.
God on High said, ease comes after hardship,[144]
spring pastures will bloom after drought.
Fireworks of lightning rip into the clouds'
billowing mass gently driven by a breeze.
Gusts grab and shake the cloud deck's crest:
the womb slashed, water comes gushing out,[145]
Splashes down in torrents that rage ever higher
along the hilly edges, while people are fast asleep.
The land, stirred by showers, bursts into flower,
herbage and plants of exquisite varieties.

Three kinds of strangers were permitted to enter:[146]
thunder, lightning, and a breeze from the west.
Passionately in love, they sob and shed hot tears;
for whom do they rise and are goaded, I wonder?
Winds lift and crowns of palm trees sway:
their gracious fronds swing up and down;
Bending to each other, they move to and fro:
Sufi worshippers of Badriyyah and Rifāʿī schools;[147]
Dance of unveiled girls who whirl and twirl,[148]
swing their loosened hair to the wedding's beat;
Bunches of dates hang from stalks, dark as ravens;
flow down loosely or in plaits like braided hair.[149]
My pursuit did not quench my burning desire:
crestfallen and terror-stricken, I returned.
When my hair became flecked with gray—
the color of haggard wolves with spotted fur—
I felt certain that gray was extinction's harbinger:
youth's halcyon days were not here to stay;[150]
Forsaken, left behind, not through our fault,
I hold firm to my resolve: no use in quarreling!
I was aggrieved, caught off-guard by her departure—
it's unforgivable to go and not to bid farewell![151]
I'm sick at heart, thinking of the days of yore,
agonies of memory, aggravated by a cooing dove:
Why do you sicken me with cruel tunes?
May God never forgive you, wicked bird,[152]
For wailing in heartrending notes,
mournful laments of turtledoves and rock doves.[153]
Gaiety headed south and a dreaded guest arrived[154]
at a breathless gallop: tears welled up in my eyes.
My youthful clothes made a nice, comfortable fit:
now I must wear a rough and threadbare coat.[155]

The visitor hit me in the eyes, teeth, everywhere,
indifferent to my anguished appeals for help.
People scour the firmament for the new moon,
except me—I can't tell a straight from a curving line.[156]
I conclude with prayers for the Prophet Muḥammad,
as many as handfuls of seed sown by peasants.

Dance of the Zephyr

Relatively short, this is one of two poems discovered after the early collections had been published. It offers a bucolic vision of Bedouin life with its customary vignettes of the abandoned camp, the camel caravan of the beloved, and palm trees. It exhibits the poet's signature smooth thematic transitions, the contrasting pair of youth and old age, and verses of wisdom. The poem also borrows from the Banū Hilāl cycle of verse, whether by design or because of later insertion we do not know. 6.0

6.1 Wise al-Māyidī ibn Ẓāhir recites his verses
on a sandy knoll, his perch in the dunes.
Eastern breezes formed sand into mounds;[157]
all other winds have ceased to blow.[158]
The zephyr twirled over the gazelle's traces;[159]
over firmer stretches the sands nimbly move.
Before dusk, dry valleys filled and ran with water:
healing rains of Canopus from beyond the rising sun.[160]
6.5 In a sprawling tree, a dove cooed with abandon,
singing its heart out for faraway mates.[161]
The tribe's caravan, marching across vast wastes,
emerged at an unflagging pace from the dunes.
Sturdy, muscular camels suffering in silence,
as if vexed by mistreatment, thirsting in hot winds.
The tribe's chattels were carried by fleet camels,
high-humped, hooves turned slightly inward,[162]
Silent as palm trees lined along rippling water—[163]
dense crowns brushed up like a full head of hair
6.10 Evoke baskets of succulent dates or pressed sugarcane—
sprightly camels swerved from the caravan's line.
Time came for the Bedouin to prepare for departure[164]
when the palm trees' sweet fruits are harvested.
If decided to go, they go; ordered "Stay!" they stay,[165]
heedful that Canopus reigns with blistering heat.
They took the supple-bodied damsel with her long lashes;
no host ever treated a guest to tastier morsels!
Wasp-waisted, she keeps admirers on a string:
her scent wafts over the site she left behind.
6.15 Good Lord, those sweet lips and eyes, that nose!
Cheeks? The svelte white gazelle of the sands![166]
I disobeyed my critics' orders: "Forget your romance!"
Grudgingly, I bowed to the dictates of distance.[167]
Old age crept up on me: frail, I walked with a stoop;
my limbs and faculties crumbled as I fell apart.

Decrepit, dim of vision, an old man doesn't respond,
    not even if hands are waved before his eyes.[168]
If adulthood arrives without common sense,[169]
    abandon all hope: the case is lost.[170]
If irrigation comes too late, the harvest fails: 6.20
    a flood cannot rescue wilting ears of grain.[171]
It is advisable to dress in robes of recent make:
    you can't hide threadbare hems and tatters.
If you're healthy and fine, life is enjoyable;
    once it's over, a gravestone is your company.[172]
People haggle with the world, seeking profit,
    asleep, oblivious to a death ready to pounce.
Say prayers for Muḥammad, the best of men,
    as many as a dove's coos on its perch.

Don't Be Hard on Friends

7.0 *After just one verse of introduction (the signature verse), the poet launches straight into the subject of this monothematic piece: advice on how to navigate the perils of this world. In doing so, the poet mines the store of practical wisdom that enjoyed wide currency as part of Arabian popular culture of his time. In the somewhat unexpected and abrupt closing verse, a nugget of gnomic wisdom is couched in imagery derived from camel husbandry: how the weak are easily intimidated by the powerful.*

These are the words of al-Māyidī, a discerning poet 7.1
whose well-knit verses find favor with reciters.
Take my advice: stay away from offensive talk;
empty prattle will not redound to your credit.[173]
A silly remark tossed at you is best ignored;[174]
if you hear a shrewd observation, ask for more.
Do not purvey the vile gossip of the depraved;
honest men decline a drink of melted fat.[175]
Don't delay treatment of a slight indisposition: 7.5
tarry, and you run the risk of serious disease!
Better spare a trifle for the cupper of blood,[176]
or get ready to pay a real doctor's hefty bill.
If a shady patch eludes you while it's cool,
you'll be roasted by the sun, merciless.
Don't forget: your spot in shade may yet fade;
comfort one who bakes in scorching heat.[177]
Repair sandals while you have a moment's rest,
or barefoot deal with thorns and red-hot stones.
Better to countenance your fellows' foibles 7.10
than face oppression friendless and alone.
If a hunter sets his trap too wide,
startled game bounds away in panic:
Make the place reassuring, congenial,
welcoming, and warm: then you'll catch it!
Be smart, overlook a friend's shortcomings:[178]
your kin may turn a deaf ear to your appeals;
The enemy gloats at seeing the back of you:
a solitary lightweight can't carry a little sack.[179]
Like a cameleer who fails to adjust a load: 7.15
when bags slip from the back, balance is lost.
A falcon should tend to its flight feathers
or it will not be deft on the wing to strike:
Unable to give chase and catch, it flags,[180]
its talons groping for the prey in vain.

A fearless warrior is given a wide berth;
    the kindhearted make for a soft target.[181]
Be the first to move and forestall others:
    If you don't attack, you'll be assaulted.
7.20 At the sound of a stud roaring from afar,
    a young she-camel grunts and raises her tail.[182]

Rain Poem

In this major poem, the second longest, Ibn Ẓāhir's favorite themes and motifs find full expression. On the bobbing meter of al-mutadārik, *the polythematic* qaṣīdah *is propelled forward by verses arrayed in a series of interlocking binary oppositions between a desirable quality and a less desirable one: in poetry, pearls, dates, water sources, speech, swords, people's character, drought, and lush meadows. The last contrasting pair is the stepping-stone for one of the dexterous transitions for which the poet is praised. The prelude leads into an outstanding section of thirteen verses that paints a rainstorm as an exciting game of love, lust, violence, and deceit waged by clouds, lightning, and thunderclaps. In the oeuvre, the poem is one of the few, together with Poem 5, in which the rain scene immediately follows the prelude and the wisdom section. The spectacle of celestial fireworks merges into lively scenes of palm cultivation and date harvest, the beloved's arrival and departure with her tribe, and paeans on the huge stallion camel that carries her in her howdah. From there, the mood is all downhill. Presaged by the violence of the rainstorm, the poet's struggle to turn the tide of lovesickness descends into a ferocious brawl: a tug of war between youth (in its incarnation as love) and old age that the poet is doomed to lose. The concluding verses seek to draw lessons of wisdom from these dramatic events. He does so by giving a clever Sufi twist (the* jihād al-nafs *("fighting the ego")) to its opposite: the Najdī-style wisdom of Hobbesian struggle for survival.* 8.0

8.1 Ibn Ẓāhir composes amazing verses:[183]
they surge inside for his inner ear to hear.
I lifted the cover from a hidden source:
the well water gushes from the bottom.[184]
Verses flock to my call; I pick the cream:
fastidious, I spurn the leaner rhymes.
Some poets make do with lighter weights;
the pearls I choose are sublime and heavy.
8.5 Exquisite jewels go to the highest bidder:
buyers line up to bid exorbitant amounts.
Hand-picked pearls wrapped in cotton;
the rarest gems I've kept for myself.
Traders value pearls plucked from deeper waters;[185]
the lesser sort fetches a paltry price.
Orchards treat us to a feast of sweet fruits;
some fruits, less tasty, share the shady garden.
Flowing rivers carry evil as well as good;
some wells spout water, others merely dribble.
8.10 Some speeches are heartening, others bitter bile:
colocynth is not spring water from Paradise.
Swords do not inspire awe in equal measure:
some razor-sharp, bone-shattering, some blunt and rusty.
People come in all shapes and sizes: despicable misers,[186]
big-spending lords, poltroons beneath contempt.
Lands lie denuded until their nakedness is clothed
in beautiful, ample robes by life-bringing rains.[187]
Clouds arrived at night to a din of thunderbolts,
downpours unleashed from moist mouths.
8.15 From the west they sailed in, breathless with desire,
to restore greenery with wondrous bursts of flower.
Drawing near, they flashed a smile behind a veil;
at once a deluge disgorged by their bowels
Flattened tent poles, wiped out all traces,
draped the valley's flanks in bountiful green.

A cloudburst to lift spirits and revive the dunes,
set off by angels faithful to their orders:
Heavy rains split the earth and splintered rocks,
urged by rolling thunder and lightning's blaze.
Watchtowers of bright stone and tawny buildings 8.20
turned blackish-blue when pelted with incessant showers;
A nightly bank of cumulus pours forth rain in sheets,
under the sign of Arcturus, a heavenly gift from the Lord.[188]
Thunderclaps brighten the sky; cool breezes play pranks:
the beloved's glances provoke a flood of tears.[189]
Weeping, jest, and laughter vied in the joust;[190]
ill-wishers gloated, my beloved feigned ignorance.
Longed-for blessings landed where they should:
torrents came crashing down the valley of al-Dhayd.
A marvelous sight: desert meadows, from end to end; 8.25
palm gardens greedily suck up the limpid water.
One month into summer, the first fruits appear:
its spathes protrude with yellow female flowers.
Between palm's stem and heart, they push up
graceful racemes and male flowers, waxy white.[191]
Sun-ripened, stewed without cooking:[192]
nourishment for paupers, provisions for the road.[193]
The dates, a mouthwatering delight for the eye,
briskly harvested, were weighed in baskets;
Stalks, bare of fruits, wrapped in fiber sleeves: 8.30
a year of rest for the mother, no pollination.
The Bedouin pack up, plot a route, decamp:
a wild rush, each in search of virgin pastures.[194]
It happens in fall when sizzling heat abates;
before dawn, they sight flickers of Canopus's star:[195]
A Bedouin's sign for a rush to desert pastures,
a huge, thick-haired stallion is made to kneel for my love;
The tribe's camel-in-chief, docile, easy to handle:
goaded by chanting, it gladly skips its rest at noon.

Dangling from its neck, a bell tinkles at every step;
no need for reins, the behemoth strides at unflagging pace.
Ears pricked up, it walks in tune with the driver's song,
quickens its gait as if taught by ostriches how to run.
At this rapid pace, it doesn't need a cameleer
to stay the course: self-guided homeward bound.
Three cheers for the stallion and its precious load;
though I didn't get the satisfaction owed to me—
Her tribe's departure made me frantic with despair;
her return magically cured my heart.
Her crass offences seemingly forgotten, the innocent girl!—
she flashed smiles from behind her transparent veil.
Do I see the affinity in a neck's curve and dreamy eye
with a gazelle in a dell, tree-nibbling early in the day?
Her peerless nose outshines her rivals:
bridge straight, nostrils sculpted to curve with grace.
Beauty's power is written large in domineering eyes:
bewitching gaze lurking beneath kohl-lined lashes.
Fully armed, she crushes her mesmerized lovers—
I'm helpless against her relentless assault!
I clung to my belief that she'd stand in fear of God.
How silly! No shred of evidence of her good sense!
You're elusive, an evanescent haze of a mirage;
I'm foolish, caught unawares without a waterskin.[196]
Forget to carry water on a desert journey,
risk dying from thirst in shimmering heat.
I exposed myself to ridicule—what a fool I was
to heap praise on her, hoping she'd be impressed![197]
How could I count you as a faithful friend?
Look, you're my fiercest enemy, intractable!
You're riding roughshod over poor devils like me:
why should I pay blood money? You're the killer![198]
Don't you heed how such affairs may end;
don't you recoil at catastrophic murders?

Foretelling the future is not your suit:
you didn't ask yourself or anyone else!
Be aware then that the world is a fickle place,
ruled by one law: what goes up must come down.
If you ask, in your kindness, about how I feel:
trampled on, unhinged, and brokenhearted.
Similar to fruits in lofty trees or windblown dust:
sands must slide from the dunes' peaks.[199]
Youth slips out the back door; old age knocks in front,[200]
kneels his mounts, panting from relentless gallop.[201]
A gray monster and his henchmen ambushed me:[202]
fast camel riders and horsemen in coats of mail.
I prepared for the fight; my young friend took fright,
rushing to me for safe-conduct and protection.[203]
Seeing me alone, unarmed, he drew his blades:
wielding dagger and sharp, gleaming sword,
He lunged at me, sure I was at his mercy,
as a refugee, no longer welcome, is expelled.[204]
When push came to shove, he left me in the lurch;
my callous kinsmen set about measuring my grave.[205]
If you do not sally forth with camel troops and infantry,
your foes seize a chance to grab you by the throat.[206]
Grievous injustice—perforce I looked the other way,
like lifting bags of sand to balance a camel load.
I shaded my eyes with my hands, straining to look far:
specks on the horizon, swaying canopies, faded away.
Pinning hopes on an adversary's forgiveness:
to my mind, such wishful thinking is insane.[207]
At times, noting the lion's absence, predators,
full of glee, mark their victims for murder.[208]
How I wish old age would bring me benefit:[209]
a rogue, pure and simple, his enmity is implacable.
My teeth fall out, eyes are ridden with disease,[210]
a hunchback walking slouched on unsteady feet.

In a world careening to destruction, misery is fated:
forever lurching from straight to crooked, up and down.
8.70 Dolled up like a tart, she distracts from good works;
soon enough the thrill wears off: it all ends in tears.
While we play and bustle about, life passes like a dream:[211]
in the final act a treacherous stab, the curtain falls.
My listeners, say prayers for Muḥammad, the Chosen,
as often as flashes of lightning set the sky ablaze.

Tears at the Court of Love

Without pausing to boast of his accomplishments as a composer, the poet addresses his beloved in heartrending tones: his emotions spill out like bloody entrails from an abdomen hit by a screw-shaped spearhead. Like the early Umayyad poet ʿUmar ibn Abī Rabīʿah, he alludes to a settlement in the court of love. Short interludes of wisdom verses offer implicit self-criticism of his follies. At the departure of the beloved on her camel, festooned with a cheerful flutter of ribbons, the poet sends his own camel-borne message after her, the only example of the messenger motif in the poetry, but to little avail: verses borrowed from the Banū Hilāl epic cycle underscore her tribe's haughty indifference to the plight of the powerless. The poet's rage translates into a menacing standoff between rutting bull camels, a simile for the fireworks of a devastating thunderstorm. 9.0

9.1 Al-Māyidī ibn Ẓāhir, the sage, speaks in verse:
urgings of a soul roasted on glowing embers.
Dogged by ailments beyond cure,
my stubborn heart rejected all remedy:
For a year and more, my entrails were infested
by the poisoned blade of a screw-shaped spearhead;
Blood frothed at my lips as an infant's mouth
spills milk at the corners after breastfeeding.
9.5 "Take it easy!" I said, and my eyes cried even more;
crazed by love, my eyelids shed buckets of tears.
No mistake, it's not because my soul is dim-witted:
it hankers after a lovely and elusive companion.
She gives no reason for despair—if only she did—[212]
and strings me along with lavish promises:
She never makes good, I never abandon hope;
no wonder people say I am being abused
When sages hold court to consider witness accounts
to find which of us violated hallowed rules of propriety.[213]
9.10 Drawn swords cannot force redemption of pledges:
I want a binding covenant, sealed with mighty oaths!
If you mend your ways, restore to me what I'm due;
I am at your orders, ready to give the world for you!
Forgive and forget, I say, no hurt feelings or grudges;
I'll do whatever you say: your wish is my command!
Even though you have given me the cold shoulder,
A gift-seeker at royal court, I pin hopes on reward.[214]
Forbearing, I turn a blind eye to misdemeanors;
to languish without news from you is different.
9.15 Don't cut me off! I beseech you: I gave you my all,
a friend showering you with presents and favors.
Since the year before last, I've been sick at heart;
wasted, whittled down by infatuation, thin as a pencil.
Tears fill my eyes, as water runs from a leaky skin,[215]
its leather's shoddy stitching unraveling.

Woe to a distraught traveler who stumbles on
with no more than a tiny bit of water left.[216]
In winter water is easy to get: you're drenched!
In summer you're scorched by poisonous winds.
A harebrained idea, not to take precautions:
Empty skins are no help if you're dying of thirst.
Seasoned desert travelers treasure water supplies:
a cool draft is heavenly in the heat of noon.
If the fire of youth has burnt your fingers,
you walk warily, like a warrior mauled in battle.[217]
The caravan's marching orders are shouted—not to me!
A camel is kneeled for my darling's palanquin.
All night I toss and turn, eyes blurred and red:
my heart strains to run after a distant love.[218]
Dust and bustle at departure plunged me into gloom;
God's wrath on the scout who made them leave![219]
My treasure was whisked away, an unbearable loss:
I've put all I have on her; she's my one and only.[220]
On hardy mounts they rode off to faraway countries;
young and tough she-camels, trained runners,
They whisked her across deserts, beyond my reach;
far or near, no difference, she leaves me empty-handed,
Except for heartburn blazing inside my rib cage:
fiery flames crackle, spewed out by red-hot coals.
In her haughtiness, she deigns not to condescend:
stanch my flood of tears, more than a copious well,
Enough to fill jars loaded on ships docked in harbor;
not even fully grown, strong camels lift their weight.
Listen, my messenger on a hardy desert crosser,
rested for a year, a splendid beast with drooping lips,
Fit to shuttle travelers to their destination and back;
the mount devours miles, unflagging in heat of noon:[221]
Make haste as you ride to convey what's on my mind;
give her news and greetings, my sincerest wishes;

9.35 Travel at utmost speed, faster than ships at sea,
quicker than carrier pigeons racing in the sky:
Speak to a love who trampled on my tender feelings;
trapped me in a hellish pit that would turn infants gray.
For backbiters' sake, I was slighted and shunned:
no ill-wisher lost sleep over my quandary.
They buy and sell at the dictates of whim and fancy,
not trifling with riding camels or womenfolk:[222]
Imagine swindling themselves on wanton splurges:
throwing away good money to buy degenerate brides!
9.40 Mismatches saddle a tribe's plump beauty with a dud;
some bright young men are shackled to a lazy slut.[223]
The land turned green from heavenly blessings,
sown by an angel at the Lord's command:
Rains keep up a steady beat, drumming the earth
until parched soil springs into renewed life.
Lightning illuminates pitch-black sky: lit with torches
or breechloaders fired by combat-ready warriors.[224]
Thunder crackles and reverberates—stallions' roars
when she-camels are unsaddled for pause at noon.
9.45 Aimed with raucous fury at a rival's rutting cry,
the clamor and frenzy herald their savage assault.
Say prayers for Muḥammad, the best of creation,
as often as holy books are read and messages sent.

Torn to Shreds by Passion's Agony

A gentler tone of tender love and romance reigns in this polythematic poem, all the more since it is not weighed down by the gloom and doom of old age and altercations with perfidious youth. Verses on poetry's inexhaustible well of inspiration lead to bucolic imagery of a frolicking maiden in shady palm orchards, again a close parallel to Banū Hilāl verses. The poet's darling lingers and seems open to his advances, but shows her practical side by pointing out insurmountable obstacles. The poet fails in his attempts to entrap her in the logic of her initial response. He is left with no choice but to admit defeat: grudging acceptance of life's realities, framed in twenty verses of commonsensical wisdom, including the naturally subordinate role of women in society, which seems at odds with the logic of his often servile subservience to his beloved (unless one considers that his beloved is a foil for the poet's obsession with the passing of youth). Soberness makes way for passionate ebullience when rain creates a festive atmosphere and damsels resume their dancing at the well. A detailed picture of seasons and the Bedouin peregrinations accompanies the departure of the beloved's palanquin. **10.0**

10.1 These verses were crafted by al-Māyidī, the sagacious:[225]
his deft touch molded this polished work of art:
They surged up as water gushes from a well
into a channel that waters a green orchard;
Filled to the rim from its source in the highlands,[226]
its powerful jet removes the boulders in the way.
When harvests are meager, groundwater sinks;[227]
in scorching drought, its bounty never ceases;[228]
10.5 A copious well, water fed at the wadi's outlet
by a rippling stream from sources high above.
Ask settlers about its flow and they will tell:[229]
"Seven camels can draw its water, it still won't run dry."
It irrigates rows of graceful young palm trees:
some with unripe dates, others bare of fruit.
In the orchard's shade Bedouin girls find repose,[230]
curving their necks like startled gazelles;
Voluptuous breasts peep from garments;
eyes large and black, lips succulent, moist.
10.10 With a smile they capture lovers' hearts,
teeth as dazzling as nightingales' eggs.
Silly gossip, I'm told, holds me to blame:
don't you hear the dove's pitiful cooing?
Leave me alone! The dove's mournful tune
may send empty-headed oafs into raptures.
Unlike them, I am not a fair-weather friend:[231]
my heart is torn to shreds by passion,
Spellbound by her slow and lilting walk:
she looks like a supple stalk of sugarcane—
10.15 A ravishing sight: svelte, her tresses[232]
a profusion of black tumbling down her back;
Loosened, locks curl around her temples,
scented with saffron and sandalwood.

If I ask a favor, she strings me along—
how to stop myself from asking again?
You pull the strings and wish me ill:
why not be gentle with a brokenhearted wretch?
My treasure from heaven, my gain is nil
while you strut about, with your swaying gait!
My love, bitter is the taste of separation;[233]
sweet was our dalliance in a lonely gully!
I greeted her and she returned my greeting,
similar, yet more profuse and exquisite.
She stole a glance at me and I gazed on her:
she lingered as she passed by, coy and confused,
As if her dress felt both too tight and too wide—
oblivious to how I groveled and begged.[234]
Yet she'd slake my desire if not for shame;
and I tread gingerly lest I provoke her ire.
I pleaded, "Why not grant me just one tryst?
In love, a tidbit is enough to sate my craving."[235]
She said, "I can't really tell, be it good or bad:[236]
my kinfolk decide what I can and cannot do.[237]
Let's stick to the tried and tested ways of old,
in obedience to God's command and sharia law."
If you have no say and others decide for you,
how can you promise and keep me in suspense?[238]
Horses dash about, like shapes in shimmering heat:
even reined and bridled, they shake their heads.[239]
I nurtured my desire—her gifts were so paltry:
how I wish for well-traveled and easy roads!
Isn't a man's mind his halter to keep him in control,
his tongue a key to the secrets of the heart?[240]
A rudderless ship strays from the right course—
its sail fills with breezes, then hangs listless again;[241]

Thus women grow impudent without men in charge:
fear of angering their guardian keeps them in check.
Desert travelers carry well ropes for survival;
poems fulfill a similar purpose to buckets:[242]
Hoisted up, full of water, they quench your thirst,
but if the rope snaps, that's the end of it.
Honor needs burnishing against vicious filth,[243]
like a sword's blade: if not kept sparkling clean,
Its bearer will lack the luster of a shining knight:
onlookers will take umbrage at his rusty steel;[244]
Among peers his reputation is dented—
doesn't he know what makes a man?
If you're given no reward for singing paeans,
you can hardly blame a patron—so what to do?[245]
To protest and revile is not a sensible course,
while silence leaves you choking with rage.[246]
Show a cheerful countenance to your guest,
not sullen looks or a grumpy scowl!
A guest doesn't deserve an angry grimace:[247]
he has no one else to depend on for support;
A guest has no inkling of what to expect
when he sets his face toward your place:
If he is served a dish in the afternoon,
he can wait for supper laid out late;
To do right by him, prepare what you have,
and let him rest until it's cooked and done.
The path of noble virtue is a steep climb,
otherwise it'd be a jaunt for any sluggard.[248]
Poverty's malady creeps into your bones,
cripples your attempts at getting up.
Wealth elevates a scoundrel's head;
poverty trips up a bright and cheerful lad.
If a she-goat is put in command of untold riches,
people ask, "Where dwells our lady with the horns?"[249]

Have no truck with lesser things; strive for the best;
have no truck with faithless scoundrels![250]
May God irrigate the lands of verdant youth[251]
in a deluge from skies over the higher pastures!
Billowing clouds in front chased by wild mates,
with a roar like indomitable rutting males.[252]
The cold cumulus releases torrential rains;
a flood of tears streams down its cheeks.
Infuriated by the west wind's sly whispers,
cloud calls to cloud, drenching dry wadis;[253]
Pools in the desert are filled to the brim
by bucketloads of copious rain.
In the well's precinct lissome damsels frolic,
veils discarded, black locks streaming in the wind.[254]
Uncovered, their cheeks shine bright,
rosy as unwrapped bunches of young dates.[255]
Amid the beauties, my darling reigns:
her radiance outshines their brilliance.
Ah, my ultimate quest and soul's desire,
you dissipate worries that cloud my mind.
A strong camel is brought for the day of journey,[256]
a mighty bull, onager-like, wide in the axillae,[257]
Decked out in sumptuous splendor,
ornamental cloth draped over shoulders.
When it hears the caravan leader's chant,[258]
the camel keeps pace with the pack in front.[259]
On its back she is enthroned under a canopy
in a litter weighing heavily on the camel's gait.
The Bedouin dispersed; season followed season;
nights lengthened when winter stars rose,
Until, come hot summer and ripening dates,
without paying heed to my sickness of heart,
They rode out after the first call to prayer,
at dawn's chant: "Rise up for salvation!"

In the night sky, Scorpio's heart stands low;[260]
Bedouin start on a journey from the villages,
Snatch the doe-eyed away, far over the horizon;
farewell to succulent kohl-lined beauties.[261]
Say prayers for the best of men, Muḥammad,
as often as the dove coos on its tall branch.

Glittering Mirage Led You Astray

The theme of love is conspicuously absent in this poem. At once a sharp line is drawn separating good from bad: as some verses of poetry refresh like sweet water and others are brackish, so some people are good-natured and others vicious. On a dour note of religious morality, the poem quotes popular sayings advising people to use their possessions to gain a reputation as a benefactor. Apart from such good deeds, there is little one can do to shield oneself from the world's treachery and fickleness. The best protection is to guard against enticing, but mostly false, appearances. In Ibn Ẓāhir's oeuvre, this poem offers the longest and most consistent condemnation of the world's inherent wickedness. Countervailing forces are sincere devotion and godliness: the principle of taqwā, *abiding awareness that one is well-advised to live in fear of God's judgment. It ends with a mixture of Qur'anic phrases and homespun Nabaṭī vocabulary.* 11.0

11.1 Al-Māyidī, the sage, carefully crafted his rhymes,[262]
works of art, high in wisdom seekers' esteem;
My edifying speech steers clear of aspersions;
verses recited to uplift and inspire the audience.[263]
When my poetry sessions are announced,
aficionados, afraid to miss a word, arrive in droves.[264]
Some verses refresh, drafts of sweet water;
others leave a foul brackish taste,[265]
11.5 As with people, some good-natured, others vicious:[266]
friendly folks and mean bastards are worlds apart.
Scoundrels revel in bad-mouthing others:
they ignite a wildfire of insidious gossip.
Honest men push back when evil raises its head,
crush it, laying reputation and wealth on the line.[267]
The noble-hearted use money for honor's sake,
not the reverse: selling honor for material gain.[268]
Scrooges who swim in pools filled with gold
are losers, with no friends to share the profit.
11.10 Weeds proliferate among debris and trash:
they are there for the taking, devoid of benefit.
Some amass fortunes here and in the hereafter,
favors bestowed by guidance of the Lord;
Others fail to attain both the one and the other,
forfeiting earthly goods and religious salvation.
If you appease the world and sidle up to her,
and things go well, she snaps back at you.
Orgies of sensual delights and sinful wine—
what ill-starred possessions, a rash brat's dream!
11.15 A glittering mirage led you astray from the well—
you took it for lightning splitting clouds with fire!
The world seduces with hints of tasty rewards:[269]
her whimsical breezes blow left and right,
From the far east to its western rim,
colliding and clashing, hurtling north and south.[270]

Gaudy trinkets and lures have bewitched for eons,
not failing for an instant, day and night, all week long.[271]
The months and days have been set forever:[272]
if no count is kept, the new moon brings a reminder.
Stick to counsel proffered by men of wisdom:[273]
the world is dangerously fickle and unpredictable.[274]
Don't rack your brain: leave it to the Almighty
to bring relief; you don't know how all will end.
The course of affairs is steered by the hand of God:
it is not within your power to set matters straight;
Whether you like it or not, it makes no difference:
what upsets and angers you leaves the world cold.
Amiable in appearance, she is selfish and rude:
horses' blankets for cold nights do slip off.
If you're on friendly terms, prepare for the worst:
surreptitiously, her embrace spells your ruin.
Wiles and treachery confound her patrons:[275]
woe unto people who bet on her!
Don't be a fool! Don't be deluded by her tricks:
she's a flitting shade cast by banks of fog.
Line your eyes with all the kohl you like:
when you cry, its black is washed away by tears.
Death lies in wait, as people know only too well;
the only question is when has their time come?
It is hard to fathom the heart's tortuous ways:[276]
why trudge in stony hills, and not use the highway?[277]
Reports of her tricks are abundant:
true devotees fatally ensnared by her spell.
I have understood her game from the first;[278]
once caught in error, people repeat mistakes.
To be secure, one seeks safety in godliness:[279]
the House of Permanence, your sole destination.
Certainty, absent in the world, reigns in the hereafter:
alas, people are mostly engrossed in material affairs.

How they slave away! Godliness is so simple:
doing good deeds brings lasting benefits.
In mishap, show fortitude, believe in Judgment Day;
how unwise not to think about your final station![280]
The tyranny of greed, lascivious hunger for riches,
failings to tilt Judgment's scales to one's perdition.
Build the house of piety before misery visits:
when you've fallen on hard times, it's too late.
Loads stowed on board ships in calm weather
are most difficult to unload if seas are rough.
When eyes are frozen in a terrified stare,
men and women, a piece of cloth around their loins,
Put faith in Prophet Muḥammad's intercession;
ask the Lord's forgiveness in His compassion.
If your foot loses its hold and slips,
expect the other foot to share its fate.[281]
Look at men who pull buckets at the well;
not those who failed to quench their thirst.[282]
He created livestock, the nourishment of their milk,[283]
lofty palm trees with fruits in layers—don't you see?[284]
He gave you cattle and allowed you to eat its meat,
named animals forbidden or permissible as food.[285]
He gifted horses and camels to carry your burdens:[286]
unruly animals were tamed to obey your orders.
Misery and human spirit are bound by friendship:[287]
invariably, you find them in shared intimacy.
If God has foreordained your last resting place,
you must journey there to meet your fate.
On Resurrection Day, nations are called to account:
each and every person according to their weight.
Poetry is a rope twisted in its maker's hands:
the rope finished, plucking and twining are over.
In conclusion, prayers for the Prophet Muḥammad,
as often as branches sway in the breeze.

Fatal Attraction

This poem is the opposite of the previous: gnomic wisdom is spurned, while love is all-consuming. The two poems are so engrossed in their favorite theme (salvation of the soul in the hereafter versus absorption in amorous adulation) that the perfunctory prelude makes a quick transition. Deceptively, the verses start on a contrite note, with the poet musing on the ravages of time. He laments his youth, disguised as a love affair with a Bedouin belle. His true theme reveals itself in the number of years devoted to his love: thirty years, and then ten more. The wheel of time introduces the Bedouin rhythm of migration. With it come the date harvest, camels, and the Bedouin beauties who make the poet gasp. Their pageant ushers in twenty verses of reveling that are among the poet's most colorful, startling in their similarity to verses by early classical desert poets like Dhū l-Rummah a thousand years earlier. Then the inevitable happens: the tribal council "has cast the die for departure." The poleaxed poet is left behind, as disconsolate as the Najdī poet Ibn Sbayyil three hundred years later. 12.0

12.1 The discerning poet al-Māyidī speaks up:
sleepless and sorrowful, he crafts his verse.
My heart seethes with trepidation—
it swims in a cauldron that burns my bones.
If you know the pain, you'll feel for me:
it takes a heart of stone to blame the victim!
Each day she faded and dissolved in distance,
leaving me woebegone since her departure.[288]
12.5 My heart strains to go in pursuit but fails
to catch up with her fast-paced mounts.
Eyesight grows blurry, no distant vision;
my teeth, once shiny, are full of gaps.
By God, Fate conspires to rob us of youth—
gone are halcyon days of amorous dalliance.
For thirty years we harbored deep affection,[289]
our intimacy safe from gossip and slander;
Ten further years of glum company and surliness[290]
made me despair of love and sick at heart:
12.10 Why not seek seclusion and solitude, I thought;
yet pearls can't be blamed for being beauties.[291]
Incessantly, one weaves the other into its loom:[292]
a sad story of fatal attraction and entanglement,[293]
Spun while claiming eyes, teeth, and hearing,
the bodily aids that I cannot do without.
You feel happy and on top of the world,[294]
unaware that spiteful Fate plots your demise.[295]
You're tricked into undoing of your own making,
oblivious, while the Bird of Death hovers over you.[296]
12.15 The World lasts forever and ever to eternity:[297]
the time of Resurrection remains a mystery;
Knowledge of the Hour is with God alone:
besides the Lord, no one has the faintest idea.
Year after year passes; months pile up;[298]
the zodiac spins; night and day take turns;

The four hot months, winter on their heels;[299]
soon portents of early summer are in the air.
The Pleiades, eclipsed, unleash furnace blasts,[300]
make tall palm trees shed their surplus dates;
Bunches tinged white with a reddish hue
adorn the crowns of palms, giants and young,
Lure a gazelle with soft henna-dyed hands,
a rosy-skinned damsel always kept under wraps.[301]
Bedouin rushed in from distant lands[302]
on hardy camels, some gurgling, others silent.
They make pack camels, with towering humps
from leisurely grazing on pastures of spring, kneel.
Shelters and chattels are loaded on their back,[303]
colorful clothes taken down from a shack's poles:[304]
Cloaks of Syrian make, fur-lined,
women's gowns embroidered with stripes,
Smooth like red scarves of Indian cotton,
fine work of the Turks or Christian handicraft.
Thick anklets press soundless into soft flesh
mounted on well-trained, sprightly mounts;
Her camel fidgets a little at being loaded:[305]
a touch of a thumb makes it rise.
Fast-paced legs moving at a steady beat
as is their wont, unflagging for days on end.
There goes youth's pinnacle, most sweet,
a white brilliance as stars sparkle in the dark;[306]
Delicious fragrance wafts from her breast:
its odorous perfume has a scent of musk.
Her camel train keeps pace with the driver's chant:[307]
healthy animals, unscarred by branding irons,[308]
Carry her off and dive into a shimmering mirage
like sloops at full sail running before the wind.
The camel leader is not a man to my liking:[309]
he sets the caravan in motion, a dreadful day.

The gallant rushes to the aid of the rear,
ready and willing to help mount and load.
He fixes stout litter poles onto bulging ribs:
her seat screws clamps onto my heart![310]
She's told: "The council cast the die for departure!"
they exult, while my mind clouds over.[311]
If people berate me for my choices in love,
I am silent or say, "Faultfinders are tyrants."
I held my tongue for fear of being misunderstood;
their sport is to divulge secrets I've been hiding.
What benefit do misers derive from hoarding wealth?
for the sake of heirs, they squander their honor.
Suffer through the headwinds of remorseless fate:
surely, one day tailwinds will turn your fortunes.

I Dared the Devil to Ride His Horse

This poem is one of two, the other being Poem 6, that were discovered in a manuscript after the earliest editions of Ibn Ẓāhir's poetry had appeared. Both poems are atypical compared with the body of Ibn Ẓāhir's work as a whole. Individual verses of this poem were already known from oral tradition. Especially noteworthy are verses in praise of a ruler identified as Sayf ibn Sulṭān, which have been taken as a reference to the powerful ruler of the Omani dynasty of al-Yaʿāribah, who ruled from 1692 until 1711. If so, these are the sole unambiguous historical dates for the poet and his work. The poem's most famous verse, also known from oral tradition, is the penultimate one, cherished in today's Emirates as a beloved description of the country's geographical characteristics. The "healthy sleep" enjoyed there is associated with the story of the poet's search for a suitable grave, which brought him to the area of Rās al-Khaymah. Another highlight is a ship gradually swallowed by the waves, its seasick oarsmen incapacitated: a simile for the hoariness that drowns the poet in old age. It overlaps with verses by the poet's daughter (Poem 17). The verses on his halcyon days, "riding the Devil's steed," are the oeuvre's most explicit treatment of youthful sins. These, and the quasi-boasting style of §§13.29–32, are reminiscent of examples from the Najdī tradition, and as such are atypical of Ibn Ẓāhir. 13.0

13.1 Sagacious al-Māyidī ibn Ẓāhir speaks in verses,
molded into perfect shape, straight from the heart,
A plentiful well of poetry, a ceaseless stream:[312]
he casts his bucket; the bottom gushes forth.
Opulent, its mouth flows with limpid drink:
pure, cool of taste, free of wind-driven sands.
My recitals attract crowded assemblies:
connoisseurs who savor and treasure my rhymes.
13.5 Poetry, like food, can be served raw or well-cooked,
some dishes flavored with salt, some tasteless.
Salt brings taste to dishes that are without spice:[313]
savants know vapid speech from vivid words.
By God, sound judgment is men's claim to pride;
a crabbed bigot's only care is his turban's size.[314]
Some people are remembered for noble feats;
others are merely known for having a name:[315]
Without it, they'd have been erased from memory;
livestock are only recognized by a branded mark.
13.10 Long ago, I caroused astride a spirited steed,
and raced on the wooden frame of fleet camels.
Chivalry and lofty ambition are avenues to fame,
not luxuriating in the shade of palaces and tents.[316]
As a lad, I boarded a new ship built of wood;
when favorable winds dropped, I sailed back to port.
Rows of oarsmen pulled, as if hoisting water from a well,[317]
belts loose to give sweating muscles breathing room.
My shouts, "Come on, fellows!" fell on deaf ears:
dizzy and nauseated, my sick seamen swooned.[318]
13.15 Glittering rows of teeth set in a tattooed mouth
leave gaping holes when they decay and fall out:[319]
Ebullient youth garlands itself with fancy luster;
old age takes down the festooned party set;
My vessel was sprayed by a wave of hoariness:
I bailed and bailed, fearful of drowning in the deep.

How futile to attempt to escape from death![320]
A human's days are numbered in advance.
Faultfinders blame my obsession with youth:
stop upbraiding me! What's the use of scolding?
Frantic with despair, I waved, trying to lure my youth,[321]
as one needs a rope to pull a ship back into the sea.
A reckless teen, I dared the Devil to ride his horse;[322]
I jumped into the saddle, held the reins with firm grasp,
Went on a rampage, and committed sin after sin:
I hid what I did, but God knows only too well.
One should never forget the five fundamentals:
the profession of faith, worship, and fasting,[323]
Pilgrimage as long as you find the way safe;
and paying the alms tax in full to comfort the poor.
Honorable are men who outfox the enemy,
be they Zaydis, Europeans, or Persians;[324]
Evictors of the unbelievers from their lands,
as the Prophet declared war on the idolaters.
There is no peace without the ruler of Oman!
May God grant splendor to the sublime imam:
Sayf ibn Sulṭān's sword scattered enemies far and wide;
meekly they paid obeisance, their rebellion squashed.[325]
Our good fortune was to prosper in the shade of his rampart,
and to graze our sheep and camels in far-flung pastures,
Without a care or sending scouts ahead for our safety:
peace endures while the realm's reins are in his grip,[326]
Protected by Abū Sulṭān, scourge of his adversaries,
the shining knight who climbs to the peaks of glory.
Visitors are awed by a court that's open to all:
armies of servants stagger under trays laden with food.[327]
From desert plains to coast, and waterholes in between,
this is the place where the eye sleeps in peace.[328]
Time to say prayers, my listeners, for the Prophet,
Muḥammad, our intercessor on Judgment Day.

She Left Me Baffled

14.0 *Among the original touches of this quintessential Ibn Ẓāhir poem are the comparison of his verses to colorful textiles imported from India, Syria, and the Iranian coastal province of Larestan. These wares are in high demand with visiting Bedouin, a detail that announces the transition to scenes of his belle's departure in a camel-borne palanquin. Seeing her as she bids farewell to her neighbors, but not to him, the transfixed poet nurses the wounds of his soul with a cascade of wise sayings. One cites a tale about shining cooking pots that contain a laughable amount of food, flaunted by a fake braggart lampooned by the legendary poet Abū Nuwās. The poet regains high spirits when he wakes up at night at the approach of rain and the spectacle of a thunderstorm, so ferocious that it makes sand dunes cave in. The devastation puts him in the mood to round off his musings with some pious reflections.*

Al-Māyidī recites verses of poetry, 14.1
built with care, perfect compositions,
Profound sayings scooped up eagerly
by aficionados in crowded assemblies:
Desperate with thirst, they flocked to my well;
sated, they lay down in droves at its rim.[329]
Perceptive hearts leapt with joy at my verse,
while impassive idlers were fast asleep.
I chose the merchant's unsewn cloth of silk; 14.5
his stock's most expensive wares I bought:
Precious broadcloth, the best from Larestan,[330]
colored Indian prints and red Syrian fabrics;
Praised by customers and in high demand
when Bedouin set out on their migrations;
Heading south toward al-Buraymī's marches,[331]
the camels disappeared into shimmering air:
Shading eyes with my hands, I strained to see,
thumb and middle finger used as my binoculars.
They advanced like ships crossing high seas, 14.10
sails filled with propitious western winds,[332]
On fleet mounts, carrying beauty's trophy: a lady,
etched with tattoos, her anklets sunk into flesh,[333]
Raised in the desert, her cheeks a rare brilliance
born from being concealed in tents all year long.[334]
She rides on a fine breed from distant meadows,
a high-humped camel of massive strength;[335]
An Omani thoroughbred, with low haunches,
a comely animal, civet-scented behind the ears.[336]
Colorful litter curtains are raised on its back; 14.15
a kick in its flanks makes the animal rise;[337]
Date bags are tied on its back, and off it runs,
impetuous; a nose ring must keep it in check.
It moves to the rhythm of a driver's chant,[338]
at a frisky pace, like panic-stricken ostriches.

The call went out for her; she came quietly,
 and we refrained from crying to her.
A marvelous sight, her entry on the scene:[339]
 her pigeon-toed gait as she tripped along;
Enchanted neighbors wished her farewell,
 a heartfelt goodbye of warmest wishes.
She left me baffled, confused as to what to do,
 since she did not deign to speak to me.
What use to have a friend so far away?
 like the company of the children of Ham.[340]
A friend who doesn't gladden you
 equals an enemy who swallows his wrath.[341]
Benefits of unrequited love are meager:
 a horse's gain from chomping the bit.
All I gained was a fire roaring in my breast,
 a useless oven, a bakery for loafs of misery;
Like cooking pots lampooned by Abū Nuwās,[342]
 slanderous chatter is awful assassination;[343]
Dissemblers perform one prayer, leave another;
 prayers not validated by keeping Ramadan's fast.
If you have the wherewithal, and you're in debt,
 why be tightfisted? Pay off your odious loans![344]
It's like the Pleiades watching their opposite:
 if the Seven Sisters set, Scorpio rises.[345]
Tribal kinsmen are united in fencing you off;[346]
 you string me along, my heart bridled tight.
May God stop the baleful lust of the envious,[347]
 a state of mind that begets discord and strife,
Renders hearts brutal and prone to violence,
 creates malevolence, sows invidious whispers:
Their son adds not a whit to the common good,
 nor would he be of any use in criminal gangs.[348]
Attempts at civilizing him have failed:
 he needs a nanny to hold his hand all day;

He seeks an authority figure close to him,
an infant's attachment prior to weaning.
Why do we keep serving Mammon for free?[349]
We are duped, as clearly as daylight is not dark.
There is no good in being the world's flunky—
what more do you need than food and clothes?
The world offers you distractions galore till,
caught up in its melee, you're being led astray,
Straight to life's real farewell, the truth;[350]
with no more than a jug of water and a shroud,
You're lowered into a trench dug in dusty earth—
may God reward passersby for their greetings!
Watched over by tombstones at foot and head,[351]
two mute witnesses unable to speak:[352]
A sign of good fortune allotted Muslims,
unlike the fate of unbelievers: to each his own.[353]
To learn more, listen to the wisdom of sages,
as set forth in verse by a dependable fellow:[354]
If the riding crop drops from your right hand,
watch out, don't let the reins slip from your left!
My opinion: Four qualities don't amount to anything—
any pleasure they procure will not last:[355]
Consorting with women who sing and dance;
indulgence in luxury with ill-gotten wealth;
Tyrannical rule without the semblance of justice;
thinking that the sky will be cloudless forever.[356]
In the dead of night I heard the hoopoe's call;
revival for a heart crazed with passionate love:
I woke from a deep sleep, looked up to find
a cover had been spread out in broad array;[357]
Northern winds howled from Gemini's arc
in the direction of prayer and the setting sun.
Here blinding flashes, there deafening crashes,
a spectacle of light, as torches dispel the dark.

Struck head-on by blows of stormy winds,
thunderclouds hollered with mighty rumble.
Astir at night, the storm drummed like revelers—
may it always visit my sweetheart's abode![358]
Swirling lightning swung its stick at cumulus;
sand dunes caved in, hit by cloudburst's flood.[359]
14.55 Six commandments are incumbent on you:
prayer, professing the faith, the Ramadan fast,
Performing the pilgrimage, paying alms tax,
and speaking the truth without equivocation.
Now, dear friends, say prayers for the Prophet,
as often as the dove coos and spreads its wings.

Muzzleloader's Ramrod

The poem is based on one manuscript source, as are Poems 6 and 13. Together with Poem 17, these are somewhat exceptional. Transitions are not as smooth as in other longer poems, and one senses that verses have gone missing and that thematic sections have a stand-alone character. Love, as a theme, is largely absent, and so is its associated theme of youth and the graybeard. Old age is merely mentioned as one of the scourges of human existence. Gnomic wisdom's manual of survival shows influences of the warlike Najdī tradition. This may explain the two unique verses that compare a brave man to the inner workings of a matchlock-type gun: the first reference to firearms in Nabaṭī poetry dates from the early seventeenth century. Another two verses lend color with a true-to-life simile on adroit sailing in hazardous seas. The main lesson concerning steering one's life through these risky waters to the safe harbor of the grave is not different from similar passages in other poems. The surprise comes at the end, where the poet draws an intriguing picture of scriptural and oral traditions of wisdom. In his argument in favor of the latter, though certainly not to the detriment of the former, one may detect a whiff of Sufi influence. 15.0

15.1 Al-Māyidī the sage crafts his rhymes with care:
why is a love far away so grievous to the soul?
Voracious Time can't be appeased—all is gone![360]
sweetest nights have passed without a trace.
She set great store by what we had, I thought—
our harmony: then she launched a surprise attack.
How gullible of me not to suspect hidden enmity:
detestation! Ah, my belief that good times would last!
15.5 If the world smiles on you, don't think you'll be safe
from what's brewing, ready to erupt in your face.
Dread four scourges: old age and a hunched back;
you can't tamper with Doomsday's accounts.[361]
Poverty cripples the human sense of obligation;
the horror of letting your women go hungry.[362]
You need to feed your children, and unexpected guests
whom you must regale on the house's very best.
The family head makes do with a paltry morsel;[363]
guests' leftovers are set aside for dependents.[364]
15.10 Another sort leaps with joy at dinner invitations:
greedy, though yesterday's banquet is still not digested;[365]
Snuggled up, the ne'er-do-well sleeps into the day,
gets up long after decent men have left for work.
The proof of a man's determination is in his deeds:
refusing to share your water stains your name.[366]
Warmongers, consumed by thirst for revenge,
seek to entangle fellow men in vendettas.[367]
If never unsheathed, swords become rusty;[368]
feet placed on the ground heedlessly will bleed.
15.15 Men may mobilize and gird up for battle,
until, one day, their belts start to sag.
Don't give credence to petty news of peddlers,
inveterate spreaders of slander and lurid tales.
Take my advice: Be lenient if a friend does wrong—
if good life's music stops, you may need him.[369]

Don't be beguiled by dazzling appearances:
they cast a spell that ends in your undoing.
Obey the counsel of sages who hit the mark:[370]
avoid claptrap hawked at gossip's market![371]
Noble pedigree shows in knightly strength;
a fast-paced run takes a pair of strong legs.
Smoldering matchlock fuse, cocked for retribution,[372]
charge ignited by a shower of sparks—that's him![373]
He is a firearm's trigger, a muzzleloader's ramrod,
first to rush to women and children in defense.[374]
In midsummer's sizzling heat, take water aplenty,
food for the road: real men don't stay at home.[375]
Fend off the world, dress in armor of piety:
stay safe, keep your feet from Hell's flames!
Carry a coat of mail and shield, wear a helmet:
protect your limbs from foes' searing fires.
Be early at the well if you are thirsty:
draw water at ease until your herd is sated.
If you haven't bothered to carry rope and bucket,
you'll stare at the well, crazed, wringing hands.[376]
The compassionate Lord forgives, if He so desires,
Magnificent and Almighty in His commands.
Stand in fear and awe of God, and do not despair!
Only His approval counts, not your fellows' taunts.
Pull hard on the sails if shallows are south of you:
don't drift and run aground like other ships![377]
No triumph equals reaching the safety of port,
propelled by a pleasant breeze that fills the sails.
Which of the two houses will be your abode:
the grave or your palace of glittering marble?
If I'm comfortable, snuggled up in my tomb,[378]
why care about the glitter of a sparkling mansion?
This sound and fury is none of our concern:
God is our guardian and He takes care of all;

15.35 His is life's promise and people's subsistence;
He sets our appointed time; His edicts are irrefutable.
My compositions for you are being told and retold,
heritage in scripted lines, irrefutable compositions.
Sheets lined with writing: books read by eyes;
my speech wells up straight from the heart.[379]
Say prayers for the best of creatures, Muḥammad,
as many as the compositions sung by a dove on its perch.[380]

Intelligent Speech and Borders of the Land

For Ibn Ẓāhir's Emirati following, the importance of this longest poem of the collection resides in the rain section, the most extensive of his oeuvre. At first glance a conventional prayer for rain on haunts of youthful carousing, it also presents a map of the United Arab Emirates: "From the empty deserts in the south to the north, from al-Ẓafrah to the Gulf's littoral at Dihān." The poem's other focus is on the art and importance of speech: when to speak and when not to; how to respond to verbal challenges; and in particular how to convince the beloved of one's point of view—his speech addressed to the beloved is unmatched in his oeuvre. Old age and the grave hover over his desperate plea. The audience will judge the poet on his powers of persuasion, as he affirms in the prelude. 16.0

16.1 Al-Māyidī sings his heart out in verses,
new compositions, crafted with skill,[381]
Anxious to please his circle of connoisseurs,
shrewd arbiters of taste, steeped in art's finesse.
If I'm told in confidence about someone's faults,
I know I'm next to be defamed behind my back.
Never have I stooped to bad-mouthing a friend,
nor disparaged an enemy who didn't slight me:
16.5 Too afraid of poetry's reciters catching word of it,
the public's verdict: "God's shame on him!"[382]
I never offended a love who holds me dear,
nor curried favor without a friendly response.
Yet, if I'm being humbled and trampled upon,
I don't take it lying down: I give as good as I get.
Honest to God, I am not one to act in haste[383]
against idle chatter—unless I am trifled with
By rumormongers and their smear campaign
of spreading falsehoods and malicious calumny.
16.10 They gnash their teeth if I'm happy with a friend,
gloat when I'm being snubbed by my beloved.
Let them come with goodwill and benevolence,
instead of laying into me with evil design.
If trusted friends bare their souls in confidence,
ill-wishers stew in their juices and die of rage.
This rule was handed down from our ancestors,
memorized in verse, generation upon generation:
Our friends are held in highest esteem ever more;
at news of an enemy's demise, we shrug: "No matter."
16.15 Let envious cavilers choke on rancor and pique,
shrivel like discarded waterskins in scalding winds.
May God curse backbiters who set people at odds,
inflict bitter wounds, forever engraved in memory.[384]
In assemblies, he greets me with a broad smile;
behind my back derides me with scurrilous babble.

To my mind, words exist to measure and serve truth,
weighed on Judgment Day for Muslims' reward.
My inner self is an open book for God, in Him I trust;
none other than the Lord: I lift Your name on high.
May God avenge victims of injurious oppression,
expose enemies no matter where ensconced.
It is incumbent on me to speak with caution:
not to repeat in public the secrets of our intimacy.[385]
Likewise, a ship has a rudder to stay on course;
the rudder needs the fingers' grip to steer.
Without nose ring and rope a camel can't be led;
a horse is kept in check with reins and bridle.
Women cannot do without their men;
men lose their way without strong ethics.
A foe has no choice but to go after his foe,
hell-bent to fight him tooth and nail.
Yes, my love, let me have your news;
should I pardon my ill-wishers at your behest?
I might leave them alone, for your sake
and pleasure, as you frankly let me know.
Would you tell me in no uncertain terms:
how in heaven's name could this be?
Is it your doing or the evil whisperers'?
Tell me, because time is in short supply.
You and me, we should be in close harmony,
if not driven apart by wheels of Time.[386]
By God, I am in pursuit of what you owe:[387]
make haste, for the right moment is now!
Or else go and dig a well for it in a dune,
a tumbledown affair, buried in sliding sands.
I could spend my life scouring the globe for you,
without ever seeing you again, nor you me.
This time together should be our last chance:
the debt you've incurred with me is overdue.

Being hard up, I implore you for leniency—
you turned me into a wretched nagging beggar.
I demand to be repaid what is rightly mine:
look, you tucked away what you took from me!
Satisfaction restores man's strength and pride
until his back becomes bent and hunched:
Old age's onslaught on sparkling youth—
no mistake, it will ambush you as well.
You committed more faux pas than I can recall:
let bygones be bygones, forgiveness comes first!
Seeing me down, slanderers exchange malicious winks,
while you snub me, my acts of kindness forgotten!
If things get tricky, hot words fly, arms drawn;
a word from you smooths matters over.
Stop riding roughshod over tender souls;
your cold-shouldering knocks me out.
Such unbecoming behavior is intolerable:
it makes people flee from lands considered safe.
Because of you, I lie awake in miserable nights,
as if salt has been cast into my eyes;
My stomach feels cramp and refuses food:
cut off, deserted, I have no appetite at all.
My drink is brackish: foul water from dirty pools,
as if mixed with pressed bitter-apple juice,
Forced down my throat by a cold sweetheart—
never shall I forgive her for serving vile drinks.
She broke my heart, left me wracked by pain:
her advice: rub it with black unction of tar.
I stare with an empty gaze, hardly conscious:
a bag of bones, not even a human corpse.
People look at my tragedy with unbelief:
sound in body and limb, struck with numbness.
She made me wail and sob like an orphan child,
left behind, feeble and helpless, crying out its eyes.

May God water the vales of supple, succulent youth
from clouds moving at a nimble-footed pace;
White-crested cumulus with pitch-black flanks,
thunderous reverberations rumble from afar.
A billowing bank, pregnant with masses of water,
goaded by eastern breezes, whiffs of soft, cool air.
In the west, flashes of lightning set the sky ablaze: 16.55
winds drawn by Canopus on its southern ascent.[388]
Harbingers of rain arrived in the dead of night,
a time when vacuous sluggards are fast asleep,
When predators haven't yet left their lair:
they prefer to stir at first light of dawn.
Clouds drenched lands from east to west
in an embrace of all terrain that borders Oman:
From the empty deserts in the south to the north,
from al-Ẓafrah to the Gulf's littoral at Dihān.[389]
They irrigated Līwā's dunes and al-Gharīf's plains, 16.60
as they enveloped Wādī al-Mikin in loving caresses.[390]
Rain clattered on Nazwā and around al-Habāb;
on Wādī al-Jirn it kept coming down in sheets.
Al-Ḥwēmī's sands and al-Ghadīr received their share;
as did al-Yalḥ's plain and its green sandy dales.
The clouds pelted lands with rain, from Falāḥ to al-ʿAdhīb;
for eight days and nights ever-greater floods were disgorged.
Tāhil and ʿIthmir and al-Ghwēl were not forgotten,
nor were Wadī Salām and Sīhijān passed over,
As far as Kiffā and around the borders of al-Khirīr; 16.65
al-Baṭḥā was awash with pools of water for ages.
Should we also mention al-Mizraʿ, Khaṭṭā, and al-Hzūʿ,
on the way if you're heading east for Ḥīl al-Dibānī?
They showered al-Ṣajʿah and al-ʿUshūsh's marches,
and trailed down in curtains on Miryāl Thānī,
Reached Kalbā and the mountain ranges beyond:
all of these lands, no matter how distant or close.

In the north, horns of plenty poured their gifts
on the folks of the high ledges and their gardens.[391]
Torrents, thundering down from mountains' heights,
swept up debris and soaked the desert pastures.
The earth burst into blooms of ravishing colors:
visitors flocked to marvelous desert meadows.
From afar, the tribe of my beloved drew near
to raise its lofty tents on carpets of herbage.
Worries dispelled, I enjoyed the soundest sleep:[392]
from afar they brought my sweetheart, straight to me!
Her figure ravishes, the waistline of a wasp:
a gazelle from vast desert wastes in the south.[393]
Eyes borrowed from a white gazelle of the sands;
line of neck, tinged with rose: gazelle of the plains.
Her head of hair, full and thick: a steed's tail,
color of a raven, yet of a deeper black sheen.
Now, listeners, let us say prayers for the Prophet,
as many as flashes of lightning seen in the south.

Daughter's Elegy

*In the manuscripts, this poem is headed: "What the daughter of Ibn Ẓāhir said" (*qawl bint ibn Ẓāhir*). The poem and its author have intrigued Emirati cultural circles, as shown by the book devoted to it by some of the country's foremost experts (Ghassān al-Ḥasan and ʿAlī ibn Tamīm, Sultan Alameemi,* Bint ibn Ẓāhir *(*The Daughter of Ibn Ẓāhir*)). Her talents are said to have incurred the wrath of her father: he enjoined her henceforward not to recite a single line of her own composition. The first verse's reference to her rave reviews is understood as a direct challenge to her father. According to oral tradition, she was made to pay a heavy price for her audacity. Verse eighteen is interpreted as a lament that her betrothal was broken off, perhaps on account of her compositions, and a plea to give her a new chance to marry.* 17.0

No doubt, speculations about the tragic events alluded to in the poem inspired the narrative lore on the subject. Curiously, many verses are reminiscent of verses by Ibn Ẓāhir himself: the prelude, the gnomic wisdom, the imagery taken from seafaring, the halcyon days of reckless merrymaking, the tears shed over a lost youth, and the description of senile infirmity. Overall, the poem gives the feel of an Ibn Ẓāhir poem tweaked with a shift in gender. The final verse is interesting for its geographical detail about Bedouin migration: the pivotal scene in Ibn Ẓāhir's memories of lost love and youth. This detail conforms with descriptions in Emirati sources. Ibn Ẓāhir projects the theme back to the days of the Jabrid Banū Hilāl. His daughter seems to refer to more recent Emirati practice. Therefore, her verse and subject make for a transition to the narrative lore about the poet and his daughters.

Verses of the tribe's maiden, daughter of Ibn Ẓāhir,[394] 17.1
are recited by crowds of raving connoisseurs.
Poets weave their rhymes from palm-leaf plaiting:
mine are from exquisite twigs in the palm's core.[395]
Some people's actions are guided by their eyes;
others take their cue straight from the heart.[396]
If they've spent their all, some shrug it off;
others pinch pennies without gaining dimes.
Put your feet on the ground without due care: 17.5
pay the price with crippled soles and heels.
Watch out! If you get stung in the eye,
days are spent with ointment and quacks.
If a shirt gets caught on an acacia's thorns,
pry it loose, if you're smart, without a rip.[397]
If thorns get stuck in a hothead's shirt,
he'll tear it free, the cloth in tatters.
Alone, I watch the ships of youth move away,[398]
propelled by pleasant breezes in hoisted sails.[399]
Monsoon winds drove me from a harbor's safety, 17.10
my ship cursed by misfortune, battered and leaking.
I ordered the crew to row against the headwinds.
Nothing! Pearl divers seasick, rope pullers too clumsy.
On shore, I took an oath not to hire any others:
how my expectations came to naught![400]
They laid it on thick, the self-serving scoundrels!
They came and went, and not one kept his word.
Honorable men avoid being seen in dubious light;
the riffraff bathes in it with unseemly abandon.
If you live without purpose when young,[401]
truth surfaces for all to see when you're getting old.[402]
If you don't look after a fat sheep and slaughter it, 17.15
a wolf bites its throat and does the work for you:
The brute hides in bushes and bides his time.
No one takes notice if barren spadices drop.

He effaced my path to felicity, so I said,
"You closed the road! Open another way for me!"[403]
Caught in worldly affairs, I neglected religious duty,
not punctilious in performance of daily prayers.
A light-headed girl, I left my soul to its inclinations:
dazzled by the world's carnival, I drowned in sin.
Clever men debate and expatiate on thorny issues;
once the knot is cut, words are matched with deeds.
Reason is applied to find what's right and exemplary,
for the common good, not just to blame and punish.
Faultfinding is for deranged, mangy prattlers,
scavengers scouring nooks and crannies for evil.
I cry for the days of youth that have eluded me:[404]
tears, never in short supply, drip from my eyes.
My halcyon days are gone, beyond recall, forever,
unavenged, the well's wooden cover broken.[405]
They took from me what suited them, leaving little;
done with me, the rascals made themselves scarce.[406]
They went and left me, numb and sad, to stay behind;
charitable men took care of me, not these bastards,
Who plucked out my eyes, teeth, and ears;
pulled up the pegs of the black goat-hair tent.[407]
One would wish for a perfumer's lovely scent,
not a shower of sparks from a blast in a smithy's fire.
In Kalbā they spent the hot season, then rushed off,
Bedouins from al-Jaww heading south, away from me.[408]

Narratives

Gift of Poetry

I heard[409] about Ibn Ẓāhir from our graybeards, especially my father,[410] who told me about the story of his life. His sources, the people of Rās al-Khaymah, his kinfolk, were unanimous in assuring him that without any doubt Ibn Ẓāhir originated from there. He was born there and worked in the cultivation of date palms: he owned a grove in Ḍanj. His working life started in al-Gharīf. From there he moved to al-Dhēd, and from there to al-Sāʿdī: for 35 years, or so my father's story goes. From al-Sāʿdī, he moved to al-Khirrān. While there, the tribe of al-Ẓawāhir heard about him. These events happened a very long time ago. Ibn Ẓāhir passed away about 330 years ago, or so I was told by my late father. Of course, he never met him. Ibn Ẓāhir was a contemporary of our distant ancestors: the eyewitness accounts about him stem from the earliest generations.[411] They knew every detail of his life, even the kind of she-camel he rode! 18.1

My father told me that in midsummer, during the hot season, Ibn Ẓāhir stayed in Oman, at his palm grove in Ḍanj.[412] There he stocked up on dates at the time of the date harvest—the dates we call *bū ʿasīw*, "fruits of the bunch." He carried a load of these dates on his camels. 18.2

He lifted the heavy bags onto their backs and went on his way, he and two camels that carried the dates from Ḍanj. He headed south, away from his kinsmen, and took a break around noon. In the evening, he made for al-Niwī, some distance from Maḥḍah, and in the morning he again started on his way. He rode all day and did not take a break in the shade at midday. He rode through the sands of al-ʿAnīj, and he reached Hōr al-Balmā, the flatlands that extend from al-ʿAnīj almost to al-Niwī. He rode on and on through the heat. After performing his prayers at noon, I believe, he ate some lunch. Then he resumed his journey and kept riding until he reached the sands in late afternoon. Approximately halfway through the flatland, he dismounted. A patch of rough, stony ground forced him to dismount: it was impossible to continue riding through it. He vaulted off the camel's back, took the animal by the ropes, and continued on foot, his camel in tow. All of a sudden, he heard someone screaming behind him: "Awwww, awwww!"

18.3 He wondered where the sound came from and looked around. Then he saw a woman, right there in the empty land. He halted his camel and waited until she had walked up to him. She greeted him, without uttering a word, with no more than a gesture. "Give me water! I am thirsty!" she signaled. He handed her a cup, opened his waterskin, and poured the water for her. She gulped it down, took a deep breath, and showed her gratitude by sending up a prayer for him: "May God reward you!" She asked God to grant him a talent for poetry and she sent up prayers for him to receive the Lord's blessings in this world and the hereafter. "May God requite you!" That's what she did.

18.4 He said to her, "May I ask you something, my good spirit? At first you did not know how to call to me, right? You couldn't call to me, if I am correct."

"I am a mute," she replied.

"And now?" he asked.

She said, "When I caught up with you and you gave me water to drink, all of a sudden I could speak. I also have little daughters to look after. Pour me some more water!"

18.5 He refilled the cup and put it down for her. Then she looked at the camels and their load, stretched out her hand, and cried, "I want some of those dates!"

"God willing," he said, and drew his dagger, ripped open the bag, and cut off a clump of dates. He tore about half of the dates from the bag and lowered them to her from the camel's back.

"There you go!" he said. "By the way, tell me, are you a human or a jinni?"[413]

"By God, a jinni," she said, "a mute jinni as long as I lived, until today."

Again she prayed for him: "God grant that you become a wise and learned man!" 18.6

No sooner had she uttered these words than she dissolved into thin air. The place where she stood a moment ago was empty—no one to be seen anywhere.

He resumed his journey and spent the night in the desert on his way to al-Nathrah. Sīḥ al-Nathrah, it is called. When he lay down to get some sleep at the well of Sālim, he was visited by ferocious nightmares, as happens to poets who are in the throes of inspiration. Until that moment, poetry was completely alien to him. But now, after this adventure, the event that God had sent on his path, the gift bestowed on him, verses gushed forth.

Startled, he woke, sat up, and uttered the confession of faith. Then he fell asleep again. At the first light of dawn, he lit a fire and prepared coffee. As soon as he had finished, verses of poetry started raining down on him anew. It happened spontaneously, without any effort on his part. He composed a poem or two, verses replete with wise sayings.[414]

He had had no forebodings, no indication that such a thing would happen to him. It was brought about by the female jinni who suddenly popped up in this wilderness, Hōr al-Balmā, "Flatland of the Mute."[415] It is a well-known place in the sands of al-ʿAnīj, east of al-Hiyar at the well of Sālim, on the eastern side of the Sīḥ desert. You cross over the sand hills, then take the trail toward the east in the direction of al-Niwī and Maḥḍah, and descend to the flatland. It is called Hōr al-Balmā—even women and children know it. 18.7

He rejoined his tribal group, the kinsmen he had left behind in al-Gharīf, the place where he had been born and raised and had lived. Perhaps he had married by then, or maybe not yet. After a week or so, as he and his fellows were sitting around a fire, drinking coffee, he asked them, “Have any of you heard these lines before?” and he recited verses of poetry. Astonished, they asked, “Are you the one who composed these verses or do they belong to another poet?”

“I swear by God, these are my verses,” he replied.

“Well, we had no inkling that you were a poet. We never heard you recite poetry before today!”

“Praise be to God!” he said. “I have become a poet and verses well up in me like a flood.”

18.8 There is nothing spurious in his poems, the poetry of Ibn Ẓāhir. Each and every word he speaks is right, the truth; whatever he says is true. Even in his love poetry. All poets make embellishments or omit certain facts in this kind of poetry. Except him, he doesn’t add anything in his ghazals, love poetry. All his ghazals are exactly as things are.

He settled in al-Madām, and there he stayed a long time, but all the while also traveled far and wide. In the end, he chose to move to Rās al-Khaymah, after touring all these other sites. He took a close look at various areas.[416]

Ibn Ẓāhir's Camel

Ibn Ẓāhir decided to seek a job as a hired hand with al-Miṭārīsh tribesmen who originally came from the western region, together with our ancestors. In those days, people and tribes in Arabia were constantly on the move. Our ancestors took part in those migrations. He worked for them for a long time. Upon completing a year in the job, he was paid by the man, a Maṭrūshī, who gave him his wages and a young she-camel. 19.1

When he had finished working, he had his eye on the pedigrees, the ones he knew well, so at the time of payment, he said, "Listen, So-and-So, with your permission, I'll take my leave. Would you give me the she-camel I was promised?"

The man said, "Go ahead and choose the one you like best."

"Well," he said, "I'd like to have the daughter of So-and-So." He chose one whose mother and father were pedigrees, descended from a famous stud camel, Ḍabyān.[417] As they say, a "dry, hardy she-camel."

"Are you sure? Wouldn't you like a nicer animal?"

"No, this one will do for me."

"Fine, it's yours!"

He took the young thing, raised it until it came of age, put it to work, trained it, and rode it. The she-camel was destined to become a fabled racing camel. It was capable of running so fast that not even horses could overtake it.[418] 19.2

The camel allowed him to go wherever his fancy took him, be it to travel to satisfy his curiosity or for trade—that is, buying and selling between al-ʿAyn and Dubai. He'd pick up some goods in Dubai and transport them to al-ʿAyn, sell his wares, and bring other commodities on the way back. He also went on raiding expeditions on his camel: in those days of scarcity and deprivation, it was normal practice for tribes to rob other tribes and be robbed by them.

He didn't own herds of camels, just a single she-camel. He spent much time wandering in the desert. His travels covered the entire country, no place excepted. He went everywhere by camel or on foot. It was almost as if he spent all his life on camelback.

19.3 He became caught up in a blood feud. I think his father killed someone. The victim's avengers were on the lookout for the culprit's offspring, with the aim of settling the account in blood. Indeed, they were thirsting for blood. They didn't know who he was, what he looked like, or his whereabouts. That is, until they met someone who knew him and gave them the information they were looking for, in a detailed description. Following this lead, they started observing the traffic on the desert road between Dubai and al-ʿAyn. They had learned that he made a living by transporting goods from Dubai and selling them at the market in al-Buraymī, plying regularly up and down between the two.

They searched for him a long time and kept the road under observation. They were on the lookout for a she-camel that fitted his camel's description: if you saw it, you wouldn't recognize it, but being experts they knew. Finally, they intercepted him, the three of them, as he came riding from Dubai on his way to al-Buraymī. They greeted him and he halted his camel. They exchanged greetings and spoke to him, asking who he was and where he was from. "What's the news?"

He said, "Nothing new, I have no news. How about yourselves?"

"We have nothing to tell either," they said. "Tell us with whom we have the honor to speak."

"It's none of your business," he replied. They wanted to be pleasant with him in order to make him feel comfortable, so he would tell them his name and that of his tribe. He told them, "What are you after? Why all these questions? Why do you keep asking? Haven't I told you already?"

19.4 They said, "Well, in that case, tell us about your camel. Where did you get her from?"

They feigned ignorance, as if they had not received a detailed description, and perhaps lines of poetry about the camel, none of them verses I know, or perhaps a few. They repeated, "What's your camel's breed?"

"Her mother and father are from Oman," he replied. She was sired in Oman: on both her father's and her mother's side, she is of the Ḍabyān strain. She kept her ears pricked up and her head was flat and smooth, as in the verse: "Between her reddish upper neck and the flat top of her head, a pair of pricked-up ears is a sign of her scorching speed."[419]

19.5 As he recited this verse, he kicked her flanks, broke through their line, and raced away. He had sensed that they were searching for him to take blood revenge and that they had cornered him for that purpose. He hurtled along at full speed for about four or five kilometers, as fast as a bullet. After this incident, he always took precautions.[420] I can assure you, he made his escape. That was the last they saw of him. He thanked God and asked for His kindness and protection.

This encounter and close shave changed his life. He became a different man. He decided to live somewhere else and moved to al-Madām.

19.6 Bedouin are always on the move. He was in the habit of spending the months of winter in Umm al-Khāyūs and the months of the summer's greatest heat in al-Hīlī, in the company of his family. Once, on a long night march, his camel began to yawn and that made him yawn too.

Ibn Ẓāhir said, "I yawn because my she-camel's yawning."

His companions asked, "What do you mean? Is it us or you?"

"No," he said, "I mean you!"

And he continued:

My camel is hot-tempered and fumes with rage;[421]
her speed scares the saggy-balled wolf.

And:

We sell hardy camels, gaunt from desert treks,
then buy and ride big-humped ones until they limp.

19.7 He had a suspicion that his she-camel hadn't yawned of her own accord. He felt that someone else's yawn made her yawn.

If I yawn because my she-camel yawns,
I wonder, whose yawning made her yawn?

He sang these lines in a loud voice so as to make himself heard far and wide. The others thought that he had seen them yawn, but he had not. His loud chant surprised them. "Well then, my friends, he found out about us," they said.[422]

19.8 The name of his she-camel was Khatīlah. She had grown old and feeble. He tried to improve her condition by cutting branches of a *ghāf* tree for her to munch.[423] But it did not stop her from getting weaker. In his sadness, he said,

What's the use of a *ghāf* to Khatīlah;
he lopped its branches to save her. She died.

Fishing and Pearl Diving

He built a small boat, a *shāḥūf*, also called *māshuwwah*, made from the thick bases of palm fronds. I don't know exactly. From palm leaves, materials from palm trees, that is how he built a *shāshah*: He stripped palm branches of their leaves and used the bases of the fronds to fill the space in between. He cut them, then wove them with a big needle until it was done. And yes, the thing floated. He sailed in it and went fishing at sea. For about one year he made a living as a fisherman in Rās al-Khaymah and Dihān. 20.1

The she-camel was no longer with him; she had died. This was a big loss for him. It forced him to look for a different kinds of work, so he took up fishing. He struggled to make ends meet, but remained as generous as before. He shared his food with others. He made his neighbors gifts of fish. This is the song he intoned:

"I catch the shark and pull him on shore;
    no one waiting to help me, and that's fine!
I catch the shark and pull him on shore;
    let people scold me if they like.
My catch is for my guests to enjoy:
    they must eat to their hearts' content!"

In the early days, the rulers imposed taxes (custom fee) on ships, and on the catch fishermen brought to shore and sold. The Bedouin who transported loads of firewood to ʿAjmān were made to hand over a bundle from every camel load of firewood. They levied fees on every catch of fish; on every fisherman's small boat. They took a large cut on everything. It was a source of income for the shaykhs 20.2

who were the rulers of Rās al-Khaymah. Even if all you owned was a small boat made of reed or wood, you were forced to cough up. They would send some of their men as customs officers to collect *zakāt* taxes. They demanded to be paid in riyals. In those days the currency was the French riyal, a heavy coin.

20.3 Ibn Ẓāhir had made his home in Dihān, in al-Ẓīt. One day he sailed into the harbor with a catch of fish. He also brought a load of firewood into town. In the morning, he offered it for sale in the market. That day, the collector of the custom duties arrived later than usual. He came after sunrise. "Where is Ibn Ẓāhir?" he said. "You can't escape from the law." They'd come to collect the duty from him, and he didn't like it. Ibn Ẓāhir was told,

"You must pay up!"

"I don't have any money," he said. "It is all my own work. I don't owe you anything. I built this little boat made of palm fronds with my own hands. I'm not going to pay for it."

20.4 He refused. "In that case," the other said, "you are not allowed to stay here any longer."

"So, where do I go?"

"Go and settle in Jumayrā!"

"Look here, my boy," he said, "by your leave, today I am pressed for time; there is nothing I can do. My fish and firewood have been sold. I have been at sea fishing since yesterday, and the catch I brought on shore is what I need to feed my children. I have nothing to spare. Tomorrow it will be my pleasure."

"No," the officer said, "you'll have to find the fish and firewood somewhere and give it to us. You'll have to buy it in the market yourself."

Begrudgingly, he did as he was told and went to buy what they asked for. "Here you are," he said. "Wait a minute, here is what I owe you for the custom duty. And let me also tell you that I am fed up with this place."

"How is that?"

"Well, call on your boss and tell him:

I do not command a large dhow;
I do not own lush palm groves in al-Ḥīl.
My entire capital is a boat made of reeds:
I'll sink it, set the fronds free to float!"

Ibn Ẓāhir's mind was set on traveling. Later that morning, the collector of custom duties went to see his boss, and told him, "Well, I took the custom duties from Ibn Ẓāhir, and this is what he said, and what he asked me to report to you." 20.5

"I'll tell you this," he replied. "Go back to him immediately, hurry up, and let him come to me in person!"

The official did as he was told, and said to Ibn Ẓāhir, "The shaykhs would like you to pay a visit to them, as soon as you're done."

"Yes, God willing," he replied. In those days, one would not ignore such an order. Ibn Ẓāhir went about his business and then called on them. The shaykhs had cannons that stood close to the benches of the outside sitting area where visitors tethered their camels and donkeys. Ibn Ẓāhir dismounted, entered, and greeted the shaykhs.

As soon as they saw him, they said, "Ah, the poet! Here, come over here! How are things with you?" 20.6

"May God grant you a long life," he replied, "I haven't done anything out of the ordinary: just a couple of simple words I gave your man to convey to you. I wanted him to let you know, while I went to perform my prayers."

"No, no," they said, "you are very dear to us, Ibn Ẓāhir! We must make sure that you have a good opinion of us!"

They made him a gift of rupees—that's what they called them back then: rupees. They gave him three rupees as compensation for the bundle of firewood and the fish. Two paisa, one for the wood and one for the fish. Having obtained satisfaction, he said his goodbyes, and continued on his way, Ibn Ẓāhir.

Only once did he sign up for a pearl-diving expedition. The captain needed more crewmen, but he could find no one for the last 20.7

vacancy until he stumbled on this graybeard. He did not know who he was, that he was Ibn Ẓāhir. An old man, who did not look very fit. But they needed hands on deck. They accosted him and said, "Hey, you, old guy! If you think you can do the job, come with us!"[424]

"Fine," he said, "I'll join you."

"Follow us," they said. "Let's go."

The captain led him to the house around noon. He invited him to sit inside. "Bring some snacks and coffee for him!" he instructed his daughters. They did so, and when they saw him, they were aghast. "Father, why did you bring this man along? Come to your senses—he's useless." They said so within Ibn Ẓāhir's hearing: he was in the shed just opposite. "We need the man to haul up a diver—we don't have enough of those," he said.

They were not convinced. "Father, but why this graybeard? He will give you headaches you can do without. He doesn't have the strength to pull such a heavy weight as hauling up a diver. You will rue the day you enlisted him. He'll just sit around and be a nuisance, a burden on the others. Look for someone young and energetic!"

"This is what we were able to find. There was no one else. And we have already given him our word."

20.8 Ibn Ẓāhir overheard everything they said. They came to an agreement on his wages. At sea, after a long, hard day's work of diving and hauling, the men in the water had grown tired. At a tug of the diver as a signal, the rope puller on deck started hauling. He pulled so hard that the diver almost hit his head against the underside of the ship. Ibn Ẓāhir heaved on the rope and yanked him out of the water and on board. Thereupon, he said,[425]

> "Torrid heat, calm the broad-chested diver in the deep,[426]
> while the captain rages about the crew's lack of pluck.
> If not for my fear of hurting the divers,
> my haul would fling them into the ship's hold.
> Ah, those words have turned my mood blue,
> from lovely lips that haunt me in my dreams!

Let me be old! No one stands on firmer legs!
I am a stalwart who clears all hurdles in the fray,
For the sake of belles dressed in gorgeous robes;
the glitter of teeth like dazzling white palm pollen."

The captain shouted, "Stop, stop! No more of this!" It had dawned on him who he was. He stood up and walked over to him. "Now tell me in all honesty: are you perhaps Ibn Ẓāhir?" 20.9

"Yes," he replied.

"Good," the captain said. "Be so kind as to take a rest here and leave it to the others to do the hard work."

Invited to do so, he left off working. Someone else was added to the two other members of his team. He stayed with the crew until the end of the season, when he was paid his wages in full. He spent his time relaxing in the shade, eating nice luncheons. At the end, he went on his way. That is all there is to the story.

He made his way to Jumayrā and set up his home. The people, the Arabs, lived in straitened circumstances; they were completely indigent.[427] They barely eked out a living by doing jobs in pearl diving. After a day's work, they would leave their small boats and their basket of oysters, and bed down for the night on shore. At the first light of dawn, they'd push off their boats and set out for the fishing grounds. Before departure, they would pry open the oyster shells and collect the pearls inside. He joined them in this routine. 20.10

Jumayrā was infested with gnats, the ones that bore their way into your eyes, and other nasty bloodsucking insects with a painful bite. He said,

"A land where gnats, fleas, ticks, and bugs reign,
where bloodsuckers turn stout men into skeletons.
Water and good pasture are always at hand:
no wonder they don't embark on long journeys."

Jumayrā's resources of water and pasture are excellent. He joined the pearl divers who set out to sea from Jumayrā and returned with 20.11

a harvest of pearls. Their currency at that time was the crown: twenty-four paisa made one crown. Rupees had not been introduced yet. Only paisa, black paisa; they called them "barghash."[428] They offered him twenty-four crowns for his harvest, not in Jumayrā itself, but at a nearby shore. His family was encamped a little outside of Jumayrā at the edge of the desert. He took the money and threw it into the creek, the creek of Dubai. He took the coins in his hand and, with a wide sweep of his hand, tossed the money into the water. Every single one of his paisas, excuse me for saying so, gave up the ghost.

"What's wrong with you?" the others asked. "The income of your harvest! You have been slaving away for months to earn these wages, and then you throw it away into the sea?"

He said,

> "Good riddance to that money! I don't care a whit!
> Blessed are gains made on camelback,
> not earnings from hauling ropes at sea!"[429]

20.12 No two ways about it, that was his riposte to them. "Are you in your right mind to throw your earnings into the sea?" they protested. "We would have liked to have it, we want it! So what if you have no use for it! We want it!"

He repeated his verse, on the subject of the boat. He went looking for his camels and found them grazing in the surroundings. He mounted one of them, collected brushwood, sold it in the morning, and brought what was needed to his children. In a shop, he bought whatever he needed and went home. He got out—he left Jumayrā behind and trekked to the sand dunes of al-Ẓīt.

People say that he exclaimed, as he looked out from there:

> "From the dune, I saw my desert abode: the new as of old."

20.13 In those days, people used to go diving for pearls and to catch fish in the shallow waters off the coast. But in the waters near Dihān there was nothing. He set out in the little boat he made from palm fronds, the *shāshah*. One day, he came back from the sea, pulled the boat on shore, and returned to his camp in the desert. He had had his fill of working at sea and turned his back on it.

Life at sea was wearing him out, while he went to rack and ruin, without gaining anything. Other poor devils would do odd jobs not far from home. They would scrape by without leaving their homes. And they'd still be better off than the household of Ibn Ẓāhir. As the saying goes: "Better stay at home than travel to Bengal."

On this theme, Ibn Ẓāhir intoned his chant:

"If the world smiles on you,
  life feels light as a feather.[430]
In misfortune, you flounder,
  caught in painful chains."

We were told that he signed up for pearl diving. When he received his wages, his earnings did not match what he was expecting. It was a modest sum: he did not work as a diver, but stayed on board to haul divers from the bottom of the sea.[431] It did not meet the needs of his household. It is said that he took the entire amount of money in his hands and tossed it into the sea. He could not endure life on a pearling ship. It wore him out and made his life hell. Not everyone is cut out for that kind of work. 20.14

He said, "I am made for the desert. That is where I'll go. A simple decision, there is nothing to it:

My dears, best to live off the desert:
  I have no business toiling at sea:
Pull the oars, roasted by the sun,
  my heart toasted on red-hot embers.
Ah, how about thirty young she-camels:
  ten, another ten, and ten roaming at will."[432]

Guests and Riddles

21.1 Our graybeards told us that a group of men visited Ibn Ẓāhir with the intention of putting him to the test. For that purpose, they had collected some riddles for him to solve. In those early days, people had nice customs. They enjoyed enough leisure for such pastimes, for poetry, so unlike today, when all are consumed with ambition, spending their time running about in order to amass ever more money. No, their sole ambition was to gain a good reputation and a collection of nice tales. Back then, generosity and courage were the only assets that counted.

Here in al-Khirrān, Ibn Ẓāhir acquired a son-in-law, a rich trader, as we were told. They lived as neighbors. You might say, as it were, this one on this sand hill, and the other on the next to the south. The man who married his daughter was a rich trader: he owned sheep and goats, camels, cows. A well-to-do man, he lived a life of affluence. His father-in-law, on the contrary, was a poor wretch, completely destitute, with the exception of his one she-camel. He went about dressed in a rough piece of cloth slung over his left shoulder. Wrapped in that cloak, he carried his food for the day. His hut's enclosure was made of branches of trees and brushwood, what we call *markh*, after the *markh* tree. There he lit his fire and, with his meager means, eked out a living. Such was Ibn Ẓāhir's lifestyle. Right here, near his grave, stood a tree. He used to cut branches from the tree and sell the wood.

21.2 Some Bedouin of the al-Ẓawāhir tribe paid him a visit. Their quest was to engage him in discussion and test his knowledge. Word of his fame had reached them, and they decided that Ibn Ẓāhir, because of his name, must be one of them. They carried on an argument among themselves about whether he shared their ancestry or not. "Don't bicker," others said. "You'd do better to pack up your bags and pay the man a visit." They prepared for the looming contest by taking along their savviest versifier: a poet whose lethal wit and acumen were deemed unbeatable. This chosen companion was a poet from Abu Dhabi or al-ʿAyn, or a place somewhere along the coast: a very strong poet. The plan was to spring a surprise on Ibn Ẓāhir with a baffling riddle in verse and dumbfound him.[433] They were keenly aware of Ibn Ẓāhir's renown in this domain.

The poet said, "I will throw down the gauntlet to Ibn Ẓāhir. I bet you I will prevail." He meant, I will trounce him in an exchange of versified riddles.

"No, you can't!" the others said. "You are no match for Ibn Ẓāhir, not by a long way."

He insisted: "I will beat him easily. It will be a breeze. I'll mark his vulnerable spot and hit him right there, as sure as hell. This Ibn Ẓāhir, don't make too much of him. I will challenge him, baffle him, wipe the floor with him."[434]

They decided that he must be their man. They mounted their camels and headed off, a group of seven. They did not stop until they had arrived at his place: today's al-Khirrān and the site of his grave at a sand hill with a growth of *ghāf* trees, Ibn Ẓāhir's Dune, as it's known.[435] That's where they found him.

That morning, before their arrival, another guest stopped at his 21.3
place. A man of the Bū Swiʿiyyah tribe on his way to stock up in town. His scrawny she-camel carried a small load of charcoal. He aimed to be at the market before dawn and to sell it there. Ibn Ẓāhir entertained him hospitably and untied the knot in his headdress in which he carried some coins (I don't know what the currency was back then), and he said, "Dear fellow, buy me some coffee beans, please."

"Sure, God willing," he said, and continued on his way to town. Ibn Ẓāhir, a short man with a white beard, sank to his knees and sat down on his sand dune. With his hatchet, he lopped off branches and tied them into a bundle of firewood. He looked up, and there were the mounted men. They had arrived at Ibn Ẓāhir's place, and what they saw was an unassuming figure, dressed in a long cloak, who collected animal droppings for his fire and carried a sack on his back.

They rode up and greeted him. They did not deign to dismount. "Come, come, welcome!" he called to them.

21.4 They said, "We are looking for the camp of Ibn Ẓāhir's group."

"Ah," he said, "let your mounts go straight ahead to where their noses are pointing." He said so while standing in front of their camels.

He continued: "Please come. There is the group of Ibn Ẓāhir," saying so even though he himself was Ibn Ẓāhir. "See that *ghāf* tree? That is his *ghāf* up there. The place where he lives, where he lops branches from the tree every night, for his enclosure. Actually, he and I, we are one and the same. Welcome, welcome! Make yourselves comfortable!"

"No, no," they said. "We are headed for the tribal group of Ibn Ẓāhir. Tell us how we can find his living quarters!"

"Well," he said, "as I said, you see that tamarisk? That's where Ibn Ẓāhir stays." Now it is the watercourse of Umm al-Khāyūs, just south of the torrent bed, called Jazzah after the tamarisk on the sand hill. It's still there today![436]

"Go!" he said. And the men rode off.

21.5 He did not tell them who he was. As they pulled away on their mounts, he collected the wood, lifted the bundle, put it on his head, and started walking. The men rode up the hill, arrived at the place he had pointed out to them, entered with loud greetings, and found that the only person there was a woman.[437] She welcomed them, and told them to come and kneel their camels on the slopes of the sand hill.

"Here, in the outside sitting area, please make yourselves comfortable, here at the *ghāf* tree," she told them. In the old days, visitors would couch their mounts at the outside sitting area, the *birīzah*, a place separate from the rest of the house—*majlis* is what we call it now. But in this case it was a *birīzah* at the shack's enclosure. It is separate from the house, with its own fireplace and coffee and other utensils. Visitors do not enter the house.

They walked up to the young *ghāf* tree. No one came to meet them. The woman carried firewood to them and put it down in front of them; they picked it up and kindled it. She brought a kettle for boiling water. No coffee, no dates, nothing at all. There was nothing: the man was hard up, because of his generosity and indigence. Visitors flocked to his place and were always made to feel welcome. 21.6

Once he was sure that they were out of sight, Ibn Ẓāhir packed his firewood into a bundle and followed them up the hill. He came from the other side, from behind his shack. He muttered under his breath, "O God, O God, God help me to find some food I can offer them." Meanwhile, the woman did not know what to do with the folks who had descended on her; she had nothing. Ibn Ẓāhir whispered to her, "Who are those you're with?" "Visitors," she said.

He waited for the other man to return, the man who had gone to town to stock up on food for his children. The firewood was at hand. He had put the bundle down and kept himself hidden inside the shack, his gaze trained on the road for the other man's arrival. Then he caught sight of him, as he came up the road. He jumped to his feet, grabbed the firewood, and hurried with an armful to the visitors. He took half of the bundle of wood he had gathered. He greeted them, threw down the wood, hurried back and brought a coffeepot, filled it with water, and handed it to them. He also brought some milk and put it down in front of them. 21.7

They looked at him quizzically, wondering who he was. Among themselves they said, "This little old guy must be one of Ibn Ẓāhir's dependents, a hanger-on, for sure."

On his return, he grabbed at his friend's sleeve. "Listen to me, man, alight from your camel, quickly!" He did as he was told, dismounted, and lowered all the luggage to the ground. When he saw 21.8

the visitors, he hobbled the camel and couched it at the side of Ibn Ẓāhir's shack, where they could not see it. He put the luggage and his market purchases on the ground. The man carried a leather bag full of dates, about eight kilos of rice, and assorted household needs.

"Carry the coffee to the guests: they are waiting for the coffee to be served! And take the mortar and the pestle to pound the beans! Go quickly, and hurry back to fetch the dates! Meanwhile, I will unload the saddle and trappings from your camel."

Ibn Ẓāhir cut the man's large clump of dates into two chunks and sent one of the two on a tray to the guests. All of it at once. The tray was set before them: "It is all yours, eat and enjoy!"

21.9 His cooking pots were renowned: he had his name engraved on them. They were huge: ten persons would find room in them. Because he was so generous in entertaining people as his guests. His friend entered, carried the dates, and sat down with the guests in order to prepare and pour the coffee for them.

As soon as his friend had gone, Ibn Ẓāhir walked to the camel, led it up the back side of the sand hill, and made it kneel to the west of his shack. He took off the saddle and trappings, hobbled it, and knifed it. He slashed its hocks, the pack camel that his friend took to town to load it with victuals for his household. He slaughtered it on the flanks of the dune. When it was dead, he began to skin it. He killed the animal while his friend was preparing coffee.

21.10 "We'd like to ask you where Ibn Ẓāhir is," the guests said to the friend.

"Didn't Ibn Ẓāhir come to see you here?" he asked.

"No, he hasn't come yet. We only saw a short old guy. He threw down a bundle of firewood and left again."

"That was Ibn Ẓāhir," he said.

"Are you serious? Is that the Ibn Ẓāhir we came all the way to see and meet?"

"Indeed, yes, that's him," he affirmed.

As he spoke, he stood up and returned to the shack. He wanted to continue on his journey home. When he entered, the first thing he saw was his camel slaughtered! Without a second's hesitation, he drew his dagger from its sheath and sat down at the other side of the carcass to assist Ibn Ẓāhir in skinning it and cutting it up. They tossed large chunks of meat into the cooking pot. When the pot was half full, he said, "Fine, brother, that will do. Let's leave the other half." They gave the meat a thorough washing. His wife lit the fire and hung over it the cooking pot with rice in it. She ground wheat and barley in a quern, scattered the ground grains over the rice, and stirred the cereals through the rice. Over the fire, it thickened into a porridge of bread-like consistency. In the other pot they cooked the meat, mixed with spices and with condiments added. This took a while.

"Poet of ours, you're ready, aren't you?" the visitors prompted their man. 21.11

"No worries," he said. "A pushover for me. Easy as pie."

They made conversation and small talk, exchanged news. When they had exhausted these topics, their poet said to Ibn Ẓāhir,

"The poetry is beautiful;
the poet's shape is bad."[438]

Ibn Ẓāhir looked like a poor wretch: his clothes were torn and full of holes, the tatters of a threadbare cloak, with large rips in front and in the back. His dress was very improper.

He shot back:

"Beautiful is a twig covered with leaves;[439]
bare of foliage, how could it please?
Worthy visitors I do not rebuff,
though my means are meager."[440]

"Hit back!" they prodded their poet. "Let him have it!"

"No, thank you," he said. "I am not in his league. I can't think of a riposte."[441]

Yes, he was thunderstruck. Dumbfounded. Ibn Ẓāhir had taken the challenge and wrestled him down. He had shot at him: "The 21.12

poetry is beautiful; the poet's shape is bad." He means, the reports we receive at a distance sound nice, but from up close it is a different story. He looked pitiful. "Beautiful is a twig covered with leaves." A Christ's-thorn looks attractive with its green leaves, its twigs swaying on a gentle breeze. But a tree with bare twigs, how could it make a delightful impression? If the bone-dry branches are stretched out, skeleton-like, they do not bend. If you try to bend one down, it does not give. A piece of bare wood, stripped of its leaves.

"Worthy visitors I do not rebuff." He says, "I do not turn my back on you. On the contrary, I receive you with warm hospitality. Though my means are meager." Even if I have nothing to offer.

21.13 I swear, he served them supper and honored them in every way. He was one of those generous men beloved to God. The next morning, they tethered two she-camels, and chose one of their mounts as a present for him, as God had decreed, before their departure. One of the visitors belonged to the ʿAwāmir tribe. He said, "How can this be? I am the owner of this purebred, Samḥah. Am I to be the only one not to leave a farewell present?"

He jumped from his camel and called, "Listen to me! Hurry up, take the camel saddle off her back!" And he tethered her with the other camels left behind as a present for their host. Stealthily, they took a bag (the kind of bag they used to keep money in) and secreted it under the carpet on which they had been sitting. Then they slunk away. When Ibn Ẓāhir's wife came to clean up after the guests, she discovered it under the carpet and called him: "Come quickly, the guests have forgotten their money, the friends of that other poet!"

"Calm down!" he said. "They haven't forgotten anything. They left it behind on purpose."

He said to his friend, "Now it is your call. Choose whatever strikes your fancy," instead of the slaughtered camel. He picked one of the very best, fast pedigrees. "Load your gear and victuals for your household on her back!" he told him, the friend who helped him out with the guests.

. . .

His son-in-law did not live far away. Ibn Ẓāhir used to regale visitors with coffee and supper. The man with the she-camel dropped by Ibn Ẓāhir's place. 21.14

The son-in-law said to his wife, the daughter of Ibn Ẓāhir, "You know what? Your father has a real problem this evening. How in heaven's name is he going to serve dinner to them?" The last time he went to see his father-in-law in his shack, he found him completely destitute: no rice, no dates, no meat, no sheep or goats, nothing. What should he prepare for his guests if anyone showed up?

"Where did you go?" she asked.

"To your father's place," he said, "the old man. And what did I see there? Nothing at all! What if a visitor shows up? What should he do?"

She replied, "What he always does: serve supper, and when they are done eating, he will bring you supper as well. You'll get your dinner from him. He will put aside food on the tray for you, then bring it to you and wake you up to have supper." 21.15

"Ha!" he laughed. "I'll divorce you if he has the means to properly feed his guests. And I'll give you both this camel and that she-camel to boot." He meant his pedigree she-camels: one she-camel of three years old with her calf, and a fast riding camel.

"Really?" she asked. "You'll give me your camels if my father dines his guests and brings you supper as well?"

"Yes!" he said. "And I am as good as my word."

The next evening, the visitors arrived and were given dinner. Once they had eaten to their satisfaction, Ibn Ẓāhir scooped up some food from the pot and carried it on a tray to his son-in-law. He chose shanks and carried them, balancing the tray on his head, supported by his walking cane. He woke them up: they had already gone to bed for the night. He knocked on the door and called in a loud voice, "Hello, hello, it's me!" 21.16

She nudged her husband and said, "Hey So-and-So, get up, eat their supper, get up!"

She pulled the bedding away from him. In those days, the Bedouin would sleep on the floor under a blanket. She pushed him out of bed. "Get up, man! Have supper! Your father-in-law's food!" She lit a fire. And, my God, there was enough food for three days. And then some more.

21.17 Early in the morning, before dawn or, as we say, when the call for dawn prayer is sounded, she, his wife, untethered the she-camel and took it to the shack of her father. It was a done deal. Didn't he say, "Yes, and yes again. I swear, or let my head be cut off"? She led the camel to the north side of the shack and he rose to see who was there.[442]

"It's me, Father!" his daughter said.

"Welcome, welcome! What did you bring?"

"A she-camel and her daughters."[443]

"Tether them there!" She did so and they exchanged greetings and news.

"This she-camel, Dad, is my present to you." "Really?" he asked. "Yes," she said.

21.18 She went back. Ibn Ẓāhir shackled the camel's legs and left the calf at her side.

His Bedouin visitors drank their morning coffee, pleased with the reception they had received, and made ready to go. They were on an excursion, wandering from one place to the next, enjoying hospitality wherever they went. His friend, who went to stock up in town, hailed from Himhām, not from Rās al-Khaymah. When the group had left, he called him: "Well, So-and-So, take a look at those young she-camels. Would they suit you by way of compensation? One for the victuals and one for the slaughtered camel. Will that do? If not, take their mother as well."

"No, no," he said, "the young ones will more than do for me."

The ladies of the household attached halters to the young camels' noses: they were skittish and needed to be broken in.[444] Then the man left to rejoin his fellows.

. . .

A party of mounted Bedouin arrived to ask him questions and to seek information about him, so as to size him up. At that time, his small livestock consisted of two she-goats and a billy goat. They tested him with riddles. They greeted him, and he asked, "Who are you?" 21.19

"The one on your right hand," the other said.

"Khātam, Finger Ring," he replied.

"Your date sack of a year?"

"ʿAtīj, Ancient."[445]

"Take three of the ten," they said.

"Welcome to the Seven!"

"Good," they said. "Where can we find Ibn Ẓāhir and his group?"

"Ibn Ẓāhir's folks? Do you see that *ghāf* tree? That's where he lives."

They halted their camels at the place pointed out to them. They 21.20 readied the utensils for making coffee and lit a fire. At that time, the Bedouin used brushwood and trees to build a hut inside an enclosure. They did not have houses as we know them.

He had been taking care of his goats. He walked up to them, made them sit down, brought coffee. He called a boy to handle the pots and boil water for the coffee.

"Who is this man carrying the firewood?" they asked the boy.

"He is Ibn Ẓāhir."

"Is he Ibn Ẓāhir?" they asked, astonished.

"Yes," the boy said.

He put down the bundle of wood at the enclosure and started preparing supper. He had sworn a dear oath: The supper is on me! He slaughtered the billy goat, cut its throat. In those days, the Bedouin did not use bowls or any other vessels for eating. They sat around a big wooden tray and dipped their hands into the food. He served their supper (the billy goat on top of the rice and other food) and invited the guests. "Come, have dinner!"

"*Tīsin wa-dīkin w-jafnah wa-ʿanzēn* (i.e, a billy goat, a turkey, 21.21 and a tray with two she-goats)!"[446]

The visitors refused to eat. "Explain this to us first!" they said.

"Didn't I say '*tīsin wadīkin w-jafnah wa'an zēn*' (i.e., a fattened billy goat and a tray, a nice vessel)?"

"Well," they said, "we were looking for the turkey and the two she-goats (*wa-'anzēn*)!"

"It is not 'two she-goats,' (*wa-'anzēn*) but a 'nice vessel' (*wa'an zēn*). Don't you see it shine? And I didn't say 'a billy goat and a turkey' (*tīsin wa-dīkin*), but 'a fattened billy goat' (*tīsin wadīkin*). There is a lot of fat (*widak*) in it. The billy goat is dripping with fat!"

"Now enjoy your supper! Say 'In the name of God,' and dip your hand into the food. I'll tell you more about it later."

"No way!" they said. "Tell us the whole story if you want us to eat supper!"

21.22 He said,

"By two stars twinkling alone,
when other stars have set:
My guest, rise, eat supper!
I ask you about fourteen,
Only two are present;
twelve went missing.
My guest, rise, eat supper:
a billy goat, a turkey, and two she-goats,
Eat as much as you can!

"I ask you about fourteen: the seven spheres of heaven, and the seven spheres of the earth. Two are present: earth and heaven. The other twelve are missing. You see? The penny has dropped."

21.23 They rose and sat down around the tray. The riddle gave them certitude that he was indeed Ibn Ẓāhir. But they had more up their sleeve.

"What lies on the ground wrapped in a shroud?"

"Ripe dates: we tasted the fresh harvest," he replied.

"A girl with a beautiful color?"

"God made the sun a clear presence."

"A girl stirred by eastern wind?"

"A ship steered by its rudder."

"A girl with screaming eyes?"

"A quern grinding grain."

No matter how hard they tried to outwit him with riddles, he always came out on top.

A party of camel riders caught up with him not far from Khat. Their aim was to confound him.[447] They were not guests in the real sense. Attracted by his fame, they had formed a plan to intercept him in a location where he'd be on his own, without anyone to whom he might turn for help and, having cornered him, to spring a surprise on him. 21.24

His sole possession was the she-camel that carried his children. He was on his way to the coastal region of al-Bāṭinah, toward Kalbā, I believe, for a stay during the hottest months of summer.[448] Just before sunset, he dismounted and his wife prepared to light a fire. They traveled alone with their daughters. Suddenly, out of nowhere, visitors appeared. They halted and watched. Ibn Ẓāhir went to greet them and invited them to come over to visit. They wondered how he would manage to receive them for dinner. He had no livestock—no camels, no young, weaned animals. How would he extricate himself from this predicament? What could he serve for dinner? Nothing he can do, they concluded.

He called them: "Come, sit down here, with my family! We have coffee and firewood. I am going to fetch more water. Our supply here is not sufficient." 21.25

He mounted his camel and trotted away, drew water from a well, and came back. He unloaded the skins with water, loosened the girths and the saddle, and took off all trappings. Then he plunged his dagger into the camel's breast. Shocked, the men came sprinting to him.

"What have you done? Have you gone out of your mind? You need this beast to carry your children! Your entire capital!"

He simply said, "There is your supper."[449]

21.26 Upon my word, God is my witness, I tell you: he slaughtered the beast, served them supper, and emerged from the ordeal with his honor intact and resplendent. Come morning, they tethered two she-camels for him to replace the camel slaughtered for food. One of them said to the others, "Never forget what happened! You were taught a lesson. You were made to eat humble pie through your own fault. How could you presume to challenge him?"

Ibn Ẓāhir installed his children on the back of these two she-camels. The men had sworn that they'd divorce their wives if he declined their gift. The others gave the spurs to their mounts, two riders each to one camel, and left for home.

They said, "He is a hopeless case. Incurable. No matter what ruse you employ to put him on his mettle, he can't be vanquished. His generosity is boundless. He is generous for the sake of the Lord, not out of a penchant for boasting. He is generous to a fault. That's all there is to it."

21.27 On that occasion, he composed a few lines, well-known verses:

"A guest has no inkling of what to expect
when he sets his face toward your place:
A guest doesn't deserve an angry grimace;
he deserves supper, even if served late."[450]

Even if it takes a month, you are not entitled to say anything until you have fulfilled your obligation toward him. "A guest has no inkling of what to expect."

He also said,

"The path of noble virtue is a steep climb,
otherwise it'd be a jaunt for any sluggard."[451]

21.28 For as long as I remember, we heard people everywhere tell anecdotes about Ibn Ẓāhir, quote his words, and recite his verses. I myself did not memorize his poetry. His verses are crammed with wisdom. We are told about his comings and goings. What people said about him wherever he went and stayed. We heard that people traveled (I don't know where from) just for the sake of getting to see him personally.

Mostly, he spent the summer in Hīlī and the winter in Umm al-Khāyūs. He left for his summer quarters from here. Halfway along the road, the old man was resting in the shade for a noon break, when a party of camel riders came hurrying toward him. In the expectation of getting the better of him, they challenged him with riddles.[452] They rested their mounts not far from the old man and invited him to join them for coffee. He came, and they exchanged greetings upon meeting. They offered fresh dates. "Please, dear old man, enjoy!"

"What takes the soil as a shroud?" they asked. 21.29

"It hardens in the soil. In the name of God, the Merciful, the Compassionate, its delicacies ripen on its branches," he replied.

"The girl with a beautiful color?"

"God made the sun a shining beauty."[453]

"How about a breeze from the east?"

"A ship steered by its rudder."

They gathered around him and struck up a conversation. 21.30

"Are you Ibn Ẓāhir?"

"Yes, that's me."

They said, "We rode all this way just to see you!" And they explained their reasons.

"You are most welcome!" he said. "Now, where are you headed to?"

"Our plan is to go home. Our mission is accomplished. We had no other aim than presenting these riddles to you," they replied.

"Fine," he said. "Anything else I can do for you?"

"That's all." They thanked him. "We wish you good health and peace!"

Daughters of Ibn Ẓāhir

21.1 He had three daughters. The story goes that with his camels he followed the coast on the way to Umm al-Quwayn. Before she died, one of his she-camels was not afraid to ford the creek, an arm of the sea, to the other side, or so they said. At the shore, his camels balked at wading into the water. They refused to cross the creek. His daughter had a bright idea: "Father, wasn't the mother of one of those she-camels the one that used to wade into the water?"

"Indeed she was," he said.

"In that case, why don't you bring her daughter to the fore and see if she is willing to take the plunge?" she suggested. "Push her, the daughter of the 'wading camel.'" They used to call her mother *khawwāḍah*, "she who takes the plunge." "Drive the daughter of the wading camel to the front and you'll see that the rest of the herd follows her!" she said.

22.2 They took hold of her and put her in pole position at the edge of the water. Undaunted, she waded into the sea and the others followed suit. He muttered under his breath, "Ah, the daughter of the resolute beast that took the plunge. Likewise, the daughter of a she-camel that raises her tail for the male will wave to the stud as her mother did.[454] Be prepared for her crafty tricks!"

"Didn't I tell you that this lady camel takes the plunge?" she proudly reminded her father.

"Ah, this question again!" he said, somewhat annoyed. There and then, the friction between them started.

. . .

He had three daughters. One of them was a little girl when Ibn Ẓāhir left her behind in al-Ẓāhirah region in Oman. Because of their way of life, the Bedouin were always on the move. One day, she was brought from al-Ẓāhirah to his place. "Here is your daughter!" they said, as they handed her over. 22.3

Some of his fellows looked askance at the girl, saying, "There is reason to be suspicious. It is most unlikely that she really is his daughter. No, she can't be a daughter of Ibn Ẓāhir."

"No problem," he said. "Cast her away, and leave her somewhere in a vast, empty desert!"

In another story, the girls were playing outside. When two men passed by and looked at them, unaware that their father was nearby, one said to the other, "Those two are his daughters, but the other one is not." They did not know that she was one of his daughters. Ibn Ẓāhir overheard what they said, but he kept quiet.

Even when she had grown up, his youngest daughter hardly ever 22.4
spoke a word. She only spoke to answer a question directly addressed to her. The other daughters composed verses—they were poets. He recognized enough of himself in them to know for sure that they were his offspring. His doubts about the other girl kept nagging him. He would ask his other daughters, "When you go out to collect firewood, and she is with you, does she say anything? Does she ever recite a verse of poetry? A nice line? Do you ever hear her sing a song?"

"No," they replied, "never, not a single word."

He voiced his concerns to his wife: "I have my doubts about this girl. She doesn't look like a daughter of mine."

"By God," she said, "do whatever you want to do and make short work of it."

"Don't you have something in mind?" he asked.

"If she isn't your daughter, it is up to you to decide what is best. Really, by God, whether she is or is not your daughter, as a matter of fact you do not consider your daughter as your daughter any longer. Do what you have to do and tell me if there is something you want me to do."

22.5 It was winter season, and here in Umm al-Khāyūs winters can be bitterly cold. An icy wind blew from the west, and freezing rain fell for hours on end: it was coming down in buckets. At dusk, he told his wife, "When you ladle supper out of the cooking pot for our daughters, leave her food aside for later. Let me handle this. It will become clear whether she is my daughter or not. I am going to find out."

He went looking for her and said, "Daughter, go outside, dig a hole, and place this bundle of wood in it so that it stands upright."

She didn't say a word. She remained completely silent, though she was not a mute: if questioned by her sisters, she would reply. But she did not sing or recite verses of poetry. No, not at all. For that reason, he doubted her parentage, because her sisters had a talent for poetry, and she didn't.

22.6 She planted the bundle of wood firmly in the ground, as she was told, and returned to him. He took her with him and tied her up tightly to the pile of wood and left her there. Her supper was kept waiting under a cover. She remained in that position the whole night, while he sat hunched over the fire. First, the flames danced, then the fire gradually died down. He huddled inside a winter cloak that he had pulled over his head, and warmed his hands over the embers as he listened intently for her to make a sound.

Seeing that the fire had burned out, she reckoned that the old man had fallen asleep. But he was wide awake. It must have been three or four o'clock in the morning when the girl thought that the cold would kill her. The icy rain and the razor-sharp western wind, the freezing cold of al-Khirrān, cut into her wet body and she was about to breathe her last.

22.7 "There is no God but God," she said. "How long before morning comes, and the night ends, and God makes me feel well again."

"Say that again!" he shouted to her. "Repeat what you just said!" She repeated what she had said. "May God protect you!" he said. He jumped to his feet and ran to her, lifted her up, and rushed back with her in his arms. He blew on the fire, rekindled it, and let her warm herself. He handed her supper to her, told her to eat, and was reconciled with her.

His wife asked, “Are you satisfied now?”

“Yes,” he said, “and please, no hard feelings! This night I found out that she is really my daughter.”

In this manner, he learned the truth. The words she spoke offered him the key to discover what had been kept hidden for him. As soon as she spoke, he felt certain that she was his daughter. No longer was he beset by his vexing doubts about her.

He had four daughters. Earlier narrators who say that he had no daughters, or no children for that matter—they were wrong. He had four daughters, and one of them was a lively, outgoing character who would come forward to welcome visitors with open arms. She encouraged guests to come and visit them. Once, a woman came to her and told her, “So-and-So has an eye on you.” 22.8

Ibn Ẓāhir’s daughter said, “What do you mean? In accordance with the customs and practice of God and the Prophet?”

“No,” she replied, “he fell in love with you and he would like to see you and have a chat.”

“Who do you think I am?” she said. “I am the daughter of al-Māyidī ibn Ẓāhir!”

Some people grumbled that when she went outside she was not properly covered. They would warn young men interested in her not to ask for her hand. “Get married to one of the others,” they’d say. Accordingly, her three sisters found a husband, while she became a spinster. 22.9

She never married. She grew old; her teeth fell out.[455] She was at a disadvantage because she composed poetry. I did not memorize her verse, but it was along these lines: “My sail hangs listlessly, hugging the mast without motion.” If the sail is slack and sags, it means that there is no wind and that the ship cannot set out for the sea. No one is interested in such a vessel. On the contrary, if the sail fills with a brisk breeze, the ship will run. She said:

> “Poetry of the tribe’s maiden, daughter of Ibn Ẓāhir,
> is recited by raving crowds of connoisseurs.”[456]

22.10 They all married, except for the girl shunned by suitors. She alone stayed behind. The oldest girl remained unmarried. She became a spinster due to this poem. Still, she kept composing verses until her work rivaled that of her father, or perhaps she even surpassed him.

Therefore, he decided to outwit her and put her in her place. He thought of a convoluted question that would baffle her and make her give up poetry. She had become too good at it for his comfort. With her savvy, she had surpassed him. He was incapable of matching some of her verse. Yes!

He boasted to her: "My poems are so numerous. Countless! What is there left for you? I have swept up all there is to say: theme by theme, motif by motif. The air, the earth, the trees, people, animals. I have expatiated on everything under the sun. Huge experience. Loads of poetic riches. After these efforts, do you think it is conceivable that there is any ground I have not already covered? What is there left for you to say? Borrow from my poems?"

22.11 "Dear father," she said, "you do not have a monopoly on poetry. That is an impossible ambition, for you and for others."

"In that case," he replied, "if I cannot exhaust all poetic themes, as you aver, it will settle the matter for me if you compose three lines, each ending with the word *no*."

"Daddy," she said, "you insist on giving me tough love."

"As you like," he replied. "It's your call."

She took up the challenge and said,[457] "A son and your son's son, great! A daughter's son—no!"

"That is the first," he said.

"People can be sated with all. Except money—no!"

"That makes two."

"Hair grows on every part, but inside the hand—no!"

"Well done," he said. "You've completed the three rounds. But make no mistake: from now on, if I ever hear you utter verses of poetry again, I will cut out your tongue. You'll have to make do with the poems you have composed so far."

"As you say," she replied.

Search for a Grave

For thirty-five years, he lived at the well of al-Sāʿdī. Before that, he had settled in al-Gharīf, near al-Milīḥah and al-Miryīl. When he decided to move here, he started taking samples of the land. He searched for the kind of earth in which bones do not decay. He was quite a character! 23.1

He took three skins filled with clarified butter and went on his way. One he buried in al-Rassah, the place where there is now the camel racing track of Wshāḥ. A second bag, made of goat's leather of the sort we make (*ʿikkah*, we used to call it), he buried in al-Yitīmah. He pumped them full of air, pulled the fetters tight shut. He buried one in al-Yitīmah at Umm al-Falay—Umm al-Falay to the south of al-Dhēd, at the graveyard. The third one, he buried at a place called Miḥḍāb, to the east of where his grave is. He did not tell anyone he had buried them there.

A year later, he returned to dig them up. The thongs were all that was left of the one he buried in al-Rassah. The earth and worms had eaten the rest of the skin, all of it and its contents. He cast it away, muttering, "In this land my bones will rot." He continued to the one he had buried in al-Yitīmah. He put his spade in the ground in several spots until he found it. When he unearthed it, one year later, the only thing he found was the neck of the skin with the leather thongs still attached to it, like a bridle. He pulled it out and threw it away. "This place doesn't suit me," he thought. He continued to inspect the one he had buried in al-Khirrān, where he was to be interred. Lo and behold, it had not changed a bit. It was exactly the same as it was on the day he put it in the ground. It had not rotted 23.2

at all, had not decomposed, had not been touched by the worms. "This is the place!" he exclaimed.[458] "Here I want to live and die. Here, where my bones are not eaten by the worms!" He packed up his belongings and came to live there.[459] He went to the mountains, loaded two slabs of stone on the back of his camel, and transported them to his new quarters.[460] He informed the folks there: "When I have passed away and I have been laid in my grave, you must put these slabs of stone over it!" The oblong slabs he had chosen made perfect tombstones. They are still standing at his grave, for all to see.

23.3 As soon as he arrived in his new place of residence, he climbed a low hill, the one where the ruler Sulṭān ibn Sālim has his palace now. As he took in the view, he said to himself,

> "This is the place where the eye sleeps in peace:
> from desert plains to coast, waterholes in between."[461]

And this indeed is the place where he died and where he was buried. The headstones he brought from the mountain were raised at both ends of the grave, and the shaykhs of the town enclosed the graveyard with a protective wall, may God reward them.

23.4 He felt happy in the land of Umm al-Khāyūs. He enjoyed the grand view of the nearby high mountains; the pleasant greenery and pastures; a clean, sandy soil. Bedouin flocked in great numbers to his new quarters to see him and engage him in conversation. The location of his grave is known to all and the tombstones are well preserved. A sister and members of his family are also buried there. Inspired by his example, the Bedouin started to inter their dead there. Today, the graveyard is enclosed by a wall to fence it off from the street that runs along it. The grave of Ibn Ẓāhir is considered a famous landmark. He admonished his kinfolk: "Perhaps people will pass by and remember me well, saying, 'By God, this is the grave of Ibn Ẓāhir!'"[462]

The cemetery is called "Cemetery of al-Miḍāwiyyah."

23.5 I have known the grave of Ibn Ẓāhir since the day my father told me about it. People have known it for more than a hundred years.

"This is the grave of Ibn Ẓāhir," they'd say. It was considered an indisputable fact. It became customary for the Bedouin to issue invitations for meetings at the grave.[463] For instance, someone would say, "If you are truly generous, let's meet at the grave of Ibn Ẓāhir. If you are generous and hospitable, a stalwart whose name is not invoked in vain in times of distress, then you should meet me at the grave of Ibn Ẓāhir." Such an open invitation would be issued by a man who owned sheep and goats, camels, and other possessions: a well-to-do man who liked to show off and let others share in his riches.

They'd congregate at the grave of Ibn Ẓāhir. One of them would shout: "Is So-and-So present?" And you'd hear the other shout in reply: "Yes! I am here, present! Join us here at the grave of Ibn Ẓāhir!" It was as if you were attending a lavish roast given by Ḥātim al-Ṭāʾī.[464] The Bedouin would slaughter animals at the grave, invite guests to share the roast, and exchange lines of poetry. Whoever knew some verses or pithy sayings would pitch in, as if they were in competition. Gatherings at that location were an occasion for displays of hospitality, for making business deals, and for vying with one another in reciting poetry, so I heard. This is what my father and grandfather always told us, may God have mercy on them.

We have grown up knowing that this was his grave from the time 23.6
we were old enough to understand and move around town. "And this is the grave of Ibn Ẓāhir," we'd hear. He lived before our time; we did not witness these events.[465] But we know. About sixty, seventy years ago we became aware of these things. We were told that he lived here a long time ago and that he always kept a fire alive at his place. In the morning he'd fetch wood and rekindle his fire. He loved his "Noble Abode," as he called it. His cabin stood on top of the sand hill, under his *ghāf* tree. There, high on that dune. No one knows what his quarters looked like. In the old days, there were no houses. Our ancestors lived under an awning made of sackcloth and a roof made of palm-leaf matting. Under his *ghāf* tree stood his palm-branch hut with its sackcloth awning: those were the living quarters in the olden days.

23.7 Originally, al-Khirrān was where the Bedouin spent the months of the most intense summer heat. In winter, they used to migrate to the sand hills. We knew Ibn Ẓāhir from what we were told: that he was a poet and generous to a fault. His grave has always been a well-known landmark. Visitors came flocking to it from all around. It was always talked about as being a famous place. At night, people gathered around campfires to chat, prepare coffee, drink cups of warm milk, and eat freshly baked flatbreads. They would pound grain and spices in a mortar and mix it with milk and clarified butter. After supper, they kept the fire burning. Come morning, Ibn Ẓāhir only had to strike a match to rekindle it. This is the Noble Abode, he used to say. We have walked by the grave and looked at it since we became old enough to be aware of its importance. "There, look! The grave of Ibn Ẓāhir," they'd say in an excited voice as they pointed it out to us children.

NOTES

1 The poet boasts that his words are an eloquent expression of what is on his mind. For the formulaic character of this opening, see Introduction p. xxix–xxx and the section "Signature Verse" in the online "Glossary of Style, Themes, and Motifs."

2 As in the poetry of, for instance, Dhū l-Rummah, in Ibn Ẓāhir's preludes the winds give expression to the vehemence of emotions roused by memory.

3 "Cooing dove": The customary musical accompaniment to a lover's torment, repeated in countless poems. Even more lethal is the Jabrī poet Fayṣal al-Jumaylī's cooing dove: "At the stream I was stabbed to death by the cooing of a dove, / a colorful bird domiciled in the valley's foliage" (*w-anā sibab dhabḥī ʿalā l-mā ḥamāmah, mkhaḍḍibtin wargā ribuwwat wād*) (Sowayan, *al-Shiʿr al-nabaṭī*, 394).

4 "Days of dalliance": lit. "time of youthful behavior (*tiṣābī*)." The seventeenth-century poet Rumayzān ibn Ghashshām uses the same expression, *ʿaṣr at-tiṣābī*, in a poem that opens on a mournful note: "The world's heavy hand of separation oppresses people: / no one is spared from having to say farewell. [. . .] I pine for my days of youth and blissful trysts: / a natural confluence of senses enveloped by night; all of a sudden separation assaulted us with cattle prods, / and inflicted grievous wounds deep in my soul" (*yad al-bayn bi-d-dunyā ʿalā n-nās ghāshimih, walā hī li-ḥayyin min frāgih bi-ḥāshimih* / [. . .] / *shifīgī ʿalā ʿaṣr at-tiṣābi w-shamlanā, dimājin ʿalā ṭīb al-liyālī mlāyimih* / *shaʿab lāmanā al-bayn al-mfājī bi-ghārih, aṣāwībahā fī lājī ar-rūḥ wājimih*) (Sowayan, *al-Shiʿr al-nabaṭī*, 441–42).

5 The pursuing enemy is a metaphor for the onset of old age, exemplified by the appearance of streaks of white hair in place of youth's raven-black locks.

6 The gray hairs of old age, *al-shayb*, are seen as a cover of white that settles over the black hair of youth, *al-ṣiba*, as in the verse of al-Mutanabbi: "If I could, I'd show youth beneath my cover / because gray has enveloped my head before its time" (*law kāna yumkinunī safartu ʿan al-ṣibā, fa-l-shaybu min qabli l-awāni talaththumū*) (*Dīwān al-Mutanabbī*, 4:123). In hadith, white hair is considered "one of two deaths," i.e., a "sign that the end is near" (Arazi, "al-Shayb wa 'l-shabāb" in *EI2*). Here, *al-nigāb* is the plural of *al-nagbah* "hair between the eyebrows over the nose" (oral communication from Sultan Alameemi) (CA *nuqbah* "the outer parts of the face").

7 "That loathsome thing": *min lā ahtiwētih*, lit. "whom I do not like"; see also §12.34 for the same expression in a different context and n. 309. "The other": A reference to old age, the "unwanted and spurned guest, a guest who never comes alone, but is accompanied by a retinue of evils," such as "worries, solitude and physical decrepitude," and "mental decay, decline and imminent death." Revulsion at old age is summed up by its mirror image: "the disgust of beautiful women" which it provokes (Arazi, "al-Shayb wa 'l-shabāb" in *EI2*).

8 As explained to me, in §§1.13–25 the poet represents youth and old age in dialogue with his inner self. He implores youth not to abandon him to the enemy who is catching up with him in pursuit: old age. In doing so, he employs the imagery of Bedouin heroic poetry: tribal warfare and theft of camels, the owners' pursuit of the raiders, and the moral duty to protect a refugee. Unable to accept that he is past his prime, the poet challenges youth, his "friend," to remain at his side and ward off the onslaught of old age, his "enemy," and threatens violence to coerce his friend. The latter accepts the invitation to duel but then becomes inert, i.e., at that stage youth is a mere phantom and desperate struggle cannot avert the ineluctable advance of age. As from §1.19 the poet's interlocutor is *al-shayb*, "grayness, old age."

9 Jabr ibn Sayyār makes the same point as Ibn Ẓāhir does in this line, i.e., that no matter what sacrifices one is prepared to make, youth will not return: "There I stood, lost in thought and sighing with regret: / those days have rushed by and can't be caught" *wigaft adīr al-fikr w-agḍī ḥawāsif, wa-l-ayyām mā yifdā fawātin ṭrūdhā* (Sowayan, *al-Shiʿr al-nabaṭī*, 468). It is similar to the ghazal stereotype of paying any price were the age of dalliance for sale, as in the eighteenth-century lines of Ibn Dawwās: "If the times of youthful passions were on offer for thousands, / or were sold to the highest bidder / I'd have bought them for you, Jabr, / and brought them, whether your folks liked it or not" (*law ʿṣūr aṣ-ṣibā tishtirā bi-l-ulūf, aw tiḥaggag bi-sōmin yibīʿūnih / ishtirēnāh yā-Jabr fīmā ʿanāk, law bi-l-ikrāh rabʿik yijībūnih*) (Sowayan, *al-Shiʿr al-nabaṭī*, 482–83).

10 From here it is only one step for Ibn Ẓāhir to replace love and beauty with youth itself, for rejection at the hands of the beloved to be replaced with old age, and for the poet to engage in a direct dialogue with both.

11 Here the poet addresses his youth.

12 This verse is the closest the poet comes to reconciling himself to the inevitability of old age, an attitude recommended by the Emirati saying, "If time does not do your bidding, acquiesce and take him as your friend" (*in mā ṭāʿak az-ziman ṭīʿah ḥattā tiṣīr ribīʿah*) (Ḥanẓal, *Jāmiʿ al-amthāl wa-maʾthūr al-aqwāl wa-l-ḥikam wa-l-kināyāt ʿind ahl al-Imārāt*, 475). Ibn Ẓāhir's default position is to regard grayness as an implacable enemy (§8.67).

13 In this verse, the poet ends his soliloquy by saying farewell to youth, his treasured companion (lit. "neighbor of joy," *jār al-surūr*). The poet's lament about the departure of his beloved, here the personification of youth, and his agitated dialogue with youth and old age, give way to a calm tone of wisdom gained from this bitter experience, starting in the next line.

14 This and the preceding verse warn against complacency and despair by giving examples of the unpredictability of fate: contrary to expectation, a young person may die young and an old person may live even

longer than thought possible. A similar counsel of patience, equanimity, and resignation in the face of adversity is found in §§3.28–33, §7.8, and §9.40. Often the point is introduced by the interrogatory and exclamatory particle *kam* ("how many, how often!").

15 His contemporary Ḥmēdān al-Shwēʿir derives similar grim pleasure from describing the ravages of old age (e.g., in Kurpershoek, *Arabian Satire*, 123). Often it is made to contrast with the alacrity of the old man's mind and the wealth of experience that gives him a further advantage over younger and fitter men, just as Nestor towers over his younger fellows in *The Iliad*.

16 "The venom of ants is chosen because, unlike the venom of snakes, it is painful but not lethal" (Thānī, *Ibn Ẓāhir*, 96).

17 One might argue that "I believe" (*arā*) is merely there for the sake of meter, but it is not untypical of Ibn Ẓāhir to use a note of caution and to allow for the possibility of other views and truths. The rhyme word for "disappearance" (*dhahāb*) is used in the editions, but all MSS give "torment" (*ʿadhāb*, the torments of the grave, may be meant).

18 "These three" are life, death, and afterlife subsequent to divine judgment. The rules of "Holy Scripture" is the translation of *āyāt al-kitāb*, which of course means the Qur'an, but elsewhere Ibn Ẓāhir also mentions the Torah and the Psalms. The translation allows for their inclusion.

19 This verse seems to bear no relation to the context. Perhaps other verses are missing. The meaning, as explained to me, is that an old *lōḥ* (CA *lawḥ* "board, plank, slab") might not make a good fit if one tries to join it with another new piece of wood. As a proverb, it may express the idea that living beings are better left alone if they have become accustomed to a certain way of life. Commentators have speculated that the verse might refer to the grave in the sense that each person is buried alone (and not together with one's beloved, for instance), or that *lōḥ* refers to the heavenly tablet, *al-lawḥ al-maḥfūẓ*, on which the Qur'an is preserved, and that *qābī* should read *ghābī*, hidden in *al-ghayb*, "the unknown" (Abū Shihāb and Abū Malḥah, *Ibn Ẓāhir*, 130; Thānī, *Ibn Ẓāhir*, 98). Both interpretations seem

far-fetched: *gibā* derives from CA *qabā*; *al-qabw* "a layer joined with another one"; *al-qabw* "joining two things together"; *iqtabaytuh* "I collected, put together" (Ibn Manẓūr, *Lisān al-ʿArab*, 3523).

20 Here the poet resumes the more upbeat tone of §1.25, where he bids farewell to his halcyon days.

21 In some of his stereotyped comparisons of the beloved to a gazelle, Ibn Ẓāhir uses the conceit that she would be a real gazelle were it not for certain aspects as mentioned here and more extensively in §§2.19–22.

22 It was explained to me that *mastūr al-ḥijāb*, lit. "hidden behind a veil, partition," here refers to a partition or screen (*sitr*) inside the tent, and not the facial veil.

23 The beloved maiden is the one who ornamented and embroidered the cushions and tassels on the camel that bears her litter. This is an example of the smooth thematic transitions (*ḥusn al-takhalluṣ*) for which Ibn Ẓāhir is admired in the Emirates: the focus switches imperceptibly from the camel to its precious load, the beloved, through a description of her stitching work loaded on the camel's back.

24 "Circumspect": *akhif khōfin*, lit. "I hide my fear." "Gloat": a standard expression, as in the line of the early Nabaṭī poet Abū Ḥamzah al-ʿĀmirī: "Fearful that our enemies will rejoice and gloat" (*min khōftin tashmit binā al-aʿdā'*) (Sowayan, *al-Shiʿr al-nabaṭī*, 282).

25 In this primeval scene of departure, the camels that carry the tribe's litters and those left behind crane their necks to throw a last glance at their loved ones, as expressed by Dhū l-Rummah: "They packed up and departed, throwing longing glances: / resolved on a migration against the will of Mayy and her court of lady friends" (*wa-ajlā naʿāmu l-bayni wa-nfatalat binā, nawwa ʿan nawā Mayyin wa-jārātihā shazrū*) (*Dīwān*, 566–67).

26 "Empty-handed": *mā ʿiṭānī minh ṭōʿ*, lit. "she did not accede to any of my wishes (*ṭōʿ*, CA *ṭawʿ*)." This has been translated into a humdrum proverb: "When the Bedouin depart on a migration, I want her to stay" (*widdī ilā shadd al-ʿarab mā yishidd*), i.e., one wishes to stay close to one's loved ones (al-Juhaymān, *Amthāl*, 9:27).

27 The Bedouin year moves in a circle. "Year": *ḥūl* (in the Emirati dialect thus pronounced, in Najd as *ḥōl*, closer to the CA diphthong in *ḥawl*) means that the wheel of seasons has made a full turn. The new year starts with the appearance of the star Canopus (*shēl*, CA *suhayl*) toward the end of August in the morning. This is the time of the date harvest and the departure of the Bedouin from their summer residence at the wells of an oasis, i.e., the time of the year described in these verses.

28 Another nice transition: the simile of the thirsting traveler, anxious to reach a copious well, acts as a prelude to the fervent prayer for rain on the beloved's journey. It is customary for poets to clarify that their prayers do not stem from a particular predilection for that land but from passion for the Bedouin girl who followed her tribe in its migration to those desert pastures, or a dear one who has been buried there, as expressed by the early poet Mutammim ibn Nuwayrah: "It is not because I love the land that I pray for this boon, / but only that rain may quicken the earth where my darling lies; / a greeting from me even though my love is far away" (*fa-wa-llāhi mā usqī l-bilāda li-ḥubbihā, wa-lākinnanī usqī l-ḥabība l-muwaddaʿā / taḥiyyatuhū minnī wa-in kāna nāʾiyan*) (*al-Mufaḍḍaliyyāt*, 1:537; 2:208). Rains that arrive at night are considered the best, followed by the rains in the evening; least desirable are rains during the day, according to al-Aṣmaʿī (*al-Mufaḍḍaliyyāt*, 1:536).

29 "Rutting": *tṣūl bhā*, the female suffix in this position makes it more likely that this hemistich refers to the clouds of the previous line (Thānī, *Ibn Ẓāhir*, 102), not the torrents that follow, though that is also a possibility.

30 The wind, especially the east wind, *al-ṣabā*, "milking" the clouds for water is a stock image of Bedouin poetry, e.g., "Fresh-fallen rain from clouds at night, milked by the east wind: / water limpid and clean when it settles in ponds" (*b-gharīḍi sāriyyatin adarrathu l-ṣabā, min māʾin asjara ṭayyibi l-mustanqaʿī*) (*al-Mufaḍḍaliyyāt*, 1:54; 2:17); "when winds from the east milk the clouds, joined by / southern breezes, their soft strokes make the rain run from the udders" (*idhā*

mā stadarrathu l-ṣabā aw tadhaʾʾabat, yamāniyyatun amrā l-dhahāba l-manāʾiḥū) (Dhū l-Rummah, *Dīwān*, 871).

31 "Two weeks": here separate from the period of one month in the preceding verse. Added up, the one month and two weeks would approximately be equal to the period that elapses between copious rainfall and the full growth of grazing in the desert pastures mentioned in Jabrid poetry by the name *mīqāt Mūsā*, "the time set by Moses" for this growth, based on Q Baqarah 2:51, "We made an appointment with Moses for forty nights," as in the verse of ʿĀmir al-Samīn: "There desert pastures dry up and bloom / as in the appointment of God the Exalted with Moses" (*dammār ʿammār al-maghānī bihā kamā, mīqāt Mūsā li-l-wiliy jall min qāl*) (Sowayan, *al-Shiʿr al-nabaṭī*, 332–35); and Jabr ibn Sayyār: "After forty days you will see the shoots of green" (*ʿigb arbaʿīnin thumm tanẓir nabtahā*) (Sowayan, *al-Shiʿr al-nabaṭī*, 454). Perhaps the period of "two weeks" refers to the herbage's early shoots, enough to attract the Bedouin.

32 A stereotyped phrase of boastful praise: the tribe is so strong that it routinely wanders through lands considered too dangerous by others; *tarʿā ba-l-khaṭar* "the camels graze in the area of danger (an expression conveying the tribe's confidence in its ability to repulse any enemy attack)" (Musil, *The Manners and Customs of the Rwala Bedouins*, 550) (CA *khaṭar* "imminent danger, peril, risk").

33 "Cheetahs for the hunt": *ṣēd nimr*, lit. "hunting with panthers," is attested in the earliest known Nabaṭī poetry; see "Banū Hilāl and Hunting with Cheetahs" in the online "Glossary of Style, Themes, and Motifs."

34 Again, a standard expression of praise. Cowards and misers would pitch their tents in a dip in the terrain so as not to attract unwanted visitors. These generous stalwarts, however, raise their tents on an elevation as an invitation to all comers. *Ḥumr*, "the red ones," are explained as tents made of red leather, while *sumr*, "the dark ones," are tents woven of the black hair of goats (Thānī, *Ibn Ẓāhir*, 104).

35 "Take no ruler's orders": *ʿtāt al-amr* (CA *ʿātin*, pl. *ʿutāt* "inordinately proud, averse from obedience" Lane, *Lexicon*, 1951). Among the

Bedouin, tribes that openly flout orders of town-based rulers come in for special admiration. Their recalcitrance is matched, and made possible, by the quality and training of "obedient" horses.

36 This is the only mention of a tribe by name in Ibn Ẓāhir's poetry and it has been the subject of much speculation among experts in the Emirates. For a discussion of this subject, see Introduction, p. xx. "Intrepid stalwarts": *shalāghīf*, one of the archaic epithets in vogue with tribal poets (*shallaghf*, "a word heard among tribesmen of Qays with the meaning of 'turbulent, agitated,'" Ibn Manẓūr, *Lisān*, 2316). The exact meaning is often unknown, and they have become omnibus terms for all kinds of chivalrous virtue.

37 See §1.32 above, where love has set the poet's heart ablaze. As his Bedouin belle belongs to Banū Hilāl, and since she stands for his youth, as the poet explained, the poet's nostalgia for her tribe, the epitome of romantic desert chivalry, is by implication also a requiem for the merriment of his young years.

38 That is, the Prophet Muhammad, who hails from the Meccan tribe of Quraysh.

39 The word for "verses," *amthāl*, also means "proverbs." The epithet "discerning, wise" (*fihīm*) is repeated in many of the poet's signature verses; it is also used for self-description by the eighteenth-century poet Ḥmēdān al-Shwēʿir: "Listen carefully, my boy, to this wise old man" (*yā-ṣbayy iftihim min ʿwēdin fihīm*) (Kurpershoek, *Arabian Satire*, §26.1); and is mentioned in the story about the genesis of Ibn Ẓāhir's talent through the intervention of a female jinni; see pp. <?>–51.

40 See also §10.34, where the poems are compared to buckets full of water. Like water, poetry is indispensable for survival, especially when crossing deserts in the hot season, a metaphor for demanding episodes in one's life. Similarly, the early Najdī poet al-Khalāwī says: "My tongue drew the verses from the well, molded / and adorned them with every beautiful shape" (*jidhabhā lsānī min janānī w-ṣāghih, ʿalā gālibin min kill mā zān jāt bih*) (Ibn Khamīs, *al-Khalāwī*, 305).

41 "Devotees": *rāmis*, lit. "speaker." Here it means an educated audience, connoisseurs of poetry whose judgment the poet fears and who

may question him on the meaning and quality of verses. If he captivates this elite, they will perpetuate his verses and cause his renown to spread far and wide.

42 "Doom-laden course": *ḥawādith ashyā*; like *ṣurūf al-dahr*, "the whimsical turns taken by fate." The "events" (*ḥawādith*) in poetry invariably mean "unfortunate events, events that dash hopes and optimistic expectations," even though grim outcomes are the only thing one can expect with certainty, as expressed in the verse of the early classical poet Mutammim ibn Nuwayrah: "The one thing I know for sure is the inevitability / that I am destined to be the sport of fate, but should I lament that?" (*wa-laqad ʿalimtu wa-lā maḥālata innanī, li-l-ḥādithāti fa-hal taraynī ajzaʿū*) (*al-Mufaḍḍaliyyāt*, 1:77; 2:23); see also §§11.16–18 on the inexorable march of the World that crushes everything in its way.

43 "Halcyon days": *ʿaṣr aṣ-ṣibā*, as in a poem of Rumayzān to Jabr ibn Sayyār: "After this, how I wish that those days would return, / my halcyon days, they belong by rights to me!" (*w-min ʿigb dhā yā-lēt al-ayyām tinthinī, bi-ʿaṣr aṣ-ṣibā f-anā bihin ḥagīg*) (Sowayan, *al-Shiʿr al-nabaṭī*, 477); also *ʿaṣr at-tiṣābī*, see §1.7, §1.38.

44 A close parallel to an image used by Ḥmēdān al-Shwēʿir: "I have packed up my equipment at the well: let someone else take my job, if he feels like it" (Kurpershoek, *Arabian Satire*, §5.15). The expression's popularity at the time is attested by a verse of Fayṣal al-Jumaylī, a poet of the Jabrid period: "I take my leave from the well, sling the leather trough over my shoulder: / another man with new buckets may take my job" (*anā ṣādrin ʿāllagt ḥōḍī bi-mankibī, wa-khallētha l-illī dlāh jdād*) (Sowayan, *al-Shiʿr al-nabaṭī*, 394). The same expression occurs in a verse by the late-nineteenth-century poet ʿAdwān al-Hirbīd: "I take my leave from the well, sling the leather trough over my shoulder: / my congratulations, you folks with new buckets") (*anā ṣādrin ʿallagt ḥōḍī bi-mankibī, w-hannātkum y-ahl al-ʿdād al-jidāyid*) (Sowayan, *Ayyām al-ʿArab*, 211).

45 See nn. 189 and 253 (§§8.22–23, §10.54) and §5.51 on the anthropomorphizing imagery used for thunderstorms that inundate the

land. "Laughter": It is a common trope in poetry for lightning to be compared to the flashing smile and glittering teeth of a beautiful woman, e.g., in the verses of the earlier Nabaṭī poet Ibn Zēd: "From where the sun sets rose clouds flashing with light, / like the faces of young beauties who dropped their veils; / to moisten the robes of the night and then tear them to shreds / with bursts of lightning that blind the beholders' eyes" (*sarā min mighīb ash-shams yāḍī lakinnih, wjūh al-ʿadhārā ṭāyḥāt al-bakhānig / tarwā bi-thōb al-lēl thummin yishiggih, sanā bārigin yaghshā ʿyūn ar-rawāmig* (Sowayan, *al-Shiʿr al-nabaṭī*, 307).

46 That is, one should not risk standing in the way of whatever takes a preordained, natural course, as in the saying, "A torrent does not deviate from its usual course" (*sēl an-naḥā mā yinʿadil ʿan majārīh*) (al-Juhaymān, *Amthāl*, 3:291, and Kurpershoek, *Arabian Romantic*, §14.2.56, §29.20).

47 Ḥawāmī's wells: Ghadīr al-Ḥuwaymī (Abū Shihāb and Abū Malḥah, *Ibn Ẓāhir*, 205).

48 The first hemistich is identical to the first hemistich of §12.22.

49 In recent times, the poet Ibn Batlā included such reports about the whereabouts of rainfall in his verses, starting: "When visited by a wayfarer traveling in the wake of the clouds, / we press him for more of his glad tidings as he brings us the news" (*lā minnih lifānā ṭ-ṭurgī illī gifā l-ghēmāt, lifā bi-l—khabar wi-nkhaṣṣisih min tisārīrih*) (Kurpershoek, *Bedouin Poets of the Dawāsir Tribe*, 143–63).

50 Perhaps Ghadīr al-Ḥuwaymī is meant (Thānī, *Ibn Ẓāhir*, 369).

51 "Frenzied" because big herds of thirsty camels have arrived and must be restrained and watered, an arduous job, see n. 282.

52 "No doubts": *walā ankart minh*, as in the line of Abū Qays ibn al-Aslat, "You did not recognize my face when you scanned its features" (*ankartihī ḥīnā tawassamtihī*) (*al-Mufaḍḍaliyyāt*, 1:565; 2:225). The poet's conceit is that it is not the maiden who looks like a gazelle, but a gazelle who looks suspiciously like a maiden.

53 "Assault" is how *ghāsh* was explained to me; also, synonym of *jāsh, yijīsh* "to rage, boil" (Abū Shihāb and Abū Malḥah, *Ibn Ẓāhir*, 161);

and in the saying, "flies descend in swarms on date syrup" (*adh-dhibābah mā tghāwish illā ʿalā d-dibs*), on the tendency of people to be attracted in masses to whatever is desirable (Ḥanẓal, *Jāmiʿ al-amthāl*, 154). Locusts are the Bedouin's image of choice to convey the notion of overwhelming multitudes that cannot be resisted. This imagery is also used to describe the poet's anxious state of mind when he is in the grip of inspiration, e.g., "Woe unto a heart swarmed over by creeping young locusts, / wave after wave alighting on the heart's branches at dusk" (Kurpershoek, *The Poetry of ad-Dindān*, 127). The Tihāmah in the Hijaz, in western Arabia along the coast of the Red Sea, is frequently mentioned as the region where swarms of locusts originate.

54 "Stray camels," *garāyif*, pl. of *girīfah* (pronounced in Emirati dialect as *jirīfah*; the root is related to CA *qarifa*, "to loath, feel disgusted," i.e., the stray camel's discomfort with the unfamiliar place), explained to me as "camel that has come from elsewhere," for instance if sold, and keeps longing, *tiḥinn*, for its place of origin. The metaphor is meant to convey that the poet knows many verses by poets from other tribal groups, but is careful to keep those separate from his store of home-grown poetry. The early classical poet al-Musayyab ibn ʿAlas pictures verses of poetry that move and gather at waterholes like camels, and their owners' curiosity at the appearance of powerful strangers among the herds: "I will dedicate an ode carried on the wings of the winds, / passing through the lands on its way to al-Qaʿqaʿ; / it waters at the wells as an exotic marvel, / recited over and over to rapturous crowds," *fa-la-ʾuhdiyanna maʿā l-riyāḥi qaṣīdatan, minnī mughal-ghalatan ilā l-Qaʿqāʿī / taridu l-miyāha fa-mā tazālu gharībatan, fī l-qawmi bayna tamaththulin wa-samāʿī* (*al-Mufaḍḍaliyyāt*, 1:96–97; 2:31). And in the same vein, al-Mutanabbī: "My camels for you are on the move: / they do not sojourn in a fixed abode; / As soon as my rhymes have been spoken, / they jump over mountains and cross the seas" (*wa-ʿindī laka l-shurradu l-sāʾirā-, -tu lā yakhtaṣiṣna mina l-arḍi dārā / qawāfin idhā sirna ʿan miqwalī, wathabna l-jibāla wa-khuḍna l-biḥārā*) (*Dīwān*, 2:95).

55 As in the narratives about Ibn Ẓāhir, other poets and aficionados would travel from afar for a meeting with the famous poet, listening to his recitations and memorizing his work for transmission, and in order to put his reputation to the test. This verse gives a concise picture of the oral nature of his poetry.

56 Climbing a solitary height or high dune is a common motif in the prelude, which may or may not be part of the poet's real efforts to come to grips with the onset of inspiration. See Kurpershoek, *The Poetry of ad-Dindān*, the section on "The lonely mountain scene," 38–39.

57 This poem stands out for its more than usual abundance of rhetorical effects. In this verse, tearfulness is accentuated by repetition of the wiping: *misūḥ* [. . .] *misūḥ* [. . .] *al-masḥ*.

58 Cf. the verses "The callous won't even let you squeeze water from moist earth" (*wa-l-khibl mā yasgīk min raṭb ath-tharā*) (Kurpershoek, *Arabian Satire*, §12.25), and "The ground's moisture dissipates and clouds evaporate" (*w-abʿad tharā nagʿih w-kannat mzūnih*) (Kurpershoek, *Arabian Romantic*, §32.6, 234n368). Cool, moist earth found deeper in the ground is applied to reduce pain.

59 That is, there is no medicine for lovesickness.

60 As explained to me, the cruel lady stands for the World (*al-dunyā*), and its whims and fickleness. A wise person does not expect any good from her and does not seek to mollify her, because the inevitable disappointment will only make him suffer even more.

61 The verse alludes to the expression "the rope of hope" (CA *ḥabl al-rajāʾ*), i.e., "to cut off all hope."

62 A hyperbolic way of saying that the beloved's promises to her creditors (that is, those who have acted with sincerity toward her and have kept their word) are just empty words. Even hardship itself, *al-ʿisir* ("the scarcity of food that prevents people from exercising their duty of hospitality and generosity as they would wish"), complains about her unfaithfulness (Abū Shihāb and Abū Malḥah, *Ibn Ẓāhir*, 164; Thānī, *Ibn Ẓāhir*, 144). "Promises," *wʿādhā*, for *wʿūdhā*, because of the exigencies of rhyme.

63 In verses §3.23 and §3.24 the poet reveals the true identity of his beloved: his own lost youth. Sultan Alameemi avers that old age and youth (*al-shayb wa-l-shabāb*) is the main theme of Ibn Ẓāhir's work, and behind it, of course, the search for answers to the question of life and death.

64 "Grim reaper": *ṣayyād al-arwāḥ*, lit. "hunter of spirits," explained as the Angel of Death, Izrāʿīl. A similar expression occurs in al-Khalāwī's poetry: "Poems of infinite value to the audience, / when the spirit's adversary is lurking, ready to snatch up the soul" (*giṣāydin lā bidd al-malā tistifīdhā, l amsā gharīm ar-rūḥ li-r-rūḥ ṣāyid*) (Ibn Khamīs, *al-Khalāwī*, 365). See also §4.27.

65 Here, *ardāf* is not the plural of *ridf*, "rump," but of *ridīf*, "co-rider, person who sits behind the saddle, holding on to its rear knob."

66 The sequence of verses starting with the exhortation *lā tāmin*, "you are not safe from, should not be confident that mishaps will not befall you," and *lā tāyis, tayyis, yayyis*, "you, he, should not despair of (things taking a turn for the better)," occurs in other poetry of the period (e.g., Sowayan, *al-Shiʿr al-nabaṭī*, 418). For the common motif "beware of the world," i.e., unexpected blows of fate (*lā tāmin ad-dunya*), and its use by Rumayzān, see n. 177 to §7.8.

67 This verse is similar to one by Abū Ḥamzah al-ʿĀmirī, perhaps the earliest Nabaṭī poet: "Be patient! One day your suffering will abate, / make way for ease, as dry watercourses are filled with torrents" (*iṣbir fa-lā budd ash-shadāyid tinjilī, bi-rakhā wa-lā budd al-misīl yisīlā*) (Sowayan, *al-Shiʿr al-nabaṭī*, 275). And al-Khalāwī: "A dry valley that ran with water must do so again, / if not this year, then the year after" (*w-wādin jarā lā bidd yajrī min al-ḥayā, immā jarā ʿāmin jarā ʿām ʿāyid*) (Ibn Khamīs, *al-Khalāwī*, 56). Arabic editions end the verse with *sayyal ʿitādha*, where *ʿitād* (CA *ʿatād* "equipment, materiel") was explained as meaning "all of its parts, foundations, basis." However, some MSS give *sēlin ʿtādhā*. For the sake of meter, the *tanwīn* of *sēl* ("flood") should be assimilated to the following verb, *iʿtādhā*, which is used for a valley that has received a torrent following

life-bringing rains, in the sense of *aʿādhā*, "brought back (the herbage)," e.g., "May (the tree) be irrigated by rains of al-Thurayyā's star" (*ʿasāh min wabl ath-Thrayyā tʿād*) (Sowayan, *Ayyām al-ʿArab*, 288), and "May rains shower your land and return the green, O Jabr" (*laʿall al-ḥayā yā-Jabr yiʿtād dārkum*) (*al-Shiʿr al-nabaṭī*, 463).

68 "Dark spots": *ath-thalāth jānī* (*gānī*, CA *aḥmar qānī* "dark red"; in the MSS, the *qāf* has been replaced by *jīm*, in accordance with Emirati pronunciation); *siwādhā*: "the three (slabs of stone under the cooking pot, *al-hawādī*), (left) dark black (stains)."

69 Lit. "(as much as) what is carried in the vessels, gushed forth in tears"; in Bedouin poetry and usage, *maʿāmīl*, sg. *maʿmūl*, has the meaning of "utensils needed for the preparation of coffee," but here it is explained as "the spouts of the waterskins, the place where they are closed and tied up" (Thānī, *Ibn Ẓāhir*, 150).

70 Tersely, this verse makes a point readily understood by those steeped in desert and oasis culture. The Bedouin await the end of the hot season (*al-gēḍ*, CA *al-qayẓ*), the time of the date harvest, to stock up on dates in preparation for departure to desert pastures. This ends the poet's proximity to his beloved: she leaves with her tribe. Therefore, the poet compares himself to a cultivator who rejoices in the hot season's harvest, i.e., the presence of the beloved, but is sorry to see the Bedouin depart as a result of this harvest. See Kurpershoek, *Arabian Romantic*, where this cyclical movement of the seasons and love is the principal theme. Here *al-gēḍ* "the hot season" means the dates, *ruṭab*, that ripen in the summer; *himād* is explained as "ripe dates, ready to be harvested."

71 In this verse, the poet gives expression to the notion that there is no chain of cause and effect independent of God's will. Causal relations exist because they are in accordance with certain habits of God, which could change at His pleasure. Similarly, in a verse by al-ʿUlaymī in praise of Qaṭan ibn Qaṭan ibn Qaṭan, who ruled Oman in the second half of the sixteenth century: "I said, 'These are God's beautiful habits, / how many times did we not travel far, only to return'" (*fa-gilt ʿawāyid allāh al-jimīlah, fa-yāmā gid tagharrabnā w-jīnā*) (Sowayan,

al-Shiʿr al-nabaṭī, 358); and the famous verse of al-Ḥuṭay'ah: "One's good works will not go unrewarded: / the covenant between God and humans will not cease" (*man yafʿali l-khayra lā yaʿdam jawāziyah, lā yadhhabu l-ʿurfu bayna llāhi wa-l-nāsī*) (al-Iṣfahānī, *al-Aghānī*, 2:185; al-Ḥuṭay'ah, *Dīwān al-Ḥuṭay'ah bi-riwāyat wa-sharḥ Ibn Sikkīt*, 120).

72 The notion that a generous soul, especially one who skimps on his own outlay in order to entertain guests, will end up with a reward bigger than his sacrifice, is prominent in popular wisdom and poetry; see p. xxxiii of Introduction and n. 135 to §12.40.

73 "Lofty castles": *banāyā gṣūrhā*; the plural of *gaṣr*, "castle," receives the emphasis from its rhyme position. The physical origins of the imagery are referred to in the poetry of Ibn Ẓāhir's era, e.g., by Jabr ibn Sayyār in his advice on how to rule a "city state" like his town of al-Qaṣab: "If you wish your land to be held in respectful regard, / make sure to have it fenced with walls; / And with fortified buildings and buttressed towers, / towers that rise up like mountain bluffs; / Once you've completed your constructions, sleep in it, / and let your armed men be its battlements" (*ilā baghēt ad-dār yithbit ʿizzahā, f-ijʿal ʿalā awṭānahā ḥīṭānahā / w-ḥaṣṣan mibānīhā w-timm brūjahā, kinn al-brūj an-nāyifāt rʿānahā / fa-lā stitamm lik al-binā' f-nimhā, w-ijʿal ḥamām al-gaṣr rūs ikhwānahā*) (Sowayan, *al-Shiʿr al-nabaṭī*, 453).

74 Cf. §3.3 and §§15.36–37. "Centuries old" might be connected to the same phrase in §4.34: one may learn from history or neglect its lessons at one's peril. It is also a common trope in the poetry of his era, e.g., al-Khalāwī: "Our witness are our precursors' works of poetry: / consult them and they'll tell you all you need" (*w-lanā sābigin tashhad dawāwīn ghērnā, salūhā w-tinbīkum bi-l-akhbār jāyibih*) (Ibn Khamīs, *al-Khalāwī*, 305).

75 "Read": lit. "verses recited by many (written) in letters (or messages, *risāyil*)"; see next note.

76 This verse, like §3.1, §4.5, and §§15.36–37, might be cited in support of the assumption that these poems existed in writing from the outset. However, the paraphernalia of writing (ink, pen, paper) and reading (letters, messages, reciting from paper) are ubiquitous in the

work of poets who were illiterate or flourished in a predominantly oral culture; see Sowayan, *Nabaṭī Poetry*, 101. The pre-Islamic poet Thaʿlabah ibn ʿAmr pictures "a scribe, bent over his work, inkpot in hand, / moving his fingers forward and back again" (*akabba ʿalayhā kātibun bi-dawātihī, yuqīmu yadayhī tāratan wa-yukhālifū*), accompanied by Lyall's perceptive comment: "He was probably himself unable to read and write, and the details he mentions seem to show that the art of writing had a curiosity for him as an outsider rather than as one who practiced it" (al-Mufaḍḍal, *al-Mufaḍḍaliyyāt*, 1:561; 2:222–23).

77 Being remembered as a poet forever is already a common trope in the earliest known Arabic poetry, e.g., this passage in a famous poem by al-Muzarrid: "For certain, the exquisite verses I throw at my opponent / will be the song of travelers at night and the chant of camel drivers; / They will be memorized by multitudes of reciters / and resound in lands far and wide; / Gaining in brilliance as they are repeated / by devotees who taste and weigh the verses on their tongues" (*zaʿīmun li-man qādhaftuhu bi-awābidin, yughannī bi-hā l-sārī wa-tuḥdā l-rawāḥilū / mudhakkaratin tulqā kathīran ruwātuhā, ḍawāḥin la-hā fī kulli arḍin azāmilū / tukarru fa-lā tazdādu illā stināratan, idhā rāzati l-shiʿra l-shifāhu l-ʿawāmilū*) (*al-Mufaḍḍaliyyāt*, 1:179; 2:61). And in poetry from Ibn Ẓāhir's era, e.g., al-Khalāwī: "Perhaps those who recite our work will remember us / with a prayer that imbues our bones with new life" (*laʿalla allidhī yarwūnhā yadhkirūnī / bi-tarḥīmtin tūḍiʿ ʿẓāmī jidāyid* (Ibn Khamīṣ, *al-Khalāwī*, 365).

78 See §3.6 and n. 56.

79 Love lost to distance is a major theme in poetry. See the section "Departure, Separation, and Loss: Love Near or Far" in the online "Glossary of Style, Themes, and Motifs." The theme in Dhū l-Rummah's poetry has entered popular sayings currently in use: "How far Mayy has traveled from the camp where her camels had kneeled" (*yā-biʿd Mayy ʿan manākh al-rikāyib*) (al-Kuwaytī, *Yaqūl al-mutawaṣṣif: amthāl wa-aqwāl shaʿbiyyah jumiʿat min manṭiqat*

al-ʿAyn, 1:117). In the poetry of our period, *niyā* is a common indication of distance, e.g., in an ode in praise of Qaṭan ibn Qaṭan by the poet Muwāfiq, composed in a mixture of classical and Nabaṭī Arabic: "If the one I love has traveled far away from me, / at a great distance, it means great calamity" (*w-frāg min nahtiwīh in bāt muntaziḥan, ʿannā biʿīd an-niyā miḥanun min al-milan*) (Sowayan, *al-Shiʿr al-nabaṭī*, 349); and Jabr ibn Sayyār: "For me, your life is worth more than all those I'd gladly see cast beyond India, / or dumped on distant islands beyond China" (*fidētik illī mn warā al-hind bi-l-mnā, warā aṣ-ṣīn maglūʿ an-niyā fī jizāyirih*) (Sowayan, *al-Shiʿr al-nabaṭī*, 486). In this context "distance," *niyā*, is presented as an active agent, responsible for removing the beloved to an unbridgeable distance, as in the verse of Rumayzān: "Callously indifferent, distance caused the lovers to separate" (*wa-ṣarf an-niyā bēn al-mḥibbīn fārig*) (Sowayan, *al-Shiʿr al-nabaṭī*, 478); it is similar in early classical poetry, e.g., in a line of ʿAlqamah ibn ʿAbadah: "to the land of a man who lives far off" (*dāra mri'in kāna nā'iyan*) (*al-Mufaḍḍaliyyāt*, 1:776; 2:330) (CA *na'ā* "to be far away, remote"; *na'y* "remoteness"). See also §1.11, §6.16, §10.64–65. "Time": *ftūrha*, explained as *fatrāt* "periods of time."

80 This bleak scene presages the landscape of the end time of §§4.59–61. The melancholy view of the beloved's deserted abode is one of the most common tropes of Arabian poetry and, later mostly in a metaphorical sense, in Arab love poetry in general. For instance, this verse's wording parallels Ibn Sbayyil's: "The resting places' cattle droppings have crumbled / to fine dust blown about the abandoned site" (*minzālhum taḍri ʿalēh al-maʿāṭīn taḍri ʿalēh mn al-ḍuwāri habūbih*) (Kurpershoek, *Arabian Romantic*, §3.3).

81 The first word of the verse, *ʿamīdarah*, is explained as "empty site" by Abū Shihāb and Abū Malḥah, *Ibn Ẓāhir*, 67, but this probably amounts to a guess. In some MSS, the word occurs as *ghamīdarah*, and Sultan Alameemi informed me that he encountered this word in Kuwait with the meaning of "chaos, disturbance."

82 The old she-gazelle, *ʿanz*, "which leads and guards a herd of gazelles, takes her post on a height, scenting the enemy," as in the line of

poetry: “Oh, the eye of the gazelle, who stamps noisily on the rocky slope / scenting the breeze, while the other gazelles follow her” (*yā-ʿēn ʿanzin tiṣaffag bi-l-ʿarāǵībī, tatlī mahabb al-hawā wa-ṣ-ṣēd yatlīhā*) (Musil, *Rwala*, 200–1).

83 Lit. “ugly appearance” (*gibḥ al-yimā*, CA *qubḥ al-jimā*) is explained as *umm ṭawq* (Abū Shihāb and Abū Malḥah, *Ibn Ẓāhir*, 67): the small tawny desert owl, and the related Omani owl, is known for its hair-raising shrieks, which can be heard on http://twitter.com/natgeomagarab/status/838087346289520641.

84 Lit. “without a friend who comes to your aid” (*yighūr*).

85 “Hoots”: “The owl, *būm*, as the embodiment of a dead person’s soul, is always savage and shrieking, and it is alone in the desolate dwellings and the sepulchers and where slain men fall and where death occurs” (Homerin, “Echoes of a Thirsty Owl: Death and Afterlife in Pre-Islamic Arabic Poetry,” 168). The shrieks may be taken as a slain man’s cry for revenge, as in Dhū l-Iṣbaʿ’s line: “I will strike you down in the place where the owl [*al-hāmah*, which rises from a dead person’s skull] is calling, ‘Quench my thirst!’” (*aḍribka ḥaythu taqūlu l-hāmatu sqūnī*) (*al-Mufaḍḍaliyyāt*, 1:321; 2:115–16); Ibn Ẓāhir’s aim is to strike the melancholy note of loss, not the Najdī one of tribal boasting sounded in ʿAbīd ibn al-Abraṣ: “And many the desert wherein the owl hooted and the screech-owl shrieked (I crossed)” (Lyall, *The Dīwān of ʿAbīd ibn al-Abraṣ*, 31).

86 Here *būm*, the generic name for “owl,” is used. It may refer to the common barn owl. The rhyme word, *khūrhā*, might be a plural derived from CA *ākhir*, “the last,” according to Sulṭān Alameemi. The monotonous, funereal calls of the owl will go unanswered, as the cries of a drover who leads the herd from the front will not be heard by camels that trail behind the herd.

87 “Women terrified by news”: An ancient motif, graphically depicted in the scene where the news of Hector’s death dawns on his wife, Andromache, and her handmaidens (*The Iliad*, 469).

88 Note the consonance between the words *ruwābī*, “hills” (CA *rabwah*, pl. *rubā*), and *marābī* “place where one has grown up, habitually

lives" (CA *marbā*). According to Abū Shihāb and Abū Malḥah, *Ibn Ẓāhir*, 68, the plural *marābī* here means "small birds." "Soft chirps of the bird": *ḥisūs* (CA *ḥasīs* "faint noise, soft sound of voices").

89 This verse occurs only in the edition of Alameemi and, with slightly different wording, in two MSS. "Separation," *hayr* in the Emirati dialect (CA *hajr*). As explained to me, the rhyme word *wgūrhā* is the plural of *wagr* "affliction, injury; burden, load." Here its meaning is similar to the expression "the load of (sinful) passion" (*ḥiml al-ghayy*), as in the 1703 poem by Khalīl ibn ʿĀyid, nicknamed Muṭawwaʿ al-Maskūf: "You burdened me with heavy loads of sinful passion" (*ḥammaltnī bi-ḥmūl ghayyin thigīlāt*) (Sowayan, *al-Shiʿr al-nabaṭī*, 494).

90 "Grief": *mishtikā* "complaint, injured feeling." A tautological figure of speech: it became so bad that the complaint itself started complaining. The conceit is similar to the one used in §3.19: hardship itself complaining about the rigors.

91 "Youthful succulence:" *rayyāntin ghuḍḍat aṣ-ṣibā*; *rayyān* (CA *rayyān* "well-watered, luxuriant, lush, verdant, full, plump, succulent, juicy," derived from the verb *rawiya* "to drink one's fill, to be irrigated") is one of the key words in this poetry. It occurs as an epithet of fulsome love (*aṣ-ṣibā*) and youth (*shibāb*), represented by the beautiful beloved, in Ibn Ẓāhir's poetry a metaphor for his own youth, invariably connected with lamentations over its departure and the onset of old age, as also in §6.13, §10.51, §10.68, and §16.52. It carries the same connotations in other poems of the period.

92 "Chamomile": *jiḥwān* (CA *quḥwiyān*); the flower was rinsed (*jalā*, "to clean, polish") with dewdrops to attain its famous beauty. In this verse occurs a seeming incongruence of features that are pristine and tender, like flower petals, praised in one breath with rippling layers of fat, *ḥaḍāya* (synonym of CA *aʿkān*). In fact, both answer to the canon of stereotyped beauty found in traditional Arab poetry: in this case, finely chiseled white teeth and ample haunches. The chamomile in this verse is already implied in the previous line: the smiling front teeth (here a metonymy for the lips and mouth) have just burst from

the soft soil (*finīgin rbāha*, CA *fanaq* "plentifulness, softness, delicacy in living," (Lane, *Lexicon*, 2450) and *rubā* "hilly ground").

93 As explained to me, the perfume, *ʿuṭr*, came from a bottle, as a fluid, *dimā*. "Sprinkled on her locks": *mdāwi ghdūrha*, explained as perfuming, *taʿṭīr*, of her hair.

94 In almost the same words, the prominence of a smiling mouth occurs in a poem by the former head of state of the Emirates, Shaykh Zāyid: "You are resplendent, with a ravishing smile" (*lak mibsamin zāhiyyin tizahhīh*). "Ravishing": *tāyih*, as explained to me, "extraordinary, the pinnacle (of beauty)" (CA *tāha*).

95 An ancient and well-worn trope in Arab poetry: the beloved is the reason for the disease, and only she is capable of administering the medicine that will cure the poet's agony, e.g., the eighteenth-century Najdī poet Rumayzān: "She is my ailment, misery, and disease, and she is the cure that revives the dead" (Sowayan, *al-Shiʿr al-nabaṭī*, 458). The beloved is the expert who knows it all (for the sake of rhyme, *khabūrhā* stands for *khabīrhā*, "expert").

96 "Snatch my soul": *mishtāg rigīb*, lit. "watching me with hungry anticipation," i.e., for the moment that I expire. That is, old age and a premonition of death. For *rigīb* (CA *raqīb*), see nn. 260 and 345. The expression is reminiscent of the scene in which the early poet Mutammim ibn Nuwayrah imagines himself being watched by death in the shape of a hyena: "Woe is me for the long-maned creature, with tufts of hair on her neck / that comes to me limping on three legs; / She watches me through the day and looks about her: / the spark of life that is left in me gives her pause, but it is I she craves" (*yā lahfa min ʿarfāʾa dhāti falīlatin, jāʾat ilayya ʿalā thalthin takhmaʿū / ẓallat turāṣidunī wa-tanẓuru ḥawlahā, wa-yurībuhā ramaqun wa-innī muṭmiʿū* (*al-Mufaḍḍaliyyāt*, 1:75; 2:22).

97 "Warning": The absence of warning ("warner" *nidhīr*) at the appearance of the calamities plotted by the "world, fate," including old age, is a standard trope in poetry. Arazi notes that in edifying poetry gray hair is considered "a portent (*nadhīr*) of death [. . .] God sends this advance warning to allow men to prepare themselves on the eve of

imminent decease" (Arazi, "al-Shayb wa 'l-shabāb" in *EI2*). The world attacks (*tighīr*), as old age launches its assaults by surprise (*dahā*): the world, time, and evil fate operate as a triad. See n. 298.

98 For a similar expression, the Jabrid poet Ibn Zayd: "(May God annihilate) those who put their faith in this world and its people, / even if they are skilled and smart" (*w-min yāmin ad-dunyā w-min yāmin ahalhā, ilā kān min dhāt al-glūb al-ḥadhāyig*).

99 "On parting": *lī ḥaggat al-fargā*, lit. "when separation became a fact, happened" (CA *ḥaqqa* "to be confirmed as a truth or a fact; to become manifest as an indubitable fact; to happen without doubt or uncertainty," Lane, *Lexicon*, 605), as in the verse of Dhū l-Rummah: "I became certain that separation had become an indubitable fact, / and that my hopes for the tribe's maiden were dashed" (*fa-ayqantu anna l-bayna qad jadda jidduhū, wa-anna llatī arjū min al-ḥayyi lā hiyā*) (*Dīwān*, 1305).

100 The usual expression is "the millstone of war" (which crushes all and sundry). Here, separation (*al-bayn*) is given a kindred meaning. The same expression is used in a verse by the nineteenth-century poet Muḥammad ʿAbd Allāh al-Qāḍī: "The turns of the quernstone on its support sent me off / and the decrees of fate drove me to the left, away from our unison" (*ʿan ad-dār dāratnī raḥā al-bayn b-athfālī, wa-l-agdār dāratnī ʿan ash-shaml bi-shmālī*). The verse may have the literal meaning: "Not everyone who tries his hand at it knows how to make it turn," or "none of those who tried succeeded in turning it," i.e., knew how to deal with the pain of separation. Given the context (the advent of the enemy, to wit old age), I have opted for the latter. An Emirati proverb reflects this meaning: "Separation or blindness" (*al-bayn wallā al-ʿamā*), i.e., separation is a better choice than blindness, because the latter is irrevocable (Ḥanẓal, *Jāmiʿ al-amthāl*, 199).

101 It is customary for the poets of the period to paint the "world" and "fate" as "conceited, fickle, and teasing beauties who smile at their victim, feed him with illusions and false promises," only to leave the lover in the lurch, much worse off than before he had been ensnared.

Sowayan, *al-Shiʿr al-nabaṭī*, 371; see also Abū Shihāb and Abū Malḥah, *Ibn Ẓāhir*, 63.

102 "For ages": *gidāmin ʿṣūrhā*, a repetition of the same phrase in rhyme position in §4.4. In both instances, the message is that people should have known better from past experience and available knowledge. This wisdom is reinforced by the final conclusion of §§4.57–60. Hence, the references to human experience across the ages of §4.4, §§4.34–35, and §§4.57–60 are embedded as waymarks in the poem's natural and psychological cycle, and its compressed repetition in the verses that start with the Flood (§4.51) to the end; see n. 117. At the stylistic level, these references, and the distribution of other key words, are instrumental in stitching the poem's intricate structure together.

103 Here the choice for translation has not been a generic "holy books," but the specificity of *tawrāthā w-zabūrhā*: "Torahs and Psalms." The juxtaposition points in that direction: Torah revealed to Moses and the Psalms to David. According to al-Ṭabarī, *zabūr* "is the name of the book that was revealed to David, just as He named the book that was revealed to Moses as the Torah and that which was revealed to Jesus as the Gospel and that which was revealed to Muḥammad as the Furqān, because that is the name by which what was revealed to David was known. The Arabs say *zabūr Dāwūd*, and because of that the rest of the peoples know this book" (J. Horovitz and R. Firestone, "Zabūr" in *EI2*). In the Qur'an, the three references to *zabūr* are associated with revelation given to David, while the plural *zubur* may refer to certain heavenly books ("Zabūr" in *EI2*). Possibly the poet had in mind this latter meaning of the Qur'an, and heavenly books mentioned in it (also, *zabūr* fits this poem's rhyme).

104 Lit. "my liver (*kabd*)," an organ considered the locus of rancorous feelings, hatred, and spite. A *ṣifriyyah* is "a large copper cooking pot" (Holes, *Dialect*, 3:121). The water inside boils on a high fire (CA *ḥamasha* "to enrage, infuriate") and stews the meat with such violence that the pot's lid is almost blown off (*naww ash-shuwāyā*, *naww*, explained to me as "meat"; CA *nuyūʾ*, "raw meat," *laḥmun niʾun*, vernacular *nayy* "fat").

105 In his portrayal of emotions at their highest pitch, the poet presents a hyperbolic image of a cooking pot that almost explodes because of the outsized fire lit under it. "Rag": *khām* (lit. "raw material; linen, calico"); "a fire was set ablaze" (*ṭimā* "to increase, become more than usual"; *ṭāmī* "water that rises to the highest level in the well"). "Lid's valve": *mahzam* (lit. "place of escape"). The boiling and violent bubbling of the water is expressed by *ṭufūrha* (*ṭifar* "to increase suddenly").

106 "Brings relief": *yhawwin min adhāhā*, lit. "eases the harm it does," as in the line "all beings are made to taste from the good and the bad" (*kill ḥayyin dhāyigin ṭībih w-adhāh*) (CA *adhan, adhāh* "damage, harm, pain, injury, trouble") (Sowayan, *al-Shiʿr al-nabaṭī*, 531). "Boiling insides": *min ṭimāhā*, lit. "(the pot's) violent bubbling." "Erupt anew": *yizīdhā*, lit. "increases"; it is a common topos in love poetry and other genres that whenever the pain seems to subside, it returns with a vengeance, as also in §9.5; e.g., Ibn Zayd's verse: "May God requite you, as you have wronged them / with evil that worsens as soon as it seems to ease" (*athābk fīhā allāh ḥēthik ẓalamtahā, bi-sharrin ila gilt hawwan zād*) (Sowayan, *al-Shiʿr al-nabaṭī*, 300).

107 "Tight-lipped": a traditional virtue of the lover and generally, as expressed in the proverb "Keep silent and your tongue in check, and you will succeed" (*qad aflaḥ as-sākit aṣ-ṣimūt*) (al-Juhaymān, *Amthāl*, 10:255).

108 The poet reiterates that not for the first time he is being abandoned by his faithless friend. It seems as if she has dissolved into thin air: an allusion to the ancient motif of the beloved's abandoned dwelling with such remains as the blackened spot where the cooking pots stood, and a few windswept traces in the sand. In this case, there is no sign of human habitation: all has disappeared (*ghabāya*, pl. of *ghabiyy* "hidden," CA *ghabbā* "to cover, conceal"; and *duthūr* "obliterated," CA *dathara* "to fall into oblivion; to be blotted out, effaced"). The word is repeated twice in the next verse (*adthārin, duthūrhā*) to mark the transition from being buried to revival by the advent of rain. It may also mean that this separation has renewed the painful memories of previous separations.

109 Presumably, "works" (*ʿimāyil*, CA *ʿamal*) here is used in the passive sense of "undergoing the effects of," hence "travails," with similar connotations. This thematic transition, and its contrasting pair of a desolate, battered heart and revival of scorched earth, recalls Ibn Sbayyil's reversal of private and public values: his heart's springtime is the hot season's advent, i.e., the presence of the beautiful Bedouin girls at the wells of his village; see Kurpershoek, *Arabian Romantic*. But it has an additional layer as a transition from the desolation of the deserted camp, itself an expression of lost love. It is another example of *ḥusn al-takhalluṣ*, dexterity in moving from one theme to another without friction, humorously mocked as: "he (the poet) holds the locks of the one he loves in his hand, until he clings to the beard of the one he praises" (van Gelder, *Beyond the Line: Classical Arabic Literary Critics and the Coherence and Unity of the Poem*, 205).

110 The grass was so plentiful that the sheep found enough grazing in one desert dale (*hōr* "a wide expanse of low and soggy ground"; CA *hawr*) and did not have to be driven to any other spot.

111 The thunderstorm that engulfed the coastal area, and mountain ranges to its east, is compared to a noisy wedding party where the beating of sticks (*ganāh* "spear; short loaded club, heavy cane ending in a knob"; CA *qanāh*, pl. *qanā* "spear, shaft") resembles the thunder crashes, while the flickering lights of the torches are like streaks of lightning.

112 This verse has engendered much discussion among Emirati historians and literary circles, amplified by the scarcity of historical fact in Ibn Ẓāhir's poetry. The narrator Khalīfah ibn ʿAlī al-Kitbī believed that the flood was God's punishment for the arrogance and the riches in gold hoarded by the inhabitants (Alameemi, *Ibn Ẓāhir*, 223). However, available sources make no mention of a tsunami-like calamity or huge flood (called *al-ṭabʿah*, "drowning, flood," Alameemi, *Ibn Ẓāhir*, 223; Thāni, *Ibn Ẓāhir*, 422–24) that could account for such a large number of victims in a natural disaster in the seventeenth century. The only possible occurrence is a severe flood in the nineteenth century, which some have taken as an argument to situate Ibn Ẓāhir

in that period, an untenable proposition. Quite possibly, the verse refers to a calamitous flooding within living memory at the poet's time. In any case, the most likely explanation is that "ninety thousand" is a formulaic number, as is common in Arabian oral poetry and narratives (see "Formulaic Numbers" in the online "Glossary of Style, Themes, and Motifs"). For instance, in the poems ascribed to Banū Hilāl, the number ninety or multiples of it are recurrent. In these cases, it simply means a lot of people. The number thousand has been tagged on to the formulaic ninety. See the Jabrid poet Fayṣal al-Jumaylī: "I stayed with her for ninety years, suffering / her oppression and cracking of the whip" (*agamt bihā tisʿīn ʿāmin w-ṣābir, ʿalā ḍēmhā w-illī yijī min ṣgūʿhā*) (Sowayan, *al-Shiʿr al-nabaṭī*, 397). The word for "unbeliever," *gūr*, derives from Turkish *gāvur* (also written as *gawur* or *giaour*) "infidel." According to Abū Shihāb and Abū Malḥah's comment, *Ibn Ẓāhir*, 73, in this context it denotes *al-bānyān*, a word derived from Gujarati used to denote traders from the Indian subcontinent.

113 This sequence of verse (§§4.51–55, and see the introduction to this poem) is part of a concept that is found in several poems of the era: creative destruction, i.e., nature's seasonal cycles of destruction and revival, *dammār ʿammār* (lit. destroying and bringing to bloom) that come with the alternation of drought and rain, e.g., in the line of al-Shuʿaybī (see, on this poet and Ibn Ẓāhir, Introduction p. xviii) as part of prayers for rain: "A wild, roaring torrent that sweeps up all things, / destroying and fertilizing the lands in its path" (*jarrāf dharrāfin difūgin rāfig, dammār ʿammārin li-mā yitʿahhadā*) (Sowayan, *al-Shiʿr al-nabaṭī*, 373–76). Accordingly, it is fitting that the sequence itself is a repetition of a similar cycle in §§4.40–48 (and in other poems): separation and loss, followed by rain and revival, which then leads to destruction in a flood that somewhat later results in lovely aromas and fruits (the dates that herald the beloved's departure with her tribe once they have loaded up on dates and victuals) until it all ends in death for the present generation and finally the end of the world.

114 The highest date palms are called *ʿiwwānah*, pl. *ʿawāwīn* (al-Maṭrūshī, *al-Lahjah al-Imārātiyyah*, 104); the small and young ones are called *baks*. The rhyme word in the previous verse, *jdhūrhā*, means "roots," but in the context of this verse it has been given the other possible translation of "stem, lower end."

115 The delicious scent of a palm tree's flower and pollen is graphically described in this Emirati newspaper article "Scent of a Date Palm Stirs Emotions," *The National*, July 21, 2012: https://www.thenational.ae/uae/scent-of-a-date-palm-stirs-the-emotions-1.597758. "Brides," *ʿarāyis*, does not have to be taken literally; the word can also be used for girls dancing on festive occasions.

116 "Ninety days": The hot season (*al-gēḍ*, CA *qayẓ*) lasts ninety days, until the appearance of Canopus (CA *suhayl*) just before dawn: the period in which the dates ripen. In this period, the Bedouin sojourn at the wells of an oasis, and traditionally in poetry this is the season for amorous affairs. In the poet's mind, the harvest of sweet dates and the delights of love merge: delicious dates become a metaphor for the forbidden, but irresistible, fruits of love. In this passage, love is not mentioned, but it is subsumed in the wording, as are the looming pain of separation and the ravages of time. It is made explicit in this seventeenth-century verse of Rumayzān, in which the date harvest and the fruits of love merge in one delight: "Ninety days I luxuriated in love's enchantment, and ninety / nights in reaping its fruits in the gardens" (*giḍēt al-hawā tisʿīn yōmin w-mithlhin, liyālin bi-tagṭīf al-jinā min ḥadāyigih*) (Sowayan, *al-Shiʿr al-nabaṭī*, 446). As is the case here, *gēẓ* may also mean the date itself. "Fruits": *ḥaml*, lit. "load, weight," refers to a palm tree's entire production of dates. The rhyme word, *zūrhā*, means the palm's frond (*saʿaf*; *zūr*, pl. of *azwar* "inclined, curved," in reference to the curved shape of the fronds).

117 One would expect the poet to make a transition from the end of summer to the departure of the beloved and her tribe, but here a bigger leap is taken: one's departure from life and the world as such. For a more usual transition in a similar setting, see §§10.62–67. The cycle of the poem (grief at loss and memories of life's fullness;

attainment of wisdom when the world takes off its mask and death makes its presence felt; resumption of sweet memories and the pain of separation; a transition to the upbeat rain section through a comparison of nature's cycles with the ups and downs experienced by the soul) is repeated for greater effect in compressed form for the poem's coda in §§4.53–60. The flood's destruction leads to joy at blossoms and fruits (the concept of *dammār ʿammār*, see n. 113), followed by sadness at love's departure, belated wisdom (a stronger version of §§4.34–35), death, and the end of the world.

118 "The world ends": as in the saying, "the world will last longer than its people," *ad-dinyā aṭwal min ahalhā*, used not in an eschatological sense, but as an admonition to relax, i.e., the world will continue without you (al-Juhaymān, *Amthāl*, 3:97).

119 This postapocalyptic landscape, as the poet visualizes it, is clearly modeled after Qur'anic descriptions of the world's unmaking on the Day of Resurrection, as in Q 14:48, 20:105–7, 21:104, 52:9–10, 56:1–6, 75:6–9, 77:8–10, 81:1–3, 82:1–3, 84:1–5, 89:21, and 99:1–2, with some Bedouin touches added to it (the words *ṣaḥṣaḥ* and *mudamlak*).

120 Q Zumar 39:68: In Islamic tradition, the angel blowing the trumpet is associated with Isrāfīl. "On the horns of a cosmic bull" (*garn thōr*) refers to the belief (not mentioned as such in the Qur'an, but found in hadith) that the world is carried on the back or horns of a giant bull, according to medieval Islamic cosmography, and is thus inherently unstable (see Streck and Miquel, "Ḳāf," in *EI2*).

121 "Spread from mouth to mouth": *ar-rwāt*; as in the first line of Poem 2, the poet shows his concern for the reception of his verses by a critical audience of connoisseurs (CA *ruwāh*, sg. *rāwī*). *tarāthāh* "inherited from one another" (CA *tawāratha*); an alternative reading is "told each other, recited to each other" (*tarāwāh*). The same expression occurs in the first line of a poem by Ibn Ḥammād in his reply to Ibn Zayd's poem in praise of the Jabrid ruler Ajwad ibn Zāmil (r. 1471–1506): "Verses composed by the masterful Ibn Ḥammād, / a perpetuated inheritance to spite the enemy" (*yigūl ibn Ḥammādin w-min lā yikūdih, mithāyilin tirthā bi-l-hijā wi-tʿād*) (Sowayan, *al-Shiʿr*

al-nabaṭī, 302). However, the importance of not taking a transmitter's words at face value is stressed in the saying, "Transmitters are the blight of oral reports" (*mā āfat al-akhbār illā rwāthā*) (al-Juhaymān, *Amthāl*, 7:5).

122 It is a stereotypical image to compare one's verses to expensive wares that are in high demand at a market.

123 The poems (*giṣīd*, CA *qaṣīdah*) are presented as delicious dates that come in weighed quantities (*kēl* "fixed measure, especially of rice or grain") (Holes, *Dialect*, 1:471; CA *kayl* "measure, load"), selected with utmost care, and picked one by one from the sack with the help of pincers, *mijlā'/miglā'*, pl. *migālī'* (CA *qala'a* "to pluck out, tear out"). Once extracted, and held in the pincers, they are a mouthwatering sight for hungry onlookers (Thānī, *Ibn Ẓāhir*, 288).

124 Here the poet directly addresses advice to his listener. Similarly, on the theme of love, direct address produces the most vivid passage. Many verses in Ibn Ẓāhir's poetry stress the importance of having good, reliable friends. These are similar to the numerous sayings on the same subject, e.g., "a true friend shares your worries" (*rifīgak min gāsamak hammak*); "having a good friend with you is more important than the road you travel on" (*ar-rifīg gabl aṭ-ṭirīg*) (al-Juhaymān, *Amthāl*, 3:198–99). Al-Khalāwī takes eighteen verses to recommend himself as the best of friends, "closer to his friend than his friend's closest relatives" (*li-ṣidīgih agrab min ṣalāyib girāybih*), an observation often made at the time (Ibn Khamīs, *al-Khalāwī*, 211–14).

125 "Sucking up to Mammon": *khādim ad-dunyā* "servant of this World," i.e., "devoting one's life to the pursuit of riches and sensual pleasures," as implied in the service of Mammon.

126 "Coddled": *ad-dinyā lidhīdh rḍā'hā*, lit. "sucking the world's delicious milk," as in the first verse of al-Nābighah ibn Ghannām in praise of the Jabrid prince Muḥammad ibn Ajwad: "Night of felicity, not ill-starred and doom-laden / laid out for us a delicious banquet of wonders" (*s'ūd al-liyālī 'an nḥūs an-nuwāyib, tizahhabat bi-ladhdhāt al-liyālī l-'ajāyib*) (Sowayan, *al-Shi'r al-nabaṭī*, 289).

127 The meaning of the second hemistich seems to be that if the sack is empty, there will be no dates to extract with the pincers, which should be understood in the light of the first hemistich's warning that one's worldly successes will add up to very little at the end of life (since the Last Judgment applies different criteria). The dates might be taken to represent life's pleasures and temptations. This verse has intrigued commentators. Speculating on its deeper meaning, Thānī suggests that "emptiness" (*al-khalā*) is implicit in the action of the pincers used to extract the delicious dates from the vessel, and that therefore it is "an existential truth that life forsakes someone who comes to it empty-handed. Life itself renders this life null and void, exactly as pincers empty a sack of dates of its contents. Emptiness, lack of substance, is a result of life's pincers having emptied the vessel of its dates" (Thānī, *Ibn Ẓāhir*, 290).

128 See §15.32.

129 "Natural": lit. "a human being is joyful," *l-insān yifraḥ*; in Arabic it is written *al-insān* but in Emirati dialect pronounced as *l-insān*.

130 That is, Judgment Day, after the second trumpet blast when people rise from their graves, Q Qāf 50:41–42. Imagining oneself being lowered into a dusty grave has a long tradition, e.g., the section of verses by ʿAbdah ibn al-Ṭabīb beginning with: "I know that I'll be carried to my resting place, / a grave dug out in the dusty soil" (*wa-laqad ʿalimtu bi-anna qaṣrī ḥufratun, ghabrāʾu yaḥmilunī ilayhā sharjaʿū*) (*al-Mufaḍḍaliyyāt*, 1:103; 2:103). The passage reminds one of Sufi practices, such as the teachings of the influential Turkish shaykh of the Naqshbandi order, Mehmet Zahid Kotku, whose exercise "the bondage to death" instructed his disciples to close their eyes and imagine as vividly as possible being lifted on a bier, lowered into the grave, and lying there in absolute solitude, waiting to be interrogated by God's angels (Betsy Udink, *Meisjes van Atatürk, Zonen van de Sultan, verhalen uit Turkije*, 2015, 307; Elisabeth Őzdalga, *Naqshbandis in Western and Central Asia*, 1999).

131 The point is brought home by the consonance of *tigā* "piety, pious works" (CA *tuqā* "godliness, piety") and *shigā* "misfortune, distress,

misery" (CA *shaqā'*); *tigā* occurs in two other poems almost exclusively devoted to verses of wisdom §11.33, §11.35, §11.38, and §15.24; it is also used with the general sense of "right and exemplary conduct," as *tagwā* in §17.22.

132 A similar verse by ʿAbd al-Raḥīm, nicknamed Muṭawwaʿ Ushayqir: "There is no hand but that the hand of God hovers over it, / as no bird flies but that it must alight" (*tarā mā yidin illā yid allāh fōgahā, walā ṭāyirātin illā wi-hinn wgūʿ*) (Sowayan, *al-Shiʿr al-nabaṭī*, 389). The Muṭawwaʿ (meaning: "man of religion") shares his Hilālī tastes with Ibn Ẓāhir. The line is also attributed to the saga's hero, Abū Zayd al-Hilālī: "There is no hand but that the hand of God hovers over it, / and no bird but that it must alight" (*mā yidin illā w-yid allāh fōgahā, walā ṭāyirāt illā wi-hinn wgūʿ*) (al-Saʿīd, *al-Mawsūʿah*, 46).

133 The same verse occurs in a long poem by al-Kulayf: *wi-ʿrif bi-ann aṭ-ṭēr siʿdih rīshih, w-in giṣṣ mā lih ḥīltin yiḥtālahā* (Sowayan, *al-Shiʿr al-nabaṭī*, 296); see also §§7.16–17. It was a common simile at the time, e.g., this line in a poem composed in 1735: "A bird needs its wings to fly" (*fa-lā ṭērin illā bi-l-jināḥēn ṭāyir*) (Sowayan, *al-Shiʿr al-nabaṭī*, 514). See the Emirati sayings, "A bird can only fly with its own wings" and "A bird needs its own beak to sustain itself" (*kill ṭēr yiṭīr bi-janāḥah, kill ṭēr yishbiʿih mingābah*), an admonition to be self-reliant (Ḥanẓal, *Jāmiʿ al-amthāl*, 242).

134 "All-knowing": *ʿallām l-ashyā*, lit. "knowing all things"; in Arabic it is written *al-ashyā* but in Emirati dialect pronounced *l-ashyā*, see n. 129.

135 That is, in the hereafter. In the narrative saga, the reward follows immediately on the eagerly made sacrifice. See n. 72.

136 "Starling": *al-giʿgāʿ* "weak bird that cannot protect itself" (Abū Shihāb and Abū Malḥah, *Ibn Ẓāhir*, 100), i.e., one should not be deceived by appearances: a hunting falcon is a falcon, regardless of its colors, and a little bird is its prey (*rizg*) or of no consequence, even if its feathers have a nice shine. In the stories about Ibn Ẓāhir, one of his defining traits is his ragged appearance, which misleads visitors before they discover his true identity and character. This is an old motif in Arabic poetry, as in Bishr ibn ʿAmr's verse: "You see that their

best clothes are full of holes, / but their swords of tempered steel are sheathed in gold brocade" (*wa-tarā jiyāda thiyābihim makhlūlatan, wa-l-mashrafiyyata qad kasawhā l-mudhhabā*) (*al-Mufaḍḍaliyyāt*, 1: 555; 2:219).

137 "Good old virtue": *l-aḥsān al-awwilī*, lit. "the good of old"; the assumption is that earlier generations (*al-awwilīn*) enjoyed moral superiority. Just as Nestor in *The Iliad* boasts of having consorted with mythical heroes and of being the only one old enough to credibly claim such a distinction, al-Farazdaq does so for his literary ancestry, and ʿAbīd ibn al-Abraṣ for his tribal fellows of yore (A. A. Bevan, *The Naka'id of Jarīr and al-Farazdak*, 39:51–61; Lyall, *The Dīwān of ʿAbīd ibn al-Abraṣ*, 31–32; Homer, *The Iliad*, 82). Shāyiʿ al-Amsaḥ, a poet closer to Ibn Ẓāhir's time, puts it more bluntly: "I am the last survivor of a virtuous generation" (Sowayan, *Ayyām al-ʿArab*, 293). See also nn. 410 and 411.

138 The verse is a proverb: "He raises the alarm with the shepherd and connives with the wolf" (*yiṣīḥ maʿ ar-rāʿī w-ydigg maʿ adh-dhīb*) (Ḥanẓal, *Jāmiʿ al-amthāl*, 542; Ḥasan, *al-ʿĀdāt*, 135). It is similar in meaning to "run with the hare and hunt with the hounds," or the Arabic "he murders the man and walks in his funeral procession" (*yaqtil al-qatīl wa-yamshī fī jināzatuh*) and "to play a double game, work both sides of the street" (*laʿiba ʿalā ḥablayn*). Lit. "he knocks on the wolf's door when the shepherd does not pay attention, but if he senses danger he pretends to warn the shepherd about the wolf."

139 A recurrent trope in Arabian poetry: a profiteering miser who prefers to live at the expense of his fellow men comes in for special disdain.

140 An obnoxious person risks humiliation, as in the expression "If you show up at someone's dinner uninvited, you may not be well served" (*min jā blā daʿwah gaʿad blā frāsh*) (al-Juhaymān, *Amthāl*, 8:137).

141 The same point is made by the poet's Najdī contemporary, al-Khalāwī: "If you exert yourself, you can't be blamed: / the promised subsistence cannot be attained by force" (*al-ajhād ʿaddā l-lāyimāt ʿan al-fitā, wa-l-arzāg mā tātī l-fitā bi-l-ghaṣayib*) (Ibn Khamīs, *al-Khalāwī*, 63).

142 Lit. "girls who entertain men with song and dance" (*al-muṭribāt*), whose vows are idle words (*ḍyāʿ*, "futile, a waste, lost").

143 A saying also found in *Arabian Satire*, §28.24: "He who lets a viper wrap its coils round his leg will regret it, / and he who trusts a sworn enemy will be abused."

144 The poet echoes the words of Q Sharḥ 94:5 *fa-inna maʿa l-ʿusri yusran*, here rendered as *wa-l-yisr baʿd al-ʿisr*, "ease and comfort after hardship." For the Bedouin, this translates into a succession of drought and nature's revival after rains, as in the next hemistich. The verse makes for a smooth transition from gnomic wisdom to descriptions of a thunderstorm and cloudburst.

145 This verse, and the one preceding it, elaborate on the familiar simile comparing rainclouds and heavy showers with the huge udders and abundant milk of pregnant camels; see the section "Rain Clouds" in the online "Glossary of Style, Themes, and Motifs." Wind and lightning play their part in delivering the clouds of their water and come to the rescue of the scorched earth.

146 "Strangers": *mustaʾmin*, "non-Muslim foreigners who are given a safe-conduct to visit Muslim lands" ("Amān," *EI2*).

147 This line only occurs in the MSS of al-Mazrūʿī and Lūtah, and in the editions of Alameemi and Thānī (not in the edition of Abū Shihāb and Abū Malḥah). Perhaps it was omitted on purpose by the manuscript writers from al-Aḥsāʾ. Named after its founder, Aḥmad ibn ʿAlī al-Rifāʿī (d. 578/1182 in southern Iraq), the Rifāʿiyyah quickly became one of the most prominent Sufi orders, and the Rifāʿī dervishes were known for their extravagant feats ("Rifāʿiyyah," *EI2*). It had a presence in Kuwait, Bahrain, and the Emirates (http://aman.dostor.org/show.aspx?id=33720). The Badriyyah school is named after Badr al-Dīn ibn ʿUmar ibn Aḥmad ibn Muḥammad al-ʿĀdilī (d. 975/1567), who spent time in al-Aḥsāʾ; "it spread in Bahrain, al-Qaṭīf, al-Aḥsāʾ and other areas in the eastern part of Arabia where it played a prominent role in the purification of the soul," and organized celebrations of the birth of the Prophet Muḥammad (*mawālid*) (http://bashaaralhadi.blogspot.com/2017/12/ and communication of Thāni ʿAbd Allāh Ṣaqr al-Muhayrī).

148 "Dance of unveiled girls": *nāʿishāt* "young girls who dance and sway with their supple bodies, while tossing their long hair in the air on the rhythm of dancing tunes like *al-ʿiyālah* (traditional Emirati stick dance), *al-razf*, and *al-ḥarbiyyah* (war dances)" (Ḥanẓal, *Muʿjam al-alfāẓ*, 688); see also §6.3. The comparison of palm trees' crowns swaying in the wind to dancing girls tossing their long tresses, and to camel-borne litters, is common in the earliest Arabic poetry, e.g., al-Marrār ibn Munqidh: "The fronds of the palms wave in the wind, / like dancing girls pulling one another's tresses" (*ka-anna furūʿahā fī kulli rīḥin, jawārin bi-l-dhawāʾibi yantaṣīnā*) (*al-Mufaḍḍaliyyāt*, 1:125; 2:42); and the image is found in prehistoric rock carvings near Jubbah, where the long tresses show an uncanny resemblance to the crowns of palm trees (http://www.bradshawfoundation.com/middle_east/saudi_arabia_rock_art/index.php).

149 "Bunches of dates": *min dhāt ḥamlin,* lit. "from the ones that carry a load," i.e., heavy bunches of dates, as in the verse of Ibn Ẓāhir's contemporary in Najd, Jabr ibn Sayyār: "Often I dallied there with stunning beauties, / whose tresses are as heavy as date bunches" (*fa-yā ṭāl mā māzaḥt fīhā kharāyid, lākin ganāwīn ar-ruwāyā jʿūdhā*) (Sowayan, *al-Shiʿr al-nabaṭī*, 468). And the early classical poet Rabīʿah ibn Maqrūm: "On the morning of her departure, she showed her tresses, flowing down / over her back like clusters of ripe black dates" (*qāmat turīka ghadāta l-bayni munsadilan, takhāluhū fawqa matnayhā l-ʿanāqīdā*) (*al-Mufaḍḍaliyyāt*, 1:442; 2:159); and Imruʾ al-Qays: "Her pitch-black tresses stream down her back, in a profusion as dense as the tangled growth of a date palm's bunches" (al-Zawzānī, *Sharḥ al-muʿallaqāt al-sabʿ*, 22). In this verse, the poet ends his excursus on the subject of palm trees and their ripe fruits. The connection between the girls' hair and the palm trees is made through the trees' "raven black" dates, a color normally associated with the jet-black hair of beautiful girls.

150 "Extinction": *fnā,* CA *fanāʾ* "passing away, vanishing, extinction"; as the poet's focus is on his feeling of personal loss, he foresees the

extinction of his individual consciousness, rather than death in a religious sense. In this verse, he explicitly mourns the disappearance of his youth, not a particular Bedouin belle.

151 "Not to bid farewell": the lover's complaint through the ages, also in regard to the departure of youth, as in this verse by a late eighteenth-century poet, Zayd ibn 'Uray'ir, the last ruler of the Āl Ḥumayd dynasty in eastern Arabia when it was overrun by the forces of the House of Saud in 1789: "Youth turned its back on me without farewell, / and what came in its place brought the opposite" (*agfā ash-shibāb 'annī walā wāda'nī, wa-lākinn ba'd al-yōm mā nāb khālafih*) (Sowayan, *al-Shi'r al-nabaṭī*, 512).

152 "Wicked bird": *ḥamām al-gā'ī*, lit. "dove of the flat, featureless plain" (CA *qā'*); obviously, the word was chosen for the sake of rhyme.

153 "Doves": "different varieties of doves, *rā'ibī* medium-sized, *ganṭirī* the smallest, *gfā'* the biggest" (Abū Shihāb and Abū Malḥah, *Ibn Ẓāhir*, 106); the first one is mentioned in a poem by Khalīl ibn 'Āyiḍ, known as Muṭawwa' al-Maskūf (a mosque in the town of 'Unayzah), a poet counted among the "martyrs of love": "I must respond to your sad tune, O dove of doves, / cooing on your steep ledge from behind the parapets" (*'alēk ajāwib rā'ibī al-ḥamāmāt, fi kill mashdhūbin rifī' al-migāṣīr*) (Sowayan, *al-Shi'r al-nabaṭī*, 494).

154 "Headed south": *shām* is "to travel, go north," but here it means "to go away and disappear," as in the expression "to go south."

155 Verses such as these may have given rise to the narrative saga's image of Ibn Ẓāhir as a poorly dressed old man who lives in utter simplicity; see §21.11.

156 "New moon": *al-hlāl*, to determine whether the fasting month of Ramadan has come to a close. Due to his loss of eyesight, the old poet has trouble distinguishing the shape of the most apparent things.

157 "Eastern breezes": *ṣibā*. These verses are reminiscent of the Banū Hilāl verses: "The vast desert to its west is the haunt of gazelle and oryxes, / to the east the drifting sands of the dunes" (*gharbiyyahā zīzan bhā r-rīm wa-l-mahā, w-sharqiyyahā yadhrī 'alēh nfūd*) (Sowayan, *Ayyām al-'Arab*, 1031).

158 As in §1.3, the traces of the abandoned camp are erased by winds from all directions. Here the *ṣibā* is given prominence: in the next verse, this breeze "dances" around a gazelle, the symbol of female beauty. The other winds have calmed and become soft (*rāyfih*). Hence, it is intertwined with its other meaning of youthful dalliance: in this poetry, the pronunciation of CA *ṣabā* "east wind" and *ṣibā* "youth, amorous dalliance" is identical. The image of winds from all directions, swirling like dancing girls, has been inherited from the early classical poetry, e.g., Dhū l-Rummah: "The winds of Gemini (i.e., hot summer) raise shrouds of fine dust, / hot blasts of sand from all directions; / Three years, a year more, a further six / as dancing girls sweep with the hem of their dress" (*ḥadā bāriḥu l-jawzā'i aʿrāfa mūrihī, bihā wa-ʿajāju l-ʿaqrabi l-mutanāwiḥū / thalātha aḥwālin wa-ḥawlan wa-sittatan, kamā jarrati l-rayṭa l-ʿadhārā l-mawāriḥū*) (*Dīwān*, 861).

159 "Twirled": *naʿish*, in reference to the movement of dancing girls who sway their long tresses with each step. Cf. §5.55.

160 "Rains of Canopus": *shēliyyah* "rains in the season that begins with the rise of the star Canopus just before dawn, approximately early September" (CA *suhayl*). See §16.55, winds of Canopus.

161 Here and in §§1.4–5, §§5.62–63, and §10.12, the dove's cooing is the musical accompaniment of grief at separation from the beloved, as in Dhū l-Rummah's lines: "Must the coos of hidden doves pile on the grief? / They commiserate and lament without end / about their love but their eyes stay dry" (*ḥamāmun tughannī fī l-diyāri wuqūʿū / tajāwabna fa-stabkayna man kāna dhā hawan, nawā'iḥu mā tajrī li-hinna dumūʿū*) (*Dīwān*, 1077–81).

162 The printed text gives *al-garāshib* (CA *qirshabb* "a very big, tall man," Ibn Manẓūr, *Lisān*, 3587), but Alameemi explained that more likely it should be read as two separate words: *al-garā shabb* "(the camel's) back towered."

163 "Palm trees": *banāt al-ghīl*, lit. "daughters of the rivulet"; in §§6.8–11, the images of camel-borne litters, majestic palm trees in rows beside irrigation channels, succulent dates, and beautiful Bedouin girls present a subtle mixture of classical imagery and similes. The expression

recurs in §10.8 as *banāt al-baduw,* "daughters (or girls) of the Bedouin," in a similar context. See also §5.55 and §10.56. In the poet's mind, the scene is probably associated with the Banū Hilāl of §1.63.

164 "Prepare for departure": *shāmū li-niyyah* "they made up their mind to depart," a recurrent trope in Bedouin poetry, as in *Arabian Romantic*, Poems 2 and 3. This verse continues where §6.8 paused for an excursus in §§6.9–10 with glimpses of the date harvest and the beloved. The sequence of §§6.8–12 is a condensed, allusive version of the Bedouins' arrival and departure in the summer season and, most importantly, the poet's beloved Bedouin beauty. The departure coincides with the harvest of dates that taste as sweet as the Bedouin belle: here "sugar" (*sikkar*) is another word for *jummār*, "heart of palm" (cf. Sowayan, *Ayyām al-ʿArab*, 201). On closer inspection, the transition from §6.8 to §6.9 is not as abrupt as it seems, considering that it fits the conventional comparison of litter-carrying camels to swaying crowns of palm trees, e.g., in the verse of one of the earliest Arab poets, al-Muraqqish the Elder: "They came down from litters like doom palms, the backs of which fluttered in the breeze, sides adorned with embroidery" (*tanazzalna ʿan dawmin tahiffu mutūnuhū, muzayyanatin aknāfuhā bi-l-zakhārifī*) (*al-Mufaḍḍaliyyāt*, 1:476; 2:176). Here a further element links the image to the Bedouin beauty carried inside the litter—namely, the brushed-up profusion of hair that in its turn is used as a simile for the dense crown of palm fronds, the subject of another verse that likens palm crowns swaying in the wind to girls who swing their long hair from side to side while dancing, §5.55.

165 A line in the style of Banū Hilāl.

166 "Cheeks": *khaddin dimā*; it was explained that *dimā* means "like, similar to," as in *dimathum wāḥid* "one is a spitting image of the other."

167 As is the custom in ghazal, the verse is built on opposition between "to disobey, revolt against" (*ʿaṣēt*) and "to obey" (*ṭāwaʿt*): the poet did not listen to carpers who told him not to fall in love with her. Instead, he obeyed the inclinations of his heart. "Distance": *maṣrūf al-niyā*, lit. "the dictates of distance," as in Abū Ḥamzah al-ʿĀmirī's

line: "If the machinations of distance took you away or me" (*law bān bik ṣarf an-niyā aw bān bī*) (Sowayan, *al-Shiʿr al-nabaṭī*, 264); see §1.11.

168 A standard description of old age (Kurpershoek, *Arabian Satire* §§30.1–5). The verses of gnomic wisdom (§§6.19–23) flow from this self-description as a physically frail but clever sage. The first hemistiches of verses eighteen and nineteen are only partly legible in the sole MS and some of the words have been left open, marked with dots, in the edition of Alameemi.

169 It is not uncommon for the aging poet-lover to mock his own infirmity and foolishness in a transition to verses of wisdom, as in the wisdom poems of Ḥmēdān al-Shwēʿir (*Arabian Satire*, 190–91 sub lemma "old (age).") "Common sense": *an-naṣḥ* not only means "advice, good advice," but *niṣaḥ* is also "to do a job properly, diligently; to mean well, try to do the right thing" (Holes, *Dialect*, 1:521); cf. Rushaydān's line: "The best poetry is composed for good counsel's sake: / for the inexperienced and ignorant, as friendly advice" (*niʿm ibtidā naẓm al-guwāfī niṣāyiḥ, li-min jāhilin ḥagg aṣ-ṣidīg wṣāt*) (Sowayan, *al-Shiʿr al-nabaṭī*, 430).

170 This saying affirms that once a person has reached young adulthood his or her character is fixed. Usually it has a negative slant: one cannot expect any improvement, e.g., a verse by the Jabrid poet ʿĀmir al-Samīn: "If a man has committed a wrong, know that he / perforce will reoffend later in life" (*ilā dās rajlin zallitin f-iʿlam innih, lizūmin ʿalēh in ʿāsh sawwā niẓīrih*) (Sowayan, *al-Shiʿr al-nabaṭī*, 345); and Zuhayr ibn Abī Sulmā: "An old man, if he is a fool, will never see reason, while rash youngsters may still hope to attain wisdom" (al-Zawzānī, *Sharḥ al-muʿallaqāt*, 89).

171 If the crops are watered after a dry season, it is too late, no matter how much water is poured on it, i.e., the timing of measures must be right, as expressed in the similar saying, "Irrigation of crops only in the final stage will bring no benefit and the harvest will be lost" (*az-zarʿ ilā waddaʿ mā yanfaʿih māh*) (al-Juhaymān, *Amthāl*, 3:221); and "dry stalks do not yield a harvest" (*al-ghuffah mā tinfiḍ*) (al-Rawāḥī, *al-Amthāl al-ʿUmāniyyah al-shaʿbiyyah*, 126).

172 As expressed in the saying, "You do not take friendships with you into the grave (lit. the slanted tombstones)" (*mā min warā ʿūj an-niṣāyib ṣidāgah*) (al-Juhaymān, *Amthāl*, 7:165); and ʿAbdah ibn al-Ṭabīb: "I'll be left alone in a dusty place, shunned by all, / buried in sand by the winds that sweep over it" (*wa-turiktu fī ghabrāʾi yukrahu wirduhā, tasfī ʿalayya l-rīḥu ḥīna uwaddaʿū*) (*al-Mufaḍḍaliyyāt*, 1:302; 2:103); see also §5.17.

173 A variation on one of the most popular Arab sayings: "Keep it short and sweet," or "be economical with words and to the point when you speak" (*khayru l-kalām mā qalla wa-dalla*). The Jabrid poet ʿĀmir al-Samīn has worked it into a wisdom poem: "As in a verse of wisdom coined ages ago: / short speech brings more profit than lengthy talk" (*ʿalā mithl bētin gīl fī māḍiyyin miḍā, al-agwāl yighnī gillahā ʿan kithīrahā*) (Sowayan, *al-Shiʿr al-nabaṭī*, 345).

174 "Ignored": *fa-khallhā*, as in the saying, "If a fool makes a silly comment about you, do not react" (*lī ʿūyā yatk min sifīhin f-khallhā*) (Ḥanẓal, *Jāmiʿ al-amthāl*, 179). Similar advice was given in the early Arabian days by ʿAwf ibn al-Aḥwaṣ: "At improper speech I leave to others to listen, / and do not ask for clarification" (*idhā qīlati l-ʿawrāʾu wallaytu samʿahā, siwāya wa-lam asʾal bihā mā dabīruhā*) (*al-Mufaḍḍaliyyāt*, 1:351; 2:128). See also the saying, "If a madman speaks, the wise man keeps silent" (*idhā tikallam al-majnūn al-mistimiʿ ʿāgil*) (al-Rawāḥī, *al-Amthāl al-ʿUmāniyyah*, 11).

175 "Melted fat": *ad-dahn al-mdhāb*, a common expression, e.g., Shāyiʿ al-Amsaḥ's verse: "Real men do not take clarified butter as food" (*wla yākil az-zibd al-mdhāb rajjāl*), i.e., they do not practice dishonesty and dissimulation, a virtue expressed by Abū Qays ibn al-Aslat: "Prudence and firmness are better than / dissimulation, weakness, and wavering" (*al-ḥazmu wa-l-quwwatū khayrun mina l, -idhāni wa-l-fakkati wa-l-hāʿī*) (*al-Mufaḍḍaliyyāt*, 1;568; 2;226). The first hemistich shows contempt for purveyors of malicious gossip in almost the same words (similarly: *wla yangil al-yangūsh rajlin ṭayyib*, Sowayan, *Ayyām al-ʿArab*, 248).

176 "Cupper of blood" (*ḥajjām*): one who bleeds someone, especially as a remedy for headaches, so that the corrupt blood (*damm fāsid*) is let

out; *maḥājim*, cupping glasses, are the utensils in which the cupper collects the blood.

177 The poet cautions that circumspection in and of itself may not protect one from the fickleness of fate: the benefits you enjoy today may go to someone else tomorrow. Almost the same words are found in a poem with the same rhyme and meter by Rumayzān (mentioned in Kurpershoek, *Arabian Satire*, xliv, xlv, 146n98): *w-kam gāʿidin bi-ẓ-ẓill w-inzāḥ ẓillih, w-kam gāʿidin bi-sh-shams jāh ẓlāl* (Sowayan, *al-Shiʿr al-nabaṭī*, 425); and of Shāyiʿ al-Amsaḥ: *yā gāʿidin bi-ẓ-ẓill zāḥ ẓillik, w-yā gāʿidin bi-sh-shams jāk ẓlāl* (Sowayan, *Ayyām al-ʿArab*, 249).

178 Lit. "a friend will not seek you out, be loyal to you," *mā liya mink ṣāḥib* (CA *laja'a*). The advice in §§7.10–12 to be gentle and forgiving if a friend does not always live up to your expectations, if only out of self-interest, is given repeatedly in poetry. It is worse to depend on the tender mercies of relatives, as expressed by Mutammim: "If fate brings misfortunes on me, / I do not burden my kinfolk and humble myself for them" (*wa-lastu idhā mā l-dahru aḥdatha nakbatan, wa-ruz'an bi-zawwāri l-qarā'ibi akhḍaʿā*) (*al-Mufaḍḍaliyyāt*, 1:540; 2:209). Similarly, Rumayzān (Sowayan, *al-Shiʿr al-nabaṭī*, 432).

179 "Lightweight": lit. "a light load is easily lifted (or: carried away)." Perhaps this can be read in conjunction with the preceding verse: if you are friendless and your relatives let you down, you carry little "weight" and become easy prey for enemies. This makes for a smooth transition to the next verse about the correct distribution of loads on a pack animal's back.

180 A bird's wing is a symbol for ambition and able resolve: "I renounced love's play and lowered my wing" (Kurpershoek, *Arabian Romantic*, §2.2 and 204n122).

181 A popular saying on the wholesome effect of deterrence, e.g., Rumayzān: "Many aggressors are left alone, safe because feared, / and many peaceful men are ever being harassed" (*w-kam ʿāyilin dōmin ykhallā makhāfah, w-mistaslimin dōmin ʿalēh yʿāl*) (Sowayan, *al-Shiʿr al-nabaṭī*, 425); and Ḥmēdān al-Shwēʿir: "A rabbit lies down and does not fight, / yet you don't see people leaving it alone; / Ferocious lions

do not crouch and hide, / no one ventures into their domain" (*Arabian Satire*, §34.12).

182 The little she-camel, *ḥijj* or *ḥigg* (CA *ḥiqq*), a she-camel in the third year, raises its tail, frightened at the domineering sound produced by the rutting male. The old simile continues in use, especially in mocking verses (*hijā'*) (e.g., in William Tamplin, *Poet of Jordan, the Political Poetry of Muhammad Fanatil al-Hajaya*, 77), as in the saying, "whimpering groans after threatening roars are a humiliating retreat" (*ar-rghā 'igb al-hdarān gibīḥ*) (al-Juhaymān, *Amthāl*, 3:196).

183 "Amazing verses": *migālin 'ajīb*, similar to *gharīb al-gīl*, "my peerless verse" (Kurpershoek, *Arabian Satire*, §20.12); and al-Khalāwī: "When people prick up their ears and feel pleased: / revelers stay up late to hear his exquisite verse" (*wlā shannaf al-asmā' wānis nfūshā, walā ashar as-sammār illā 'ajāyibih*) (Ibn Khamiṣ, *al-Khalāwī*, 54). In early poetry, this curiosity-piquing "strangeness" of words is termed *ābidah*, i.e., "unknown, rare word," hence *awābid al-shi'r*, i.e., "poetry that is not readily comprehensible," in the sense of *mustawḥish*, "wild, not tamed, domesticated" (*al-Mufaḍḍaliyyāt*, 1:862, in a comment to a verse by Abū Dhu'ayb). It is understood that poets wish to blow away their audience with amazing wordings (*ābidah*, pl. *awābid* "unusual thing; wild animal"): "So-and-So uttered unusual, wondrous words in his verses" (*abbada fulān fī shi'rih idhā aghraba fīh*); "rare, interesting expressions in verse that excite curiosity" (*awābidu l-shi'ri gharā'ibuhu*) (*al-Mufaḍḍaliyyāt*, 1:136, 179). Similarly: "For certain, if I fling my rare verses at my opponent, / they will be sung by travelers at night and the drivers of caravans" (*za'īmun li-man qādhaftuhu bi-awābidin, yughannī bihā l-sāri wa-tuḥdā l-rawāḥilū*, *al-Mufaḍḍaliyyāt*, 1:179; 2:61). See also §3.3.

184 In oral tradition, this is said to be the first verse spoken by the poet after he received the gift of poetry through intercession of a female jinni; see §18.6 (al-Ḥasan, Tamīm, Alameemi, *Bint ibn Ẓāhir*, 37, where only the first hemistich corresponds to the verse in this edition). In the docudrama series about the poet, with a scenario written

by Alameemi, aired during the month of Ramadan by Abu Dhabi TV in 2019, it was presented in the same way.

185 Similarly, the Najdī poet al-Khalāwī compares composing poetry to pearl diving: "My verses are like carefully selected pearls, / pure white jewels of a noble kind; / Culled from deep waters where divers drown. / Only the best collect these rare gems from the bottom; / Many took the plunge but came to grief: / countless shipmates never surfaced again; / The sea's rollers will only submit to Rāshid: / he does not need to pull the ropes to secure his catch" (*w-dirrin nifīsin mintagā kill mintagā, ka-d-dānat al-ʿafrā lidhī r-rāy nājibih / min lajjitin yaghrag bihā min yighūṣhā, w-min ghāṣahā ghirrin ghadā fī ghayāhibih / w-gad zārahā gōmin ghadaw dūn khadhhā, w-yāmā markabin damm ṣāhibih / ghibbāt baḥrin mā lahā kūd Rāshid, miʿtādhā min dūn ḥablin w-jādhibih*) (Ibn Khamīs, *al-Khalāwī*, 304). The verse reflects a view common among the divers. See "Appendix D22" in John Gordon Lorimer, *Gazetteer*; and see "Pearling and Poetry" in the online "Glossary of Style, Themes, and Motifs."

186 "People come in all shapes and sizes": *an-nās ajnās* (CA *jins*, pl. *ajnās* "kind, sort, species"); "a saying that people come in different sorts" (al-Rawāḥī, *al-Amthāl al-ʿUmāniyyah*, 204); as in §5.44.

187 The Emirati editor and poetry expert Ḥammād al-Khāṭirī drew my attention to this transition as an example of the poet's mastery: the association of avarice and a cloudless sky that withholds its blessings, the life-bringing rains, from the earth.

188 "Arcturus": *simākiyyah*; the rains of *al-simākān*, Arcturus and Spica Virginis, come toward the end of spring, in Arabia around March.

189 "Breezes": *shartā*; *shartā* is a strong wind, usually accompanied by rains, hence the saying, "a *shartā* without rain," in reference to a false promise (Ḥanẓal, *Jāmiʿ al-amthāl*, 401). Here, as in other passages, the poet compares the thunderstorm to stock-in-trade figures of ghazal: "The verse is about the angel who has been tasked to steer the clouds from one location to another and to order the release of rains or to prevent it; the thunder is the angel's voice and lightning his

whip, as alluded to in the words 'thunderclaps bring delight'" (Thānī, *Ibn Ẓāhir*, 236).

190 "Laughter": i.e., lightning, as in the verse "with a smile, lightning flashed its glittering teeth, / dazzling white like chamomile freshly rinsed by drops of rain" (*tabassamu lamḥi l-barqi ʿan mutawaḍḍiḥin, ka-lawni l-aqāḥī shāfa alwānahā l-qaṭrū*) (Dhū l-Rummah, *Dīwān*, 580; cf. §5.15 on the chamomile).

191 "Racemes and male flowers": *ligāḥ al-ʿiṭīl*; *ʿiṭīl* is the male spadix, or spike, at the end of which the flowers are. The date palm flowers form inside a sheath, or spathe (CA *ʿaṭīl* "the stalk of a raceme of a male palm tree" Lane, *Lexicon*, 2082). I am grateful to Professor Clive Holes for his following elucidations on the Arabic terminology concerning date palm pollination: "The date palm's spathes (*dhirā*) protrude with their thick female flowers, which are yellow. This protective (as the word *dhirā* itself suggests) spathe looks a bit like a long leather pouch which bursts open to reveal the mass of female spikes inside it which form the flower heads (*ṭalʿ*) ready to receive the male pollen. Here *ligāḥ* is another word for *nibāt* 'pollen' and what carries the pollen is the white flower of the male spike (*ʿiṭīl*). In modern times, the male pollen (these days in the form of an extracted powder) or the pollen-bearing spike has to be brought to the female tree to impregnate it."

192 "Sun-ripened": *ṭahyah niḍay/niḍaj* lit. "properly cooked, stewed until it was well-cooked" (CA *ṭahā* "to cook, stew"; *naḍija* "to ripen, be well-cooked").

193 "Nourishment for paupers": In Arabian custom, poor people are allowed to gather dates that have fallen off the trees. In the echo chamber of Nabaṭī poetry, they are similar to locusts, as in the riddle of the poet ʿAdwān al-Hirbīd: "Gathered in by paupers who stand with empty hands" (*ḥāḍūh khālīn al-yidēn aḍ-ḍʿāfī*) (Sowayan, *Ayyām al-ʿArab*, 195).

194 A line reminiscent of similar scenes of Bedouin departure after a stay at a palm oasis during the hot season in the poetry of Ibn Sbayyil (e.g., Kurpershoek, *Arabian Romantic*, Poem 32). "Wild rush": *fī*

hawāh, lit. "as their fancy dictates," is shorthand for the more explicit line of Ibn Sbayyil: "While chasing his young she-camels' pastoral dream: / virgin tracks of desert herbs, as yet untrodden" (Kurpershoek, *Arabian Romantic*, 132).

195 "Sizzling heat": *gēẓ* "the hot and dry season, extending over four months from about the beginning of June to about the first days of October, when the Bedouins encamp in the settled territories" (Musil, *Rwala*, 8, 164, 338; CA *qayẓ*). In poetry, this is the season of love when tribes and people mix in anticipation of the date harvest, in recent premodern times and in antiquity, e.g., the verse: "Ṣaydā', will there be another summer at al-Ramādah, / its enjoyable nights and days?" (*a ṣaydā'u hal qayẓu l-ramādati rājiʿun, layālīhi aw ayyāmuhunna l-ṣawāliḥū*) (Dhū l-Rummah, *Dīwān*, 868).

196 The simile was still current in more recent times, e.g., Ibn Sbayyil's verse: "Do not act from surmises and guesswork: / a cool spell is no reason to travel without a waterskin" (*wlā takhidh ad-dinyā khrāṣin w-hagwāt, yagṭaʿk min nagl aṣ-ṣimīl al-barād*) (Kurpershoek, *Arabian Romantic*, §14.2.55, and the identical proverb in al-Juhaymān, *Amthāl*, 9:301).

197 "Impressed": *illā sibīl*, explained as "without anything in return, for nothing." Similarly, but in a different vein, Ḥmēdān al-Shwēʿir: "My eulogies were wasted on that miscreant, / like perfume on the bosom of an old hag" (Kurpershoek, *Arabian Satire*, §11.32).

198 "Roughshod": *tidūs al-ʿanīf*, lit. "you step on (i.e., commit, see n. 170 on 'to step on an offense') violence, outrages." "Blood money": *diyah*; see §3.7 "martyr of love"; and the poet-lover of Ibn Sbayyil who invokes sharia law against his mistress and similar examples in ghazal from ʿUmar ibn Abī Rabīʿah's poetry (Kurpershoek, *Arabian Romantic*, §36.10, 309 under ʿUmar).

199 Lit. "even if it takes a long time, (in the end) sands will slide down from the top of the dune," i.e., all things, no matter how tall they stand, will come to an end; even proud men will die. The world as sliding sands in the words of al-Khalāwī: "In this world, humans are exposed to dangers and extinction: / they teeter on a sandy slope that

caves in, assailed by devils" (*wa-l-ʿabd fī d-dinyā li-l-akhṭār wa-l-fanā, ʿalā jurf hārin wa-sh-shiyāṭīn wāthbah*) (Ibn Khamīs, *al-Khalāwī*, 66).

200 The following section (§§8.57–61) is a variation on the scene presented in §§1.13–22: love is merely another word for youth, which proves ephemeral when it treacherously abandons a friend invaded by the gray armies of old age, in the poet's view an inescapable truth of life that is better understood earlier than later. As in this verse, the redoubtable graybeard of old age spurs on his mount and arrives in haste, with great sense of urgency: *yiḥithth ar-raḥīl*, running as quickly as the lover's tears at the departure of youth, *ḥathāyith* (§5.65).

201 "Youth slips out": *wallā sh-shibāb*. The language is similar to the first verses of a poem by the pre-Islamic poet Salāmah ibn Jandal al-Saʿdī: "Gone is lovely youth, that marvelous time, / gone! It bolted, too fast to be overtaken; / It fled swiftly, with old age's graybeard in vain pursuit; / if only those galloping steeds might catch it! / Gone is fair youth, and its glorious achievements, / its succulent delights, delights so strange to old age"(*awdā* [*wallā* in another reading] *al-shabābu ḥamīdan dhū l-taʿājībī, awdā wa-dhālika sha'wun ghayru maṭlūbī / wallā ḥathīthan wa-hādhā l-shaybu yaṭlubuhū, law kāna yudrikuhū rakḍu l-yaʿāqībī / awdā l-shabābu lladhī majdun ʿawāqibuhu, fīhī naladhdhu wa-lā ladhdhāti li-l-shaybī*. As the scholion puts it, "if youth makes off, it can't be caught and retrieved" (*wa-lākin al-shabāb idhā wallā lam yudrak*) (*al-Mufaḍḍaliyyāt*, 1:224–26; 2:79). Ibn Sbayyil turned it into a joke: "Love is on the run; they are giving chase; [. . .] love left them behind and they can't catch up" (Kurpershoek, *Arabian Romantic*, §§31.2–3). See also §5.65.

202 "A gray monster": The onset of old age frightens beloved and lover in equal measure, as al-Mutanabbī tells the object of his admiration: "My scary white sidelocks frightened you, / but if it had come first, you'd be as terrified by seeing black" (*rāʿatka rāʾiʿatu l-bayāḍi bi-ʿāriḍī, wa-lawa nnahā l-ūlā la-rāʿa l-asḥamū*) (*Dīwān*, 4:123).

203 "Protection": *dikhīl*; an important concept in Bedouin culture; the right of asylum given by the owner of a tent and the need to respect it on pain of losing one's good reputation; *dakhal* "to seek

protection from;" *dikhīl* "one who places himself under the protection of [someone]"; *dkhālah* "protection granted by request, e.g., when an oppressed or pursued person enters the tent, or its sacred precincts, of [someone] whose protection he desires" (Musil, *Rwala* 441). In this case, the most flagrant violation imaginable occurs: the person who has been granted protection in accordance with hallowed custom turns on his benefactor when he discovers his host's vulnerability. Even worse, in §8.60 the chivalrous owner of the tent is ejected and chased away in dishonor as if he had committed a grievous wrong. Cf. Ibn Sbayyil's appeals to tribal law (*ʿurf*) (Kurpershoek, *Arabian Romantic*, 297, the lemma "law"). The young friend represents the poet's youth; see the next note.

204 This most explicit passage of one of the poet's principal themes, §§8.56–61 and §§1.12–22, depicts an imaginary life-and-death struggle between the poet's youth and the onslaught of old age: initially, youth seeks shelter with the poet, only to betray and attack him, leaving him defenseless, like a refugee who is thrown out by those with whom he sought safety. He cannot expect help from any quarter, including his own kinsmen, who calmly set about preparing his grave. The poet's message is: it is understandable that the appearance of the first gray hairs is an alarming reminder of one's mortality and the prospect of future infirmity, but any thought of resistance is futile.

205 "Measuring my grave": lit. "they started measuring the depth of a *ghilīl, ghilīlah*, digging a shallow trench in salt flats or rocky bottoms where brackish water gathers following rains" (Thānī, *Ibn Ẓāhir*, 246); *yablidūn* "they measure depth at sea with a sounding-lead, *bilūd*." As explained to me, this is a metaphor for preparations to start digging a grave.

206 A piece of common wisdom that is more current in the down-to-earth, combative tribal poetry of Najd than in Ibn Ẓāhir's introverted musings. Clearly, they have been borrowed by Ibn Ẓāhir as suitable metaphors for the kind of advice the poet-lover should have minded instead of clinging to unrealistic expectations about the loyalty of his beloved, i.e., trusting that his youth was there to stay forever.

Given Ibn Ẓāhir's acquaintance with Sufi practices and the context of inner life as a reflection of the outer world, the metaphorical use of this wisdom is at a far remove from the reality of the Najdī power struggles among city-states. The closest parallel is the Sufi "war on the soul's base instincts" (*jihād al-nafs*). The hard-boiled truths of this verse and §8.65 correspond to the verses of the quintessential Najdī poet Ḥmēdān al-Shweʿir: "March on your foe before he pays you a visit: / if you hesitate you'll find him smashing down your door"; "Do not display a sign of softness to an adversary / or to an enemy plotting your doom"; and "beware of heavenly bliss offered to you by a foe" (Kurpershoek, *Arabian Satire*, §30.11, §30.10, §29.9, and passim).

207 This verse reflects a common sentiment in the poetry of the period, e.g., ʿĀmir al-Samīn: "To pin hopes on pleading friendship with an enemy / is like an unwise person who takes a snake under his protection" (*w-min yarjī al-aʿdā bi-rajwā ṣidāgah, ka-l-afʿā ilā jāhā jihūlin yijīrahā*) (Sowayan, *al-Shiʿr al-nabaṭī*, 345).

208 "Predators": *as-sabʿ*, a word commonly used for "lion," but here it possibly refers to wolves. The line is a variation on the saying, "when the cat's away, the mice will play." Perhaps the sense is that in the absence of the main predator, lesser predators (or the lion's cubs) feel free to settle scores with those who have in the past eluded them, or thwarted them (in which case the translation should be "mark their ill-wishers for revenge").

209 Similarly, §1.24. Obviously, the poet does not share the view that an older age may also bring advantages, see introd., n. 62. Rather, he shares Jabr's view: "Old age starts with failing limbs: / Young beauties recoil without hiding their revulsion / [. . .] / No longer held in respect, his mind full of holes, / like a dry waterskin discarded at the rim of a well; / They'd rather have a dashing, merry youngster, / a ball of fire like a horse that bursts the fetters around its forelegs" (*mibtidā sh-shēb ʿēbin yijī bi-l-ʿḍā, jimlat al-bīḍ ʿamdan yaḥgirūnih / [. . .] / ṣār gadrih rakhīṣin w-ʿaglih nigīṣ, mithl shannin ʿalā l-jāl yarmūnih / yishtihūn al-ʿawaḍ fī ṣibiyyin gharīr, amradin yagṭaʿ al-gēd bi-gyūnih*) (Sowayan, *al-Shiʿr al-nabaṭī*, 481).

210 "My teeth fall out": One of the ubiquitous and grim signs that accompany the onslaught of old age, as also in §§1.26–30, §5.67, §6.18, §12.6, §12.12, §17.28, and the work of other poets, e.g., Zayd ibn ʿUrayʿir (also quoted in n. 151 to §5.61): "Old age took my teeth, eyes, and then all of my body, / leaving me prey to the approaching end" (*khadhā as-sinn wa-l-ʿēnēn wa-l-jism baʿd dhā, wa-gaffā wa-ʿāwaḍnī bi-shayyin ḥatāyifih*) (Sowayan, *al-Shiʿr al-nabaṭī*, 512). Early Arabic poetry invokes physical weakness of old age in combination with a sharp wit, honed by long experience, as defining traits for the poet-sage who dispenses wisdom, as in the opening verse of ʿAbdah ibn al-Ṭabīb: "Sons of mine! I have reached old age and eyesight fails me; / yet my wisdom is beneficial for its seekers" (*a-baniyya innī qad kabirtu wa-rābanī, baṣarī wa-fiyya li-muṣliḥin mustamtaʿū*) (*al-Mufaḍḍaliyyāt*, 1:294; 2:101; Kurpershoek, *Arabian Satire*, 90–91).

211 Lit. "she (the world) does not last."

212 See §10.26 and n. 236. Despair is easier to bear than protracted uncertainty.

213 On lovers' litigation at a tribal court, see Kurpershoek, *Arabian Romantic*, §36.10, 241n408.

214 "Gift-seeker": *gaṣd al-ʿaṭiyyāt*; cf. the use of the word *gaṣṣād* for the visitors who come from afar to meet Ibn Ẓāhir, "someone who travels with the express purpose of visiting someone in particular," see introd., n. 94.

215 "Tears": The hyperbolic volume of tears is outdone by a reprisal of the trope in §9.30.

216 The second hemistich, lit. "he has not preserved but" (*w-lā yaḥfiẓ illā*) is also understood as "he does not remember except," but in this context it may refer to water, or rather the lack of it.

217 It is not spelled out, but obviously the reference is to the poet-lover's struggle with treasonous youth and the advance of old age, a theme fully developed in Poems 1 and 8.

218 The somewhat contorted phrasing of the second hemistich is open to various interpretations, though the general meaning is not in doubt.

In other poems, the scene of departure features the caravan leader whose chant guides the camels, *al-ḥādī* (here in the previous verse *al-mnādī*), and in classical poetry the poet's heart cannot resist the call and follows, as in the lines of Suwayd ibn Abī Kāhil: "In the morning they departed, resolute and determined, / surging forward led by the chant of the caravan leader; / The noble heart was dragged along in shackles, / slave-like, forced to follow in the steps of their company" (*bakarat muzmiʿatun niyyatahā, wa-ḥadā l-ḥādī bihā thumma ndafaʿ / wa-karīmun ʿindahā muktabalun, ghaliqun ithra l-qaṭīni l-muttabaʿ*) (*al-Mufaḍḍaliyyāt*, 1:396–97; 2:143); see also Kurpershoek, *Arabian Romantic*, 196n80.

219 Blaming the scout or passing traveler whose news about rainfall makes the tribe rush off toward fresh pastures to fatten their animals is a common motif in "Bedouinist" love poetry, e.g.: "May God's reward elude the bearers of such tidings" (Kurpershoek, *Arabian Romantic*, §3.7). It is another indication of Ibn Ẓāhir's sedentary roots: a true Bedouin like Ibn Batlā of the Dawāsir would of course be grateful for such reports: "We replied, 'You've brought us joy, may your heart likewise be gladdened!'" (*Bedouin Poets of the Dawāsir Tribe*, 161, 143).

220 "One and only": *dūn kill al-ḥalāyil* "the one who eclipses all other candidates for marriage," i.e., the ideal beloved.

221 "Heat of noon": Usually desert travelers pause to spend the hottest time of the day in the shade, but boastful poetry stresses the endurance and suffering of marching on in order to cross the greatest distance possible in the shortest time. Hence, the saying, "Marching at noon time takes a toll on camels and riders" (*mashy al-guwāyil mihūnah*) (al-ʿUbūdī, *Amthāl*, 4:1351.)

222 This and the following verse seem to bear no relation to the foregoing. It is a direct quote from one of the poems ascribed to ʿAlyā, the beloved of the hero of the Banū Hilāl cycle of stories and poems: *yibīʿūn mā bāʿū w-yashrūn mā sharaw, w-lā ghibnin illā bi-n-niḍā wa-l-ḥalāyil* (al-Saʿīd, *al-Mawsūʿah*, 317–18); or *nibīʿ ilā bāʿū w-nashrī lyā sharaw, walā ghibnin illā bi-n-biḍā wa-l-ḥalāyil*) (in Sowayan, *Ayyām*

al-ʿArab, 1026; also quoted in the first published collection of Nabaṭī poetry, al-Faraj, *Dīwān al-Nabaṭ, majmūʿah min al-shiʿr al-ʿāmmī fī Najd*, 8; and noted in Thānī, *Ibn Ẓāhir*, 420–22). An ironic comment by the settled population is the saying, "Selling and buying is the raiding of the believers" (*al-bēʿ wa-sh-sharā ghārāt al-mūminīn*), i.e., not the plundering expeditions of the Bedouin (al-ʿUbūdī, *Amthāl*, 1:290).

223 Again, a verse from the same Banū Hilāl poem noted above: *kam min ṣimūt al-ḥijl tiblā bi-ʿāgah, w-kam ʿāgtin tablī bi-ḍāf al-khaṣāyil.* "Plump beauty": *ṣimūt al-ḥayy*, see n. 333 to §14.11.

224 See also §15.21 on the use of firearms.

225 The poem is in the same meter and rhyme as a poem by Abū Ḥamzah al-ʿĀmirī, which might be the earliest known Nabaṭī poem, and is almost the same length (Sowayan, *al-Shiʿr al-nabaṭī*, 263–65). This opening formula is repeated in all poems, in many cases accompanied by the same qualification, *al-fihīm* (CA fahīm). The epithet "sagacious, discerning" is also used by the central Arabian poet Ḥmēdān al-Shwēʿir, who was probably a somewhat younger contemporary of Ibn Ẓāhir: "These are the words of a learned and discerning (*al-ḥabr al-fihīm*) poet" (Kurpershoek, *Arabian Satire*, §14.1). The two poets seem to have shared a common understanding of their role as a sage and skilled artist whose role is to enlighten society on values and stratagems for life.

226 "Filled to the rim": *faljin ghashā sagf as-simām ila ṭimā*, explained as "a *falj*, pl. *aflāj*, the traditional Omani system of underground aqueducts carrying water from where it pours out, its *simām* (*miṣabb, manbaʿ al-falaj*), with the result that the aqueduct has been filled to its top, *sagf*, when the water rises, *ṭimā* (because of rains)."

227 See §3.13; as a sign that the hot season has started, the water in the earth has dried up to an arm's length as far as the elbow, I was told.

228 The early classical poet Suwayd ibn Abī Kāhil boasts of the inexhaustible supply of verses provided to him by his genius, his "demon" or familiar spirit: "My companion brings me new supplies of water; / swift-footed, he made sure my store never becomes

depleted" (*wa-atānī ṣāḥibun dhū ghayyithin, zafayānun ʿinda infādi l-quraʿ*). The scholion explains that the analogy is "with a well that is said to be always replenished (*dhātu ghayyithin*) and can always count on a fresh supply of water before it is in danger of running dry" (*al-Mufaḍḍaliyyāt*, 1:408; 2:146). As in §10.3 above, the flood unleashed by inspiration sweeps away everything in its path: "It surges like a foaming wave swells, / and arrogantly sweeps up and scatters pieces of rock" (*dhū ʿubābin zabidun ādhiyyuhū, khamiṭu l-tayyāri yarmī bi-l-qalaʿ*) (*al-Mufaḍḍaliyyāt*, 1:409; 2:146). The Najdī poet who is roughly contemporary with Ibn Ẓāhir, Rāshid al-Khalāwī, boasts of his talents in similar terms, see n. 273.

229 "Settlers": *ḥiddār*, lit. "those who have come down (to stay at the well)."

230 Again, a touch of Banū Hilāl: "You will find the daughters of Bedouins playing in its watercourses" (Lerrick, *Taghribat Banī Hilāl Al-Diyāghim: Variation in the Oral Epic Poetry of Najd*; Sowayan, *Ayyām al-ʿArab*, 1031). This paradisiacal scene of water, dense greenery, and fruits bears close resemblance to similar passages in early classical poetry, including its setting in a whimsical world and the opposition of youth and old age. It shares much of the vocabulary with the sixth-century poet ʿAbīd ibn al-Abraṣ, e.g., the words *jadwal, falaj, ẓilāl, nakhl, al-taṣābī*: "Like a water channel at the bottom of a wadi, / tears stream since her departure; / Or like a rivulet gurgling softly in the shade of palm trees, / its water runs with a whisper; / You are in love, whence this passion? / And how is it that gray hair has startled you?" (*aw falajun mā bi-baṭni wādin, li-l-māʾi min baynihī sukūbū / aw jadwalun fī ẓilāli nakhlin, li-l-māʾi min taḥtihī qasībū / taṣbū fa-ʿannā laka l-tiṣābī, annā wa-qad rāʿaka l-mashībū*) (ʿAbīd ibn al-Abraṣ, *Dīwān*, 24–25). The scene is a common one in poetry of Ibn Ẓāhir's era, more explicitly so in verses by Jabr ibn Sayyār: "I ask you for a warm welcome and an intimate majlis, / a serious gathering with worthy people; / And lofty palm trees in a shady garden around a mighty well, / amid merry songs and chanting of the crowds; / At the sides of a broad watercourse

rows of luxuriant palms, / dropping dates for wayfarers on foot to enjoy; / And a spacious abode, O Ibn ʿĪsā, and a luscious girl: / if she turns your head, you can't be blamed; / She walks with pigeon-toed steps, anklets sunk into fleshy calves, / and mesmerizes legions of love-crazed admirers; / Her finely chiseled figure and brilliant eyes shorten / the nights with an aroma of precious incense; / She resembles the houris of paradise, her resplendence / outshines light spread by candelabra" (*abī mink tarḥībin w-tagrīb majlis, rifīʿin maʿā nāsin rfāʿin gdūrahā / w-ghīnin ẓilīlātin ʿalā jāl ʿēlam, ka-mā al-ḥashr tazjīj al-ghnā maʿ zjūrahā / ʿalā jānib al-baṭḥā min al-ghīn bissag, yinūsh an-nimā māsh al-wiṭā min hjūrahā / w-bētin fisīḥin yā-bn ʿĪsā wa-ʿandal, law aṭ-ṭaraf mashghūfin bhā mā yiʿūrahā / giṣīrat khaṭw ar-rijl mā dann ḥijlahā, ilā l-ghayy tatlā sirbahā fī smūrahā / makhdūmatin rigrāgat al-ʿēn lēlahā, giṣīrin w-mijnī ʿūd al-azrag bkhūrahā / lahā min ṣifāt al-ḥūr nūrin w-bi-l-bahā, yifūg ʿalā nūr al-ganādīl nūrahā*) (Sowayan, *al-Shiʿr al-nabaṭī*, 490).

231 A standard expression, as in a verse by ʿĀmir al-Samīn: "Most fair-weather friends are whimsical: / if the going gets tough, they turn flaccid and unresponsive" *tarā akthar khillān ar-rkhā gallibiyyah / ilā shtaddat ash-shuṭṭah tarākhā kithīrahā*; and "The number of the friends you can count is astonishing, / how fast it dwindles in the hour of your need" (*alā mā akthar al-khillān yōm tʿiddhum, kithīrin w-ʿind al-mūjibāt gilīl*) (Sowayan, *al-Shiʿr al-nabaṭī*, 345, 592); and al-Khalāwī: "Many come forward, saying, 'At your service!' / only to make themselves scarce in your hour of need" (*f-kam ghimr gōmin gālhā ḥadd ḥāḍir, w-fī ḥill mūjibhā yittigī rikāyibih*) (Ibn Khamīs, *al-Khalāwī*, 301). The expression also features in a proverb: "If a friend does not come to my aid when I'm in difficulty, I don't want him as a friend when all is well" (*ṣidīj ʿalā sh-shaṭṭāt mā yiʿīn, w-allā ʿalā r-rāḥāt mā abāh*) (Ḥanẓal, *Jāmiʿ al-amthāl*, 185). "When push comes to shove, you and he share the load; / a partner in adversity, not a fair-weather friend" (Kurpershoek, *Arabian Romantic*, §21.12). See also §14.23 and "Friends" in the online "Glossary of Style, Themes, and Motifs."

232 The poet frequently employs assonance to reinforce his meaning, in this case by a repetition of the sweet-sounding long vowel *ū* (*-ūl*, *-ʿūdhā*, *-ʿūdhā*) for the soft allure of the beautiful girls.

233 "Bitter": The ancient motif of separation in Arabic poetry is kept alive in proverbs such as "If you wish for separation, ask for the impossible" (*ilā baghēt al-frāg f-iṭlib mā lā yṭāg*) (al-ʿUbūdī, *Amthāl*, 1:139).

234 "Begged": *tawassilī*, "my pleas, supplications" (CA *tawassul*), addressed to the beloved or in a plea to the poet's correspondent to intercede on his behalf with the beloved as part of the poem's conceit, as in Rumayzān's plea to Jabr ibn Sayyār: "Patience is a believer's protective armor; / by God, I come to you as a humble supplicant" (*wa-ṣ-ṣabr dirʿ al-mūminīn yiṣūnhum, yā-allāh anā lik migbilin mitwassilī*) (Sowayan, *al-Shiʿr al-nabaṭī*, 459).

235 "Enough to sate": *agnaʿ*, as in the Emirati saying, "Be content with little until much more comes your way" (*tjāniʿ bi-l-gilīl ḥattā iyīk al-kithīr*). For the lover it is the lesser option, as expressed in the saying, "It is your choice to be a fearless knight or to live in humble poverty" (*immā tikūn shijāʿ māniʿ wallā figīr gāniʿ*) (al-Rawāḥī, *al-Amthāl al-ʿUmāniyyah*, 19; Ḥanẓal, *Jāmiʿ al-amthāl*, 199); and "All that comes from the beloved is received in gratitude, even a single raisin" (*illī yātī min al-ḥabīb magbūl w-law ḥabbat zibīb*) (Ḥanẓal, *Jāmiʿ al-amthāl*, 307).

236 "Good or bad": lit. "I will not put you to the test (CA *manā*) by granting despair or hope," i.e., the worst torture, because despair may be easier to bear than a protracted period of anxious uncertainty, as expressed in the line of al-Ḥārith ibn Ḥillizah: "I despaired from ever attaining my heart's fond desire, / and at the bottom of despair lies sad consolation" (*wa-yaʾistu mimmā qad shughiftu bihī, minhā wa-lā yuslīka ka-l-yaʾsī*) (*al-Mufaḍḍaliyyāt*, 1:264; 2:91), and the saying, "despair is a gift of mercy" (*al-yaʾs raḥmah*). Another saying counseling despair is "If the door of greed opens, throw it shut with the door of despair" (*ilā infataḥ lak bāb ṭamaʿ f-siddah bi-bāb al-yās*), with reference to the verse by Muḥammad al-ʿAbd Allāh al-Qāḍī, "(O my heart,) sell your hopes for an affair with her in exchange for despair,

and you will be fine" (*bīʿī rijāh bi-yās waṣlah w-tabrīn*) (al-Juhaymān, *Amthāl*, 1:237–38). The religiously correct view is expressed in the saying, "One should not despair of God's mercy" (*mā min raḥmat allāh yās*) (al-Juhaymān, *Amthāl*, 7:166).

237 "My kinfolk decide": *illā bi-mā yāz/jāz li-halī*, the beloved's excuse that she must defer to the authority of her male guardians is a common trope in the dialogue between lovers, e.g., Rumayzān in his lover's litany to Jabr ibn Sayyār: "If I ask her why she's reserved toward me, / her excuse is: 'I must be on my guard against my kinfolk'" (*in gilt lih wēsh as-sibab fī dhā l-jifā, ʿidhrih yigūl innī aḥādhir min halī*) (Sowayan, *al-Shiʿr al-nabaṭī*, 458).

238 For similar dialogue on love, marriage, status, and religious and tribal rules, see Kurpershoek, *Arabian Romantic*, Poems 28 and 35.

239 That is, the innate nature of a character and things are unchangeable, no matter what the circumstances and constraints. In this case, spirited horses are always on the move or trying to be. This verse marks a transition to a section of wise sayings. The poet's musings in §§10.29–31 are presented as lessons drawn from his trials in love. Verse §10.31 paves the way for §§10.32–33 on the more general theme of relations between men and women; §10.34 introduces the conventional wisdom of circumspection in all matters.

240 Exercise of control by the mind and watching one's tongue are often compared to keeping a camel in check, e.g., in the words of al-Khalāwī: "A virtuous man is able to shackle his tongue, / as camels are hobbled to keep them in check" (*al-ḥirr yakfī fīh gēdih lsānih, wa-l-bill yakfīhā ʿgālin thāṭ bih*) (Ibn Khamīs, *al-Khalāwī*, 301). Similarly, the Emirati saying, "Your tongue is your horse; if you care for it, it will care for you and if you treat it with disregard, it will treat you likewise" (*lsānik ḥṣānik, in ṣintih ṣānik w-in hintih hānik*), i.e., if you use improper language, others will treat you accordingly; therefore, watch your tongue (Ḥasan, *al-ʿĀdāt*, 119).

241 "Sail": Strings of sayings like these are common in poetry of Ibn Ẓāhir's epoch, usually in the context of a deception and as a reminder that certain desirable things will only happen if certain conditions

have been met, e.g., the same image in a verse by the Jabrid poet al-Kulayf: "Likewise a ship will not move smoothly / unless its sail and ropes have been pulled taut" (*ka-dhā as-sifīnah mā yizīn misīrhā, illā bi-shadd shrāʿhā wa-ḥbālhā*) (Sowayan, *al-Shiʿr al-nabaṭī*, 297).

242 "Buckets": "The poet compares poems to buckets that are hoisted up from wells either full of water or empty" (Abū Shihāb and Abū Malḥah, *Ibn Ẓāhir*, 177). However, with reference to §2.2, the simile here may point to poetry's role in providing wise guidance, in the same way as a supply of water is essential on desert crossings.

243 "Honor needs burnishing": See §11.8.

244 See also §15.14. "Their neighbors live not in fear of treachery / from them, and are not afraid of a stained sword" (*lā yakhāfu l-ghadra man jāwarahum, abadan minhum wa-lā yakhshā aṭ-ṭabaʿ*), where *ṭabaʿ* is explained as rust on a blade, i.e., a stain on one's honor (Suwayd ibn Abī Kāhil, *al-Mufaḍḍaliyyāt*, 1:393; 2:142). Keeping white armor sparkling is an ancient metaphor for a man's energy and joyful readiness for combat, as in the line of Abū Dhu'ayb, "with a point of steel, freshly furbished, shining with a fiery glow like a beacon's light" (*fīhā sinānun ka-l-manārati aṣlaʿū*) (*al-Mufaḍḍaliyyāt*, 1:882; 2:359).

245 This verse is regarded as a statement of the poet's reasons for not touching the genre of *madīḥ*, panegyrics. The exception might be the reference to Oman's Yaʿrūbī (pl. al-Yaʿāribah) ruler Sayf ibn Sulṭān, nicknamed Qayd al-Arḍ ("Registrar of the Land"); see §13.28 and Introduction p. xii.

246 The dilemma is summed up in the Emirati saying, "If I speak up, it will be overheard by the neighbors and the entire quarter will know; if I keep silent, I will bear an unspoken grudge that will eat my heart out" (*in tiḥikkēt simʿat al-jīrān wa-l-ḥillah w-in sikitt hū ḍumar fī l-galb wu-hū ʿillah*) (Ḥanẓal, *Jāmiʿ al-amthāl*, 245). To suppress one's rage is a common counsel given by poets, e.g., Rumayzān: "Many a good man was forced to disguise his rage, / from fear that his adversary would take notice" (*fa-kam min fitan qad kann bi-l-karh ghēẓhā, makhāfat an yadrī bi-dāhā khaṣīmhā*) (Sowayan, *al-Shiʿr al-nabaṭī*, 427).

247 "Doesn't deserve": *mā tūjib ʿalēh*; the guest has a right to being hospitably received, *ḥaqq*, as expressed in the verse of al-Marrār: "He skimps on the guest's right, a blameworthy act, / and lets his fellows pick up the tag" (*yaḍannu bi-ḥaqqihā wa-yudhammu fīhā, wa-yatrukuhā li-qawmin ākharīnā*) (*al-Mufaḍḍaliyyāt*, 1:124, 2:41–42); and *al-ḥaqq* is explained as "one's obligations in tribal burden sharing and feeding guests" (*al-Mufaḍḍaliyyāt*, 1:701; 2:297).

248 "Sluggard": *dinbil* "billy goat" (Abū Shihāb and Abū Malḥah, *Ibn Ẓāhir*, 179; Alameemi, *Ibn Ẓāhir*, 229); however, it is more likely a variation of *tanbal*, "lazy sailor, slacker who shuns arduous tasks" (al-Rūmī, *Muʿjam al-muṣṭalaḥāt al-baḥriyyah fī al-Kuwayt*, 172). The verse is almost identical to a verse by the poet al-Shuʿaybī from al-ʿUnayzah in the al-Qaṣīm area of central Arabia, addressed to Barakāt al-Sharīf (d. 1616), a member of the Mushaʿshaʿ emirate in Arabistan, now the Khuzestan province of Iran: *tarā al-marājil ṣaʿbitin mirgātha, lō lā ṣʿūbathā rigathā az-zimmalī.* The verse by al-Shuʿaybī is identical in meaning to this verse of Ibn Ẓāhir, with the only differences being *al-marājil* instead of *al-jimāyil* and a different rhyme word (Sowayan, *al-Shiʿr al-nabaṭī*, 382). The verse's guiding idea is one of frequent occurrence (e.g., Sowayan, *al-Shiʿr al-nabaṭī*, 514, 517); and verses by Ḥmēdān al-Shwēʿir (Kurpershoek, *Arabian Satire*, Poem 20), though it is not typical of Ḥmēdān or of Ibn Ẓāhir. Rather, it belongs to the raw boasting of the Najdī Hilālī tradition in the style of al-Khalāwī and Shāyiʿ al-Amsaḥ, as the latter's line in a poem of wide-ranging self-praise: "If you die without glory and high achievement, / you've lived the life of a downtrodden weakling" (*min māt ma ḥāsh ath-thanā w-adrak al-ʿlā / mamshāwh min jōf al-ʿbād ḍiʿīf*) (Sowayan, *Ayyām al-ʿArab*, 293). It is the subject of many wise sayings, such as: "To achieve your lofty ambitions, you must ride your mounts to exhaustion" (*illī yabī aṭ-ṭōlāt titʿab rkābih*) (al-Juhaymān, *Amthāl*, 1:348).

249 Again, this verse is very similar to a line in a poem with the same rhyme and meter by al-Shuʿaybī: "If a she-goat were rich, she'd be respectfully consulted, / and they'd ask, 'Where is the mansion of the

lady with fine horns?'" (*wa-l-māl law hū ʿind ʿanzin shīwirat, wi-ygāl yā umm grēn wēn al-manzilī*) (Sowayan, *al-Shiʿr al-nabaṭī*, 382). Nevertheless, a rich goat is still a stupid goat and considered so, as expressed in a similar proverb: "A beggar was lodged in a palace, but he kept stretching out his hand to implore passersby, 'Put some of God's gifts on the windowsill'" (*aṭ-ṭarrār ḥaṭṭūh fī gaṣir, madd īdah w-gāl: min māl allāh yā-rōzanah*) (Ḥanẓal, *Jāmiʿ al-amthāl*, 155). And the line of the poet Khalaf Abū Zwayyid: "I am like a goat that scratches the soil in search of its own slaughter" (*anā ka-mā ʿanzin tḥarrith zawālih*) (Sowayan, *Ayyām al-ʿArab*, 595). Similarly, the Emirati saying, "A goat is still a goat, even if it flies" (*ʿanz w-law ṭārat*, Ḥasan, *al-ʿĀdāt*, 108).

250 "Scoundrels": *wa-l-kiffar ẓilmin*; "And the disbelievers: they are the wrongdoers" (*wa-l-kāfirūna humu l-ẓālimūna*) (Q Baqarah 2:254). From this verse, the poet makes a transition to the theme of rain: a customary way of invoking blessings on the beloved or dear ones. The poet enjoys particular renown for these rain sections, *maṭariyyāt*.

251 The conventional prayer for rain on the land where the beloved sojourns, as with his contemporary Jabr ibn Sayyār (Sowayan, *al-Shiʿr al-nabaṭī*, 454).

252 As in §9.45.

253 See §8.22 for a similar role of sly intrigue by the west wind, *shartā*. In the poet's imagination, the wind acts as a mischievous informer whose whisperings set cloud against cloud, male against female, as he travels swiftly from one to the other, spreading his calumnies to devastating effect. The clouds clash, thunder roars, and forked lightning splits open the pregnant bellies of the female clouds, who release their store of water—to the delight of the poet who sent up verses of prayer for the land of the beloved's tribe to be irrigated with rain.

254 One might argue that veils have to be discarded for the poet to describe the beauty of the girls' hair in fitting similes. On wattled enclosures of the Bedouin, see n. 304. Modern Bedouin poets follow the same sequence: scenes of exuberance and delight triggered by the lush green brought forth by the rains of an abundant springtime,

all the more joyful following a period of severe drought; see the poem of al-Dindān, introduced by his words: "We suffered from the drought and asked God to send us rain" (Kurpershoek, *The Poetry of ad-Dindān*, 139–41). It is part of the cycle of "destruction and revival" (*dammār ʿammār*), frequently cited by poets of Ibn Ẓāhir's era; see n. 113.

255 Bunches of dates are often protected against birds by being wrapped in a cover.

256 In this verse, the poet strikes the elegiac note appropriate to "the day of departure" (*yawm al-ẓaʿīnah*) topos of classical poetry.

257 A very strong male camel carries the ornamental litter, howdah, in which the tribe's principal ladies are seated. It is also called "the camel of the throne" (*jimal al-takht*). Though the generic word for the species "camel" is of Semitic origin, in Arabian poetry *jimal* only refers to male camels of a certain age: "stud camel between its sixth and twentieth year" (Musil, *Rwala*, 330–31).

258 "Leader's chant": See §12.32.

259 The "pack in front" is the *salaf*, the tribe's warriors who ride in front on fast she-camels, while the horses trot alongside, tied to the camels. To attribute this kind of speed to the heavily laden animal is a hyperbolic way of stating the pack camel's strength. Though this camel carries the caravan's heaviest load, it still outpaces the other camels, as in the verse of the pre-Islamic poet Bishr ibn ʿAmr: "Do you see the camels carrying the litters, driven / at a pace that leaves the other camels behind?" (*bal hal tarā ẓuʿunan tuḥdā muqaffiyatan, lahā tawālin wa-ḥādin ghayru masbūqī*) (*al-Mufaḍḍaliyyāt*, 1:553; 2:217).

260 Lit. *al-rijīb* (CA *al-raqīb*) "opposite star," which in this case is Capella, the brightest star in the constellation Scorpio, the star opposite to the Pleiades, see n. 345.

261 "Succulent [. . .] beauties": *rayyān ash-shibāb*, lit. "verdant youth," see §10.51 above.

262 "Crafted": *binā*, lit. "to build, construct"; see n. 73 on the comparison of composition to the construction of impregnable buildings and fortresses.

263 The self-righteous tone of these verses is repeated in the prelude of Poem 16.

264 "Aficionados": *al-rāmisīn*, lit. "those who talk, have conversations, memorize and recite poetry," see §3.4.

265 A common saying, as in Kurpershoek, *Arabian Satire*, §6.9, §28.13: "Their conceit was rewarded with poverty and shame, / and sweet water replaced by brine"; and "Even if I have to drink brackish water mixed / with bitter apple, I value self-respect more."

266 "As with people": *an-nās ajnās* "people are of different kinds"; this saying is an introduction to verses of gnomic wisdom about desirable characteristics and their opposites. It is followed by generalized comments, not advice in direct address to a listener; see §5.6. More than elsewhere, this moralistic poem strikes a dour tone as it separates the good from the bad in terms of religion.

267 "Crush it": *taṭfīhā*, lit. "extinguish it." Ibn Ẓāhir makes the point that good people are always the ones left with the unenviable duty of cleaning up the mess created by irresponsible, asocial troublemakers, like Ḥmēdān in his poem about conflagrations and strife: "Some ill-starred wretches let war loose and it ran free [. . .] Leaving it to you to quench the fire" (*Arabian Satire*, §§6.2–4).

268 See "Wealth and Poverty" in the online "Glossary of Style, Themes, and Motifs" for the poet's appreciation of the balance between the two.

269 "Tasty rewards": The ephemeral nature of these rewards is a classical motif, based on the notion that death is "tirelessly lying in wait" (Arazi, "al-Shayb wa 'l-shabāb" in *EI2*). These physical pleasures are associated with youth; old age is supposed to put an end to that.

270 The winds may bring or withhold precious rain and fortune. On winds, see n. 388 on the winds of fortune, and §6.2.

271 The enumeration of measurements of time, as part of the poet's brooding on the vicissitudes and inequities of this world, is echoed by another poet of the period, Rumayzān: "A ferocious world unleashes its days and months; / its years pour out for you bitterness after bitterness" (*dunyan tighīẓ ayyāmaha wi-shhūrahā, wi-snīnahā tasgi ar-rjāl*

mrūrahā), followed by the common description of role reversals between owls and falcons, real men and feral cats, and peregrines and sparrows, while chicken live in castles (Sowayan, *al-Shiʿr al-nabaṭī*, 460).

272 "Set forever": *sarmidiyyāt* "the permanent sequence of days and nights" (CA *sarmad* "lasting and permanent, without interruption"). Cf. Q Anʿām 6:96. It occurs in the saying, "Expressions of hope do not slake one's thirst" (*mā yirwī aẓ-ẓamyān kithr as-sarāmīd*) (al-Juhaymān, *Amthāl*, 7:212).

273 Wise poets commonly exhort listeners to follow their advice, e.g., the Jabrid poet ʿĀmir as-Samīn, "When at a loss, take counsel with a wise guide, / with experience of what happened in days past" (*akhbir dilīl an-nās ilā kunt jāhil, b-afʿāl ma kid mā miḍā min misīrahā*) (Sowayan, *al-Shiʿr al-nabaṭī*, 345); and al-Khalāwī: "Ask: 'Who is the sea of poetry?' 'Rāshid!' / His verses surge up like a flood of cresting waves" / [. . .] / "The borders of composition and meaning / as far as knowledge stretches he has reached; / A dictionary for those seeking answers, that is Rāshid [his first name, with the meaning 'rightly guided'] / the sultan of all poetry that hits its mark" (*w-in gīl man baḥr ash-shiʿr gīl Rāshid, fī l-ashʿār tayyārin tiṭāmā ghabāyibih* / [. . .] / *nihāyāt mā yinshā w-ghāyāt ma ḥawat, ṣdūr ar-rjāl mn al-maʿānī w-jāt bih* / *gāmūs ahl ar-rāy fī r-rāy rāshid, w-silṭān man anshā min al-gīl ṣāybih*) (Ibn Khamīs, *al-Khalāwī*, 52–53, 300); and Ḥmēdān al-Shwēʿir: "Learn from a man clever, tested, and wise, / a penetrating mind, prescient about the blows of fate" (Kurpershoek, *Arabian Satire*, §2.2). The connection with poetry is made in the saying, "Proverbs are an excellent guide for intelligent people" (*al-amthāl li-dh-dhhanā khēr dilīl*); verses with wise sayings or similar content are also called "proverbs" (*amthāl*) (see n. 39) (al-Juhaymān, *Amthāl*, 1:353).

274 The instability of the world is exemplified by the image of the world as a sphere balanced on the horn of a bull, *garn thōr* (personal communication from Saad Sowayan); see §4.61 and n. 120.

275 "Wiles and treachery": *makkāritin ghaddāritin*, a use of energetics beloved by poets of the era, e.g., Jabr ibn Sayyār: "She's full of tyranny,

treachery and vile tricks; / the depth of her sea of wonders can't be plumbed" (*jawwāritin ghaddāritin ʿayyāritin, w-min al-ʿajāyib mā tgās bḥūrahā*) (Sowayan, *al-Shiʿr al-nabaṭī*, 463); and his correspondent Rumayzān: "She's full of wiles, hostility and treachery: / with brute injustice she casts off ties with lovers" (*makkāritin nakkāritin ghaddāritin, tinfiḍ ḥbāl al-ʿāshigīn bi-zūrahā*) (Sowayan, *al-Shiʿr al-nabaṭī*, 462).

276 "Tortuous": lit. "hearts are deep," as in the Emirati saying, "this person is a deep well shaft" (*ghazīr al-yāl/jāl*), explained as "someone who is hard to fathom, who keeps his thoughts to himself and does not show his intentions" (Ḥasan, *al-ʿĀdāt*, 109).

277 The poet blames his unreasonable heart for his mishaps, see §9.24 and n. 218.

278 At this point, the poet gets ready to take up the slack and steer people with a firm hand to the right course.

279 "Godliness": *tigā*. See n. 131 for the use of *tigā* (CA *tuqā*, *taqwā*) in this verse, and §11.35 and §11.38 hereafter.

280 Another reading gives *shirwā andhālhā*, and the meaning of the hemistich would be: "despair not: many folks have no truck with worthless trash" (Thānī, *Ibn Ẓāhir*, 195).

281 The verse is almost identical to a verse by the poet al-Kulayf, also written in accordance with the eastern dialect, al-Julayf, in his long ode (105 verses), considered one of the best poems of the period, in praise of the last ruler of the Jabrid dynasty of the al-Aḥsāʾ region in eastern Arabia, Muqrin ibn Qaḍīb ibn Zāmil, before the Ottoman governor of Basra took over in 1525. The verse is: *f-ilā zlifat rijlik w-ḥall bhā al-gḍā, f-idr ann al-ukhrā ḥālahā min ḥālahā* (Sowayan, *al-Shiʿr al-nabaṭī*, 296).

282 A graphic description of the scene is given in three verses by Bashāmah ibn al-Ghadīr: A deaf man, not distracted by the maddening noise at the well, races against time as he pulls frantically at the well rope that lifts the bucket to fill the troughs for camels that press around the well, crazed with thirst. He does so after waiting for his turn on the morning after the night of the third day. "He steadies the

shaking of the rope, and if his hands fail, he seeks assistance from his upper arm" (*fa-aqāma hawdhalata l-rishā'i* [the rope of the bucket] *wa-in, tukhṭi' yadāhu yamuddu bi-l-ḍab'ī*) (*al-Mufaḍḍaliyyāt*, 1:828–29; 2:344–45). Therefore, this verse's advice is to have a laserlike focus on the issue at hand and not to waver when others are seen to be giving up on the task.

283 Q An'ām 6:136.

284 Q Qāf 50:10.

285 Q Ḥajj 22:37.

286 Q Naḥl 16:8; Q Āl 'Imrān 3:14; the latter verse is this poem's message in a nutshell, in particular its end, and the gist of much of his *dīwān*: "Made attractive to the people is the love of desires [. . .]; such are the goods of this present life, but with Allah is the best place of resort" (Richard Bell, *The Qur'ān*, 1:45–46).

287 "Bound by friendship": *bāb ṣidāgah*, "a door of friendship," i.e., misery is woven into human existence; the expression is similar to the line of 'Amr ibn al-Ahtam: "Among the virtuous, there is always a way of doing good" (*wa-li-l-khayri bayna l-ṣāliḥīna ṭarīqū*), i.e., a virtuous person will find ways of doing good works (*al-Mufaḍḍaliyyāt*, 1:254; 2:85).

288 In an artful allusion, the poet takes the conventional image of the beloved's departure and identifies it with the concepts of time and memory. As in the first poem and elsewhere, love and the beloved are made to represent the poet's youth, which falls victim to usurpation by old age, as depicted in the following verses.

289 The poet gives the length of time spent in harmony with his beloved (see following note). Similarly, Rumayzān measures the time he spent in amorous felicity in his verse: "In this manner we spent two thousand days and then more, / three hundred days with no fatigue" (*akhadhnā kadhā alfēn yōmin w-zōdhā, thalāth miyat yōmin walā nīb zāhig*) (Sowayan, *al-Shi'r al-nabaṭī*, 479).

290 The ten years and the thirty years of the preceding verse are said to allude to the approximate age given to the poet when he started to compose verses. The poems' preoccupation with the passage of time

and old age leads to similar conclusions, though in Ibn Ẓāhir's era it is a common conceit in poems concerned with gnomic wisdom.

291 That is, a woman cannot be blamed for the suffering caused by her beauty.

292 The subject of the verb is left undefined. The explanation given to me is that as youth retreats, old age gradually takes over. In the poem's thematic sequence, this note of resignation is followed by amorous revival at the return of the beloved's tribe in the next cycle of the Bedouin year's seasons of migrations, similar to poems by the nineteenth-century central Arabian poet Ibn Sbayyil (see Kurpershoek, *Arabian Romantic*, xviii–xix and 235n374 on the pivotal role of the star Canopus in this cycle).

293 "Entanglement": *maʿānīh daljah* "its spirit is weak, corrupt" (Abū Shihāb and Abū Malḥah, *Ibn Ẓāhir*, 189); as explained to me, in Emirati dialect *dalj* carries the meaning of "mixed up, interwoven, entangled." Another meaning is *daljāt* "ship that is unstable at sea because of lack of a proper keel and because its low boards are close to the water so that waves easily spill into the ship's hold," as in the verse "Ramshackle boats, unfit to sail at sea" (*fī daljātin kharāyib / mā yigṭaʿin l-ibḥūr*) (*Dīwān Ibn ʿAtīj*, 58); *diljah*, *dalājah* (CA *dalqāʾ* "old, decrepit she-camel with broken teeth; when she drinks, the water runs from her mouth"; also, *dilqim al-asnān* "teeth, molars that fall out because of age," Ibn Manẓūr, *Lisān*, 1411).

294 See n. 292. Here the subject is mentioned: *al-dinyā* (CA *dunyā*) "the world."

295 "Spiteful Fate": *bi-l-ghēẓ al-khabīth kiẓūm*, lit. "harboring spiteful rage," i.e., "repressing its hate in order not to show it while waiting for the right moment to pounce on the object of its rancor"; see n. 246.

296 "Bird of Death": *ṭēr al-manāyā*; *miniyyah*, pl. *manāyā* "destiny, death;" *ḥōḍ al-manāyā* "the pool of death" (Musil, *Rwala*, 183, 224; CA *manīyah*, pl. *manāyā* "death foreordained by God, fate").

297 The world is described as *sarmadin* (CA *al-sarmad* "lasting a long time, forever"; see n. 272). In Sufism, it denotes duration without beginning or end, an eternity outside the measurement of time.

298 "Year after year": The enumeration of different categories of time serves the poet's purpose of contrasting humankind's condition in the world's ebb and flow with the permanency of the afterlife, as in these seventeenth- or early-eighteenth-century verses by Fāyiz ibn Nḥēṭ: "Days are half blind and nights give birth to events: / there is no escape from their volleys of calamity; / They come when you least expect taking a hit: / they do not send messengers or warners ahead" (*w-al-ayyām ghimsin wa-l-liyālī ḥawādith, wlā min dawāhī ramyihin mnīr / tijīh ʿalā ghirrin wu-hu mā darā bhā, wlā jāh minhā ṭārish w-nidhīr*) (Sowayan, *al-Shiʿr al-nabaṭī*, 550–51); and Rāshid al-Khalāwī: "We count the nights and the nights count us; / life is evanescent, but the nights will endure" (*nʿidd al-liyālī wa-l-liyālī tiʿiddna, wa-l-aʾmār tafnā wa-l-liyālī bi-zāyid*) (Ibn Khamīs, *al-Khalāwī*, 58, 369). See §4.29 for the same observation: "You're assaulted (by the world, fate) without warning or reconnaissance."

299 "Four hot months": i.e., the four months of the traditional season of pearl diving during summer when the sea of the Gulf is calm and the water not cold.

300 "The Pleiades, eclipsed" (*al-kannah*): the disappearance of the Pleiades from April 28 to June 6, which traditionally signals the onset of the great summer heat (al-ʿUbūdī, *Muʿjam al-anwāʾ wa-l-fuṣūl*, 248–50; Kurpershoek, *Arabian Romantic*, 189n38). Similarly, in the earliest Arabic poetry, traveling in the desert at the time of the eclipse puts the poet's intrepidness on display, as in verses of Rabīʿah ibn Maqrūm: "Often I visited wells [with foul water] when the Pleiades fall at the end of night, / under my saddle a stout and fast riding camel" (*waradtu wa-qad tahawwarati l-Thurayyā, wa-taḥta waliyyatī wahmun wasāʿū*) (*al-Mufaḍḍaliyyāt*, 1:377; 2:137). In this poem, §§12.19–20 are a concise summing up of the seasons of the Bedouin year.

301 As explained by Alameemi, this verse telescopes three images of color into one: the red-white color of *ruṭab*, fresh, ripe dates; the reddish and white hues of a gazelle; and the red-brown dye of henna on a woman's fingers and palm. "Soft hands": *ghuḍḍin ʿagābih*, lit. "soft at the backside, at the haunches"; again, it might refer to the hind parts

of a gazelle or to the palms of a henna-dyed hand. “Under wraps”: lit. “about whom (her beauty) there is no misunderstanding (among the Bedouin),” i.e., she is not seen, but her singular beauty is known to all. The reference is to a tribal habit of keeping young unmarried women secluded in a tent away from sunlight that might alter the whiteness of their skin. The color of *ruṭab* dates is also compared to camel litters for women: “With ruddy coverings to their litters, like the upper sides of ripening clusters of dates” (*al-Mufaḍḍaliyyāt*, 2:217). The second hemistich reads literally: “Or news of someone whose reputation is not a figment of the imagination.”

302 The first hemistich is identical to the first hemistich of §2.17.

303 “Shelters”: In this case, the “house” is not a tent but an improvised structure made of wood and other natural materials, cf. this early description: “The houses of the Arabs were made of hair [i.e., tents], or a shelter made of camel wool, or a tent [*khaymah*] made from tree material, or made of stone” (*al-Mufaḍḍaliyyāt*, 1:808).

304 The Bedouin of the southern Gulf littoral did not live in tents but would build temporary shelters from wood and other materials, see §21.20, §23.6. In essentials, these probably did not differ much from such construction in recent times. Wooden frames, especially from acacia and prosopis trees, “are covered with a variety of materials, including dry brushwood, palm fronds, palm leaf matting, blankets, goat hair cloth, canvas tarpaulins, and sheets of plywood and corrugated aluminium” (Roger Webster, “The Bedouin of the Wahiba Sands: Pastoral Ecology and Management”; a more detailed description of such structures is given in Webster, “Notes on the Dialect and the Way of Life of the Āl Wahība Bedouin of Oman”).

305 “Fidgets”: When the couched camel is loaded it makes slight bodily movements, but otherwise remains calm and does not try to shake off the load or rise to its feet before it should; *mistikīn* (CA *kāna* “to humble oneself, submit”) used for a loaded camel, “submissive,” (*dhalīl al-nafs*) (*al-Mufaḍḍaliyyāt*, 1:468).

306 “White brilliance”: *jalāhā al-khibā*, lit. “the little tent (in which she was kept) kept her (skin) light”; i.e., she did not have to work outside

like the common women but was sheltered from the sun so as to preserve her "aristocratic" whiteness of skin (CA *jalā* "to clean, polish; to be brilliant"), see n. 334 and §12.21 above.

307 "Driver's chant": A standing expression in the departure scene, see n. 218. In Arabian desert poetry, as in this volume, it is part of the departure scene of the poet's beloved, as prelude to his effusion of sorrow; or it may herald her arrival, which is also a harbinger of heartbrokenness because of her inevitable departure. As such, the camel trains' appearance or disappearance are intimately connected with the change of seasons, such as the summer months spent in palm oases.

308 Wounds and ulcers were treated with the same red-hot iron used for branding the animals.

309 The poet admits that the caravan leader is an admirable fellow, but at the same time he is jealous of the man's close proximity to the beloved. Also, the man leads the group that carries the poet's sweetheart away. However, the verb used, "I did not like him, a man not to my liking" (*mā ahtiwētih*, CA *hawiya* "to love, like"), is used in exactly the same form in §1.17, where it refers to the arrival of old age and the departure of youth. Therefore, while this and similar scenes may resemble those of Dhū l-Rummah and other classical poets, in Ibn Ẓāhir's poetry they have been firmly set in the context of the "graybeard and youth" theme (*al-shayb wa-l-taṣābī*) that matches the poet's philosophical ruminations.

310 The poet compares the pain inflicted by this sight to the tight grip of a clamp screwed onto his heart.

311 It is an ancient conceit that the beloved's departure comes as a surprise to the poet-lover, e.g., the verse of ʿAlqamah ibn ʿAbadah: "I did not know about their departure until they had resolved to be gone: / all their male camels were bridled for a start before dawn" (*lam adri bi-l-bayni ḥattā azmaʿū ẓaʿanan, kullu l-jimāli qubayla l-ṣubḥi mazmūmū*) (*al-Mufaḍḍaliyyāt*, 1:788; 2:334). "Clouds over": see §14.47.

312 A person's energy and talents are often compared to a well, as in the saying, "He drew water in copious amounts and then he watered the

palms or crops one more time to make sure that they were fully irrigated" (*sigāh ʿalalin baʿd nahal*) (al-Juhaymān, *Amthāl*, 3:265).

313 "Salt": lit. "salt is salt for the food (*zād*)." The word for salt, *milḥ*, is repeated four times in this and the previous line to emphasize the superior quality of his verses.

314 For similar criticism of sour narrow-mindedness masquerading as religious righteousness, see Kurpershoek, *Arabian Satire*, Poems 12 and 27.

315 As in the previous verse, the poet hints at the exercise of power and social interactions in a manner more common in Najdī poetry of his era. Cf. Kurpershoek, *Arabian Satire*, §4.21: "He said, 'I was a shaykh long before you; / my ancestor took possession of it.' / 'Congratulations to your father and grandfather! / What a shame they sired a dunce like you.'" This would fit the political message (the only one found in Ibn Ẓāhir's oeuvre) in the final part of the poem.

316 "Lofty ambition": *al-ʿlā* (CA *ʿulan* "heights, peaks"), see n. 248. Many lines of Bedouin poetry make the binary distinction between the indefatigable knight whose face is blackened by the sun from riding all day long on his raids and a good-for-nothing who lazes in the shade of the tent while being served by womenfolk who secretly despise him (e.g., the chapter "A Face Marked by the Sun" in *The Story of a Desert Knight*, 168–78).

317 "Oarsmen": *miyādīfī* lit. "my oars" (CA *mijdāf*, pl. *majādīf*). It is a reference to the saying, "my oars are broken" (*kisar miyādīfī*). If it is said that someone's oars are broken, it means that he has sustained a big loss and is completely helpless, similar to the expression "his keel is broken" (*inkisar bīṣah*), i.e., his ship is lost beyond repair (Ḥanẓal, *Jāmiʿ al-amthāl*, 219); see also §17.11.

318 The situation described in the verse is expressed in the Emirati saying, "At your orders, we hoist the sails and pull the oars" (*akhadhnā bi-shrāʿ w-miydāf*), an ironic comment aimed at someone who monopolizes the discussion and has no time for others (Ḥanẓal, *Jāmiʿ al-amthāl*, 245). The implied meaning is that the poet shouts orders at his crew in order to steer the ship of youth away from old

age's depredations, but to no avail. The same images and meaning are found in §17.11.

319 The same word, *wshām*, occurs in rhyme position and as the final word of the first hemistich. Alameemi (*Ibn Ẓāhir*, 59) suggests that the word in the latter position derived from *shām* "to travel." The poet's purpose is to underline a contrast in meaning. The word often has the meaning of tattoos or traces (of green) left by rains, and it also has the general meaning of "trace." Here it may associate the traces of teeth with traces of former habitation at an abandoned campsite of the beloved's tribe (CA *awshama fīh al-shayb* "hoariness, old age became visible in his traits").

320 "Escape from death": The futility of trying to escape from death, or fear of death as a reason to be overcautious, is one of the most popular subjects in sayings, as in this Emirati proverb: "Aḥmad and his servant were on the run from death, when they found that they had run straight into death's arms" (*Aḥmad w-khaddāmah shārid min al-mōt, ligā l-mōt jiddāmah*) (Ḥanẓal, *Jāmiʿ al-amthāl*, 354). And on caution: "Being circumspect does not postpone your decreed time of death" (*al-ḥadhar mā yadfaʿ al-gidar*) (Ḥanẓal, *Jāmiʿ al-amthāl*, 356). The theme reminds us of its most famous version: the anecdote in Rumi's *Mathnawi*, (in Behrooz Mahmoodi-Bakhtiari and Farhang Farbod, "Fleeing Destined Death")

321 Lit. "I wished for resplendent youth to take me back."

322 Riding horses and racing camels symbolize the devil-may-care attitude of reckless youth (§13.10), as Ḥmēdān not only "swam in a sea surging with sinful rapture," as Ibn Ẓāhir in §13.22 below, but also "struggled through gullies surrounded by hyenas, clambered on rocky hills haunted by demons" (Kurpershoek, *Arabian Satire*, §26.7). Riding "the Devil's steed" is a common expression, as in recent times people of Najd used to call a bicycle "the vehicle of Satan." The Najdī chronicles record that one of the tribal chiefs routed by the Wahhābī troops of the Āl Saʿūd was nicknamed *Ḥuṣān Iblīs*, "the Horse of Satan" (Kurpershoek, *A Saudi Tribal History*, 557n39).

323 "Worship": *ʿbādah*; obviously here more specifically "prayer (*al-ṣalāh*)" is meant. In the books of *fiqh* (the science of religious law in Islam), prayer follows religious purity as the first subject in the treatment of the *ʿibādāt* (religious practice) (G.-H. Bousquet, "ʿIbādāt," *EI2*). The poet makes the whole represent a part, the opposite of synecdoche. One reason for the choice in favor of the broader term might be that *wi-ʿbādah* fits the meter, while *wi-ṣ-ṣalāh* does not.

324 "Zaydis, Europeans, or Persians": *Zīdiyyihā w-Farniyyihā w-Āʿjāmahā*; the female personal suffix *–hā* refers to "the enemy," but is mostly padding for the meter's sake. These three groups would have represented the sum total of strangers against whom the Yaʿāribah rulers led a successful uprising that aligned more indigenous elements of society against the threat of foreign overlords: the Zaydī imams of Yemen had expulsed the Ottoman Turks from Yemen in 1645. The Europeans, the *Farniy* powers (lit. "the Franks," the Emirati pronunciation of *ifranjī* by substitution of *yāʾ* for *jīm*, as usual in the Emirati dialect, see Introduction p. xlii), is a synonym for the Christian powers in the Gulf, foremost at the time being the Portuguese whose last stronghold, Muscat, was conquered by Sulṭan ibn Sayf in 1650. The Persians, *al-aʿjām* (plural of *ʿajamī*; *ʿajam* are "people who are not Arabs, foreigners, especially meaning Persians," Lane, *Lexicon*, 1967), had long been present, particularly after the accession of Shah ʿAbbās and his conquest of Hormūz in 1624.

325 "Meekly they paid": *wagfin ʿala z-zahdā*, lit. "behaving with modesty, humbleness," explained as "surrender and good behavior (following the punishment for their uprising)." "Rebellion": *gyāmhā* (CA *qiyāmah* "resurrection; upheaval, resolution").

326 The verses §§13.30–32 are not in the MS but were added in Alameemi's edition from oral tradition (as explained in his *Ibn Ẓāhir*, 66–67). Indeed, the Omani chronicles laud the hitherto unknown level of security that reigned in the domains of Sayf ibn Sulṭān, see introd., n. 7.

327 A similar scene at the nineteenth-century Bedouin court of Ibn Rashīd: "In the kitchen, cooks jostle about / like thirsty camels pressed around a waterhole" (Kurpershoek, *Arabian Romantic*, §23.51).

328 In today's Emirates, this famous verse is considered a succinct description of the country's coastal and inland desert areas. "Desert plains": *sīḥ* "extensive flat desert area with many pebbles" (in CA it refers to small streams of water running on the land's surface, al-Khāṭirī, *Muʿjam mawārid al-miyāh al-qadīmah bi-Imārat Abu Ẓabī*, 18).

329 An alternative rhyme word is *ymām/jmām* ("welling up"). "Flocked": The amateurs of oral tradition, *ar-ramisīn, ar-rimmās*, always gather in sizable crowds, *ẓōl*, as in §13.4.

330 "Larestan": a region in Iran, Larestan county in the Fars province with a Sunni majority; *lāriyyah* "people of Iranian origin in Dubai who speak the Iranian dialect of their ancestral home, *Lārih*" (Ḥanẓal, *Muʿjam al-alfāẓ*, 593); *lāriyyah* "Persians, *ʿajam*" (al-Maṭrūshī, *al-Lahjah*, 288).

331 Lit. "toward the south," explained as a broad reference to the area of the oasis of al-Buraymī (Abū Shihāb and Abū Malḥah, *Ibn Ẓāhir*, 219). This also goes for the last verse of this collection, the final line of the poem by Ibn Ẓāhir's daughter, about the direction of the Bedouin migration.

332 "Like ships": In the earliest Arabic poetry, the camels that carry the women's litters are compared to the swaying crowns of palm trees (see n. 164) and ships that sail on heaving waves, e.g., al-Muraqqish the Elder: "To whom belong the camels bearing women's litters, that float in the shimmering heat of the forenoon, like doom palms or great seagoing ships" (*li-mani l-ẓuʿnu bi-l-ḍuḥā ṭāfiyātin, shibhuhā l-dawmu aw khalāyā safīnī*) (*al-Mufaḍḍaliyyāt*, 1:467; 2:173); al-Muthaqqib al-ʿAbdī: "The camel-borne litters cut through Falj / like burdens laden upon ships" (*wa-hunna ka-dhāka ḥīna qaṭaʿna faljan, ka-anna ḥumūluhunna ʿalā safīni*) (*al-Mufaḍḍaliyyāt*, 1:577; 2:228); Ṭarafah: "The litters of Banū Mālik set out in the morning, / looking like big ships on their way down Wadi Dad" (*ka-anna ḥudūja l-Mālikiyyahi ghudwatan, khalāyā safīnin bi-l-nawāṣifi min Dadī*); and the camel itself in the line of al-Musayyab ibn ʿAlas: "Its neck stretches taut the length of the rein, as tall as a ship's sail" (*wa-tamuddu thinya jadīlihā bi-shirāʿī*) (*al-Mufaḍḍaliyyāt*, 1:95; 2:31).

333 “Anklets”: *ṣimūt al-ḥijil*, i.e., her legs and calves are so fleshy that her anklets (CA *ḥijil*) have no space to move and do not clink as she walks; they are “silent” (*ṣimūt*). It is regularly encountered in stereotyped descriptions of female beauty, e.g., the Jabrid poet al-Shuʿaybī: “A tall beauty, fleshy in the calves, robes wafting with perfume” (*hayfā ṣimūt al-ḥijl fāyḥat ar-rdā*); the lady is plump and her skin is white, because she is kept in the shade of her tent (as in §12.30 and n. 306) and does not venture out to perform the menial tasks in the sun usually reserved for women, such as collecting firewood, i.e., she is privileged and belongs to an aristocratic family, such as that of a Bedouin shaykh; hence, the expression is often put in the context of her being hidden in her own little tent, as in the lines of the Jabrid poet Abū Ẓāhir: “Anklets clasped around fat calves, dark tattoos around the lips; / A glimpse of her from behind the curtain of her tent / blinds as when the sun breaks through the clouds” (*ṣimūt al-ḥijl gāniyat al-wshām / turā min khidrahā min ʿigb sitrih, ka-shams al-ufq b-ftūg al-ghamām*) (Sowayan, *al-Shiʿr al-nabaṭī*, 375, 289); and in early Arabic poetry such a glimpse is gained through the curtains of the camel-borne litter, as in the playful verses of Bishr ibn Abī Khāzim, where “among the dames in the litters is one kind and playful,” “plump where the anklets go round, soft and tender, and svelte in flanks and belly” (*nabīlatu mawḍiʿi l-ḥajilayni khawdun* and *wa-fī l-kashḥayni wa-l-baṭni ḍṭimārū*) (*al-Mufaḍḍaliyyāt*, 1:664; 2:278–79).

334 “Concealed in tents”: see previous and §12.30.

335 “Camel”: *ʿibīhī* “strong camel”; see §12.23.

336 See introd., n. 142.

337 “Colorful litter curtains”: see nn. 23, 303, and 304; “makes it rise,” as in §12.28.

338 “Driver’s chant”: see §12.32.

339 The poet transitions from the camel’s pace to the gait of his beloved who had been carried on the animal’s back. In accordance with the usual thematic sequence, in §14.24 the subject of unrequited love is followed by wise sayings on the world’s inequities and ways to avoid its pitfalls.

340 I.e., slaves. The implied meaning is that slaves are on a different level of society and that for people of the poet's class there can be no true companionship with them.

341 Sayings that correspond to "With friends like you, who needs enemies?" are common in poetry's complaints about insufficiently loyal friends, e.g., al-Mutanabbī: "There may be benefit in some enmity, / while some friendship may harm and hurt" (*wa-mina l-ʿadāwati mā yanāluka nafʿuhū, wa-mina l-ṣadāqati mā yaḍurru wa-yuʾlimū* (*Dīwān*, 4:130); the Jabrid poet ʿĀmir al-Samīn in a string of wise counsels similar to the ones given by Ibn Ẓāhir (Sowayan, *al-Shiʿr al-nabaṭī*, 345); and in 1735 the headman of al-Bīr, Muḥammad ibn Manīʿ al-ʿAwsajī al-Badrānī al-Dawsarī: "To entrust your secret thoughts to the rabble / is shortsighted and will not further your goals" (*w-min waddaʿ awbāsh al-barāyā sdūdih, fa-hū ʿādim ash-shōfāt mikhṭī gṣūdihā*) (Sowayan, *al-Shiʿr al-nabaṭī*, 514).

342 "Al-Raqāshī had made a boasting poem on the cooking pot of his kin [. . . .] Then Abū Nuwās stepped in with an epigram on the cooking pot that sustains a whole family (*umm ʿiyāl*), but which is filled completely with a locust's breast; [. . . .] It is described with damning praise for its whiteness like the full moon, whereas other cooking pots are black from the fire; [. . .] if al-Raqāshī's honour were as unsullied as his pot, his glory would be second to none" (van Gelder, "Some Types of Ambiguity: A Poem by Abū Nuwās on al-Faḍl al-Raqāshī"). "When Abu Nuwās, for his part, went on repeatedly about the cooking pots of his antagonist Fadl al-Raqashi being pristine white rather than blackened with soot, he was accusing him (in a standard image) of never cooking and certainly, therefore, of never being the generous host at a feast" (Philip Kennedy, *Abu Nuwas: A Genius of Poetry*, 97). Here it means that, like the bakery of misery's loaves, it does not live up to expectations created by appearances and in fact is completely useless.

343 The poet blames the stock figure of *al-wāshī*, the slanderer, for his misfortunes. From there it is a small step to the wider context of popular sayings and wisdom in the next verses. The train of thought

started with the poet's disappointment at the lack of farewell (§14.21), followed by bitter thoughts about unfaithful friendship being worse than open enmity and its similarity to the deceit of false appearances and lies. This in turn brings him to reflect on the damage wrought by slanderous troublemakers and lack of sincerity in general.

344 In oral tradition, another verse runs: "They tell me not to lay myself out for a guest: / they wish for me to grow a hump of contemptible meanness" (*yigūlūn lī darb aḍ-ḍēf lā ti'tinī bah, yibūn ar-ridā yabnī 'alayy sanām*) (Alameemi, *Ibn Ẓāhir*, 190). This verse, and the one that precedes it, are identical to verses of Shāyiʿ al-Amsaḥ, and are probably borrowed from his legend (Sowayan, *Ayyām al-ʿArab*, 269). It is part of the well-known tendency for verses from different poems in the same meter and rhyme to become entangled in the course of oral transmission.

345 See §10.67. The poet refers to certain conditions that are most unlikely to be met: a miser is as unlikely to turn into a generous host as a star is to meet its opposite star. In the commentary on Abū Dhu'ayb's verse about wild asses that come to drink toward the end of night, it is explained: "The wild ass came to the water before dawn when the Pleiades fall toward the western horizon and Capella (*al-ʿayūq*) follows behind as closely as the man posted above the shufflers (*al-raqīb* 'the watcher') in the game of *maysir* to see to it that the shuffling is done fairly." This means that the wild asses came to drink at the hottest time of the summer, when Capella is in the position as described toward the end of night (*al-Mufaḍḍaliyyāt*, 1:864–65; 2:357, 360). *Al-raqīb* is a star that "watches" a star about to set farther to the west, as Capella is the "watcher" of the Pleiades. With reference to the poetry of al-Khalāwī, *al-raqīb* of Pleiades is considered to be the star named *qalb al-ʿaqrab*, "the heart of the scorpion" (http://www.mekshat.com/vb/showthread.php?302901).

346 A common topos: the beloved's kinsmen fiercely defend her honor and keep predatory suitors away from her.

347 Lit. "a greed that needs leads to hatred" (*miṭmiʿin yūzī al-bighīḍ*), as explained in Abū Shihāb and Abū Malḥah, *Ibn Ẓāhir*, 223.

348 In the following verses, the poet embroiders on this conclusion: the only solution for such a state of mind is a heavy dose of tough love.

349 In this verse, the poet reaches for the root causes of the spiritual malady described in the previous verses: an unjustified belief in the false promises of this world. Having laid these foundations as a stepping-stone, the poet is ready for his grand leap toward the ultimate remedy: the unshakable certainties of the true faith.

350 "Real farewell": i.e., the inevitability of death, as prefigured by the beloved's departure and separation, as expressed in the saying, "Separation from the beloved is fated and written in the stars" (*mgaddar w-maktūb frāg al-maḥbūb*) (al-Juhaymān, *Amthāl*, 10:313).

351 "At foot and head": *mitʿātibīn*, perhaps derived from *ʿatabah*, "doorstep, lintel," i.e., facing one another at both edges of the grave. See §5.17 and §6.22.

352 The tombstones are as mute as the dead, sharing a grim silence expressed by the early classical poet ʿAbdah ibn al-Ṭabīb: "They fling to him a farewell, 'Peace!,' that goes unanswered; / once keen of hearing, he is deaf to the call") (*nabadhū ilayhī bi-l-salāmi fa-lam yujib, aḥadan wa-ṣamma ʿani l-duʿāʾi l-asmaʿū*) (*al-Mufaḍḍaliyyāt*, 1:302; 2:103).

353 "To each his own": *killin lah siwām*, explained as "signs, marks" (*ʿalāmāt, simāt*); perhaps from the root *w-s-m* by transposition of consonants.

354 It is not clear who is meant. Many poets before Ibn Ẓāhir stressed the importance of being circumspect by using images such as this one, or the need to make sure of keeping a firm foothold in case one of your feet slips; the poet may also be referring to himself in this regard. "Verse": *waṣf*, lit. "description," also used for "spoken verse"; see §11.50 and §16.13 (memorized in verse, *waṣfin min zimān*).

355 An enumeration of four qualities is a recurring motif in the poetry of the period, e.g., ʿĀmir al-Samīn, in praise of Qaṭan ibn Qaṭan: "May he remain in the possession of these four, as long as he lives" (*dāmat tḥāẓīh ṭūl al-ʿumr arbaʿat*) [. . .] "May his enemies always suffer from these four" (*wi-mḥāẓiyin kill min ʿādāh arbaʿat*) (Sowayan, *al-Shiʿr*

al-nabaṭī, 330). And with the same rhyme and also in praise of Qaṭan ibn Qaṭan, al-ʿUlaymī, not to be outdone by the other poet, refers to two times four qualities ascribed to the addressee: "May these four always accompany him as long as he lives" (*ʿasā ybārīh fī dunyāh arbaʿat*) [. . .] "Let his enemies be plagued by these four" (*wi-mlāzimin kill min ʿādāh arbaʿat*) (Sowayan, *al-Shiʿr al-nabaṭī*, 354). In another poem, al-ʿUlaymī reserves three qualities for himself: "Three noble qualities I jealously pursue" (*thalāth khṣāl bī ḥirṣin ʿalēhin*) (Sowayan, *al-Shiʿr al-nabaṭī*, 357).

356 Possibly, this is the fourth element mentioned in §14.45. In Arabian poetry, clouds are mostly welcome harbingers of rain: the promise of relief after hardship, as illustrated by the rain verses that follow. In this proverb, however, clouds are signs of trouble ahead, as in the saying, "There are clouds in the sky" (*saḥāb fi s-simā* or *fī s-simā ghēm*), explained as a warning to watch your words because there is a rumormonger present in the assembly (Ḥanẓal, *Jāmiʿ al-amthāl*, 228). On the rhyme word *ghamām*, "clouds" (CA *saḥāb aghamm* "an unbroken bank of clouds, full cover of clouds," Ibn Manẓūr, *Lisān*, 3303), see also §12.37.

357 "I woke": It is a common trope in early Arabic poetry that the poet is the only person to stir from sleep as he senses the approach of rain, e.g., in Dhū l-Rummah's description of deadly quiet and the stealthy approach of rainclouds that soon will unleash a deafening spectacle of sound and light, similar to the picture painted by Ibn Ẓāhir: "I woke up while all the others slept because of a cloud / and faintly, surreptitiously, distant flashes burst across the sky; / It woke me up, alone among my friends, / as it slowly rose from the depths of the Tihāmah precipice, / Gently urged forward by a southern wind / like a man whose broken arm had healed and then broke again; / On its approach, climbing to the right of the protected pasture, / the clouds cast their anchors and released torrential rains from their hold" (*ariqtu wa-qad nāma l-ʿuyūnu li-muznatin, talaʾlaʾu wahnan baʿda hadʾin wamīḍuhā / ariqtu lahū waḥdī wa-qad nāma ṣuḥbatī, baṭīʾan mina l-ghawri l-tihāmī nuhūḍuhā / wa-habbat lahu l-rīḥu l-janūbu*

tasūquhū, kamā sīqa mawhūnu l-dhirāʿi mahīḍuhā / fa-lammā ʿalat ʾaqbāla maymanati l-ḥimā, ramat bi-l-marāsī wa-stahalla faḍīḍuhā) (Dhū l-Rummah, *Dīwān*, 707–9). Traditionally, rains that arrive at night are considered the best, as explained on authority of al-Aṣmaʿī in *al-Mufaḍḍaliyyāt* in the scholion concerning a verse by ʿAlqamah (*al-Mufaḍḍaliyyāt*, 1:771.)

358 The customary prayer for rain on the lands where the poet's beloved resides.

359 "Sand dunes caved in": *takhākhā min mighārīh al-ḥizām*; *mighārī* "slots in a belt in which pearls or bullets are placed" (Abū Shihāb and Abū Malḥah, *Ibn Ẓāhir*, 226), where it is explained that the splash of rain is compared to the sound of gunshots; *al-ḥizām* "belt" is explained as "a belt of sands." The verb *takhākhā* also occurs in §3.25 and §15.15.

360 "Time": *ayyām*, lit. "days." In this instance, "the days" are almost synonymous with "love," as in this early classical verse: "If the days give us trouble, Mayy, / I will not divulge our secret, nor will my feelings change" (*fa-in tuḥdithi l-ayyāmu yā-Mayyu baynanā, fa-lā nāshirun sirran wa-lā mutaghayyirū*) (Dhū l-Rummah, *Dīwān*, 618). In general, it refers to the changeability of fortune, as expressed in the saying, "Inevitably, the wheel of time keeps turning" (*lā bidd dōrāt al-liyālī yidūrin*) (al-Juhaymān, *Amthāl*, 6:190).

361 "Dread": *yiḥtā*; also *ḥātā, yḥātī* "to pay attention to, be concerned, worried about" (Thānī, *Ibn Ẓāhir*, 334). Judging by what follows, the poet seems to have in mind the following four scourges: old age, poverty, avarice and sponging off others, and strife and rumormongering.

362 "Your women": The worst humiliation for a man is to be unable to defend the women in his household, as put in an early verse of al-Muzarrid ibn Ḍirār: "O Zurʿah ibn Thawb, the women in your household / became thin while you binged on fresh, foaming camel milk" (*a-Zurʿa bna Thawbin inna jārāti baytikum, huzilna wa-alhāka rtighāʾu l-raghāʾidī*); the scholion adds that the scholar al-Aṣmaʿī, with respect to a verse of invective by al-Aʿshā, remarked that the poet did not mention men, because it is a much greater shame for men if their womenfolk perish or suffer (*al-Mufaḍḍaliyyāt*, 1:132; 2:45).

363 "Family head": *fī majd bētih*, explained as "all that is found in the house"; (CA *al-mājid* "someone who excels in good works"; also in the expression "give the animal plenty of food" (*imjud al-dābbah fī ʿalafih*) (*al-Mufaḍḍaliyyāt*, 1:696); and the notion of sufficiency, which is also present in the line of Abū Dhu'ayb: "each man had lived a life of distinction" (*wa-kilāhumā qad ʿāsha ʿīshata mājidin*), explained as "*al-mājid* is a person who has garnered a sufficient amount of honor and power" (*al-Mufaḍḍaliyyāt*, 1:884); and the seventeenth-century poet al-Surayḥī: "The cooks in his household do not deviate from two ways: / they turn day into night and the night into day" (i.e., they are cooking day and night) (*ṭibābīkh majdih bihim shāritēn, nahārih ka-l-lēl w-lēlih nahār*) (Sowayan, *al-Shiʿr al-nabaṭī*, 520). "Make do": *yijūz*; the head of the family is resigned to not being able to have a full meal himself.

364 "Set aside": *lāyim*, explained as "part of the food prepared for guests but not eaten by them; if a whole roasted sheep is served, the guests leave part of the tray uneaten so that they will not be blamed (*lōm*) by the members of the household for being impolite"; *al-lāymah* "portion of a slaughtered animal's meat that is not set before the guests but kept apart" (Abū Shihāb and Abū Malḥah, *Ibn Ẓāhir*, 210).

365 "Another sort": There is no transition from the previous verse, but it cannot be a continuation of the foregoing: sympathy with a hard-up man who struggles to live up to the demands of hospitality without doing so to the detriment of his dependents, and who makes do with very little himself. It is a common conceit for poets to depict themselves as hardworking family men, e.g., Ḥmēdān al-Shwēʿir and al-Ḥutay'ah, who receives praise for his concern for his daughters (Kurpershoek, *Arabian Satire*, xlii). In this verse, the poet derides the opposite: a sluggard who is a burden on others and consumes without contributing anything himself. Therefore, one or more verses may have gone missing.

366 "Stains your name": *wijāymah*; *wagm* was explained to me as "value, worth"; *wijām*: "a cairn of stones erected in the desert to serve as a waymark"; here it means that someone who is not guided by spiritual

signposts loses his way and becomes confused (Thānī, *Ibn Ẓāhir*, 336) (CA *wajam* "waymark"). The MSS read *walāymih*, a repetition of the rhyme of §15.10. The sense of the hemistich remains clear.

367 A common warning at the time, as in Ḥmēdān al-Shwēʿir's poems: "Discord and strife slumber / until roused by mean rascals" (Kurpershoek, *Arabian Satire*, §34.2, Poem 6).

368 Similar to the verse of al-Khalāwī: "If you unsheath the sword of pride, you will lead the lion; / if you fail to do so, you'll be led by monkeys" (*fa-min sall sēf al-ʿizz li-l-lēth gādih, w-min lā yisill as-sēf f-al-gird gād bih*) (Ibn Khamīs, *al-Khalāwī*, 197); and the eighteenth-century poet ʿAbd al-ʿAzīz ibn Kathīr: "If you do not wield the sword, the enemy will wipe the floor with you" (*w-min lā ymaḍḍī as-sēf amḍat bih al-ʿdā*) (Sowayan, *al-Shiʿr al-nabaṭī*, 517). And the Jabrid poet al-Kulayf: "Bring reckless troublemakers to their senses / by giving them a taste of steely swords; / A thorough treatment with straight talk and sharp blades / chastises the insurgents and silences their clamor" (*yihdī al-glūb al-ʿāyilāt ʿan al-ʿayā, illā ann yiḥill as-sēf fī jihhālahā / f-ilā ētifā ḥaggin w-sēf ṣārim, hadat al-ʿṣāt w-ṭāwaʿat ʿidhdhālahā*) (Sowayan, *al-Shiʿr al-nabaṭī*, 297). See also the heading "Poet of War and Peace" in Kurpershoek, *Arabian Satire*, xxiii–xxvi.

369 "Good life's music": *ayyām at-taghānī*, lit. "days of luxury." The idea expressed here, that one should always deal gently with friends (if only for the reason that one may need them one day) is a very common piece of wisdom in poetry; see nn. 124, 178, and 231.

370 As in §11.20, an encouragement to take the advice of wise poets, similar in wording to al-Khalāwī's verse: "Apposite, discerning are the verses he pondered; / incontestable speech and hard-hitting truth" (*sidīdin rishīdin yāzin al-harj bi-l-ḥashā / walā yikhrij illā ṣāmil al-lafẓ ṣāybih*) (Ibn Khamīs, *al-Khalāwī*, 300).

371 Lit. "Do not buy the idle chatter being sold in the marketplace."

372 A smoldering rag is given to smell to a person possessed by an evil spirit in order to exorcise the jinni, as in the sayings, "Like a jinni and a smoldering rag" (*ka-mā al-jinnī wa-l-ʿiṭbah*), i.e., two mutually

exclusive things or incompatible characters (al-Rawāḥī, *al-Amthāl al-ʿUmāniyyah*, 155); and "The burning rag and the jinni" (Ḥanẓal, *Muʿjam al-alfāẓ*, 459).

373 The panache of the hero is described in terms of firearm technology: the matchlocks and early flintlocks used in the seventeenth century. The first reference to firearms in Nabaṭī poetry occurs in a poem, called "the clove poem" (*al-qaranfuliyyah*), dedicated by al-Shuʿaybī to Barakāt al-Sharīf al-Mushaʿshaʿī, see Introduction p. xxix. "Igniting": *girrāʿah* (pronounced *kirrāʿah*) "ignition of fire by striking two stones together in order to produce a spark" (Ḥanẓal, *Muʿjam al-alfāẓ*, 523). Perhaps the spring-loaded hammer of a flintlock firearm is meant. "Sparks": *ṣalbūkh garrā*, lit. "small stones from Garrā, a place near Aflāj Banī Qatab and Wādī al-Jazī" (Abū Shihāb and Abū Malḥah, *Ibn Ẓāhir*, 212); *ṣalbūkh* "flints, small stones, also called *girrāʿah*, that are struck together to produce a spark and ignite the kindling for a fire" (Ḥanẓal, *Muʿjam al-alfāẓ*, 393).

374 "Trigger": *ʿagrab al-makwā*, lit. "scorpion of the place against which the branding iron is held," explained as "trigger." Perhaps it refers to the curved lever, the so-called serpentine, that lowers the smoldering match into the flashpan of a matchlock. This may explain the origin of these terms. "Ramrod": *sāyig ad-dawā*, lit. "the person who drives, applies the medicine," explained as "the person who loads the gunpowder." The terminology may stem from the way gunpowder was loaded in a muzzleloader by pouring black powder from a flask into the barrel and using a ramrod to push the bullet up against the powder. "Women and children": *ḍimāyim*, sg. *ḍimīmah*, explained to me as "a dependent" (CA *ḍamīm* "adjunct," Lane, *Lexicon*, 1801).

375 A common maxim and conviction: to carry a sufficient supply of water is a synecdoche for the wisdom of taking precautions when a man must travel across deserts in search of a livelihood, as expressed in the Emirati saying, "Carry a sufficient amount of water until you reach water and do not die from thirst" (*shall al-mā li-l-mā gabil lā yalḥagk aẓ-ẓmā*) (Ḥanẓal, *Jāmiʿ al-amthāl*, 229; also Kurpershoek, *Arabian Romantic*, §11.16); see §8.46 and §9.21 for similar advice.

376 “Wringing hands”: *ḥāyimah*, lit. *ḥāyim* means “circling around,” e.g., vultures over a field of battle or camels circling around a well, crazed with thirst and without a shepherd to draw water for them. Here the word conveys the latter meaning of desperate thirst and lack of means to satisfy it: to endure the pangs of Tantalus. See §15.23 and note above about taking precautions, such as carrying enough water in the desert.

377 “Other ships”: *sinyār* “a fleet of pearling boats that sail caravan-like in line, one following the other” (Ḥanẓal, *Muʿjam al-alfāẓ*, 338).

378 “Snuggled up in my tomb”: *ṭāb lī bēt al-mimāt*; see §13.33, “where the eye sleeps in peace.” Verses such as these may have given rise to the legend of Ibn Ẓāhir’s search for a suitable grave.

379 In this and the preceding line, the poet seems to draw attention to a distinction between written lines of poetry and poetry recited and perpetuated in oral performance, while claiming superior authenticity for the latter tradition. It is not necessary to draw conclusions from these verses as to the poet’s familiarity with writing or the lack of it. Rather, it resembles a trope that may have been common at the time. Rāshid al-Khalāwī, a Najdī poet of the period whose compositions are somewhat similar in style, makes cognate boastful claims: “My poems tower above the other versifiers as / the faith of Ṭā Hā ranks before all other religions” (*giṣīdī ʿalā min fōg al-ashʿār mithilmā, ʿalā dīn Ṭāhā fōg al-adyān gāṭbih*) (Ibn Khamīs, *al-Khalāwī*, 307). The “scripted lines” in §15.36 might be a metaphor for the transmission of the poet’s verses in oral culture: done with as much attention and precision as what is scripted to fix memory; or it might point to the existence of early written versions. Given that much of this poetry proceeds by opposition of contrasting pairs of statements, it seems that the poet claims a status for his Nabaṭī verses, composed within the framework of oral culture, at least equal to the one enjoyed by written tomes that lend prestige to bearers of literate culture, especially in the field of religion. The unmediated truth that wells up straight from the heart and is given expression by the tongue to be caught fresh at the source by an appreciative audience (to borrow an

image repeated in the prelude of earlier poems) could be interpreted as an expression of the immediacy of the Sufi experience. It is also a notion with ancient roots. The eighth-century poet Dhū l-Rummah, suspected of being literate, was asked: "'Do you write?' He put his hand on his mouth. 'Don't tell anyone,' he said. 'This is a bad thing where I come from!' (*fa-innah ʿindanā ʿayb*)" (al-Iṣfahānī, *al-Aghānī*, 18:30). See also §4.5 and n. 76.

380 These final verses with a prayer for the Prophet are a customary ending for a poem. They may have been added at a later stage of oral transmission. Here the rhyme word draws attention because it is a repetition of the end of §15.36, *niẓāyimih* ("compositions"), where the verb and a noun of the same root are also used in the first hemistich. Normally, verses about the art of poetry occur in a poem's prelude and not at the end as here. To include the dove in "irrefutable compositions" might be a Sufi-like way for the poet to point to the divine spirit that suffuses all living nature.

381 "Crafted with skill": lit. "structures, buildings, soundly built" (*ʿadlāt al-mibāni*); similar expressions are used in this opening verse of the Jabrid poet Ibn Zayd: "This is the speech of Ibn Zayd, who molds his verses / into a new building, the delight of connoisseurs" (*yigūl Ibn Zēdin gīl bānī mithāyil, jdād al-bnā li-l-fāhimīn tishūg*) (Sowayan, *al-Shiʿr al-nabaṭī*, 312); in a similar vein, Shāyiʿ al-Amsaḥ wrote: "Lofty buildings of a major tribe" (*rfāʿ al-mibāni kbār al-ḥamāyil*) (Sowayan, *Ayyām al-ʿArab*, 290).

382 "Poetry's reciters": *akhāf min al-rwāt*, i.e., fear of a descent into a mudslinging contest, as pictured in a verse of Jarīr that impressed al-Rāʿī: "Verses in hot demand with poetry lovers, / hard-hitting like an Indian sword that cuts to the bone" (*kharūjin bi-afwāh al-ruwāti ka-annahā, qarā hunduwāniyyin idhā huzza ṣammaʿā*) (al-Iṣfahānī, *al-Aghānī*, 24, 212). How much a poet stands in awe of the court of public opinion is expressed in the saying, "Better to be burned in fire than shamed in public" (*an-nār walā al-ʿār*) (al-Rawāḥī, *al-Amthāl al-ʿUmāniyyah*, 204). The verse echoes this line of the Najdī poet Rāshid al-Khalāwī: "Beware of saying poetry that is met with

disapproval: / souls, my alert friend, have a taste for vile aspersions" (*w-min gāl shiʿrin fīh mā yaskhaṭ al-malā, fa-sh-shēn yā-ṣāḥī lih an-nafs shāribih*) (Ibn Khamīs, *al-Khalāwī*, 173).

383 Similarly, the early poet Suwayd ibn Abī Kāhil counsels restraint and determination: "It is not in the character of these tribesmen / to be rash with foul speech or to waver in the hour of need" (*min unāsin laysa min akhlāqihim, ʿājilu l-fuḥshi wa-lā sūʾu l-jazaʿ*) (*al-Mufaḍḍaliyyāt*, 1:392; 2:142).

384 One transmitter interprets this verse as a reference to gossips who rumored that one of his daughters was not really his, see §22.3 and Alameemi, *Ibn Ẓāhir*, 180.

385 "In public": *bi-l-ghibā w-bi-l-biyānī*, lit. "hidden, covert; clear for all, openly." The verse's wording leaves open the possibility that the poet believes he must say the same thing in private and in public, especially on sensitive subjects like amorous feelings, as when al-Aḥnaf was asked about the meaning of chivalrous conduct (*al-murūʾah*) and said, "It means that you do not think of doing something you'd be ashamed to do openly" (*ʾallā tafʿala fī l-sirri ʾamran wa-anta tastaḥyī ʾan tafʿalahu jahran*) (Ibn Manẓūr, *Lisān*, 4166). The choice of words is similar to the saying, "A person consists of a heart and a public face (or public speech)" (*al-insān galbin w-bayān*), explained as "a person has his 'two small ones,' his heart and his tongue, and his bodily features, i.e., one should not judge a person by appearances only" (al-Juhaymān, *Amthāl*, 1:388–89). Here the poet may prelude on the transition to the subject of love in §16.26: lovers are sworn to keep their trysts secret.

386 "Wheels of Time": as in the saying, "the world assembles and disperses" (*ad-dinyā mā jmaʿat illā farrigat*) (al-Juhaymān, *Amthāl*, 3:96).

387 "Pursuit": *ant aṭ-ṭilīb* "I am in hot pursuit of you," e.g., as when camel raiders are pursued by the owner of the robbed herd (CA *ṭalaba* "to desire, seek, pursue"). Explained to me as: "I want urgently what you owe to me."

388 "Winds drawn by Canopus": *w-habb lhā shēliyyin yimānī*, lit. "the wind of southern Canopus (CA *suhayl*);" see §6.4 for "rains of

Canopus." It does not mean that the wind blows from the direction of Canopus's rise just before dawn. The rain falls in the season named after that star, starting at the end of August and in early September, when the most intense heat begins to abate.

389 "Empty deserts": *fjūj/fyūy*, sg. *fajj*, may refer to a "gap, mountain pass," or to "wide, empty tracts of land." Given the place names mentioned in the second hemistich, here it must be the latter: "All the sands between al-Ẓafrah and al-Jaww in Oman, including Ramlat al-ʿAtīq and its surrounding area" (Abū Shihāb and Abū Malḥah, *Ibn Ẓāhir*, 88). "The south": In Ibn Ẓāhir's poetry, "the south" refers to the area of al-ʿAyn and al-Buraymī (Thānī, *Ibn Ẓāhir*, 450); see n. 408.

390 "Līwā": the text simply says *ar-raml*, "the sand," but this is understood to refer to the Līwā oasis at the foot of the first of the great Empty Quarter dunes (Abū Shihāb and Abū Malḥah, *Ibn Ẓāhir*, 89). "Caresses": *dānāh al-mdānī*; this can be understood in two ways: First, the approach and closeness of clouds and rain to the location (*danā*). Second, in the dialect, *dānā* means "to love and be close to," and *mdānī* "person who loves"; here it is the cloud who is in love with the location, "*mdānī*" (CA *danā* and *dānā*).

391 "Folks of the high ledges": *al-bdā*; *al-bdā*, sg. *badwāwī*, live on the ridges of the mountain ranges north of Rās al-Khaymah; they belong to the tribe of al-Shuḥūh (the tribal *nisbah* Shiḥḥī). "Gardens": *sāḥibt al-jnān*; there is no comment on it in the editions and the meaning is uncertain; *sāḥib* means "pulling, drawing," e.g., the hem of a robe over the ground, and it is used for curtains of rain that clouds draw over the land in similar fashion; and *jnān* might be the plural of garden (CA *jannah*, pl. *jinān*).

392 "Worries": *hmūm* (CA *hamm*, pl. *humūm* "anxiety, concern, worry, distress"). In §1.33 and §12.1, it is related to the anxieties about love and premonitions of old age that keep the poet awake at night. Here the poet celebrates the moment his worries are dispelled by the arrival of the beloved, at the height of youthful beauty, and he is able to enjoy sound sleep again.

393 Probably the Omani fringes of the Empty Quarter are meant.

394 "Tribe's maiden": *fitāt al-ḥayy*. The opening words are in the style of the Banū Hilāl poetry, as in the famous verse quoted by the historian Ibn Khaldūn, in Sowayan's translation: "The gallant lady of the camp, Umm Salāmah, proclaims: / 'May God strike with fear those who do not have pity on her'" (*tagūlu fatātu al-ḥayyi Ummu Salāmah, bi-ʿaynin arāʿ allāhu min lā rithā lahā*) (Sowayan, "The Hilali Poetry in the *Muqaddimah*: Its Links to Nabaṭī Poetry," *al-Shiʿr al-nabaṭī*, 243; Ibn Khaldūn, *Muqaddimah*, 593). The expression dates to the earliest days of Arabic classical poetry, as in the line of ʿAwf ibn al-Aḥwaṣ: "The cherished maiden of the tribe is among those who kindled the cooking fire" (*wa-kānat fatātu l-ḥayyi mimman yunīruhā*) (*al-Mufaḍḍaliyyāt*, 1:349; 2:128); the commentary explains that even this aristocratic girl, who is kept in her tent and absolved from the obligation of performing menial tasks, did not hesitate to come out of her tent and lend a hand in cooking a dinner for guests, i.e., part of the poet's boasting of his hospitality; and al-Muraqqish al-Aṣghar's shorthand description of a noble-born beauty: "She does not get up to light a fire at night / and prepare food, but sleeps as long as she likes" (*lā taṣṭalī l-nāra bi-l-layli wa-lā / tūqaẓu li-l-zādi balhāʾu naʾūm*) (*al-Mufaḍḍaliyyāt*, 1:505; 2:192); see also nn. 301, 333.

395 "Core": *glūb*, lit. "hearts" indicates *jummār*, "palm core, edible tuber growing at the upper end of the palm trunk" (Wehr, *Dictionary* under the root *j-m-r*). Here it refers to tender twigs deep in the palm's crown, near the core, that are not directly exposed to the sun.

396 Cf. §15.37 on the superiority of poetry uttered straight from the heart.

397 "Acacia's thorns": *shikil/shičil*, "Christ's-thorn" (*sidr*). This verse's wisdom is situational. Similes with thorn trees are also used to warn against a certain type of person, as in the saying, "Like a boxthorn, he rips the shirt of anyone who comes close" (*mithil al-ʿōshazah min garabhā shaggat thōbih*) (al-Juhaymān, *Amthāl*, 7:348). Similarly: "If your hand gets stuck under the stone of a quern, try to pull it out very slowly" (*yom īdik taḥt ar-raḥā jirrhā shwayy shwayy*) (Ḥanẓal, *Jāmiʿ al-amthāl*, 212).

398 Metaphorical usage of sailing imagery, in particular favorable or adverse winds that influence the course of one's ship of life, occurs

in the poetry of Ibn Ẓāhir and his daughter, but the latter's verses on the subject have especially drawn the attention of Emirati students. In the lemma devoted to the daughter of Ibn Ẓāhir, listed as "Salmā," Ḥanẓal writes: "Once, Ibn Ẓāhir submitted the following riddle to visitors in his majlis: 'What thing repels the crossers / that follow one another and are not held by a rope attached to a nose ring?' (*wish illī yridd al-ʿābirāt ʿalā l-gifā, mittābiʿātin wlā ygād zmām*). When they were lost for an answer, he called his daughter Salmā, who solved the riddle with a verse of her own: 'If the breeze blows from the south it turns the ship back / and it will keep going to the north' (*in dhaʿdhāʿ al-jinūb yriddhā, yāzim shimāl misīrahā w-amāmhā*)." He mentions the belief that she composed her poem when she had reached the age of forty and given up hope of ever marrying; and that most people do not believe that her father had killed her by cutting off her tongue out of jealousy because she had surpassed him as a poet (Ḥanẓal, *Muʿjam al-alfāẓ*, 331–32). The key word in the riddle, "crossers" (*al-ʿābirāt*), reminds one of §14.10. The word for "nose ring" in the riddle alludes to a train of camels, a caravan, that are led by a rope attached to the nose ring. The word "following one another" (*mittābiʿāt*) might refer to the camels, but as this has been excluded, it refers to a number of ships in one line, a ship caravan (*sinyār*), see n. 377.

399 Verses §§17.9–12 closely parallel §§13.12–14. The comparison between love's misfortunes and shipwreck also occurs in poetry from central Arabia, as in this verse by Rumayzān: "I was battered by fate in the sea of love; / O Jabr, waves of passion smashed and sank my vessel" (*w-aṣbaḥt fī baḥr al-gharām msammar, baḥr al-hawā yā-Jabr gharrag miḥmalī*) (Sowayan, *al-Shiʿr al-nabaṭī*, 458). Ḥanẓal gives the following first hemistich: "My dear, the frivolities of youth have passed me by" (*yā-būy ghayyāt aṣ-ṣibā qad ʿadannī*), where "youth" may also mean the wind called *aṣ-ṣibā* (*Muʿjam al-alfāẓ*, 332).

400 Cf. §§13.12–14. These verses' disappointment with the quality of the crew hired for the ship is echoed in the story of Ibn Ẓāhir's recruitment as a hauler on a pearling ship.

401 "Without purpose": lit. "if you do not know at a certain age what happened, passed (*mā miḍā*, in your life)."

402 The implied maxim is that someone cannot be expected to show ability at a later age if he has not shown promise in his youth, as stated in verses of al-Khalāwī and other poets of the period, see nn. 169 and 170.

403 This is perhaps the most mysterious verse of the poem. Sulṭān Alameemi told me that in the Emirates it is interpreted in the context of the two preceding verses. If so, her fate is compared to a sheep that does not serve its intended purpose, but falls prey to a predator; or to the spadix of a date palm that likewise does not serve its purpose, because if it is not impregnated, it falls off and disappears without a trace. Similarly, the poet has remained unmarried and childless: a huge disappointment for a bright-eyed girl who started out in life with extraordinary gusto and optimism. According to Alameemi's version, a kinsman had promised to marry her and had reserved her for himself, but in the end he did not make good on his promise. Therefore, in her desperation, she pleads with him to release her and remove obstacles in the way of another marriage.

404 In this arrangement of poems according to rhyme, it so happens that the final verses reprise the note of lost youth struck at the beginning of Poem 1. "Days of youth": *ʿaṣr aṣ-ṣibā*, see n. 43. "Eluded me": *fātnī*, "it passed me by"; here it has the connotation "for good," as in the saying, "The dead are gone; the past is dead" (*min māt fāt*) (al-Juhaymān, *Amthāl*, 8:238).

405 "Beyond recall, forever, unavenged": *la min tithannī wlā riḍā thārin*, lit. "no turning back and no satisfaction of revenge" (CA *inthanā*, *tathannā* "to turn away, turn back"; *tha'r* "revenge, blood revenge"). "Wooden cover": *mithānī*, sg. *mithnā*, as explained to me, "a piece of wood laid over the shaft of the well as support for the man who hoists up the bucket." In this case, the wooden piece is broken, hence there is no way to draw water from the well. In this context, the well is a metaphor for the woman, marriage, and procreation. According to

another interpretation, *mithānī* means "promises." The translation of the second hemistich is uncertain.

406 This verse corresponds to the story of Ibn Ẓāhir's daughter, whose marriage plans were thwarted by her predilection for poetry. One transmitter of oral lore opined that in this verse the poet blames the Banū Hilāl (*tirjaʿ ʿalā li-Hlāliyyīn*) for her discomfiture (Alameemi, *Ibn Ẓāhir*, 274), see introd., n. 61.

407 See §12.24.

408 "South": i.e., the area of al-ʿAyn and al-Buraymī, see §16.59 and n. 331. "They spent the hot season" (*ḥḍaraw ḥiḍḍār*), explained by Ḥasan (*al-ʿĀdāt*, 48–49) as "this migration, called *al-ḥiḍārah*, usually is toward al-Buraymī, al-ʿAyn, and its adjacent areas, Ḍank [regarded as Ibn Ẓahir's location early in life, see §18.2], Līwā, and al-Bāṭinah region of Oman with its many villages on the Arabian Sea; and to the crests of the mountains near the Straits of Hormuz between Rās al-Khaymah and al-Fujayrah [. . .] This journey on camelback takes several days and is called *sēr al-ḥiḍḍār* ['march of those who come to stay, be present at a location'], because of their slow pace; they spend the last night of the journey in the proximity of their destination; next morning, they arrive in the village, dressed in their best clothes, where the inhabitants say, *ṣabbaḥaw al-ḥiḍḍār*, 'this morning the migrants have arrived'" (see also Ḥanẓal, *Muʿjam al-qawāfī*, 184); *maḥḍar*, pl. *maḥāḍir* "temporary settlement near gardens of palm trees during the season of the date harvest; the term is particular to Līwā" (al-Khāṭirī, *Muʿjam mawārid al-miyāh*, 17; *al-ḥāḍirūn* "those who return to the *maḥādir* during the hot season, *al-qayẓ*," Ibn Manẓūr, *Lisān*, 97). It is expressed in the saying, "During the hot season she stays in Dibā [near Kalbā, mentioned in this verse] and she spends the winter in gardens of palm trees in Oman [which may refer to al-Buraymī]" (*ash-shams tgayyiẓ fī Dibā w-tashtī fī ʿMān*) (Ḥanẓal, *Jāmiʿ al-amthāl*, 103; for the places to which the people of Rās al-Khaymah would travel on hired camels for the price of one rupee to spend the hot months of summer, see al-Ṭābūr, *Rijāl fī taʾrīkh al-Imārāt*, 137); in Najd, a village well for common use is called

ḥaḍīrah, as in the proverb, "Today is my darling's turn at the well" (*al-yōm dōr ṣwēḥbī fī l-ḥaḍīrah*) (al-Juhaymān, *Amthāl*, 9:311). "Al-Jaww": see Introduction p. xiv, the area of al-ʿAyn and al-Buraymī that like Līwā supported the Jabrid Banū Hilāl against the Omani imam. The word *jaww* also means "a flat expanse of desert." Alameemi informed me that he thinks it refers to Līwā.

409 The narrator of this paragraph is Khalīfah ibn ʿAlī ibn Khalīfah al-Kitbī (Thānī, *Ibn Ẓāhir*, 404).

410 "Graybeards": *shuwwāb*. See "Early Ancestors as Sources of Authority (*al-awwilīn*)" in the online "Glossary of Style, Themes, and Motifs" on the weight accorded to the authority of previous generations, *al-awwilīn*, lit. "those who came first, before us," and those old enough to have heard a version of a story, poem, or other oral traditions from even earlier sources.

411 "Met him": *laḥag ʿalēh* [. . .] *al-awwilīn lāḥgīn ʿalēh*, lit. "caught up with him, reached him"; the phrase conjures up an image of generation after generation reaching backward with outstretched arms in the hope of gaining a firsthand witness account from the oldest men, who in their turn had enjoyed the good fortune of collecting accounts from other Methuselahs before them. Similar expressions were used by transmitters of ancient lore almost two thousand kilometers to the north, in the Great Nafud Desert, as registered by Dr. Saad Sowayan, see n. 465.

412 "Ḍanj": i.e., Ḍank.

413 In poetry, the appearance or sound of the jinni is the mark of a particularly lonely and bleak stretch of desert crossing, as in the verse of the pre-Islamic poet Bishr ibn Abī Khāzim: "I crossed many desert wastes where the jinn are heard playing their tunes / and waterless spaces where the hot winds whistle shrilly" (*wa-kharqin taʿzifu l-jinnānu fīhī, fayāfīhī taḥinnu bihā l-sahāmū*) (*al-Mufaḍḍaliyyāt*, 1:651; 2:274, 276).

414 The story is reminiscent of the supernatural manner in which the pre-Islamic bard ʿAbīd ibn al-Abraṣ became a poet overnight without having shown earlier signs of talent, "due to a vision which he had,

while asleep under a tree in the wilderness, of a heavenly messenger who put into his mouth a rolled-up ball of poems, and predicted that he would become a famous poet and the glory of his tribe" (Lyall, *The Dīwāns*, 8). The difference is that ʿAbīd solicited heavenly aid to endow him with the powers to retaliate when he and his sheep had been chased away from a well by a man of Banū Mālik who added insult to injury with a derogatory verse (al-Iṣfahānī, *al-Aghānī*, 22, 81–82).

415 "Flatland": *hōr* "an expanse of low land, not longer than four kilometers, surrounded by sand hills" (Al-Khāṭirī, *Muʿjam mawārid al-miyāh*, 19).

416 Here the speaker alludes to the poet's search for a suitable place to be buried; see the final narrative in this volume.

417 "Ḍabyān": a famous strain of Omani camels; "Ḍabyān ibn Yuthub, the offspring of an excellent pedigree stud camel by this name" (Ḥanẓal, *Muʿjam al-alfāẓ*, 434).

418 This is a common motif in storytelling, the Arabian equivalent of the ugly duckling, used for both humans and animals. In northern Arabia, a similar version of the motif is found in the narrative lore and verse of the nineteenth- and early-twentieth-century Bedouin poet Khalaf Abū Zwayyid (Sowayan, *Ayyām al-ʿArab*, 608–9).

419 The line is not clear. Apparently, the narrator quotes words from a line or lines of poetry, without giving the line in full. It is not found in the collections of Ibn Ẓāhir's work.

420 This might also offer an explanation for his initial dissemblance toward unknown guests and visitors attracted by his reputation as a poet and sage; see §21.5.

421 Such vaguely metered and rhymed lines are common in the narratives. By these standards they would not qualify as poetry, but some of them may be mangled fragments from poems that circulated in oral culture and either survived elsewhere in a more recognizable state or were lost.

422 The story shows that the poet is shrewd and alert even after long desert treks at night: he deduces the presence of other people, or

that his companions had grown weary and yawned, from his camel's yawn.

423 Ibn Ẓāhir's shack was by a *ghāf* tree. The fruit and leaves of this tree are eaten by humans and are considered highly beneficial for animals. Fāṭimah al-Naẓūrī, *Wīn al-khīl diwā al-ʿilīl, al-tadāwī fī bādiyat Abu Dhabī*, 23.

424 "The occupation of diving, though a severe form of labor and fatiguing at the time, is not considered by those engaged in it to be particularly injurious to the health, and is practiced even by old men." See "Appendix. F: Sailing Craft of the Persian Gulf" in Lorimer, *Gazetteer*.

425 A version of these lines has been included and explained in al-Ḥasan, *al-Shiʿr al-nabaṭī fī manṭiqat al-khalīj wa-l-jazīrah al-ʿarabiyyah*, 149–52, who argues that the verses are inferior to Ibn Ẓāhir's poetry, and therefore cannot be his.

426 The calm and warm seas during the summer allow divers to stay longer in the water than in other seasons. A broad-chested diver has big lungs that allow him to remain underwater for a considerable time.

427 "The Arabs": *al-ʿarab*, in common speech, particularly among Bedouin tribes, *ʿarab* has come to mean "people, folk"; its first use in this sense is attested in a poem by the Jabrid poet ʿĀmir al-Samīn. Sowayan, *al-Shiʿr al-nabaṭī*, 340.

428 "Barghash": so-called after the Omani sultan Sayyid Barghash bin Saʿīd Āl Bū Saʿīd (1837–88), who ruled Zanzibar from 1870 to 1888. One hundred barghash were the equivalent of one rupee.

429 The first hemistich of the first verse was not recited in the oral recording and is unknown.

430 "Feather": *shaʿar*, lit. "hair."

431 Divers were paid considerably more than haulers. The divers "are mostly poor Arabs and free negroes or negro slaves but Persians and Baluchis are also to be found among them, and, in recent years, owing to the large profit made by divers, many respectable Arabs have joined their ranks. The efficiency of a diver depends more on his skill and daring than on the strength of his constitution" ("Appendix

C: The Pearl and Mother-of-Pearl Fisheries of the Persian Gulf" in Lorimer, *Gazetteer*).

432 Stories like these may have contributed to the current notion in the Emirates that Ibn Ẓāhir was a Bedouin.

433 "Dumbfound": *miʿjizah* "to render him powerless, helpless, unable to respond"; the same term is used in §21.24. It is a poet's ambition to reduce his opponent to silence, as expressed by Ibn Ẓāhir's contemporary, al-Khalāwī, "sturdy and forceful verses that silence the other poets: / even stud poets cower when I pelt them with my verse" (*mshīdin mfīdin miʿjizin kill shāʿir, fḥūl ash-shiʿr ʿan gāf mā gāl hāybih*) (Ibn Khamīs, *al-Khalāwī*, 53, 303).

434 "Wipe the floor": *mḥiṭinnah fī mikhbāyah*, lit. "stuff him into my pocket."

435 "Ibn Ẓāhir's Dune": *miḥḍāb ibn Ẓāhir*; *miḥḍāb*; *al-maḥāḍib* "an area thickly covered with *ghāf* trees of the *ḥiḍīb* type"; *al-ḥiḍībah* "a small type of *ghāf* tree on which camels feed" (Alameemi, *Muʿjam al-ghāf*, 100–2, 237).

436 Jazzah: "*jazz* is a tree that grows on mountainous slopes and in sandy areas" (Al-Ṭābūr, *al-Ṭibb al-shaʿbī*, 327; Ḥanẓal, *Muʿjam al-alfāẓ*, 154).

437 "Loud greetings": Visitors who do not belong to the family must give notice of their approach so as not to surprise and embarrass members of the host's household by an unexpected appearance; "*hūd* is the expression used by a visitor when he knocks on the door, *hūd ya-ahl ad-dār*, 'easy, inhabitants of the house'" (Ḥanẓal, *Muʿjam al-alfāẓ*, 719). Among the Bedouin, it is normal for a woman to receive unannounced visitors in the absence of the owner of the house while waiting for his return. In such a case, she will invite them to prepare their own coffee.

438 Lit. his *nibā* "reports, news."

439 These lines are part of verses not found in MSS but recited in circles of oral poetry. They have been grafted onto verses of the Banū Hilāl cycle: "The high-minded stalwart ʿAlī ibn Ẓāhir says: / Upon the repudiation of my wife: a poor man is trampled upon; / By God, I do not shrink from dueling with the brave / but in straitened condition

I have little to offer; / Beautiful is a twig covered with leaves; / bare of foliage, how could it please?" (*yigūl fitā al-ʿilyā ʿAlī ibn Ẓāhir, ʿalā ṭ-ṭalāg inn al-figīr dhilīl / fa-wallāh mā bī min mlāgāh ghilmā, lākinn mā bēn al-yidēn gilīl / yimīl ʿūd ash-shakl lī ʿād mūrig, w-lī ʿād ʿaryānin fa-kēf yimīl*) (Alameemi, *Ibn Ẓāhir*, 41).

440 A verse reminiscent of Abū Zayd al-Hilālī's verse: "These are the words of the Hilālī, Salāmah, / I swear, the indigent are to be pitied: / They rise to the challenge of generosity, / then collapse like an overburdened camel" (*yigūl al-Hlālī wa-l-Hlālī Salāmah, ʿalayya aṭ-ṭalāg in al-mgill dhilīl / yinūḍ yabghī li-l-marājil w-yinthinī, kamā yinthinī bi-l-ḥmūl hazīl*) (Thānī, *Ibn Ẓāhir*, 568–69; al-Saʿīd, *al-Mawsūʿah*, 1:45).

441 Lit. "I am not from his group (*rbāʿah*)."

442 Thānī's text (*Ibn Ẓāhir*, 473) adds the words: *w-allah, hadd hirshah*, explained by al-Ṭābūr as a Bedouin expression for "by God, he had slaughtered his camel" (*hirsh* "big, old male camel," metaphorically also used in reference to an old man, al-Suwaydāʾ, *Faṣīḥ al-ʿāmmī fī shamāl Najd*, 1056).

443 In another version, she mentions her divorce. "Ibn Ẓāhir said, 'What is the matter?' She said, 'Your son-in-law took an oath that he would divorce me if you had visitors and you would succeed in serving them dinner. Therefore, I am no longer his wife; he has no authority over me, unless he gives you what he promised.' 'What is it?' 'His livestock and all the contents of his house, which he will make a present of to you'" (Khalīfah ibn ʿAlī al-Kitbī, in Thānī, *Ibn Ẓāhir*, 464–65).

444 "Halters": *khaṭm*; *khaṭam* "to attach the halter to a camel's nose" (CA *khiṭām* "halter, cord of which one end is fastened round the nose and jaws of a camel" (Kurpershoek, *Oral Poetry*, 5:77).

445 "ʿAtīj": a name. Al-Maṭrūshī, *al-Lahjah*, 230.

446 The story is also explained in al-Ṭābūr, *al-Alghāz al-shaʿbiyyah fī al-Imārāt*, 34–36.

447 "Confound": *msawwīn lah miʿjizah* "they were scheming to render him speechless"; see n. 433.

448 "Kalbā": For his stay there during the hot season, see §17.30.

449 The poet's stealthy way of slaughtering his sole camel reminds one of the gruesome slaughter scene in a poem by ʿAmr ibn al-Ahtam: "Then I went to the huge beasts lying down asleep" (*al-Mufaḍḍaliyyāt*, 1:250; 2:84). A contemporary Najdī poet with whom Ibn Ẓāhir has much in common, Fayṣal al-Jumaylī, in an elegy, praises his brother: "As if he never served starving guests his own riding camel, / excusing himself from the meat saying, 'I'm fasting'" (*w-kannih mā ʿashshā l-guwāyā dhilūlih, w-bāt mḥarrimhā yigūl ana ṣāyim*) (Sowayan, *al-Shiʿr al-nabaṭī*, 393). According to another version, Ibn Ẓāhir cooked the camel whole, including its head, a thing not usually done, according to the narrator: "The old man cooked his sole she-camel for you, even its head" (*ḥattā rāshā ṭibakhhā ash-shēbah lkum, al-fāṭir*) (Thānī, *Ibn Ẓāhir*, 459), i.e., the camel was so precious to him that he would not even discard its worst part, as in the story in *al-Aghānī*: "Jaʿfar was called 'the she-camel's nose' (*anf al-nāqah*) because his father, Qurayʿ, slaughtered a she-camel and distributed its meat among his wives. His mother, al-Shamūs of Wāʾil, and Saʿd Hudhaym sent Jaʿfar to distribute the meat, but when he returned to his father there was nothing left except the head and neck, and his father said, 'You'll have to make do with this.' The boy put his fingers in its nostrils and dragged the head to his mother. Thus, he and his descendants were called 'the she-camel's nose'" (al-Iṣfahānī, *al-Aghānī*, 2:180–81).

450 See §§10.41–46. The Arabic wording of the verses differs slightly from this edition's version. The second verse corresponds to this edition's verse §10.42, but the second hemistich is closer to §10.44.

451 The narrator cites a verse of the Jabrid poet al-Shuʿaybī (late sixteenth and early seventeenth centuries) that was included in the work of Ibn Ẓāhir, see n. 248.

452 "Getting the better of": *awanhum* "as if they," explained as a presumption that they would prevail, born from an unrealistic estimation of their own and their opponent's powers; "how presumptuous of them to think that they would get the better of him."

453 As in the verse of Rumayzān: "Whenever she appears, she eclipses the sun of early noon" (*tighīb ḥayā shams aḍ-ḍuḥā kill mā bidat*) (Sowayan, *al-Shiʿr al-nabaṭī*, 464).

454 Here lies the nub of the story: It suddenly dawns on the poet that the daring she-camel is emblematic of the character of his self-willed daughter, and that he will be in for a hard time on account of her unconventional behavior, as explained in the verse of Dhū l-Rummah: "These camels are indomitable, / intractable thanks to the fierce Qays ʿAylān" (*lahā ḥawmatu l-ʿizzi llatī lā yarūmuhā, mukhīḍun wa-min ʿAylāna naṣrun muʾazzarū*), where it is explained that *mukhīḍ* is the person who leads the stud camel to impregnate a she-camel, the act of *makhāḍah*, and by extension acquired the meaning of someone who makes a supreme effort to attain his goal (*Dīwān*, 642–43).

455 "Her teeth": A reference to Ibn Ẓāhir's verses on the ravages of infirm old age and his daughter's verse, §17.28.

456 The loose grammar leaves open the possibility that the admiration expressed in the second hemistich might refer to the work of the father or good poetry in general. Traditionally, these signature verses are the poet's blurb about his own work and there is no reason to make an exception for the daughter.

457 See n. 398 to §17.9 for more background on the story of the daughter. Emirati commentators have been much exercised by the difficulty of making sense of these intriguing lines. As with all similar lines in these tales, they show no consistency of meter and rhyme that would qualify them as poetry, even of a questionable sort. They strike one as calques that have been handed down, mangled, and remolded along the way, and some might be fragments of lost poems. The lines might be related to Banū Hilāl materials: a version featuring Abu Zayd al-Hilālī with the repetition of "no" (*lā*) at the end of a gnomic wisdom statement has been found in the Sudanese province of Kordofan (al-Ḥasan and Tamīm, Alameemi, *Bint ibn Ẓāhir*, 112–13). Alameemi has endeavored to read a deeper meaning in these three lines on the theme of gender relations (al-Ḥasan and Tamīmī,

Alameemi, *Bint ibn Ẓāhir*, 116–17). According to this view, the first line is a straightforward statement of fact about the workings of the patrilineal descent system. The second line concerns the realm of worldly ambition, and in the view of her father women are advised to steer clear of it. The third line requires more speculative thought. The inner side of the hand (*bāṭin al-yad*) corresponds to the belly (*baṭn*). Fathers and sons are related through their spines, figuratively and because of the belief that a man's sperm is stored in the marrow of his spine. The mother's belly produces its fruit. Hence, the notion that the inside of the hand is not entitled to lineage rights, as no hair grows on the inside of the hand. Thus, the daughter denies her own rights in tribal society, worldly ambition, and reproductive rights. Even though she aligned herself with the poet's patriarchal values, she is severely punished by her father for having the audacity to formulate them. Perhaps because he suspected an ironic intent.

458 "This is the place": A similar concern with the quality of the soil is conspicuous in early classical Bedouin poetry and among the central Arabian Bedouin in more recent times. They show a strong preference for sandy soil, untouched by the impurities of towns and cultivated areas, as in the verse of Dhū l-Rummah: "Their camel-borne litters avoided the villages, / and did not tread on paths among irrigated fields" (*ẓaʿāʾinu lam yaslukna aknāfa qaryatin, bi-sīfin wa-lam tanghuḍ bi-hinna l-qanāṭirū*) (*Dīwān*, 1018–20). On his deathbed, Dhū l-Rummah is said to have asked, "Where are you going to bury me?" On being informed that he would be laid to rest at the usual burial ground of his folks, he refused. His preference was for Firindādayn, a high dune that travelers see from as far away as two days of riding. His fellows protested that no grave could be dug in such drifting and sliding sands. But Dhū l-Rummah instructed them to transport slabs of stone to the top of the dune and use them to construct his grave. And so it happened (*Dīwān*, 388–89). The grave is known until this day, and its location in Dhū l-Rummah's beloved sands of al-Dahnāʾ, on the upper flanks of a high dune, was pointed out to me on an expedition to visit the place in 2017.

459 In one version, the test of the earth is also conducted by fire: "Ibn Ẓāhir lived in Umm al-Khāyūs. According to our ancestors [*al-awwilīn*, see nn. 137, 410 and the online 'Glossary of Style, Themes, and Motifs'], he would bury a spool of wool and if it had rotted when he unearthed it after a while, he moved away from the place. Before sleeping, he buried the fire under ashes: if the fire had died out at dawn, he left the place. When it was still burning as it was when he lit it the evening before, he said, 'Yes, this is my land!' He no longer felt a desire to go anywhere else" (*w-ywarrī aḍ-ḍaww w-yōm iminnih b-yirgid, radd ʿalēhā ar-rmād hādhāk w-khallāhā, yōm ynishsh al-fajr, min yigūl b-hā čīh, w-yilgīhā čāybyah al-bigʿah, rifaʿ ʿanhā mā yiskinhā, w-yōm yalgāha baʿadhā čanhā mwarrinhā al-maghrib, al-jamr maḥallih, gāl, ʿiyal hī hadhī ad-dār, wlā jāzat lah ghēr hnāk*) (Thānī, *Ibn Ẓāhir*, 543).

460 "Slabs of stone": similar to the instructions given by Dhū l-Rummah for his burial; see n. 458.

461 A slightly different reading of §13.33. Similarly, a verse by al-Khalāwī: "A fellow is not constrained in his choice of land: / his land is where he feels well and does well" (*fa-d-dār mā yiḥṣar ʿalēhā wlēdhā, dār al-fitā mā ṭāb fīhā mikāsbih*) (Ibn Khamīs, *al-Khalāwī*, 59; itself a version of the Latin *ubi bene ibi patria*, "where it is well, there is the fatherland").

462 "Remember me well": see §4.6 and n. 77.

463 "Meetings at the grave": i.e., the wish of the poet was fulfilled. As presented here, the scene at the grave is reminiscent of a similar desire formulated by the sixteenth- or seventeenth-century poet Fayṣal al-Jumaylī: "When I die, bury me in a place close to a copious well, / with healthy sandy soil, with throngs of visitors; / Erect eight stone slabs at my grave: / the corpse rots but they always shine as new; / Let the ladies' litters come and go at my grave, / the pack camels of Bedouin marching to market towns; / They will say, 'Here lies a man so generous, / for a prodigious host every night brings visitors!'" (*ilā mitt ḥiṭṭūnī ʿalā jāl manhal, ʿadhiyy al-jibā dubb az-zimān yrād / ḥiṭṭū ʿalā gabrī thimānin ṣifāyiḥ, yibīd al-fitā w-asmālihinn jdād / bāghin ilā marrat ʿalayy ẓaʿāyin, ẓaʿāyin badwin gāṣdīn blād / yigūlūn rāʿ al-gabr*

yāmā min aṣ-ṣikhā, w-rāʿ aṣ-ṣikhā dubb al-liyāl yrād) (Sowayan, *al-Shiʿr al-nabaṭī*, 394).

464 Ḥātim al-Ṭāʾī: A pre-Islamic poet proverbial for his reckless generosity and for slaughtering all his camels to prepare lavish dinners for his guests.

465 "We did not witness": *mā liḥignā ʿalēh*, lit. "we did not catch up with them," i.e., we are not old enough to have heard their stories ourselves. Narrators commonly introduce their stories with the caveat that they cannot be held responsible for the veracity of their words and that they can only go by what they have heard from older people, who likewise inherited these stories from their predecessors. E.g., "Even though we did not live in those old times, we have met and come in contact with old men [. . .] who in turn knew old men older than themselves. So, men memorize old stories. They hand them down to each other, pass them on from one to the other, the father bequeathing them to his son" (*w-ḥinnā lō kān ḥinnā mā liḥiǵnā ʿalā haka-d-dōr al-awwal hadhāk, lākin liḥiǵnā linā rjālin* [. . .] *wu-hum lāḥǵīnin rjālin warāhum. wi-tḥafaẓ ar-rjāl. taʿāṭā l-ʿlūm, ytanāgalōnh ar-rjāl min wāḥdin l-wāḥid, wa-l-wāld ywarrthah lu-wldiduh*) (Sowayan, *The Arabian Oral Historical Narrative*, 87).

Bibliography

ʿAbīd ibn al-Abraṣ. *Dīwān*. Beirut: Dār al-Ṣādir, 1964.

Abū Shihāb, Muḥammad. *Turāthunā min al-shiʿr al-shaʿbī*. Abu Dhabi: Nādī Turāth al-Imārāt, 1998.

Abū Shihāb, Muḥammad, and Ibrāhīm Abū Malḥah. *Al-Mājidī ibn Ẓāhir: Hayātuh wa-shiʿruh*. Abu Dhabi: Abu Dhabi Authority for Culture and Heritage, Poetry Academy: 2012.

Alameemi, Sultan [al-ʿAmīmī, Sulṭān ibn Bakhīt]. *Al-Mājidī ibn Ẓāhir: Sīratuh wa-ashʿāruh wa-qaṣāʾid tunshar li-awwal marrah*. Abu Dhabi: n.p., 2004.

———. *Safarjal: Dīwān Rāshid al-Khiḍr*. 2nd ed. Abu Dhabi: Cultural Programs and Heritage Festivals Committee, Poetry Academy, 2015.

———. *Muʿjam al-ghāf*.

Al-ʿAmārah, ʿAbd Allāh Salīm. *Al-Qiyam al-ijtimāʿiyyah fī al-amthāl al-shaʿbiyyah al-Imārātiyyah*. Dubai: Hamdan bin Mohammed Heritage Center, 2015.

Badger, George Percy. *Imāms and Seyyids of ʿOmān by Salīl ibn Razīq from A.D. 661–1856*. New York: Burt Franklin, 1963.

Bell, Richard. *The Qurʾān*. 2 vols. Edinburgh: T. and T. Clark, 1960. First published 1937.

Bevan, A. A. *The Nakaʾid of Jarīr and al-Farazdak*. 3 vols. Leiden, Netherlands: E. J. Brill, 1905–7.

Dhū l-Rummah. *Dīwān Dhī l-Rummah*. Edited by ʿAbd al-Qudūs Abū Ṣāliḥ. Beirut: Muʾassasat al-Īmān, 1982.

Encyclopaedia of Islam, Second Edition [*EI2*]. Edited by P. Bearman, Th. Bianquis, C. E. Bosworth, E. van Donzel, and W. P. Heinrichs. Leiden: Brill Online, 2012.

Al-Faraj, Khālid, ed. *Dīwān al-Nabaṭ, majmūʿah min al-shiʿr al-ʿāmmī fī Najd*. Vol. 1. Damascus: Maṭbaʿat al-Taraqqī, 1952.

Gelder, Geert Jan van. *Beyond the Line: Classical Arabic Literary Critics and the Coherence and Unity of the Poem*. Leiden, Netherlands: E. J. Brill, 1982.

———. "Some Types of Ambiguity: A Poem by Abū Nuwās on al-Faḍl al-Raqāshī." *Quaderni di Studi Arabi* 10 (1992): 75–92.

Ḥanẓal, Fāliḥ. *Al-Mufaṣṣal fī taʾrīkh al-Imārāt al-ʿArabiyyah al-Muttaḥidah*. Abu Dhabi: Lajnat al-Turāth wa-l-Tārīkh, 1983.

———. *Amīr al-shiʿr al-nabaṭī al-Mājidī ibn Ẓāhir: Dirāsah fī fikrih min khilāl fannih al-shiʿrī*. Abu Dhabi: Ittiḥād Kuttāb wa-Udabāʾ al-Imārāt, 1992.

———. *Muʿjam al-alfāẓ al-ʿāmmiyyah fī dawlat al-Imārāt al-ʿArabiyyah al-Muttaḥidah*. Abu Dhabi: Wizārat al-Iʿlām wa-l-Thaqāfah, 1998.

———. *Jāmiʿ al-amthāl wa-maʾthūr al-aqwāl wa-l-ḥikam wa-l-kināyāt ʿind ahl al-Imārāt: Dirāsah fī al-thaqāfah al-shaʿbiyyah wa-l-qiyam al-fikriyyah*. Abu Dhabi: Abu Dhabi Tourism and Culture Authority, 2016.

Ḥasan, Muḥammad ibn Aḥmad ibn. *Al-ʿĀdāt wa-l-taqālīd fī Dawlat al-Imārāt al-ʿArabiyyah al-Muttaḥidah*. Abu Dhabi: n.p., n.d. Printed at the expense of Shaykh Zāyid ibn Sulṭān Āl Nahāyān, president of the United Arab Emirates.

Al-Ḥasan, Ghassān Aḥmad al-Ḥasan. *Tajalliyyāt al-ghawṣ fī al-shiʿr al-nabaṭī fī dawlat al-Imārāt al-ʿArabiyyah al-Muttaḥidah*. Abu Dhabi: Hayʾat Abū Ẓabī li-l-Thaqāfah wa-l-Turāth, Akādīmiyyah al-Shiʿr, 2011.

———. *Al-Shiʿr al-nabaṭī fī manṭiqat al-khalīj wa-l-jazīrah al-ʿarabiyyah, dirāsah ʿilmiyyah*. 2 vols. 2nd ed. Abu Dhabi: Wizārat al-Iʿlām wa-l-Thaqāfah, 2002.

Al-Ḥasan, Ghassān, ʿAlī ibn Tamīm, and Sultan Alameemi. *Bint ibn Ẓāhir: Abḥāth fī qaṣīdatihā wa-sīratihā al-shaʿbiyyah*. Abu Dhabi: Academy of Poetry, 2018. First published 2008.

Holes, Clive. *Dialect, Culture, and Society in Eastern Arabia*. Vol. 1, *Glossary*; vol. 2, *Ethnographic Texts*; vol. 3, *Phonology, Morphology, Syntax, Style*. Leiden, Netherlands: E. J. Brill, 2001–16.

Homer. *The Iliad of Homer*. Translated by Richmond Lattimore. Chicago: University of Chicago Press, 1962.

Homerin, T. Emil. "Echoes of a Thirsty Owl: Death and Afterlife in Pre-Islamic Arabic Poetry." *Journal of Near Eastern Studies* 44 (1985): 165–84.

Al-Ḥumaydān, ʿAbd al-Laṭīf ibn Nāṣir. "Al-Ṣirāʿ ʿalā as-sulṭah fī dawlat al-Jubūr: Bayn mafāhīm al-qibaliyyah wa-l-mulk." *Dirāsāt taʾrīkhiyyah* 2 (1995): 43–102. Riyadh: Markaz al-Buḥūth, Kulliyat al-Adāb, King Saud University

Al-Ḥuṭayʾah. *Dīwān al-Ḥuṭayʾah bi-riwāyat wa-sharḥ Ibn Sikkīt*. Edited by Mufīf Muḥammad Qamīḥah. Beirut: Dār al-Kutub al-ʿIlmiyyah, 1993.

Ibn ʿAtīj al-Hāmilī, Saʿīd ibn Rāshid. *Dīwān Ibn ʿAtīj*. Edited by al-Kindī Muṣabbiḥ al-Mirar, ʿAlī ibn Muṣabbiḥ al-Mirar, and Ghassān al-Ḥasan. Abu Dhabi: Lajnat al-Turāth bi-Nādī Turāth al-Imārāt, 1999.

Ibn Khamīs, ʿAbd Allāh ibn Muḥammad. *Rāshid al-Khalāwī: Ḥayātuh, shiʿruh, ḥikamuh, falsafatuh, nawādiruh, ḥisābuh al-falakī*. Riyadh: Maṭābiʿ al-Farazdaq, 1985. First published 1972.

Ibn Khaldūn, ʿAbd al-Raḥmān ibn Muḥammad. *Muqaddimat Ibn Khaldūn*. Edited by Darwīsh al-Juwaydī. Beirut: al-Maktabah al-ʿAṣriyyah, 1999.

Ibn Manẓūr. *Lisān al-ʿArab*. Cairo: Dār al-Maʿārif, n.d.

Ibn Ruzayq, Ḥamīd ibn Muḥammad. *Al-Fatḥ al-mubīn fī sīrat al-sādah Āl Bū Saʿīdiyyīn*. Edited by ʿAbd al-Munʿim ʿĀmir and Muḥammad Mursī Abd Allāh. Muscat: Ministry of National Heritage and Culture, 1983. First published 1857.

Ibn Ẓāhir. *Dīwān al-shāʿir al-shaʿbī Ibn Ẓāhir*. Dubai: Al-Maṭbaʿah al-ʿUmāniyyah, 1963. Printed at the expense of Shaykh Ḥamdān ibn Rāshid al-Maktūm.

Al-Iṣfahānī, Abū l-Faraj. *Kitāb al-Aghānī*. Cairo: Maṭbaʿat Dār al-Kutub al-Miṣriyyah, 1928.

Al-Juhany, Uwaidah M. *Najd before the Salafi Reform Movement: Social, Political and Religious Conditions during the Three Centuries preceding the Rise of the Saudi State*. Reading, UK: Ithaca Press, 2002.

Al-Juhaymān, ʿAbd al-Karīm. *Al-Amthāl al-shaʿbiyyah fī qalb al-jazīrah al-ʿarabiyyah*. 10 vols. Riyadh: n.p., 1982.

———. *Al-Asāṭīr al-shaʿbiyyah min qalb al-jazīrah al-ʿarabiyyah*. 5 vols. 7th ed. Riyadh: n.p., 2014.

Kennedy, Philip. *Abu Nuwas: A Genius of Poetry*. London: Oneworld Academic, 2012.

Al-Khāṭirī al-Nuʿaymī, Ḥamād ibn ʿAbd Allāh. *Ashʿār qadīmah wa-abyāt yatīmah*. 2 vols. Abu Dhabi: Abu Dhabi Tourism and Culture Authority, 2014.

———. *Al-ʿArīj fī ashʿār Ibn ʿAtīj*. Abu Dhabi: Hay'at Abū Ẓabī li-l-Siyāḥah wa-l-Thaqāfah, Dār al-Kutub al-Waṭaniyyah, 2016.

———. *Muʿjam mawārid al-miyāh al-qadīmah bi-Imārat Abu Ẓabī*. Abu Dhabi: Abu Dhabi Tourism and Culture Authority, 2015.

———. *Al-Ẓafrah, Shiʿr wa-shuʿarā'*. Abu Dhabi: Department of Culture and Tourism, National Library, 2018.

Kurpershoek, P. Marcel. *Oral Poetry and Narratives from Central Arabia*. 5 vols. Leiden, Netherlands: E. J. Brill, 1994–2005.

———. *Bedouin Poets of the Dawāsir Tribe: Between Nomadism and Settlement in Southern Najd*. Vol. 3 of *Oral Poetry and Narratives from Central Arabia*. Leiden, Netherlands: E. J. Brill, 1999.

———. *The Poetry of ad-Dindān: A Bedouin Bard in Southern Najd*. Vol. 1 of *Oral Poetry and Narratives from Central Arabia*. Leiden, Netherlands: E. J. Brill, 1994.

———. *A Saudi Tribal History: Honour and Faith in the Traditions of the Dawāsir*. Vol. 4 of *Oral Poetry and Narratives from Central Arabia*. Leiden, Netherlands: E. J. Brill, 2002.

Kurpershoek, P. Marcel, ed. and tr. *Arabian Satire: Poetry from Eighteenth-Century Najd*. Ḥmēdān al-Shwēʿir. New York: New York University Press, 2017.

———. *Arabian Romantic: Poems on Bedouin Life and Love*. ʿAbdallāh ibn Sbayyil. New York: New York University Press, 2018.

Kurpershoek, P. Marcel, and Claude Lorentz. "Charles Huber, voyageur en Arabie: Sur deux manuscrits de poésie bédouine de la Bibliothèque nationale et universitaire de Strasbourg." *La Revue de la*

BNU (Bibliothèque Nationale Universitaire de Strasbourg) 17 (2018): 100–11.

Al-Kuwaytī, al-Ḥaẓẓ Muṣabbiḥ Farḥān. *Yaqūl al-mutawaṣṣif: Amthāl wa-aqwāl sha'biyyah jumi'at min manṭiqat al-'Ayn.* 2 vols. Abu Dhabi: Abu Dhabi Tourism and Culture Authority, 2015.

Lane, Edward William. *An Arabic-English Lexicon.* London: Williams and Norgate, 1863–93.

Lerrick, Alison. *Taghribat Banī Hilāl Al-Diyāghim: Variation in the Oral Epic Poetry of Najd.* Vol. 1, *Introduction, Overview, Description*; vol. 2, *Arabic Composite of Text.* PhD diss., Princeton University, 1984.

Lorimer, John Gordon. *Gazetteer of the Persian Gulf, 'Oman, and Central Arabia.* Leiden, Netherlands: Brill Online, 2015.

Lyall, C. J. *The Dīwāns of 'Abīd ibn al-Abraṣ of Asad and 'Āmir ibn aṭ-Ṭufail of 'Āmir ibn Ṣa'ṣa'ah.* Cambridge, UK: E. J. W. Gibb Memorial Trust, 1980. First published 1913.

Mahmoodi-Bakhtiari, Behrooz, and Farhang Farbod. "Fleeing Destined Death." *Mawlana Rumi Review* 8, no. 1 (2017).

March, Jennifer R. *Cassell Dictionary of Classical Mythology.* London: Cassell, 1998.

Al-Maṭrūshī, Khamīs Ismā'īl. *Al-Lahjah al-Imārātiyyah.* Abu Dhabi: al-Majlis al-Waṭanī li-l-A'lām, 2013.

Al-Mufaḍḍal, Abū 'Abbās ibn Muḥammad aḍ-Ḍabbī. *Dīwān al-Mufaḍḍaliyyāt.* Edited by Charles James Lyall. Vol. 1, Arabic text (1921); vol. 2, translation and notes. Oxford: Clarendon Press, 1918–21.

Musil, Alois. *The Manners and Customs of the Rwala Bedouins.* Oriental Explorations and Studies 6. New York: American Geographical Society, 1928.

Al-Mutanabbī, Abū al-Ṭayyib. *Dīwān Abī Ṭayyib al-Mutanabbī bi-sharḥ Abī al-Baqā' al-Akbarī.* 4 vols. 2nd edition. Cairo: al-Ḥalabī, 1956.

Al-Naẓūrī, Fāṭimah. *Wīn al-khīl diwā al-'ilīl: al-Tidāwī fī bādiyat Abū Ẓabī.* Abu Dhabi: Dā'irat al-Thaqāfah wa-l-Siyāḥah, Dār al-Kutub, 2018.

Özdalga, Elisabeth. *Naqshbandis in Western and Central Asia: Change and Continuity.* Transactions 9. Istanbul: Swedish Research Institute in Istanbul, 1999.

Philby, H. St. J. B. *Sa'udi Arabia*. Beirut: Librairie du Liban, 1968.

Al-Rawāḥī, Sālim ibn Muḥammad ibn Sālim. *Al-Amthāl al-'Umāniyyah al-sha'biyyah*. Al-Seeb, Oman: Maktabat al-Ḍāmirī, 2012.

Al-Rūmī, Aḥmad al-Bishr. *Mu'jam al-muṣṭalaḥāt al-baḥriyyah fī al-Kuwayt*. Kuwait: Markaz al-Buhūth wa-l-Dirāsāt al-Kuwaytiyyah, 1996.

Al-Sa'īd, Ṭalāl. *Al-Mawsū'ah al-nabaṭiyyah al-kāmilah*. Vol. 1. Kuwait: Dār al-Salāsil, 1987.

Al-Sālimī, Nūr al-Dīn 'Abd Allāh ibn Ḥamīd. *Tuḥfat al-a'yān fī sīrat ahl 'Umān*. Ruwī, Oman. Self-published by Zāhir and Zuhayr, sons of the author's grandson, Sa'ūd ibn Ḥamad at al-Maṭābi' al-Dhahabiyyah.

Samhūdī, 'Alī ibn 'Abdallāh. *Wafā' al-wafā' bi-akhbār dār al-muṣṭafā*. Beirut: Dār al-Kutub al-'Ilmiyyah, 1984.

Al-Shaybānī, Muḥammad Sharīf. *Dīwān al-jawāhir fī shi'r Ibn Ẓāhir, Shā'ir al-Khalīj*. Beirut: Maṭābi' Dār al-Kutub, 1967. Printed at the orders of Shaykh Zāyid ibn Sulṭān Āl Nahayān, ruler of the Emirate of Abu Dhabi.

Sowayan, Saad Abdullah. *Nabaṭī Poetry: The Oral Poetry of Arabia*. Berkeley, CA: University of California Press, 1985.

———. *The Arabian Oral Historical Narrative: An Ethnographic and Linguistic Analysis*. Wiesbaden, Germany: Otto Harrassowitz, 1992.

———. *Al-Shi'r al-nabaṭī: Dhā'iqat al-sha'b wa-sulṭat al-naṣṣ*. Beirut: Dār al-Sāqī, 2000.

———. *Ayyām al-'Arab al-awākhir: Asāṭīr wa-marwiyyāt shafahiyyah fī l-ta'rīkh wa-l-adab min shamāl al-jazīrah al-'arabiyyah ma'a shadharāt mukhtārah min qabīlat Āl Murrah wa-Subay'*. Beirut: Arab Network for Research and Publishing, 2010.

———. "The Hilali Poetry in the Muqaddimah: Its Links to Nabaṭī Poetry." *Oriente Moderno* 83, no. 2, *Studies on Arabic Epics* (2003): 277–306.

Al-Suwaydā'. *Faṣīḥ al-'āmmī fī shamāl Najd*. 2 vols. Riyadh: Dār al-Suwaydā', 1987.

Al-Ṭābūr, 'Abd Allāh 'Alī. *Rijāl fī ta'rīkh al-Imārāt al-'Arabiyyah al-Muttaḥidah*. Rās al-Khaymah: n.p., 1993.

———. *Al-Alghāz al-sha'biyyah fī al-Imārāt*. 3rd ed. Rās al-Khaymah: Nādī Turāth al-Imārāt, Markaz Zāyid li-l-Dirasāt wa-l-Buḥūth, 2015.

———. *Al-Ṭibb al-sha'bī fī al-Imārāt al-'Arabiyyah al-Muttaḥidah*. 3rd ed. Dubai: Maṭba'at Ibn Dismāl: 2008.

Tamplin, William. *Poet of Jordan: The Political Poetry of Muhammad Fanatil al-Hajaya*. Leiden, Netherlands: E. J. Brill, 2018.

Thānī, Aḥmad Rāshid. *Ibn Ẓāhir: Baḥth tawthīqī fī shi'rih wa-sīratih al-shakhṣiyyah*. Abu Dhabi: al-Mujamma' al-Thaqāfī, 1999.

Tibbetts, G. R. *Arab Navigation in the Indian Ocean before the Coming of the Portuguese, Being a Translation of Kitāb al-Fawā'id fī uṣūl al-baḥr wa-l-qawā'id of Aḥmad ibn Mājid al-Najdī*. Oriental Translation Fund. New Series 42. London: The Royal Asiatic Society of Great Britain and Ireland, 1981. First published 1971.

Tolstoy, Leo. *The Death of Ivan Ilyich and Other Stories*. Translated by Ronald Wilks, Anthony Briggs, and David McDuff. London: Penguin, 2008.

Shaykh Sirḥān ibn Sa'īd al-Azkawī. *Kashf al-ghammah al-jāmi' li-akhbār alummah li-muṣannif majhūl*. Edited by Aḥmad 'Ubaydalī. Nicosia, Cyprus: Dilmun, 1985.

Al-'Ubūdī, Muḥammad ibn Nāṣir. *Mu'jam al-uṣūl al-faṣīḥah li-l-alfāẓ al-dārijah*. 13 vols. Riyadh: n.p., 2008.

———. *Mu'jam al-anwā' wa-l-fuṣūl*. Riyadh: n.p., 2011.

———. *Mu'jam wajh al-arḍ wa-mā yata'allaq bih min al-jibāl wa-l-ābār wa-l-ajwā' wa-naḥwahā fī al-ma'thūrāt al-sha'biyyah*. Riyadh: Dār al-Thalūthiyyah, 2014.

———. *Al-Amthāl al-'āmmiyyah fī Najd*. 5 vols. Riyadh: n.p., 1979.

Udink, Betsy. *Meisjes van Atatürk, Zonen van de Sultan, verhalen uit Turkije* [*Girls of Atatürk, Sons of the Sultan: Stories from Turkey*]. Amsterdam: Uitgeverij Augustus-Atlas Contact, 2015.

Webster, Roger. "Notes on the Dialect and the Way of Life of the Āl Wahība Bedouin of Oman." *Bulletin of the School of Oriental and African Studies* 54, no. 3 (1991): 473–85.

———. "The Bedouin of the Wahiba Sands: Pastoral Ecology and Management." In *The Scientific Results of The Royal Geographical*

Society's Oman Wahiba Sands Project 1985–1987, edited by R.W. Dutton. *Journal of Oman Studies*, Special Report no. 3: 443–52.
Wehr, Hans. *A Dictionary of Modern Written Arabic*. 3rd ed. Edited by J. Milton Cowan. Wiesbaden, Germany: Harrassowitz, 1961.
Al-Zawzānī, Abū ʿAbd Allāh al-Ḥusayn ibn Aḥmad ibn al-Ḥusayn. *Sharḥ al-muʿallaqāt al-sabʿ*. Beirut: Dār Bayrūt, 1982.

Further Reading

Faraj, Maryam Jumʿah. *Al-Ghawṣ ʿalā al-luʾluʾ: Al-ghawṣ niẓām iqtiṣādī, ijtimāʿī, thaqāfī; al-Imārāt namūdhajan.* Dubai: Hamdan Bin Mohammed Heritage Center, 2014.

Ghubāsh, Muḥammad Saʿīd. *Al-Fawāʾid fī taʾrīkh al-Imārāt wa-l-awābid.* Reviewed by Fāliḥ Ḥanẓal. Dubai: Nadwat al-Thaqāfah wal-ʿUlūm, 1998.

Al-Ḥamdān, Muḥammad ibn ʿAbd Allāh. *Ṣabā Najd: Najd fī al-shiʿr wa-n-nathr al-ʿarabī.* 2nd ed. Riyadh: Maktabat Qays, 1984/1985.

———. *Al-Bīr: Hādhā bilādunā*, 63. Riyadh: King Saud University, 2001.

Ḥanẓal, Fāliḥ. *Muʿjam al-qawāfī wa-l-alḥān fī dawlat al-Imārāt.* Sharjah: Ittiḥād Kuttāb wa-Udabāʾ al-Imārāt, 1987.

Al-Ḥijī, Yaʿqūb Yūsif. *Ṣināʿat al-sufun al-shirāʿiyyah fī al-Kuwayt.* Kuwait: Markaz al-Buḥūth wa-l-Dirāsāt al-Kuwaytiyyah, 1998.

Holes, Clive. "The Language of Nabaṭi Poetry." In *Encyclopaedia of Arabic Language and Linguistics On-Line Edition*, edited by R. De Jong and L. Edzard. Leiden, Netherlands: E. J. Brill, 2012.

Holes, Clive, and Said Salman Abu Athera. *The Nabaṭī Poetry of the United Arab Emirates: Selected Poems, Annotated and Translated into English.* Reading, UK: Ithaca Press, 2011.

Imruʾ l-Qays. *Dīwān.* Beirut: Dār Bayrūt, 1986.

Al-Khāṭirī al-Nuʿaymī, Ḥamād ibn ʿAbd Allāh. *Al-Ibl fī al-turāth al-Imārātī.* Abu Dhabi: Abu Dhabi Tourism and Culture Authority, 2015.

Kurpershoek, P. Marcel. "Free and/or Noble? The Hunting Falcon and Class in Arabian Nabaṭi Poetry." In *Falconry in the Mediterranean Context during the Pre-Modern Era*, edited by Charles Burnett and

Baudouin Van den Abeele. Bibliotheca Cynegetica 9. Geneva: Droz, 2018.

Kurpershoek, P. Marcel. "Heartbeat: Conventionality and Originality in Najdi Poetry." *Asian Folklore Studies* 52 (1993): 33–74.

———. "Politics and the Art of Eulogy in Najdi Nabaṭi Poetry: Ḥmēdān al-Shwēʿir's (al-Shuwayʿir) Apologies to Ibn Muʿammar and Ibn Sbayyil's Ode on Ibn Rashīd." *Quaderni di Studi Arabi*, n.s. 13-2018, 87–101.

———. "Praying Mantis in the Desert." *Arabian Humanities* 5 (2015).

Al-Qamzī, ʿAlī ibn Dumaythān. *Riḥlat al-ghawṣ*. Dubai: Dāʾirat al-Mawāniʾ wa-l-Jamārik, 2000.

Al-Shāmisī, Aḥmad Khalīfah, ed. *Lamḥāt min al-turāth al-baḥrī.* Al-Fujayrah, UAE: Ḥukūmat al-Fujayrah, Idārat al-Turāth wa-l-Āthār, 2002.

Al-Suwaydāʾ. *ʿAbd al-Raḥmān ibn Zayd: Al-nakhlah al-ʿarabiyyah; adabiyyan wa-ʿilmiyyan wa-iqtiṣādiyyan.* Riyadh: Maṭbaʿat al-Jazīrah, 1993.

Al-Ṭābūr, ʿAbd Allāh ʿAlī. *Julfār ʿabra al-taʾrīkh*. Dubai: n.p., 1998.

Al-ʿUbūdī, Muḥammad ibn Nāṣir. *Muʿjam al-nakhlah fī al-maʾthūr al-shaʿbī.* Riyadh: Dār al-Thalūthiyyah, 2010.

Weipert, Reinhard. *Der Dīwān des Rāʿī an-Numairī.* Beirut: Commissioned by Franz Steiner Verlag, 1980.

Al-Ẓāhirī, Abū ʿAbd al-Raḥmān ibn ʿAqīl. *Dīwān al-shiʿr al-ʿāmmī bi-lahjat ahl Najd*. Riyadh: Dār al-ʿUlūm, 1982.

Index

abandonment, §§4.9–12, §4.44; of Bedouin camp, xxviii, §§1.65–66, §§4.8–14, §4.46, §6.0, §8.64, 135n80, 142n109; of the beloved, xxvii; by youth, §1.0, §1.17, §2.0

ʿAbd al-ʿAzīz ibn Kathīr, 195n368

ʿAbd Allāh ibn Sbayyil. *See* Ibn Sbayyil, ʿAbd Allāh

ʿAbdah ibn al-Ṭabīb, 147n130

al-ʿAbdī, al-Muthaqqib, 187n332

ʿAbīd ibn al-Abraṣ, lxxivn62, 136n85, 149n137, 168n230, 205n414

Abu Dhabi, xiii, xix, xxi, xxiv, lviii–lxi, §21.2

Abū Dhuʾayb, 172n244, 190n345, 194n363

Abū Malḥah, lxi, 135n81, 136n83, 137n88, 140n101, 143n112, 190n347

Abū Nuwās, §14.0, §14.26

Abū Qays ibn al-Aslat, 128n52, 156n175

Abū Shihāb, lxi, 135n81, 136n83, 137n88, 140n101, 143n112, 190n347

Abū Ẓāhir, 188n333

Abū Zayd al-Hilālī, xxvii, xxxv, li, lxxxiiin110, 148n132, 209n440, 211n457

al-ʿAdhīb, liv, §16.63

agonies of love, §3.0, §§4.40–44, §10.13, §§10.17–25

al-Aḥnaf ibn Qays, 199n385

al-Aḥsāʾ, xxi, xxii, xxiii, xxiv, xxv, xxviii, xxix, xxx, xxxiv, l, lvi, lix, lx, lxi, lxiii, lxixn15, lxxiiin50, lxxvn67, 150n147, 178n281

ʿAjmān, lx, §20.2

Ajwad ibn Zāmil, xx, xxii, xxiii, xxx, xxxiv, lxviiin8, 145n121

Āl Ḥumayd, xxii, xxviii, xxxiv, lxxiiin50, 152n151

Āl Maktūm, Shaykh Ḥamdān ibn Rashīd, lxi

Āl Maktūm, Shaykh Rashīd, xix

Āl Maktūm, Shaykh ʿUbayd ibn Jumʿah, lx

Alameemi, Sultan, lviii, lxi–lxii, lxviiin1, lxviin5, lxixn21, lxxxivn115, 131n63; on *al-garā shabb*, 153n162; on *ʿamīdarah*, 135n81; on color imagery, 181n301; on Ibn Ẓāhir's daughter, 203n403; on *khurkhā*, 136n86

Albuquerque, Alfonso de, xxii

ʿAlqamah ibn ʿAbadah, 135n79, 183n311, 193n357

ʿAlyā, 166n222

ʿĀmir al-Samīn, xxviii, lxxvin69, 125n31, 155n170, 156n173, 164n207, 169n231, 177n273, 189n341, 191n355, 207n427
al-ʿĀmirī, Abū Ḥamzah, xxvii, xxviii, xxxiii, lxxiiin57, 123n24, 131n67, 154n167, 167n225
ʿAmr ibn al-Ahtam, 179n287, 210n449
al-Amsaḥ, Shāyiʿ, xxvii, xxxiv, xli, xlvi, xlviii, lxiii, 149n137, 156n175, 157n177, 190n344, 198n381; self-praise, 173n248
ancestors, xxvii, §16.13, §18.1, §19.1, §23.6, 184n315, 205n410, 213n459. *See also* graybeards
Angel of Death, xxxix, 131n64
angels, lxxviiin76, §4.61, §8.18, §9.41, 145n120, 147n130, 159n189
anklets, §12.27, §14.11, 169n230
ants, §1.31
Apocalypse. *See* Judgment Day
Arcturus, §8.21
al-Aʿshā, 193n362
al-Aṣmaʿī, lxxxiin109, 124n28, 193n357, 193n362
assembly rooms, xlviii
audiences of poetry, §§4.4–5; aficionados, §§11.2–3, §§14.2–4; connoisseurs, §3.0, §3.4, §13.4, §16.2, §17.1, §22.9, 126n41, 145n121, 198n381; devotees, §2.3, §3.5; judging the poet, §16.0; lovers of, §§5.1–2, 197n379, 198n382; savants, §13.6
ʿAwf ibn al-Aḥwaṣ, 156n174, 201n394
al-ʿAyn, xxiii, l, lxviin2, lxxxin103, lxxxvn133, §19.2, §19.3, §21.2, 135n79, 200n389, 204n408
Badriyyah Sufis, §5.54
Bahrain, xxii, lxi, lxixn13, lxixn15; Sufism in, lxxvn67, 150n147
Banū Hilāl, xx–xxv, xxviii, xxix, xxxii–xxxvii passim, l, §1.0; on dancing girls, 168n230; departure of, xxviii; Ibn Ẓāhir and, xx; Jabrids, xx–xxii, l; migrations of, §17.0; nostalgia for, 126n37; saga, xxix, xxxii, xxxiv, xxxv, §6.0, §9.0, §10.0, 152n157, 166n222, 208n439; *taghrībah*, xxxv; thunderstorms and, xxxvii; verse style of, 154n165, 201n394. *See also* Hilālī poetry characteristics
Banū Jabr (al-Jubūr), xxii, xxiii, xxxi; Ajwad ibn Zāmil, xx, xxii–xxiii, xxx; Hilāl ibn Zāmil, xxiii; Ḥusayn ibn Ajwad ibn Zāmil, xxiii; Muḥammad ibn Ajwad, xxii, 146n126; Muqrin ibn Qaḍīb ibn Zāmil, 178n281; Muqrin ibn Zāmil, xxii; Qaṭan, xxii; Sayf ibn Ajwad, xxii. *See also* Jabr ibn Sayyār
Banū Yās, xxiv, li
Barakāt al-Sharīf, xxvii–xxviii, xxix, xxxii, lx, lxxn27, lxxiiin52, 173n248, 196n373
Barrāk ibn Ghurayr, xxxiv, lxxiiin50
Bashāmah ibn al-Ghadīr, 178n282
Basra, xxiii, lxxvn67, 178n281
al-Baṭḥā, liv, §16.65
al-Bāṭinah, liv, 204n408
battles. *See* combat
beauty: of Bedouin women, §2.0, §§2.17–18, §3.37, §§10.8–10, §§10.56–58, §10.67, §12.10, §12.21, §§14.11–12; of the beloved, §§1.40–41, §§4.21–25, §§6.13–15,

§§8.40–44, §§10.14–16, §10.58, §§16.74–76; and disgust for old age, 120n7, 164n209; gazelle as simile of, §6.15, §12.21, §§16.74–75, 153n158; of women's hair, §5.56, §16.76, 151n149, 174n254
Bedouin, lxviiin5, §§1.60–64, §2.0, §3.0, 162n203, 184n316, 212n458; abandoned camp of, xxviii, §§1.65–66, §§4.8–12, §4.46, §6.0, §8.64, 135n80, 142n109; Banū Yās, xxiv, li; beauty of women, §2.0, §§2.17–18, §3.37, §§10.8–10, §§10.56–58, §10.67, §12.10, §12.21, §§14.11–12; camel caravan, §6.0, §§6.6–11, §9.23, §§12.22–29, §§12.32–35, §§14.7–18; cyclical year of, §3.40, §12.0, 124n27, 180n292; hospitality and, xliv, §21.5, §21.16, §21.18, 125n34; Ibn Ẓāhir considered as, xlix–lii, 208n432; love for imported textiles, §14.0; migrations of, xxx, xl, lii, §§6.6–12, §§8.31–33, §10.0, §17.0, §19.6, 166n219, 204n408; seclusion of unmarried girls, §14.12, 181n301, 182n306, 201n394; shelters of, §12.24, §21.20, §23.7; use of the term, l. *See also* Banū Hilāl; Banū Jabr (al-Jubūr); Banū Yās; beloved, departure of
begging, poet's, §10.23, §16.35
beloved, departure of, xxv, xxix, xxxvi, xxxviii, li, §§1.41–54, §3.0, §§6.13–16, §9.0, §§9.23–29, §12.0, §§12.30–37, §14.0, §§14.20–21; inevitability of, 191n350; palanquin of, xxxvii, lxiii, §§1.41–47, §10.0, §§10.61–63, §14.0, §§14.10–19; unexpectedness of, 183n311
beloved, the: arrival of, §§16.72–74; beauty of, §§2.20–22, §§6.13–15, §§8.40–44, §§10.14–16, §10.58, §§14.11–12, §§16.74–76; cold responses of, §§1.9–11, §1.47, §4.27, §8.23, §§9.13–15, §9.30, §9.36, §§10.17–18, §14.0, §14.21, §14.30, §§16.39–43; deserted abode of, xxviii, §§1.65–66, §§4.8–14, §4.46, §6.0, §8.64, 135n80, 142n109; dialogue with, §§10.21–27; kinfolk of, §10.26, §14.30; longing for, §4.15–27, §§10.14–28, §10.59; as metaphor for youth, §§3.15–24, §§12.4–13, §12.30; speech addressed to, §16.0, §§16.26–44
Bird of Death, §12.14
Bishr ibn Abī Khāzim, 188n333, 205n413, 279n413
Bishr ibn ʿAmr, 148n136, 175n259
black color: clouds, xl, §2.10, §16.53; cooking pots, 132n68, 141n108, 189n342; girls' eyes, §10.9; goat hair, §17.28, 125n34; gunpowder, 196n374; kohl around the eyes, §2.18, §11.28; night sky, §9.43; paisa coins, §20.11; ravens, xxxvii, §16.76, 120n5; ripe dates, 151n149; starling feathers, §5.27; unction of tar, §16.48; woolen tents, §1.61; youthful hair, xxxvii, §1.13, §3.23, §10.15, §10.56, 151n149
blind fate, xxxviii
blood feud, §§19.3–5
blood money, §8.50

boat of palm fronds and branches, liii, §§20.1–4, §20.13, lxxxin98, lxxxiin108
bravery, xli, §5.45, §15.0, §§15.20–22
Bū Sanīdah, Aḥmad ibn ʿAbd al-Raḥmān, lix
bucket metaphors, §§2.2–3, §2.9, §§10.34–35, §11.43, §§13.2–3
building metaphors for poetry, 175n262, 198n381
bull, cosmic, 145n120
al-Buraymī, xvi, xxiii, xlv, l, lxviin2, §19.3, 200n389, 204n408

camels: camel caravan, §6.0, §§6.6–11, §9.23, §10.62, §§12.22–29, §§12.32–35, §§14.7–18; carrying two riders, §3.27; as food, §§21.9–10, §§21.25–26, 210n449; given as reward to Ibn Ẓāhir, §21.13; husbandry of, §7.0, §7.15; Ibn Ẓāhir's daughter and, §§22.1–2; Ibn Ẓāhir's she-camel, lxxxivn114, §18.2, §§19.1–8, §20.1, §20.12, §21.1, §§21.24–26; of Ibn Ẓāhir's son-in-law, §21.15, §§21.17–18; in messenger motif, §§9.32–36; as metaphor for poetry, 129n54; as metaphor for self-control, §10.31, §16.23; old age and, 180n293; palanquin of the beloved, lxiii, §§1.41–47, §§8.33–8, §9.0, §§10.60–63, §§12.28–36, §§14.11–19; pedigrees of, §19.1; racing camels, §23.1, 185n322; rutting bulls, §9.0, §9.45, §10.52; stallions, §§8.33–38, §8.0, §9.44; stealing of, xxiv, lxxxin98; stray camels, 129n54; studs, §7.20, §19.1, §19.4; in trades and raids, xxi, xxiii, xxiv, §19.2; "wading camel," §22.1; yawning, §§19.6–7. *See also* migrations
Canopus, lxv, §6.4, §6.12, §8.32, §16.55, 124n27, 144n116, 180n292
Capella, 190n345
castles, §4.1
chamomile, §4.22, 160n190
cheetahs, xxviii, xxix, xxx, xxxvii, lxiv, §1.0, §1.61
Christians, xxiii, xxiv, li, §12.26, 186n324
clarified butter, xliv, §23.1, §23.7, 156n175
clouds, xiv, xxxvii, §§10.52–54, §14.47, §§16.52–54; black color, xl, §2.10, §16.53; "milking" metaphor of, §1.58, §5.48; night clouds, §§1.55–59, §2.15, §4.46, §5.49, §§8.14–22, §14.49, §16.56
coffee, §§21.5–6, §21.3, §21.8, §21.18, §21.20, §21.28
color imagery, 181n301
combat, with youth and old age, xxxviii, §1.18, §8.0, §§8.58–60, §9.22, §15.15, 120n8
common sense, §6.19
complaints, xxvi, xxxv
contrasting pairs, §3.0, §6.0, §8.0
cooking pots, §21.9; metaphors, §§4.37–39, §5.40, §12.2, §14.0, §§14.25–26
court of love, §9.0, §9.9
cure for lovesickness, xxvi, §3.7, §8.39, §9.2, 138n95
cycles, poetic, 143n113, 144n117, 174n254. *See also* Banū Hilāl: cycle of verse

Ḍabyān stud camels, §19.1, §19.4
al-Dahnā', l, lxiv, lxxiin45
dancing girls, §5.55, §10.0, §10.56, lxxvn67, 144n115, 151n148, 153n158, 153n159, 154n164
Ḍank, xxii, xxiii, xliii, lxviin2, §18.1, §18.2, 204n408
dates, §18.5, §21.8; date harvest, §3.0, §3.40, §4.0, §4.55, §6.11, §§8.28–29, §10.65, §12.0, §18.2, 124n27, 132n70, 160n194; as metaphor for beauty, §10.57, §§12.20–21, 151n149
daughter of Ibn Ẓāhir, xvi–xvii, §13.0, §§22.1–2, §§22.5–7, §22.8, §22.11, 187n331, 202n398
al-Dawsarī, Muḥammad ibn Manī' al-'Awsajī al-Badrānī, 189n341
Day of Resurrection, xlii, §4.5, §11.49, §12.15, 145n119. *See also* Judgment Day
al-Ḍayāghim, Āl Ḍaygham, xxxv, lxxiiin56
days of dalliance, §1.7, §10.21, §12.7, 121n9, 153n158
death: Angel of, xxxix; Bird of, §12.14; cycle of revival and, §§4.45–60; inevitability of, §8.55, §8.61, §11.48, §13.18, §§14.39–40, §15.6; Judgment Day, §§5.10–11; life as prelude to, §1.35; lying in wait for the soul, §§6.22–23, §11.29, 138n96, 176n269. *See also* grave, the
debt, §3.19, §14.28, §16.31, §§16.34–36
demons, 185n322. *See also* jinni
departure of the beloved. *See* beloved, departure of
dervishes, §5.55
despair, xlv, §1.16, §2.0, §4.42, §8.39, §9.7, §10.26, §12.9, §13.20, §15.27, 170n236
deterring troublemakers, §§7.18–20, §8.62, §15.14
Devil, riding the horse of the, xliii
al-Dhēd, liv, §18.1
Dhū al-Iṣba', 136n85
Dhū l-Rummah, xli, lxiii, lxiv, lxv, lxxin43, lxxiin46; on beauty of Bedouin women, §12.0; on doves' cooing, 153n161; grave site of, 212n458; on literacy, 197n379; on self-willed females, 211n454; on separation from the beloved, 123n25, 134n79, 139n99; on silent arrival of rain, 192n357; wind metaphors, 119n1, 153n158
Dibā, liv, 204n408
Dihān, §16.0, §16.59, §20.1, §20.3, §20.13, lxxxivn113
al-Dindān, lxxiiin60, 174n254
dissemblance, Ibn Ẓāhir's, xlviii, §§21.4–7, §21.10, §21.19, §21.20, 206n420
distance, love lost to, §6.16, §§9.24–28, §15.1, 134n79
divers. *See* pearling
divine decrees, §3.41, §5.25, §15.35. *See also* God
divorce, §21.15
doctors, §3.7, §7.6
dogs, §3.35, §5.36, §5.38
Doomsday. *See* Judgment Day
doves: caught in a net, §1.39; mournful cooing awakens memories of the beloved, xxxvi, §1.0, §§1.4–6, §4.13, §§5.62–64, §§10.11–12; prayers like cooing of, §6.24, §10.68, §14.57, §15.38; separation and, §6.5

dreams, xxxvi–xxxviii, xliii, li, §2.5, §8.71, §11.14, §20.8
drought, §4.56, §5.0, §8.0, §10.4, 143n113, 150n144, 175n254
Dubai, xiii, xix, xlviii, lix–lxi, §19.2–3, 187n330

emotions, passionate: cooking pot metaphor for, §1.32, §3.11, §§4.37–39; love, §10.13, §14.48; rutting bulls metaphor, §9.0; sea of love metaphor, 202n399; wind metaphor, §1.4
Empty Quarter, xxiii, li, 200n390, 200n393
end of the world. *See* Judgment Day
envy, evil effects of, §§14.31–35, §§16.15–17
Europeans, §13.25. *See also* Portuguese
evil, protection from by God, §3.25
evildoers, §§11.5–12
eyesight, loss of, §§1.28–30, §5.68, §6.18, §12.6, §12.12

Falāḥ, liv, §16.63
falcons, xxx, l, §§7.16–17
Fāliḥ Ḥanẓal, lviii, lxixn21, 202n398, 202n399
false appearances, §§5.26–27, §§5.34–35, §§5.37–44, §11.0, §§11.13–32, §13.7, §14.0, §15.18, 189n342
al-Farazdaq, 149n137
Fate: blind fate, xxxviii; calamities of, §1.7, 138n97; deceit and attacks of, §4.40, 139n101; unpredictability of, §1.26, §2.6, §3.0, §§3.28–35, §§7.7–8, §§12.40–41; youth robbed by, §12.7, §12.13
al-Fāyah, liv
Fāyiz ibn Nḥēt, 181n298
Fayṣal al-Jumaylī, xxxi, 127n44, 142n112, 210n449, 213n463
feathers, §§5.19–20, §5.27, §7.16, §20.13, 148n136
Filī, liv
fire metaphors, §3.26; emotions like a cooking pot, §1.32, §3.11, §§4.37–39, §§14.25–26; of war, §§1.63–64
firearms, §15.0, §§15.21–22
firewood, xlv, xlviii, lxxxin98, §§20.2–24, §21.3, §§21.6–27, 188n333
fishing, l, liii, §§20.1–6, §20.10, §20.13. *See also* sailing
Fiywī, liv
al-Flāsī, Muḥammad ibn Khalfān ibn Ḥzēm, lxxvin72
floods, §2.14, §3.29, §4.0, §§4.51–54, §6.20, §§8.15–18, §14.54, §§16.58–70, 168n228
fog, banks of, xxxviii, §1.66, §11.27
forgiveness: of the beloved, §16.39; from God, §11.41, §15.28
foxes, §5.37
friendship wisdom, §§5.6–7, §6.22, §7.10, §7.13, §10.13, §11.47, §§14.22–23, §15.17, §§16.12–14
frivolities of youth, §1.38, §13.16, 202n399
al-Fujayrah, liv, 204n408

gardens, §16.69; enchanted, §1.8; of palm trees, §§4.52–53, §§8.25–30, 204n408
gazelles, xxix, §1.40, §2.0, §§2.19–22, §6.3, 135n82; as simile for beautiful

women, §6.15, §12.21, §§16.74–75, 153n158
generosity: exhortations towards, §3.43, §§5.23–24, §13.24; of Ibn Ẓāhir, xix, xlii–xliii, xlvi–xlvii, §§18.3–5, §20.1, §21.3, §21.6, §21.13, §§21.15–16, §21.18, §21.26, lxxxin98; Ibn Ẓāhir's grave and, §23.5. *See also* hospitality
al-Ghabbi, xxiii
ghaḍā wood, §3.11
al-Ghadīr, §16.62
ghāf trees, §19.8, §21.2, §21.4–6, §21.19, §23.7
al-Gharīf, §16.60, §18.1, §18.7, §23.1
al-Ghashshām, Rumayzān, xxxi, lxiii, 119n4, 127n43; on the beloved's kinfolk, 171n237; on date harvest and the fruits of love, 144n116; on deterring attackers, 157n181; on fate's unpredictability, 157n177; on love being the disease and the cure, 138n95; on love lost to distance, 134n79; measuring time with the beloved, 179n289; poetic pleas of, 170n234; on the sea of love, 202n399; on the sun's beauty, 211n453; on suppressing one's rage, 172n246; on the wickedness of the world, 176n271; on the world's treachery, 177n275
ghazals, xxxv–xxxvi, xli, lxxviiin83, §18.8, 121n9, 154n167, 159n189
al-Ghiwīl, liv
girls: dancing, lxxvn67, §5.55, §10.0, §10.56, 144n115, 151n148, 153n158, 153n159, 154n164; seclusion of unmarried Bedouin, §14.12, 182n301, 182n306, 201n394. *See also* women
gloating, §1.49, §7.14, §8.23, §16.10
goats, §21.20, §21.21; metaphor for stupidity, 173n249; and riches, §10.49; tents of black hair of, 125n34
God: all-knowing, §§5.21–22, §13.22; alone knows the Hour, §12.16; decrees of, §3.41, §5.25, §15.35; fear of, §8.45, §15.29; foreordains life and death, §11.48; forgiveness from, §11.41, §15.28; judgment of, §11.0, §§11.21–22; law of, §10.27; mercy of, 171n236; protection from evil by, §3.25; provision from, §9.41, §§11.44–46, §§15.34–35, §16.19; will of, §§3.41–42
godliness, §11.0, §§11.33–36, §11.38, §15.24
gossip, warnings against, §7.4, §15.16, §15.19, §§16.3–4, §§16.7–10, §§16.15–17, §16.21
grave, the, §§5.14–17, §§6.22–23, §8.61, §§14.39–41, §§15.32–33, §16.0, 122n19. *See also* death
grave of Ibn Ẓāhir, xliv; Ibn Ẓāhir's search for, xliv, §18.8, §§23.1–3, 197n378; site of, xliv, §21.1, §21.2, §§23.4–7
gray hair, xxxvii, xxxix, lxxivn62, §3.23, 120n6, 168n230; as a warning of death, §§5.58–59, 138n97
gray monster, xxxvii, §§8.57–60
graybeards, xv, xxxvii, xlviii, lxxviiin82, §§1.19–21, §20.7, 183n309; as sources of authority, §18.1, §21.1. *See also* ancestors

greed, §11.37, §15.10, 170n236
Greek saga, li
grim reaper, §3.24

al-Habāb, liv, §16.61
halcyon days, §1.7, §2.7, §5.59, §12.7, §13.0, §17.25
al-Ḥamrāniyyah, liv
al-Ḥārith ibn Ḥillizah, 170n236
Ḥātim al-Ṭā'ī, xlvi, §23.5
hazaj meter, lvii
al-Hazzānī, Muḥsin, lx
hearing loss, §12.12
Hell, §15.24
hereafter, the, §§11.33–36. *See also* grave, the
Ḥīl al-Dibānī, liv, §16.66
hilālī meter, xxx–xxxi, xxxiii, xxxiv, xli, lviii
Hilālī poetry characteristics, xxx–xxxiv passim, xli, lviii. *See also* Banū Hilāl
al-Hīlī, l, liv, §19.6, §21.28
Himhām, liv
al-Hirbīd, ʿAdwān, lxxviin76, 127n44
history, wisdom of learning from, 133n74
al-Hiyar, liv
Ḥmēdān al-Shwēʿir. *See* al-Shwēʿir, Ḥmēdān
hoariness, §1.14, §13.0, §13.17
Holes, Clive, lvii
Holy Scriptures, §1.36, §4.0, §4.36, 122n18
Homer's Iliad, lxxxin102
hoopoe, §14.48
Hōr al-Balmā, xliii–xliv, §18.2, §18.7
Hormuz, xxii–xxiii
horses, §1.62, §3.27, §3.37, §5.41, §10.29; Devil's horse, §13.21; Ibn Ẓāhir's camel faster than, §19.2; metaphor for self-control, §16.23, 171n240; tails compared to beloved's hair, §16.76
hospitality, §§10.41–45; of Bedouin, xliv, xlvi, §6.13, §21.5, §21.16, §21.18, 125n34; of Ibn Ẓāhir, lxxxin98, §21.3, §21.6, §§21.8–10, §§21.12–14, §§21.20–21, §§21.24–26, 201n394; of Ibn Ẓāhir's daughter, §22.8; at Ibn Ẓāhir's grave, §23.5; inability to provide, §15.8; lack of, §§5.34–35, §15.12, 190n345; in Sayf ibn Sulṭān's court, §13.32. *See also* generosity
hot season, §§12.18–19, §17.30, 190n345; Ibn Ẓāhir during, §18.2, §19.6, §21.24; in al-Khirrān, §23.8; as metaphor for life's struggles, 126n40; pearling in, §20.8, lxxxin100, 181n299; as time of love, 142n109, 144n116, 161n195; wells in, 167n227; winds of as dancing girls, 153n158. *See also* dates
Hour, the, §12.16
House of Saud, xxii, 152n151
Huber, Charles, lviii
Hunting, xxix–xxx, xxxvii, lxiv, §1.0, §1.39, §1.61, §§7.11–12
al-Ḥuṭay'ah, 132n71, 194n365
Ḥuwayzah, lxxn27
al-Ḥwēmī, liv, §16.62
hyenas, 138n96, 185n322
al-Hzūʿ, liv

Ibn ʿAtīj al-Hāmilī, liii
Ibn Batlā, 128n49
Ibn Dawwās, lxxivn62, 121n9
Ibn Ghashshām, Rumayzān. *See* al-Ghashshām, Rumayzān
Ibn Ghashshām, Rushaydān, lxxiin47, 155n169
Ibn Ḥammād, 145n121
Ibn Iyās, lxviiin8
Ibn Khaldūn, xxxiii, xli, 201n394
Ibn Khamīs al-ʿAlīlī, Ḥamad, lxxvin72
Ibn Liʿbūn, lx
Ibn Muḥīn, lx
Ibn Rashīd, 186n327
Ibn Sbayyil, ʿAbd Allāh, xli, lii, §2.0, 135n80, 160n194; on Bedouins' cyclical year, 180n292; on being caught unprepared, 161n196; on loss of youth/love, §12.0, 162n201; on martyr of love, 161n198
Ibn Ẓāhir: beginnings as a poet, xliii–xliv, 158n184; designating as Bedouin, xlix–l; generosity of, xix, xlii–xliii, xlvi–xlvii, §§18.3–5, §20.1, §21.6, §21.13, §§21.15–16, lxxxin98; grave of, xliv, §18.8, §21.1, §21.2, §§23.1–3, §§23.4–7, 197n378; hospitality of, §21.3, §§21.8–10, §§21.12–13, §§21.20–21, §§21.24–26, 201n394; jealousy towards his daughter, xvi–xvii, xliv–xlvi, §22.2, §22.10; legendary status of, xlii–xlix; poverty of, §20.1, §21.1, §21.6, §21.11, §21.12, §21.14; son-in-law, §21.1, §§21.14–16; transliteration of his name, lxiv; wife, xxvi, xlv–xlvi, §§21.5–6, §21.10, §21.13, §§22.4–5, §22.7. *See also* daughter of Ibn Ẓāhir
Ibn Zayd, xxix–xxxi, xxxiv, 139n98, 141n106, 145n121, 198n381
Imruʾ al-Qays, 151n149
Indian cotton, §12.26, §14.0, §14.6
infirmity of old age. *See* old age
inspiration, poetic, 129n53; on mountains, §3.6, 130n56; nightmares and, §18.6; through a jinni, xliii, lxxviiin83, §§18.2–6; well metaphors for, §8.2, §10.0, §10.2, 168n228
Iranian fabrics, §14.0, §14.6
irrigation, lii, §6.20, §§10.2–7
ʿIthmir, liv

Jabr ibn Sayyār, xxxi, lxiii, lxxivn62, 121n9, 125n31, 133n73, 135n79, 151n149; on beauty of Bedouin women, 169n230; on ravages of old age, 164n209; on the world's treachery, 177n275
Jabrid poetry, xxi–xxxvi passim, xli, 125n31, 188n333. *See also* ʿĀmir al-Samīn; al-Kulayf; Fayṣal al-Jumaylī; Ibn Zayd
Jabrids. *See* Banū Jabr
Jarīr, 198n382
al-Jaww, xxiii, xxiv, §17.30
jinni, §18.7, 126n39, 158n184; desert spirit, xliii, §§18.2–6; exorcism of, 195n372
Judgment Day, §1.35, §4.0, §§4.59–61, §§5.10–11, §§11.36–37, §13.34, §15.6, §16.18, 135n80, 147n130
judgment of God, §11.0, §§11.21–22, §11.49
Julfār, xxiv
Jumayrā, §20.4, §§20.10–12

Kalbā, liv, §16.68, §17.30
Kawwāziyyah Sufis, lxxvn67
keywords, poetic, xxxviii–xxxix
Khalaf Abū Zwayyid, 174n249
al-Khalāwī, Rāshid, xxxi–xxxii, xxxiv, xl, xli, lxiii, 126n40, 131n64, 131n67; on “amazing verses,” 158n183; on choosing one’s land, 213n461; on deterring attackers/troublemakers, 195n368; a “discerning poet,” xl, lxxvn69, 195n370; friendship wisdom, 146n124, 169n231; on importance of public approval of poetry, 198n382; on inevitability of death, 161n199; on inspiration of poetry, 167n228; on passage of time, 181n298; on pearl diving as simile of writing poetry, 159n185; on poet’s wisdom, 177n273; on remembrance of the poet, 134n77; on rendering other poets silent, 208n433; self-praise, lxxviin76, 173n248, 197n379; on stars, 190n345; on subsistence, 149n141
Khalīfah ibn ʿAlī l-Kitbī, lxxxvin133, lxxxvin138, 142n112, 205n409
Khalīl ibn ʿĀyid, 137n89, 152n153
Khatīlah (Ibn Ẓāhir’s camel), §§19.1–8
al-Khāṭrī, Ḥammād, 159n187
al-Khirrān, liv, §18.1, §21.1, §23.2, §23.8
kinfolk of the beloved, §10.26, §14.30
knights, §15.20, 184n316
al-Kulayf, 148n133, 172n241, 178n281, 195n368

laments, xxvi, xxviii, §1.5
Lane, Edward, lxxxvin42
Larestan, lv, §14.6
laziness, §§10.46–47, §15.11, §16.56, 173n248
leftovers, §5.34, §15.9
legends: Jabrid oral culture and, xxv–xxviii; legendary status of Ibn Ẓāhir, xlii–xlix; Qaṭan ibn Qaṭan al-Hilālī, xxii; al-ʿUlaymī, xxvi–xxvii
lightning metaphors, §2.11, §4.0, §9.43
lions, §5.36, §5.38, §8.66
literacy of poets, 197n379
Līwā, xxi, xxiii–xxiv, li, liv, §16.60, 204n408
locusts, §3.2
loss motifs, xli; lost to distance, §4.41, §§12.4–7, 134n79. *See also* beloved, departure of; youth
love motifs: agonies of love, §3.0, §§4.40–44, §§10.17–25; amorous pursuits, §1.39; chivalrous romance, xxviii; court of love, §9.0, §9.9; lost to distance, §1.12, §4.41, §§12.4–7, 134n79; love as the disease and the cure, §4.26; lovesickness, xxvi, §§3.7–15, §3.23, §8.0, §9.0, §§9.1–5, §9.29, §10.65, §§12.2–5, §12.9, §12.36; martyr of love, §§3.7–15; tough love, §22.11, 191n348; trysts, §3.24, §10.25, 119n4, 199n385; youth as, 162n200, 162n201. *See also* beloved, the
lovelorn poet, xxxviii, §§1.9–11, §8.22, §§14.24–26, §14.30, §§16.44–51
lovesickness, xxvi, §§3.7–15, §3.23, §8.0, §9.0, §§9.1–5, §§9.16–17, §9.29, §10.65, §§12.2–5, §12.9, §12.36

Lyall, C.J., lxv
al-Madām, liv, §18.8

Maḥdah, liv
majlis, lix, §21.5, 168n230, 202n398
mamdūḥ, xxxv
Mammon, §5.12, §14.36
manuscripts, xxix, xxxii–xxxiii, xliv, xlix, lvi, lviii–lxi, lxxxivn115, §15.0
markh tree, §21.1
al-Marrār ibn Munqidh, 173n247
marriage, §§9.39–41, §§22.9–10, 203n403, 203n405, 204n406
martyr of love, §§3.7–15, 161n198
meadows, §2.16, §3.35, §16.72. *See also* pastures
Mecca, xxvii, lv, lxxiiin57, §4.62, §13.24, §14.56
Medina, lv, lxxiiin57
memories, xx, xxv, xxix, xxxvi, xli; people remembered for deeds or a name, §§13.8–9; permanence of the poet in, §3.5, §4.0, §4.6, §§15.36–37, §§23.4–7; stirred by cooing doves, §1.4, §5.62; stirred by scents, §§4.39–40, §4.54; wind metaphor of, 119n2. *See also* nostalgia for Bedouin glory days
messenger motif, §9.0, §9.25, §§9.32–36
meter, xxx, lvi–lvii, 167n225; *hilālī*, xxx–xxxi, xxxiii, xxxiv, xli, lviii; *hazaj*, lvii; *mutadārik*, §8.0; *mutaqārib*, lvii; *ṭawīl*, xxx, lvii; well metaphors for, §2.0
migrations: of Bedouin, xx, xxx, xl, lii, §2.17, §3.40, §§6.6–12, §§10.64–67, §12.0, §17.0, §19.1, 124n27, 166n219, 180n292, 183n307, 204n408; departure of beloved and, xl, §§6.13–16, §10.0, 124n27, 124n28; of Ibn Ẓāhir, lii, lxxxin103, §21.24, §21.28; in Ibn Zayd's poems, xxx. *See also* camels
Miḥḍāb, §§23.1–2
Milīḥah, liv
milk, §1.8, §9.4, §11.44, §21.7, §23.7, 124n30, 146n126, 193n362
Million's Poet competition, xxi
mirages, §8.46, §11.15, §12.33
Miryāl Thānī, §16.67
misers, §5.23, §5.44, §8.12, §12.40, 125n34, 149n139, 190n345
al-Miṭārīsh tribe, §19.1
al-Mizraʿ, liv
money: chasing after, §21.1; crown, §20.11; paisa, §20.6, §20.11; riyals, §20.2; rupees, §20.6
morality, religious, §11.0, §§11.5–18. *See also* godliness
Moses's appointment, §1.0, 125n31
mountains, §3.2, §4.7, §§16.68–70, §23.4; poetic inspiration on, §3.6, 130n56
al-Muʿayrīḍ's flood, §4.0, §4.51
Muhadhdhab, liv
Muḥammad, Prophet, §1.67, §3.44, §4.62, §5.69, §6.24, §8.72, §9.46; prayers for, §10.68, §11.51, §13.34, §14.57, §15.38, §16.77; prayers of, §11.41; war on unbelievers, §13.26
Muḥammad ibn Manī al-Dasarī, §§14.22–23
Muqrin ibn Zāmil, 178n281
al-Muraqqish the Elder (al-Akbar), 187n332
al-Muraqqish the Younger (al-Aṣghar), 201n394

al-Musayyab ibn ʿAlas, 129n54, 187n332
Muscat, lv
musical qualities, §3.0
Musil, Alois, l
mutadārik meter, §8.0
Mutammim Ibn Nuwayrah, 124n28, 127n42, 138n96, 157n178
al-Mutanabbī, 120n6, 129n54; friendship wisdom, 189n341; on the gray monster, 162n202
mutaqārib meter, lvii
muṭawwaʿ, lxxn31
Muṭawwaʿ al-Maskūf. *See* Khalīl ibn ʿĀyid
Muṭawwaʿ Ushayqir. *See* al-Tamīmī, ʿAbd al-Raḥmān
mutes, female, xliii, lxxixn89, §§18.2–5
Muwāfiq, 135n79
al-Muzarrid ibn Ḍirār, 134n77, 193n362

Nabaṭī poetry, xxi, xxv, xxviii–xxix, xxxiii, xxxiv–xxxv, xlii, liii, lvi–lix, lxiv–lxv; contextualization of Ibn Ẓāhir with, xxv, xxviii–xxix, xxxiii, xxxiv–xxxv, xlii, liii, lvi–lix, lxiv–lxv; dating of, xxi, xxv, lviii; geographical spread of, xxi, xxviii; Graybeard's Song and, §1.0; manuscripts of, lvi, lviii–lix; meter and, lvi–lvii; signature verses and, xxxiv
al-Nābighah ibn Ghannām, 146n126
Najd, xxi, xxii, xxv, xxvi, xxviii, xxxi–xxxvi, xlvii, lvi, lx, lxiii; Hilālī poetry characteristics, xxx–xxxiv passim, xli, lviii; literary influences from, xxv; al-ʿUlaymī and, xxvi; village wells in, 204n408
Najdī poetry, xxxv xlvii; literary influences from, xxxv; signature verses and, xxxi–xxxii; wise sayings in, 164n206
Nāṣir ibn Qaṭan, xxiii, xxiv–xxv
Nazwah, liv
night clouds, §§1.55–59, §2.15, §4.46, §5.49, §§8.14–22, §14.49, §16.56
nightingales' eggs, §10.10
Nizwā, lv
Noah's Flood, §4.0
non-Muslims. *See* unbelievers
nostalgia for Bedouin glory days, xx, xxix, li, §1.0, §§1.63–67, 168n230
al-Numayrī, al-Rāʿī, 198n382
numbers, formulaic, 143n112

oil economies, l, li, lvi, lxvi
old age, §6.0, §16.0; arrival of, §13.16, §§16.37–38, 183n309; bringing an end to physical pleasures, lxxivn62, 176n269; combat with, xxxvii–xxxix, §1.18, §8.0, §§8.58–60, §15.15, 120n8; hoariness, §1.14, §13.0, §13.17; of Ibn Ẓāhir's daughter, §22.9; loss of eyesight in, §§1.28–30, §5.68, §6.18, §12.6, §12.12; physical decay in, §§6.17–18, §8.68, §12.12; possible benefits of, §1.24, §8.67, 122n15; and premonition of death, 138n96, 138n97; as a pursuing enemy, §1.13, §§8.56–67; ravages of, §§1.28–33, §5.0, §§5.66–68, §§8.68–69, §15.6; as an unwanted guest, xxxix, §5.65, §5.67, 120n7;

wisdom of, 165n210. *See also* gray hair
Oman, xv, xx, xxi–xxxv passim, xliii, xlv, l–li, liii, lv, lvi, lix–lxiv passim, lxviin2, §18.2, 204n408; cultural connections with the Emirates, xxi; Emirati history inseparable from, xxi; Ibn Ẓāhir and, l; Ibn Ẓāhir's camel from, §19.4; under the Jabrids, xxi–xxii, Sayf ibn Sulṭān, §13.26; al-ʿUlaymī and, xxv–xxvi
Omani chronicles, xxi–xxii, xxxi, xxxiv, li, 186n326
oral culture and tradition, xiii, xvii, xix, xxii, xxvii–xxix, xxxii–xxxiv, xl–xliv, xlix, lii, lvii, lxi–lxiv, §3.5, §13.0, 186n326, 190n344; compared to written forms, §§15.36–37; oral culture and tradition, Ibn Ẓāhir's daughter in, §17.0; interpretation of poems and, xxvii, xxxii; legendary status of Ibn Ẓāhir in, xlii–xlix; transmission of Ibn Ẓāhir's poetry, xlix, lxxxivn115, §4.5, §5.1. *See also* Banū Hilāl
orchards, §8.8, §10.0, §§10.7–8
ostriches, §8.36, §14.17
owls, xxxvii, §1.13, §4.0, §§4.11–12, 136n85

palanquin of the beloved, xxxvii, lxiii, §§1.41–47, §9.0, §§10.60–63, §§12.28–36, §§14.11–19
palm trees: and camel caravans, §§6.9–11, 187n332; compared to dancers, §5.0, §5.54, §5.56; core, §17.2; cultivation, §18.1; flowers, §4.54, §§8.26–27; gardens, §§4.52–53, §§8.25–30, 204n408; orchards, §10.7; scent, §4.54; in thunderstorms, §§5.53–56
panegyrics, 172n245
Paradise, §8.10
passion, §4.0, §4.40, §5.52, §10.0, §10.13, §14.48, 168n230
pastures, §1.8, §2.0, §4.47, §5.46, §§8.31–33, §10.51, §16.70, §23.4, 166n219. *See also* meadows
patience, exhortations to, §§3.29–35, §7.10, §7.13, §§10.44–46, §§17.7–8, 122n14
pearling, xlviii, l, lii, §§8.4–7, §17.11, §§20.7–14, 181n299
pedigrees, camels', §19.1, §19.4
perfume, §4.23, §12.31
Persians, §13.25, 207n431
persuasion, powers of, §16.0
pilgrimage to Mecca, §4.62, §13.24, §14.56
Pleiades, §12.19, §14.29, 175n260
poetry: bucket metaphors for, §§2.2–3, §§10.34–35, §§13.2–3; building metaphors for, 175n262, 198n381; compared to expensive items, §5.0, §§5.3–5, §§8.4–7; competing in, §21.2, §§21.11–12; food metaphors for, §§13.5–6; Ibn Ẓāhir's beginnings in, §§18.6–7; of Ibn Ẓāhir's daughter, §§22.9–10, §22.11; importance of public approval of, §16.5; literacy and, 197n379; permanence of in collective memory, §4.0, §4.6, §§15.36–37, §§23.4–7; rope metaphor for, §11.50; sheep metaphors for, §5.0; superiority

poetry (cont.)
of Ibn Ẓāhir's, §§8.1–12; water metaphors for, §11.4, §14.3, §§18.6–7. *See also* audiences of poetry; cycles, poetic; inspiration, poetic
poison, §1.31, §9.3, §9.19
political messages, 184n315
Portuguese, the, xxii–xxiii, xxix, li, 186n324. *See also* Europeans
poverty, §11.7–9, §11.11, §20.10; godliness and, §§11.37–38; of Ibn Ẓāhir, lxxxin98, §5.66, §20.1, §21.1, §21.6, §§21.11–12, §21.14, 148n136; inability to provide for the family, §§15.7–9; unpredictability of, §§12.40–41
prayers, §13.23, §14.55; false appearances of, §14.27; for God's succor, §4.3; jinni prays for Ibn Ẓāhir, §18.3, §18.6; Prophet Muḥammad and, §5.69, §6.24, §8.72, §9.46, §10.68, §11.41, §11.51, §13.34, §14.57, §15.38, §16.77; for protection from evil, §3.25; for rain, §§1.55–59, §1.67, §10.51, §14.53, §16.0, §16.52, 175n254
pre-oil lifestyles, li, lvi
promises of the beloved, §§9.7–8, §9.10
proverbs. *See* wise sayings
Psalms, §4.0, §4.36, 122n18

al-Qāḍī, Muḥammad ʿAbd Allāh, 139n100, 170n236
Qarmatians (al-Qarāmiṭah), xxii
al-Qaṣab, 133n73
*qaṣīdah*s, xiii–xiv, xix, xxv–xxvi, xxix, xxxiii, xxxv, xxxvi, xl, xliv, xlix, lxii, lxvi, §8.0
al-Qaṣīm, xxviii, 173n248
al-Qāsimī, Shaykh Ṣaqr bin Khālid, lix
al-Qāsimī, Shaykh Sulṭān ibn Sālim, lix
al-Qāsimī, Shaykh Sulṭān ibn Ṣaqr, lx
Qaṭan ibn Qaṭan al-Hilālī, xx–xxiii, xxvi–xxviii, xxxi–xxxii, xxxv, 132n71
al-Qaṭīf, xxii, lv, lxxvn67
Qayd al-Arḍ. *See* al-Yaʿrubī (al-Yaʿāribah), Sayf ibn Sulṭān
Qur'an, §1.36, 145n119

Rabīʿah ibn Maqrūm, 151n149, 181n300
racing camels, §19.2, §§19.4–5
rage, suppressing one's, §10.40, §14.23
rags of Ibn Ẓāhir, lxxxin98, §5.66, §20.1, §21.1, §21.6, §§21.11–12, §21.14, 148n136
raiding, xxi, xxiv, xxvii, §19.2
rain, xiv, xv, xix, xxxvi, xi, xxxix, xl–xlii, §§2.11–15, §16.0; in the Emirates, xix, §§16.58–68; as God's blessing, §10.51; icy, §22.6; like prayers, §1.67; national borders and, xix, xxii, lii–liii; poet woken by, §14.49; portrayed as a game, §§8.20–24; prayers for, xxxvi–xxxvii, §1.0, §§1.55–59, §10.51, §16.52; reviving the land, xli, §4.0, §§4.46–49, §§5.48–50, §6.4, §8.15, §8.18, §9.42, 132n67; udder metaphor for, §1.58, §5.48. *See also* meadows; pastures; thunderstorms
rajaz meter, lvii

Ramadan, §14.27, §14.55, 152n156
Ramlat al-ʿAtīq, 200n389
Ramlat al-ʿUnayq, liv
al-Raqāshī, 189n342
Rās al-Khaymah, xxiv, xliv, xlix, l, liii, lix, lxii, lxv, lxviiin5, lxxixn87, lxxxin103, lxxxiin104, lxxxvn133, §13.0, §18.1, §18.8, 204n408; fishing in, §§20.1–2
Rāshid al-gharbī, liv
al-Rassah, §23.1
ravens, xxxvii, §1.13; color compared to youthful hair, §5.56, §16.76, 120n5
religion, §13.23; believers' reward, §14.42, §16.18; false appearances in, §13.7; fundamentals of, §§13.23–24, §§14.55–56; godliness, §11.0, §§11.33–36, §11.38, §15.24; Ibn Ẓāhir and, lxxviiin84; imam's authority, xxiv; morality, §11.0, §§11.5–18; *muṭawwaʿ*, lxxn31; neglect of, §§17.19–20; poet's wisdom compared with, xxxix–xl; wise sayings and, lxxvin75. *See also* God
Resurrection Day, xlii, §4.5, §11.49, §12.15, 145n119. *See also* Judgment Day
revenge motifs, xxvii, §15.13, §17.26, §§19.3–5
rewards: for believers, §14.42, §16.18; camels given as, §21.13; for generosity, xlvii, §3.43, §5.24, 148n135
rhymes, xxx, xxxiv, lvi, lviii, §2.0, §5.0, 167n225
rhythm. *See* meter
riddles, xlvii, §§21.1–2, §21.19, §§21.21–23, §§21.28–29
Rifāʿiyyah Sufis, §5.54
rivers, §8.9
Riyadh, lv
rope metaphors, §11.50; ropes of hope, §3.17
al-Rubʿ al-Khālī. *See* Empty Quarter
Rumayzān. *See* al-Ghashshām, Rumayzān
rutting, §1.57
Rwala Bedouin, l

al-Sāʿdī, liv, §18.1; well of, §23.1
al-Saʿdī, Salāmah ibn Jandal, 162n201
sagas: Greek, li; of Ibn Ẓāhir, xlii–li. *See also* Banū Hilāl
sailing, §10.32, §12.33, §13.12, §14.10, §15.0, §§15.30–31, §§17.9–11. *See also* fishing
al-Ṣajʿah, §16.67
Salmā. *See* daughter of Ibn Ẓāhir
salt, §§13.5–6
Samad al-Shān, xxiii, lv
al-Samīn, ʿĀmir. *See* ʿĀmir al-Samīn
sand dunes, §§6.1–3, §8.55, §14.0, §14.54, §20.12, 212n458; Ibn Ẓāhir's Dune, §21.2, §§21.3–5
sarcasm, xxxvii
Saʿūd ibn ʿAbd al-ʿAzīz. *See* House of Saud
Saudi Arabia, xxi, xxiv
al-Sayyid, ʿAbd Allāh, xxviii
Scorpio, §10.67, §14.29
Scriptures, Holy, §1.36, §4.0, §4.36, 122n18
sea, life at, xlix, §§20.1–14. *See also* sailing
sea of love, 202n399
seasickness, xxxviii, §13.0, §13.14, §17.11

seasonal treks. *See* migrations
seasons, xxxii, l, §10.0; cyclical movement of, xxx–xxxi, 124n27, 132n70, 180n292, 181n300, 183n307; of rains, 153n160, 200n388; rutting, §1.57; winter, §22.5. *See also* hot season
self-control metaphors, §§10.31–32, §§16.22–24, 171n240
self-praise, xxxv–xxxvi, xli, 173n248, 197n379. *See also* signature verses
senility, xxxvii, §1.27, §17.0
separation from the beloved, §1.0, §3.38, §§4.15–27, §4.32, §6.5, §6.16, §§9.23–29, §§12.4–13; bitterness of, §10.20, §12.0; inevitability of, 191n350
Seven Sisters, §14.29
Shādhiliyyah Sufis, lxxvn67
Shammar tribe, xxvii
sharia, §10.27
Sharjah, lix–lx
sharks, §20.1
Shaykh Zāyid, xix, lxi, 138n94
sheep, §3.35, §17.15
shelters: Bedouin, §12.24, §21.20, §23.7; in Greek sagas, li; Ibn Ẓāhir's, §21.1, §23.6. *See also* tents
shimmering heat, li, §8.47, §10.29, §12.33, §14.8, 187n332
ship metaphors: godly life, §§15.30–31; hard times, §11.39; loss of youth, §13.0, §§13.12–17, §§17.9–11, §22.9; self-control, §10.32, §16.22
ships: caravans of, §14.10, 197n377, 201n398; instability of, 180n293; moving with or against the wind, §5.45, §12.33, 172n241; ship of youth, xxxviii, §§13.12–17
al-Shuʿaybah, xxiv
al-Shuʿaybī, xxvii–xxix, xxxii, 143n113, 173n248, 173n249, 188n333, 196n373, 210n451
al-Shuḥūh (Shiḥḥī), 200n391
al-Shwēʿir, Ḥmēdān, xxxi, xlviii, lvii, lxiii, lxxivn62, lxxxivn119, 173n248; on the beloved's lack of response, 161n197; bucket metaphors, 127n44; on deterring attackers, 164n206; a "discerning poet," lxxvn69, 126n39, 167n225; on poets' wisdom, 177n273; on the ravages of old age, 122n15; on the sinfulness of youth, 185n322; on the strife left by evildoers, 176n267; wisdom verses of, 155n169
Sīfat Dihān, liv
signature verses, xiv, xxix–xxxiii, xxxiv, xl–xli, lxvi, §1.1, §2.1, §7.0, §7.1, §8.1
Sīḥ al-Gharīf, liv
Sīḥ al-Ṣaʿjah, liv
Sīhijān, liv
silk, §14.5
simplicity, li, liii, §2.0, 152n155
sin, xliii, lix, §11.14, §13.0, §13.22, §17.20, 137n89, 185n322
slaves, 189n340, 207n431
Sohar, xxiii–xxiv, li, lv
soil quality, §§23.1–2, §23.4
son-in-law of Ibn Ẓāhir, §21.1, §§21.14–16
southward journeys, li, §5.65, §14.8, §15.30, §17.30, §18.2
Sowayan, Saad, lvii, lxv, lxxn24, lxxiin46, lxxiiin56, lxxivn62
speech, art of, §16.0, §§16.7–12, §16.18, §§17.21–23

starling feathers, §5.27
stepmother motifs, xxvii
stray camels, §3.3
stud camels, §7.20, §19.1, §19.4
succulence, youthful, §4.21, §10.9, §10.67, §16.52, 162n201
Sufism, xxxix, xli, §5.0, §8.0, §15.0, 147n130, 164n206; dervishes, §§5.54–55; on eternity of the world, 180n297; poetic inspiration and, 198n379, 198n380
summer. *See* hot season
al-Surayḥī, 194n363
Suwayd ibn Abī Kāhil, 166n218, 167n228, 199n383
swords, §8.11, §§10.36–38, §15.14
Syrian fabrics, §12.25, §14.0, §14.6

taghrībah, xx
Tāhil, liv
al-Tamīmī, ʿAbd al-Raḥīm, xxvii–xxviii, lxxxiiin111, 148n132
taqwā, §11.0
Ṭarafah, 187n332
Tawām, xxiii, lv
al-ṭawīl meter, xxx, lvii
taxes, §§20.2–5
tears of the poet, §§3.9–10, §§3.38–39, §5.65, §9.5, §9.17, §§9.30–31, §10.53, §11.28, §16.44, §16.51, §17.24, 168n230
teeth: of the beloved, §1.48, §1.50, §2.22, §4.21, §10.10, §13.15, §20.8, §22.9; falling out, §8.68, §12.6, §12.12, §13.15, §22.9, 180n293; as a lightning metaphor, 160n190
tents, xxxvii, l, §8.64, §16.72; flattened by rain, §8.17; partitions of, §1.42; of red leather, §1.0, §1.61. *See also* shelters
textiles, imported, §12.25, §§14.5–6, §14.0
Thaʿlabah ibn ʿAmr, n76
Thānī, Aḥmad Rashīd, lxi–lxii, lxxviin78, lxxxin101, lxxxiin107, 122n16, 147n127, 209n442
thirst, §8.47, §9.20, §10.35, §11.43, §15.26, §18.3; for the beloved, §1.0, §1.54; of camels, §6.7; for poetry, §2.3, §14.3; for revenge, §15.13, §19.3
thorn metaphors, §§17.7–8
thunderstorms, xxxvii, xli, §§2.10–15, §4.0, §§5.47–56, §8.0, §§8.14–24, §§9.43–45, §§10.51–55, §§14.50–54, §§16.53–55, 174n254; as roaring stallions, §9.44; as rutting bulls, §9.0, §9.45, §10.52; as a wedding party, §4.50. *See also* rain
Tihāmah mountain, §3.2
Time, xli, lii, §1.0, §§11.18–19, §12.0; deceit and attacks of, §§15.2–4; measuring of, §§12.8–9, §§12.17–18; wheel of, §4.9, §12.0, §12.17, §16.30, 193n360
Ṭiwi al-ʿUshūsh, liv
Tolstoy, Leo, *The Death of Ivan Ilyich*, xl
tombstones, §14.41, §§23.2–4
tongue, keeping control of one's, §§10.31–32
Torah, §4.0, §4.36, 122n18
traders and trading, lxxxin98, §5.26, §8.7, §19.2, §21.1, 142n112. *See also* pearling
transitions, thematic, xl, 123n23, 142n109, 150n144; Agony of

transitions, thematic (cont.)
Love, §3.0; Dance of the Zephyr, §6.0, 155n169; Don't Be Hard on Friends, 157n179; Graybeard's Song, §1.0; Muzzleloader's Ramrod, §15.0, 194n365; Rain Poem, §8.0, 159n187; She Left Me Baffled, 188n339; Torn to Shreds by Passion's Agony, 171n239, 174n250; Wisdom Poem, §5.0
transitory nature of the world, §4.0
translation, xiii, lx–lxi, lxiv–lxvi
transliteration, lxiv–lxv
treachery: of the world, §11.0, §§11.13–32, lxxvin75; of youth, xxxviii, §8.71, 162n200
Trojan War, xx
truth, the, xxxvii, §14.39, §14.56; Ibn Ẓāhir's poetry viewed as, xl, §18.8, 197n379
trysts, §3.24, §10.25, 119n4, 199n385
turban size, §13.7
turkeys, §21.21
tyranny, §3.18, §11.37, §14.47, 177n275

'Ubayd ibn Rashīd, lx
al-'Ulaymī, xxvi–xxvii, xxxii, 132n71, 192n355
'Umar ibn Abī Rabī'ah, xli, §9.0
Umm al-Falay, §§23.1–2
Umm al-Khāyūs, §19.6, §21.28, §23.4
Umm al-Quwayn, liv
Umm Salāmah, 201n394
'Unayzah, 152n153
unbelievers, §4.51, §5.51, §§13.25–28, §14.42, 143n112, 174n250
United Arab Emirates, xv–xvi, xix–xxiv passim, xxix, xxxiv, l–li, lviii, lxiii, §13.0; geographical spread of, 187n328; historical area of, xxi; Ibn Ẓāhir and, xlii, xliv, xlix, lii–liii, lxiv; poems as geographical depiction of, §16.0, §§16.58–68, 187n328
al-'Uqaylī, Mubārak, lx
al-'Ushūsh, §16.67
al-'Utaybah, Aḥmad ibn Khalaf, lix–lx
al-'Uways, Sālim ibn 'Alī, lix
al-'Uyūniyyūn, xxii

veils, §10.56; tent partitions, §1.42
vengeance: divine, §16.20; human, xxvi, §15.13, §17.26, §§19.3–5
vipers, §§5.42–43
virtues, §5.31, §10.46, §21.27, 126n36; Bedouin, xli, xlvi, 141n107, 156n175
visitors, §§10.41–45; to Ibn Ẓāhir, xliv, xlv–xlviii, §21.2, §§21.3–8, §§21.10–13, §§21.19–26, 165n214; to Ibn Ẓāhir's grave, §§23.4–7. *See also* generosity; hospitality

Wādī al-Jazī, 196n373
Wādī al-Jirn, liv
Wādī al-Mikin, liv
Wādī Ḥanīfah, xxvi, lv
Wādī l-Ghadīr, §2.17
Wādī Salām, liv
Wahhābī, 185n322; chroniclers, xxiv; doctrine, xxxix; radicalism of, lix
warfare, §§1.63–64
wasp-waisted beloved, xxxvii, §1.41, §2.21, §6.14, §16.74
water: bitter, §11.0, §11.4, §§16.46–47; bucket metaphors, §§2.2–3, §§13.2–3; Ibn Ẓāhir gives to the jinni, §§18.3–5; irrigation, lii, §6.20; metaphor for poetry,

§11.4, §14.3, §18.6, §18.7; travelers' supplies of, §§9.17–21, §15.23. *See also* wells
waterskins, §§8.46–47, §§9.17–21, §16.15
wayfarers, §2.17, 169n230
wealth, §11.7–9, §11.11; godliness and, §§11.37–38; unpredictability of, §§12.40–41
wedding metaphor, §4.50
weeping. *See* tears of the poet
wells, §2.0, §2.15, §2.19, §§10.2–7, §11.43, §§13.2–3, §14.3, 204n408; advice on being prepared for, §§15.26–27; of al-Saʿdī, §23.1; marriage metaphors, §17.25; metaphor for poetic inspiration, §8.2, §10.0, §10.2, 167n228. *See also* water
wheel of seasons, 124n27
wheel of time, §4.9, §12.0, §12.17, §16.30, 193n360
white-spotted owl, xxxvii, §1.13
wife of Ibn Ẓāhir, xxvi, xlv–xlvi, §§21.5–6, §21.10, §21.13, §§22.4–5, §22.7
wild asses, 190n345
will of God, §§3.41–42
winds, §1.3; eastern breezes, §§6.2–3, §16.54; of fortune, §§11.16–17; in al-Khalāwī's poetry, xxxii; "milking" the clouds for water, §1.58, §5.48; mischief of, §10.54; moving with or against it, §5.45, §12.33, §15.31, §§17.9–11, §22.9, 172n241; northern, §14.50, §14.52; as simile for youth, 202n399; of thunderstorms, §§5.46–47, §§5.51–55, §8.22, §§10.52–54; western, §5.51, §10.54, §14.10, §22.5, §22.6
wise sayings, xxx, xxxi, xxxv, xxxvii, xxxix, xlii, §5.0, §§6.19–23, §14.0, §18.6, §21.28; on being prepared, 161n196; on deterring attackers, §8.62; of a "discerning poet," xl, §3.1, §11.19, §§14.43–47, 167n225, 195n370; on friendship, §§7.2–20, §§14.22–23, 169n231; of Ibn Ẓāhir's daughter, §§17.5–8; of al-Khalāwī, xxxii; against laziness, §§10.46–47; scriptural and oral traditions of, §15.0; on self-control, §§10.29–50, §16.23
wolves, §§3.34–35, §5.33, §5.58, §§17.15–17
women: beauty of, §2.0, §§2.17–18, §3.37, §§10.8–10, §§10.56–58, §10.67, §12.10, §12.21, §§14.11–12; in Bedouin hospitality, §21.5; disgusted at old age, 120n7, 164n209; hair of, §5.56, §10.57; protection of, §15.7; subservient to male kin, §10.26, §10.33, 209n443, 212n457; "terrified by news," §4.13. *See also* girls
world, the, xxxviii–xli, lii, 130n60; "beware of the world," 131n66; deceit of, §§14.36–38, §15.5, §§17.19–20; end of, §4.0. *See also* Judgment Day; eternity of, §12.15; fickleness of, §4.0, §11.20, §§11.24–27, §§14.45–47; wickedness of, §§4.28–35, §§5.12–15, §6.23, §8.53, §11.0, §§11.13–18
worms, xliv, §23.2

al-Yalḥ, §16.62
al-Yamāmah, lvi

Yanqal, xxiii–xxiv, lv
al-Yaʿāribah dynasty, xx, xxii
al-Yaʿrubī (al-Yaʿāribah), Sayf ibn Sulṭān, xx, xxv, xxxiv, §13.0, §§13.27–33, 172n245
al-Yaʿrubī, Nāṣir ibn Murshid ibn Sulṭān, xx, xxiii–xxv
al-Yitīmah, §§23.1–2
youth, xiv, xxxvii–xxxix, li, §6.0; beloved as a metaphor for, §§3.15–24, §§5.59–66, §10.51, §§12.4–13, §12.30, §16.52; combat with, §1.18, §8.0, §§8.58–60, §9.22; days of dalliance, §1.7, §10.21, §12.7, 121n9, 153n158; foolishness of, §6.19; frivolities of, §1.38, §13.16, 202n399; illusions of, §1.0, §§1.21–23; loss of, §§1.15–17, §1.25, §3.0, §8.56, §13.20, §§17.9–11, §§17.24–30; as a metaphor for love, 162n200, 162n201; physical pleasures of, 176n269; ship of youth, xxxviii, §§13.12–17; sinfulness of, §§13.21–22, §13.0, §§17.19–20; wasted time of, xliii, §2.8, §12.0, §§13.10–11, §17.14
"youthful succulence," §4.21, §10.9, §10.68, §16.52, 162n201

al-Ẓafrah, xxiv, liv, lxxxivn113, §16.0, §16.59
al-Ẓāhirah, liv, §22.3
al-Ẓawāhir, §18.1, §21.2
Zayd ibn ʿUrayʿir, xxii, lxxiii50, 152n151, 165n210. *See also* Āl Ḥumayd
Zaydis, §13.25
al-Ẓīt, liv, §20.3, §20.12
Zuhayr ibn Abī Sulmā, 155n170

About the NYU Abu Dhabi Institute

The Library of Arabic Literature is supported by a grant from the NYU Abu Dhabi Institute, a major hub of intellectual and creative activity and advanced research. The Institute hosts academic conferences, workshops, lectures, film series, performances, and other public programs directed both to audiences within the UAE and to the worldwide academic and research community. It is a center of the scholarly community for Abu Dhabi, bringing together faculty and researchers from institutions of higher learning throughout the region.

NYU Abu Dhabi, through the NYU Abu Dhabi Institute, is a world-class center of cutting-edge research, scholarship, and cultural activity. The Institute creates singular opportunities for leading researchers from across the arts, humanities, social sciences, sciences, engineering, and the professions to carry out creative scholarship and conduct research on issues of major disciplinary, multidisciplinary, and global significance.

About the Abu Dhabi Poetry Academy

The Abu Dhabi Poetry Academy is a major initiative devoted to supporting and publishing poetry in the Arab world. The first scholarly organization dedicated to studying and teaching Arabic poetry in both its Classical and Nabaṭī forms, the Academy organizes cultural activities relating to the field of poetry, as well as lectures, scholarly conferences, and literary workshops. These events attract scholars and enthusiasts from around the world.

The Academy has created a significant platform for poetic experimentation in Arabic by presenting live poetry readings featuring young poets from across the Arab world, and by publishing their work. The Academy also publishes collections by established poets, scholarly studies of Arabic poetry, and translations of Nabaṭī poetry into other languages. The Academy is currently working to establish two libraries: a public library that will make accessible scholarly works and materials on UAE folk culture, and another that will serve as a repository for poetry manuscripts.

The Director of the Academy is the Emirati author Sultan Alameemi, who has written nineteen works of fiction and non-fiction and who has served as a judge on the *Million's Poet* televised competition.

About the Translator

Marcel Kurpershoek was a senior research fellow at New York University Abu Dhabi and a specialist in the oral traditions and poetry of Arabia. He obtained his PhD in modern Arabic literature at the University of Leiden. He has written a number of books on historical, cultural, and contemporary topics in the Middle East, including the five-volume *Oral Poetry and Narratives from Central Arabia* (1994–2005), which draws on his recordings of Bedouin tribes. For the Library of Arabic Literature, he has edited and translated *Arabian Satire* by Ḥmēdān al-Shwēʿir (2017) and *Arabian Romantic* by ʿAbdallāh Ibn Sbayyil (2018). In 2016, Al Arabiya television broadcast an eight-part documentary series based on the travelogue of fieldwork he had undertaken in the Nafūd desert of northern Arabia for his book *Arabia of the Bedouins* (in Arabic translation *The Last Bedouin*). In 2018, Al Arabiya broadcast his five-part documentary on Najdī poetry. He spent his career as a diplomat for the Netherlands, having served as ambassador to Pakistan, Afghanistan, Turkey, Poland, and special envoy for Syria until 2015. From 1996 to 2002, he held a chair as professor of literature and politics in the Arab world at the University of Leiden.

The Library of Arabic Literature

For more details on individual titles, visit www.libraryofarabicliterature.org

Classical Arabic Literature: A Library of Arabic Literature Anthology
Selected and translated by Geert Jan van Gelder (2012)

A Treasury of Virtues: Sayings, Sermons, and Teachings of ʿAlī, by al-Qāḍī al-Quḍāʿī, with the *One Hundred Proverbs* attributed to al-Jāḥiẓ
Edited and translated by Tahera Qutbuddin (2013)

The Epistle on Legal Theory, by al-Shāfiʿī
Edited and translated by Joseph E. Lowry (2013)

Leg over Leg, by Aḥmad Fāris al-Shidyāq
Edited and translated by Humphrey Davies (4 volumes; 2013–14)

Virtues of the Imām Aḥmad ibn Ḥanbal, by Ibn al-Jawzī
Edited and translated by Michael Cooperson (2 volumes; 2013–15)

The Epistle of Forgiveness, by Abū l-ʿAlāʾ al-Maʿarrī
Edited and translated by Geert Jan van Gelder and Gregor Schoeler (2 volumes; 2013–14)

The Principles of Sufism, by ʿĀʾishah al-Bāʿūniyyah
Edited and translated by Th. Emil Homerin (2014)

The Expeditions: An Early Biography of Muḥammad, by Maʿmar ibn Rāshid
Edited and translated by Sean W. Anthony (2014)

Two Arabic Travel Books

Accounts of China and India, by Abū Zayd al-Sīrāfī

Edited and translated by Tim Mackintosh-Smith (2014)

Mission to the Volga, by Aḥmad ibn Faḍlān

Edited and translated by James Montgomery (2014)

Disagreements of the Jurists: A Manual of Islamic Legal Theory, by al-Qāḍī al-Nuʿmān

Edited and translated by Devin J. Stewart (2015)

Consorts of the Caliphs: Women and the Court of Baghdad, by Ibn al-Sāʿī

Edited by Shawkat M. Toorawa and translated by the Editors of the Library of Arabic Literature (2015)

What ʿĪsā ibn Hishām Told Us, by Muḥammad al-Muwayliḥī

Edited and translated by Roger Allen (2 volumes; 2015)

The Life and Times of Abū Tammām, by Abū Bakr Muḥammad ibn Yaḥyā al-Ṣūlī

Edited and translated by Beatrice Gruendler (2015)

The Sword of Ambition: Bureaucratic Rivalry in Medieval Egypt, by ʿUthmān ibn Ibrāhīm al-Nābulusī

Edited and translated by Luke Yarbrough (2016)

Brains Confounded by the Ode of Abū Shādūf Expounded, by Yūsuf al-Shirbīnī

Edited and translated by Humphrey Davies (2 volumes; 2016)

Light in the Heavens: Sayings of the Prophet Muḥammad, by al-Qāḍī al-Quḍāʿī

Edited and translated by Tahera Qutbuddin (2016)

Risible Rhymes, by Muḥammad ibn Maḥfūẓ al-Sanhūrī

Edited and translated by Humphrey Davies (2016)

A Hundred and One Nights

Edited and translated by Bruce Fudge (2016)

The Excellence of the Arabs, by Ibn Qutaybah
Edited by James E. Montgomery and Peter Webb
Translated by Sarah Bowen Savant and Peter Webb (2017)

Scents and Flavors: A Syrian Cookbook
Edited and translated by Charles Perry (2017)

Arabian Satire: Poetry from 18th-Century Najd, by Ḥmēdān al-Shwēʿir
Edited and translated by Marcel Kurpershoek (2017)

In Darfur: An Account of the Sultanate and Its People, by Muḥammad ibn ʿUmar al-Tūnisī
Edited and translated by Humphrey Davies (2 volumes; 2018)

War Songs, by ʿAntarah ibn Shaddād
Edited by James E. Montgomery
Translated by James E. Montgomery with Richard Sieburth (2018)

Arabian Romantic: Poems on Bedouin Life and Love, by ʿAbdallah ibn Sbayyil
Edited and translated by Marcel Kurpershoek (2018)

Dīwān ʿAntarah ibn Shaddād: A Literary-Historical Study, by James E. Montgomery (2018)

Stories of Piety and Prayer: Deliverance Follows Adversity, by al-Muḥassin ibn ʿAlī al-Tanūkhī
Edited and translated by Julia Bray (2019)

Tajrīd sayf al-himmah li-stikhrāj mā fī dhimmat al-dhimmah: A Scholarly Edition of ʿUthmān ibn Ibrāhīm al-Nābulusī's Text, by Luke Yarbrough (2019)

The Philosopher Responds: An Intellectual Correspondence from the Tenth Century, by Abū Ḥayyān al-Tawḥīdī and Abū ʿAlī Miskawayh
Edited by Bilal Orfali and Maurice A. Pomerantz
Translated by Sophia Vasalou and James E. Montgomery (2 volumes; 2019)

The Discourses: Reflections on History, Sufism, Theology, and Literature—Volume One, by al-Ḥasan al-Yūsī
Edited and translated by Justin Stearns (2020)

Impostures, by al-Ḥarīrī
Translated by Michael Cooperson (2020)

Maqāmāt Abī Zayd al-Sarūjī, by al-Ḥarīrī
Edited by Michael Cooperson (2020)

The Yoga Sutras of Patañjali, by Abū Rayḥān al-Bīrūnī
Edited and translated by Mario Kozah (2020)

The Book of Charlatans, by Jamāl al-Dīn ʿAbd al-Raḥīm al-Jawbarī
Edited by Manuela Dengler
Translated by Humphrey Davies (2020)

A Physician on the Nile: A Description of Egypt and Journal of the Famine Years, by ʿAbd al-Laṭīf al-Baghdādī
Edited and translated by Tim Mackintosh-Smith (2021)

The Book of Travels, by Ḥannā Diyāb
Edited by Johannes Stephan
Translated by Elias Muhanna (2 volumes; 2021)

Kalīlah and Dimnah: Fables of Virtue and Vice, by Ibn al-Muqaffaʿ
Edited by Michael Fishbein
Translated by Michael Fishbein and James E. Montgomery (2021)

Love, Death, Fame: Poetry and Lore from the Emirati Oral Tradition, by al-Māyidī ibn Ẓāhir
Edited and translated by Marcel Kurpershoek (2022)

The Essence of Reality: A Defense of Philosophical Sufism, by ʿAyn al-Quḍāt
Edited and translated by Mohammed Rustom (2022)

The Requirements of the Sufi Path: A Defense of the Mystical Tradition, by Ibn Khaldūn
Edited and translated by Carolyn Baugh (2022)

The Doctors' Dinner Party, by Ibn Buṭlān
Edited and translated by Philip F. Kennedy and Jeremy Farrell (2023)

Fate the Hunter: Early Arabic Hunting Poems
Edited and translated by James E. Montgomery (2023)

The Book of Monasteries, by al-Shābushtī
Edited and translated by Hilary Kilpatrick (2023)

English-only Paperbacks

Leg over Leg, by Aḥmad Fāris al-Shidyāq (2 volumes; 2015)

The Expeditions: An Early Biography of Muḥammad, by Maʿmar ibn Rāshid (2015)

The Epistle on Legal Theory: A Translation of al-Shāfiʿī's Risālah, by al-Shāfiʿī (2015)

The Epistle of Forgiveness, by Abū l-ʿAlāʾ al-Maʿarrī (2016)

The Principles of Sufism, by ʿĀʾishah al-Bāʿūniyyah (2016)

A Treasury of Virtues: Sayings, Sermons, and Teachings of ʿAlī, by al-Qāḍī al-Quḍāʿī with the *One Hundred Proverbs* attributed to al-Jāḥiẓ (2016)

The Life of Ibn Ḥanbal, by Ibn al-Jawzī (2016)

Mission to the Volga, by Ibn Faḍlān (2017)

Accounts of China and India, by Abū Zayd al-Sīrāfī (2017)

Consorts of the Caliphs: Women and the Court of Baghdad, by Ibn al-Sāʿī (2017)

A Hundred and One Nights (2017)

Disagreements of the Jurists: A Manual of Islamic Legal Theory, by al-Qāḍī al-Nuʿmān (2017)

What ʿĪsā ibn Hishām Told Us, by Muḥammad al-Muwayliḥī (2018)

War Songs, by ʿAntarah ibn Shaddād (2018)

The Life and Times of Abū Tammām, by Abū Bakr Muḥammad ibn Yaḥyā al-Ṣūlī (2018)

The Sword of Ambition, by ʿUthmān ibn Ibrāhīm al-Nābulusī (2019)

Brains Confounded by the Ode of Abū Shādūf Expounded: Volume One, by Yūsuf al-Shirbīnī (2019)

Brains Confounded by the Ode of Abū Shādūf Expounded: Volume Two, by Yūsuf al-Shirbīnī and *Risible Rhymes*, by Muḥammad ibn Maḥfūẓ al-Sanhūrī (2019)

The Excellence of the Arabs, by Ibn Qutaybah (2019)

Light in the Heavens: Sayings of the Prophet Muḥammad, by al-Qāḍī al-Quḍāʿī (2019)

Scents and Flavors: A Syrian Cookbook (2020)

Arabian Satire: Poetry from 18th-Century Najd, by Ḥmēdān al-Shwēʿir (2020)

In Darfur: An Account of the Sultanate and Its People, by Muḥammad al-Tūnisī (2020)

Arabian Romantic: Poems on Bedouin Life and Love, by Ibn Sbayyil (2020)

The Philosopher Responds: An Intellectual Correspondence from the Tenth Century, by Abū Ḥayyān al-Tawḥīdī and Abū ʿAlī Miskawayh (2021)

Impostures, by al-Ḥarīrī (2021)

The Discourses: Reflections on History, Sufism, Theology, and Literature—Volume One, by al-Ḥasan al-Yūsī (2021)

The Yoga Sutras of Patañjali, by Abū Rayḥān al-Bīrūnī (2022)

The Book of Charlatans, by Jamāl al-Dīn ʿAbd al-Raḥīm al-Jawbarī (2022)

The Book of Travels, by Ḥannā Diyāb (2022)

A Physician on the Nile: A Description of Egypt and Journal of the Famine Years, by ʿAbd al-Laṭīf al-Baghdādī (2022)

Kalīlah and Dimnah: Fables of Virtue and Vice, by Ibn al-Muqaffaʿ (2023)

Love, Death, Fame: Poetry and Lore from the Emirati Oral Tradition, by al-Māyidī ibn Ẓāhir (2023)